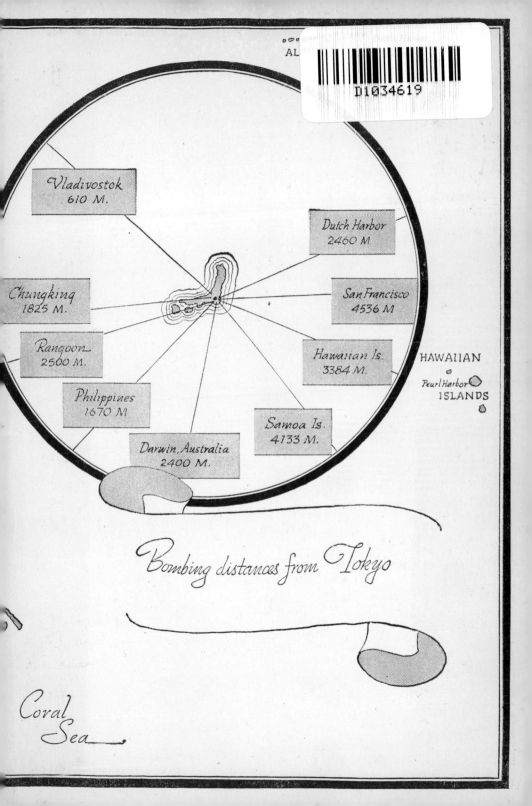

Bombing distances from Tokyo

Upton Close

Long before the outbreak of war in the Pacific, Upton Close was known as the outstanding authority on Asia and the peoples of the Pacific Basin. After graduation from college Close went to China and served as an intelligence officer for the United States government during World War I, and as advisor to the Chinese Student revolutionaries in Peking, aide of War-Lord Wu Pei-fu, and editor of the Peking Leader. Later Professor of Asiatic Culture at the University of Washington, Upton Close annually visited the Far East as leader of an Oriental seminar of students, teachers and professional people. Between travels and lectures, he has witten ten books and has contributed more than a thousand articles to magazines and newspapers. Early in 1941, when storm clouds of the Pacific War began to brew, he was invited to become National Broadcasting Company's special expert on Pacific affairs. Today his commentaries over NBC's Red Network have established him as a "must" to millions of listeners.

BEHIND THE FACE
OF
JAPAN

BY THE SAME AUTHOR

UPTON CLOSE

BEHIND THE FACE

OF

JAPAN

D. APPLETON-CENTURY COMPANY

Incorporated

NEW YORK   LONDON

1942

To
LIEUTENANT COLONEL LLOYD P. HORSFALL

Coast Artillery Corps, U. S. A., commanding the harbor defenses of Southern New
York; fellow student and fellow traveler in
the Orient who did not agree with all that
is said in this book but who has "polished"
and "ground" it, as Confucius advised.

*How lucky they that deal only with
    ancient fears
That rattle only tongues long-lost and
    old
And catalog but dry and disinfected
    years
Of destiny gone cold!*

THE AUTHOR

To The Reader

THIS book is a milestone in America's becoming adult. Demand for it is a barometer of American adult interest in the people of nations about us. Within seven years this book's first writing became either so extinct or so precious to its few possessors that only with greatest difficulty was the author, himself, able to procure a copy to prepare for this new publication. Thousands of would-be readers have asked for *Behind the Face of Japan* at bookstores. Now—here it is!

The "lost edition" was published in New York, in 1935, and during the next two years in London, Paris, Stockholm, Tel Aviv, Russia, and Tokyo. In Japan the parts dealing with Japanese history were pirated. (There is a high price on the author's head for the rest of the book, which according to the Japanese High Command, placed the author in the "knows-too-much" class.)

Just seven years to the week after the author wrote his "last word," where the question was asked: "Why should America and Japan fight?"—and answered, "They shouldn't—but will"—Japanese submarines and bombers attacked Pearl Harbor. This topped off conclusions as definite as that Japan's navy would raid Pearl Harbor without declaration *à la* Port Arthur in 1904.

In the summer and fall of 1934, the writer had stayed home from his annual journey through the Orient, to write a full-length portrait of the Japanese people and their nation. He believed his own people would be interested in such a portrait three years after Japan had leaped upon Manchuria, and two years after the first Japanese destruction and seizure of Shanghai, and Japan's defiant departure from the League of Nations, and open preparations to seize the Pacific and Asia.

The author was right about the Japanese—wrong about Americans! European-minded journalists termed the book "jingoistic" and the writer a "warmonger." At that time it was the fashion to be pacifist. Europe was played up, and the Pacific left to cash-conscious writers of popular repetitions of dusty conceptions and prejudices about Asia. The Atlantic was still the big pond.

But the book became a bible to those who knew Japan and her challenge to the world. It became a text to intelligent Army and Navy men, required in many of their classes. Secretary Cordell Hull and others expressed deep appreciation of this frank study of the nation of Japan by a man with no axes to grind and a historical background to back up his opinions. It was "digested" for the millions of *Reader's Digest* readers. Demand arose for it when the author became the far eastern expert for the National Broadcasting Company. But the time for its general acceptance was not yet ripe, and the author clung to the belief that only a war with Japan could cause this country to turn its eyes to America's real *Far West*— the Pacific.

On December 6, 1941, Upton Close, sensing time was short, en route from Washington to Hongkong, was in San Francisco. He met and interviewed on the air Maxim Litvinoff, as the Soviet Ambassador stepped off his trans-Pacific plane. What he sensed from that close-mouthed diplomat he imparted as best he could to network listeners. A few hours later, on December 7, he was in the control room of the National Broadcasting Company in San Francisco explaining the incredible, which he was so thoroughly on record as expecting, to the nation. Millions of Americans got their first news that America was in war from the scriptless broadcasts of Upton Close all through that broken Sunday.

His chore, when the first few days and nights beside the microphone had eased up, was to start a revision of his book in the hopes that what had happened during that week would never happen again. But the only insurance that it will never happen again is that the people of America know the true nature of their enemy.

This, then, is it: the profound, yet fascinating study of a rampant race as seen through the eyes of a historian who knows their past, has analyzed their present policy, and predicted their future moves.

CONTENTS

JAPAN AGAINST THE WORLD

EMOTIONAL FACES OF JAPAN

About Pronunciation,
Capitalization, and Quoting

J APANESE names are the most easily pronounceable in the world. Give the vowels their continental values, as in Italian, French, or German. Give the consonants their English values. If you are a stickler, pronounce carefully each of double consonants and elide final "u." "Katsu" is pronounced practically "Katz."

A new system of "remanji"—putting Japanese into roman or English) letters—was decreed by the militarized Ministry of Education about 1938, chiefly on the grounds of "eliminating degenerate foreign influence," although at the same time an attempt was made to accommodate the more esoteric aspirations and in-suckings of ultra-nice Japanese diction.

Examples: Fuji was made Fuhi; Tatsuta, Tatutua; and Chichibu (place, prince and ship), Titibu!

This book ignores the new official spelling, which may not, after all, survive Tojo's New Order in Asia!

Many of the quotations are in translation and Japanese journalistic translations made by Japanese are usually in fearful and wonderful English. The author has been compelled to lend a helping hand. Japanese put into English often rambles, repeats and folds back upon itself. The author has taken the liberty of eliding and transposing within quoted speeches but has preserved the sense.

The average reader will not wish to be bothered with the given names of Japanese individuals; therefore given names are put in parentheses following the surname. The common style until modern times was for the given name to follow the surname; both that and the western style are now in use in Japan. Where two different readings of the given name are in vogue both are given in the parentheses.

Japanese nouns and names have no special plural forms. But for smoothness the author uses "Fujiwaras" for more than one member or generation of the Fujiwara family, and "kimonos" for more than one kimono.

THE BACKGROUND

We struggle with men of today—
and with all their yesterdays.

Chapter I
First Word of the 1942 Edition

===

Because an Asiatic nation borrowed the tools and weapons of the West, trained itself assiduously in their use, and chose a moment when the West was in bitter civil war to strike us, the whole relationship of Asiatic and European living has changed forever.

Japan set out to enslave her neighbors and build the great empire of the Pacific, easily the best supplied empire in raw materials and manpower in the world, and therefore the strongest in all history and dominant over the rest of the world—if it can be built. The fanatic, militaristic core of Japan, proceeding with its self-assigned "divine mission" to establish the "eight pillars under one roof" (the eight parts of the world under the mikado or "great gate"), believed and preached that the people of Japan were to bring the millennium of peace to the world, war torn since the dawn of history, by the simple process of forcing all peoples to submit themselves to the government of the Son of Heaven.

Much is revealed in the following pages about this theory which only a few months ago was so fantastic to you, but which to-day affects your lives and your property and the whole reshaping of the world more than any other one thing in the world. We have to take note here in the First Word before we plunge into the story, that even if Japan loses—as millions in the West and in Asia intend she shall do even though it shall cost our last dollar and our last life— nevertheless the face of the world is altered beyond all recognition. Japan loses—we hope and resolve—yet Asia wins in the complete and final wiping out of white empire among tinted peoples of that continent. The West wins, yet loses her blissful illusion that there

3

was inherent behind white skin (as we call it) a superiority which made us better fighting people, better trading people, and better thinking people.

For many years some of us have watched the revolt of Asia brew. We have sensed that the renaissance of Asia would have as upsetting an effect on ideas and economic relations and political structures as did the renaissance of Europe, half a millennium ago. There were plenty of indications, for those willing to see, that the brief period of the white man's world dominance was nearing its end on this globe.[1]

That dominance was obtained through the explosive spiritual force with which Europeans burst out of their isolated medieval societies upon the rest of the round world, and it was implemented by the power machines which westerners—particularly from the British Isles —first developed. We westerners assumed that our advantages over the rest of the peoples of the world were due to virtue, or at least, to God's grace, instead of recognizing that they came from two temporal factors, the first of which was to lose its momentum as the adventure of discovery wore off, and the second to be neutralized as Asiatics learned to use the power tools of the West.

Our odds over the Asiatic were certain enough to disappear in time, but the white world hastened that time by drifting into unspeakable destructive civil war within itself—a civil war beginning with imperial rivalries between the European powers which exploited Asia, and ending in the knock-down, drag-out struggle for the domination of the seas and air. This war appeared as the struggle over "ideologies"; once in its brutal physical grip, its spokesmen gradually forgot that presentation.

All Asiatic peoples: Turks, Chinese, Indians, Javanese—even Tibetans—were certain to take advantage of this white man's civil war, to throw off his dominance. But Japan was the one nation of Asia which took advantage of it by explosive violence. She was the one Asiatic nation mentally conditioned and physically equipped to do so.

That is why we must know, now at long last, *something* about Japan.

As this book goes to press we are at the end of the story of the

---

[1] Some of them set forth in the author's *Revolt of Asia: the End of the White Man's World Dominance* (New York, 1928).

white man's dominant age on this planet, and fighting pretty desperately now just to hold our own. The thoughtful among us are wondering deep in our hearts how far this revolt will go before it stabilizes, and what the stabilization will be like for us and for friends and foes (who vary according to the fortunes of the moment), both Western and Asiatic.

Under these circumstances there seems no bit of hitherto neglected knowledge more needed by us than knowledge of what is the nation of Japan and who are the Japanese people and how experienced and tough are they, and what are the hopes of making world-citizens out of those who are left after the present holocaust—there will be something like fifty million left even should we destroy half of them!

The following full-length portrait of the Japanese nation—with the indications that Japan was getting ready to explode in our faces —and without declaration of war—was published in 1934. Its publication, and that of other good books on the subject, proved that the author's hunch was correct—that Americans would never take a popular interest in the Japanese until we were at war with them. *Now* it will become evident whether or not we will take that interest *because* we are at war with them.

So soon as the present war is over—one way or another—there will be plenty of wanting to know and needing to know about Japan. If, fantastically, the Japanese should technically win, they would undoubtedly make a tourist mecca out of the United States, and we would be their willing innkeepers—to receive the crumbs from *their* feast of world trade and monopoly! If we win, *we* shall make a prized tourist exhibit out of Japan, even as we did out of Germany after 1918. It will be necessary for guest and host to know a *little* about one another.

Whoever wins, trade relations will spring up exceedingly rapidly. Our "coördinators" sent to look after the affairs of defeated Japan and her empire certainly would not be less in number than the Americans who went to reconstruct and straighten out Germany after 1918. And they will need to know something about the people they are reconstructing.

So here's the book! To bring it up to date for 1942 publication, no change has been necessary in the presentation of Japanese philosophy and trends or in deductions regarding the relations of nations across the Pacific. Some things that were in the future in 1935, are now in the past, and changes have been made accordingly. Some of the thumbnail biographies have been cut in favor of sketches of personalities now dominant on the scene.

Let the author close this preliminary word with a few phrases from the 1935 edition. It is his desire that when the reader has finished this book, he will see Japan and see it whole. But it is not his claim that this book is an unabridged history or encyclopedia of Japan. The writer was not unswayed by personal likings, hopes, and apprehensions, but he tried to hold his camera steady. The data required for this book had perforce to be gathered, in many cases, from informal sources rather than from cut and dried works which have run the gauntlet of critics, statisticians, and verifiers. It is the distillation of an immense amount of research among periodicals and little known records. For some anecdotes the author is dependent upon his memory of conversations that took place over a period of years, and all sorts of situations in China and Japan. The author has no feelings to espouse, no axes to grind, no person to please, no hates to tickle. Certain Japanese, who felt entitled for the moment to dislike him very much, opined that he was as fearless, as oblivious to his own advantage, and as stubborn as a Japanese!

One thing at least the author need not worry about in this second edition—the attacks of our fashionable critics. He knew their dominant European or Russian mindedness, their unwillingness to believe that anything world-shaking could come out of Asia, their unstable pacifism, and the extent to which Japanese hospitality had disarmed them. He tried to avoid arousing them—in the original edition—by fulsome evidence of his desire to be fair and scholarly. The effort was in vain. His attitude was good enough for the Japanese themselves, who praised his book—while banning it for official reasons—but was only bait for the critics. Now, history has reversed the finger of scorn.

It would have been better had the American public read about Japan ten years ago. But we still need to know about Japan. And so with the kindness of the new publishers, this book goes out again.

Chapter II

Japan: The Face and the Spirit

W<small>E</small> westerners touched Japan's life less than a century ago, in a formative period, and partly enticed her in our direction. Now, our struggle with her reshapes our world.

Japanese diplomats and service-club executives traveling among us dwelt much on the cherry blossoms. All the while their minds were concerned with cotton, steel, and naval ratios.

Japan of cherry-blossom worshipers, wood-block prints and geisha girls; Japan of sentimental patriots who cut themselves open to show that their motives are pure, of political assassins and their sympathizers who chop off their fingers to send to the judges; Japan that assumes the position of upholder of the peace of the far east and looses her armies in other people's territory—this paradoxical Japan seemed too unreal to us.

But there were realities enough behind such bizarre phenomena—realities of steel and explosives, of freighters and ledger books. In the first two decades of this century Japan became militarily adult. In the third decade she became the West's diplomatic equal and emerged industrially adult. The fourth decade sees her full-out challenge of war against the greatest powers standing in her way. Japan's rise is the headline development of the twentieth century. It is doing more than communism to end our western capitalistic system and break up our empires.

Japan built some of the world's most efficient and up-to-date mechanized industry. In a position to buy as well as to sell, and to send ships laden both ways, she was building the world's most successful merchant marine. She was determined to have, for its complement, the world's first navy. Her old motive of military conquest began to operate in the sixteenth century, became dormant until the nineteenth, fully awakened again in the twentieth, and then combined with commercial conquests.

Japan, like most nations that can afford diplomats, censorships, and propaganda services, wears a mask. It is always possible, with more or less persistence and perhaps risk to the observer, to see the face behind the mask. But if we go behind that again—we discover the amazing, indomitable, insanely egoistic spirit which is Nippon.

Japan appears fantastic to us moderns because we have forgotten our own medieval past. We have become both too wise and too simple. We have forgotten motives that well up from deeper than "the practical idea." The survival of profit-and-pain-ignoring loyalties and prides in Japan helps to make the most interesting lives ever psychographed. No country produces more colorful, exaggerated, gorgeous humans. Know them, know their nation. Through their sayings, ambitions, loves, hates, motives; through the things they have a mighty determination to live or die for, we may understand the Japanese people and what such people, believing that their day has come, have done to our smug world.

Japanese grow in as great variety of mind and body as Americans or Englishmen or Frenchmen, but they possess a unifying faith in a national destiny lacking in modern Europe and America. In most of them survives a religious patriotism that we have outgrown, a spirit of martyrdom not known in the west since our religious martyrs chose death at the stake—a group frenzy not seen since the Crusades.

The face of a nation in any period or mood is the composite face of the men guiding or spurring it at the time. In the case of fascist Italy it is the face of Mussolini with his mouth open. In Germany and Russia it is slightly more complicated. In India it is the face of Gandhi superimposed upon the fat phiz of a money-lending maharajah. The face is not all the man, and the face changes—with tremendous experiences it changes almost beyond recognition—from age to age. But behind the face is a spirit, which in Japan has changed not since the days when a tribe (Yamato), claiming divine descent, set out to conquer the shores of Japan's Inland Sea.

After we have looked at the face of this rising nation Japan, and understood how logical and how inevitable an outgrowth of the fifteen centuries that have gone before is the challenge on her face, the trend of the Pacific era of world history becomes obvious, the unfolding drama of the human race more meaningful.

If we wish to understand why and how intensely Japan demanded racial and naval equality with the white powers, or to judge how likely of success are her plans of imperial, industrial, and maritime supremacy, we must take account of factors such as the racial stocks of her people, their unique qualities, the formation of the nation, and the logic of its development. No Japanese would think of facing or discussing America without equivalent knowledge.

We westerners, interested elsewhere, quite unanimously failed to equip ourselves for meeting our Pacific problem—now our dominant international problem. To begin with, officially there is no such thing as "Japan." The name of the country is Nippon, and its Divine Ruler is properly called the Tenno, not the Mikado. Nor, before fateful December 7, 1941, did more than one out of a hundred of us (judging from shows of hands in lecture audiences) know more than one great Japanese name—Admiral Togo!

I wish to make these people and their motives and ambitions as real to you as they are to me. I have sat with them through their moods, traded with them items of the gentle scandal they love, participated in their elegant chaffering, bandied with them phrases and puns which they adore, attended their solemn festivals, marched in their patriotic processions, worked with them in the débris of fire, flood, and earthquake, tried out the heartier humor of the west which escaped them altogether, slept peacefully on their clean mats, drunk with them in wild hilarity when all bars were down, known the intensity and motherliness of their affection, dodged the callous brutality of their militarism, and felt the sharp cut of their touchiness. I have traced the success stories of intrepid personalities of their past and present from thatched huts to national shrines where millions worship.

There is something behind all this. Nippon is, she believes, saving the world, both eastern and western. When Nippon believes a thing she believes it hard. Like Judah of old she bears a heaven-dictated commission, making her people, in the Old Testament phrase, a "peculiar people" and requiring of them readiness to make the ut-

most sacrifice, but promising them a final triumph as certain as
heaven's control of earthly affairs.

This was the phase of Japan that westerners knew, and those
who knew considered too fanciful for second thought. Yet it is the
most important phase, and the one that makes history now. Japanese
were never reticent about it. The Japanese statesman who knows
America best, who was reared and educated in America, tells us.
This is Matsuoka (Yosuke), the leader who in dark anger and challenge led Japan's delegation out of the hall of the League of Nations.

Most western of all Japanese, Yosuke Matsuoka is most intelli-
gently implacable toward the west. We may think that we of the
United States had little to do with Japan. Yet we became host to a
Japanese schoolboy, provided him an American foster-mother, educated him to manhood, then sent him home to become a publicist,
politician, railway executive, empire builder, and stiffener of the
Japanese backbone against the world. Returning to Japan from
Geneva, in 1932, Matsuoka stopped to place a headstone at the un-
marked grave of the pioneer Oregon woman who reared him. He
allowed his Oregon schoolmates of public school and state university
to banquet him. Yet to the very core of his being he resented the
white man in general and the American in particular.

His "American mother" loved him as a child and person, and he
knew it. But other Americans among whom he grew up, from professors to shingle weavers of the Oregon mills, patronized the "little
Jap kid." In his soul he resented such kindnesses more than the
curses and brickbats from young ruffians who made sport of his
slant eyes and the pigmentation of his skin. His eyes, which are not
at all slant, smoldered, but he held down his gorge and learned how
to hit "straight from the shoulder" like Americans and impress them
with "big talk."

When he was graduated from the University of Oregon, he returned to Japan and began a career that is astounding, considering
his age and the fact that for many Japanese he is "too American"
to get on facilely.

He was very useful to that clique which wanted freedom of action
and government backing for empire building on the plains of Manchuria. Japan's military lords assigned him to his special job at

Geneva over the heads of the entire diplomatic force to make sure there would be no stuttering in the presence of the white diplomats.

Matsuoka and his fellows made the second decided jog in modern Japanese history. The first was made by her swashbucklers of 1867 who plunged their nation into the whirlpool of world politics. What truly lies in the Japanese heart was never so frankly expressed as by the "American" Matsuoka, He stated:

... "The Mission of the Yamato race [Japanese] is to prevent the human race from becoming devilish, to rescue it from destruction and lead it to the world of light.

... "The general depression ... is nothing less than the deadlock of modern civilization. The hidebound, material-minded civilization of the present generation has finally plunged the whole world into its present welter of confusion. ... I cannot help feeling that the so-called civilized world has become stingy. ... Scientific and mechanical methods, the principles of individualism and profit making, provide no solution for the danger of annihilation by war, or for depression and unemployment problems.

... "Unless we Japanese change our habit of copying western civilization, it is not only impossible to accomplish the great mission of Nippon as I have stated it, but we also are doomed to destruction. [Nobody copied more sedulously in method—professedly to oppose it in aim.] Our Yamato race has a peerless tradition. We have no business being drunk with European civilization. All we have to do is to find the worthy in our own glorious ancient history. Get back to the Japanese spirit, reëxamine the national history of two thousand years!

... "Providence calls on Japan to undertake the mission of delivering humanity from the impasse of modern material civilization." [1]

These may be breath-taking statements to westerners who suppose that Japanese must have qualms about sending their armies into other people's territory or bombing cities of nations with which, professedly, they are not at war. But American-reared Matsuoka merely casts off the usual Japanese reserve in expressing what wells up in all Japanese hearts.

[1] Matsuoka in magazines *Seiji, Keisai, Giho,* 1933-1934.

The nation's feeling receives its scriptural declaration in the passage from the classics read by the court scholar, Dr. Ichimura, at the ceremonial naming of Japan's new Heir to the Throne. The language is archaic but it expresses to-day's spirit:

"The essence of ruling the people lies in the enlightening of them. If there are persons not yet properly governed, it is because they have not yet benefited by the Imperial rule. . . . If those who have not yet received enlightenment under the Imperial rule are found, they are to be subjugated." [2]

This passage, plagiarized by Japanese court scholars of the eighth century A.D. from the testament of a Chinese king who lived twenty centuries before Christ, is appropriated by the Japanese of twenty centuries after Christ as the policy to be carried out during the rule of the Heir to the line of god-rulers who form the core of the Japanese nation. In just such a manner did western churchmen appropriate scripture and tradition to document their claims: just so did Cromwell appropriate Jewish scripture to inspire and justify the victory of his Ironsides.

Perhaps all this sounds medieval beyond belief. But we do well to note the medieval-mindedness of men who built railroads in Manchuria, took Japan out of the League of Nations, made speeches over our radio networks, and organized a Japanese fascist party. If we ignore it, we are seeing Japan falsely through the glasses of our own modernism.

We of the more liberal and emotionally steady (thus far) parts of the west may gain some conception of the Japanese mind through the supernationalism which swept Germany, Italy, Russia, and Turkey. Japanese history and lives will show us, however, that the Japanese conviction has root, continuity, and drive even greater than any known in these western waves of emotionalism.

A better comparison is with our own past, beginning with the Crusades. We can remember when each respectable Christian sect alone possessed the formula for the salvation of men's souls. (We have more recently been in the midst of the era of political sects each of which is positive that it alone can save mankind.)

In the range between the Crusades and Leninism we could find

[2] *Nihon Shoki*, vol. 5.

everything Japan is to-day. The startling and serious aspect to us is that these medieval egotisms motivate a nation empowered with submarines, air fleets, the world's cheapest hydro-electric power, and spindles superior to Manchester's.

Japan's national egotism reached its apex of intensity as that of the liberal nations of the west dropped to an all time low. While Japanese students inscribed patriotic oaths in blood, English and American students proclaimed that they would never fight for their country, right or wrong. While "the white man's burden" was becoming a phrase for banter in Anglo-Saxondom, a Japanese statesman reared in Oregon proclaimed Japan's divine mission in the world. It is proclaimed with absolute sincerity, by Japanese who believe it as fervently as our ancestors who perished in the Hundred Years' War believed in the divine rights of kings. Japanese die to support this ideal—frequently by their own hands.

Japan's medieval-minded moderns are as upsetting in our sophisticated world as an ichthyosaurus navigating Fifth Avenue. Ichthyosaurian minds survive in the west, too, and they may overwhelm whole nations temporarily, but I refuse to believe that they supply the prevailing mentality of twentieth-century western society.

Matsuoka, who, in 1940, as head of the foreign office, ended Christian Missions in Japan, is himself a professing Christian. So is the editor of the *Japan Times*, who wrote this valedictory to the missionary:

... "Some decades ago it was believed that the Orient's only chance to progress would be via western civilization. The most active agency for spreading this western culture was the missionary. Due to the genius of the Japanese who seem throughout their history to have had an unerring eclectic sense, such occidental influence was checked and modified leaving only a beneficial residue. Thus with due thanks to the west in creating new Japan, we remember that Japan merely forged a new weapon with what she acquired from the west while the soul that wields it remains Japanese to the core. No people can destroy their soul and expect to acquire another over night—that is what the Chinese excessively influenced by the occident and communism are trying to do." [3]

[3] Japan *Times*, June 2, 1934; editorial.

At a time when Japan, in empire building, in manufacturing, in militarism, copied the west more furiously than ever—staked her life on beating us in our own game and outdoing us in our most selfish accomplishments—she turned to ancient ethics for her philosophy and congratulated herself that she was clean of our sordidness, and that her strength was as the strength of ten because her heart was pure.

Matsuoka's experience at Geneva was Japan's turning point. He says:

"The trend of affairs at the League of Nations deeply impressed me with the fact that Japan must stand on her own moral and spiritual integrity. The dispute at Geneva was discipline to prepare Japan for the coming great national crisis. Nations develop and degenerate, and nothing can alter this order of the universe. Peace as advocated by the western powers is nothing but a futile attempt to maintain the status quo."

The Japan which we face to-day believes: That the one nation not subject to the universal law of decline is that one ruled by a divinity and permeated by the spirit of the gods. That this nation has evolved steadily for over two and one-half millenniums. That the fated time has come to effulge its benefits to the world, *incidentally* making life more glorious and abundant for the savior race.

"The peace of the far east" can mean to Japanese only submission throughout Pacific Asia to the divine, imperial will of the House too sacred to have a name, and an order under Japanese law undisturbed by influence from abroad. This is evidenced concretely in the elaborate new shrines to the Japanese Divine Family, and contributory heroes, being built over Korea, Manchuria, Shanghai, Malaya, and wherever the Japanese foot is planted.

World peace, to Japanese, must have the same definition—enlarged. To them there can be only one peace, just as to the church universal there can be only one religion. When the secretary of the League of Nations, or President Roosevelt at Washington, corresponded with the foreign minister at Tokyo about the preservation of the peace of the far east, the two parties were, you see, talking about entirely different things.

There was a time, in the Atlantic era of world history, when lordly

Spain ruled the seas. She paid but little attention to the challenge
from a fog-bound island in the North Atlantic until it was too late.
Then, still too arrogant to compromise, she endeavored to crush
her braw young rival, England, and failed. While Spain sank to a
fourth-class power, Great Britain built an empire on which the sun
never set.

In 1934, in the original edition of this book, was written:

"That story may be repeated, in full or in part, in the Pacific.
Whether or not the historical parallel between the two great island
nations of history, England and Japan, is to go to such extreme
length, it sheds, as we are about to see, great light on Japan."

Chapter III

Japan and England—Parallels to the Seventeenth Century

JAPAN belongs to the modern family of nations. Her history is contemporary with that of Great Britain, the world's only other great island nation, rather than with China, which began milleniums earlier. Japan became increasingly Britain's rival as the world's factory and chief maritime nation, and the United States' rival in the Pacific and in Latin America. In fascinating, dangerous features, however, she differs from these contemporaries.

What lies behind the fearless, aggressive makers of modern Japan? What is the background of Nippon's history against which her empire-builders must be seen—to be seen truly?

The history of Japan paralleled that of England during formative centuries. The world's two great island nations developed equally up to the seventeenth century. Then in Japan came the most striking arrest of logical development recorded in history, while England entered upon the world's most spectacular imperial expansion. In the late nineteenth century Japan began history's most brilliant exhibition of catching up, and in the fourth decade of the twentieth, Japan showed astonishing signs of surpassing England. Then in this fifth decade Japan challenged Britain and the United States.

The likeness between Japan and England extended from the geography of their countries to the insular psychology of their peoples, and on into industrialization and world expansion. Striking contrasts of mentality and institutions show themselves. Both analogies and contrasts will help us of Anglo-Saxon heritage to see more clearly the face of Japan. For whether we are educated in English history or not, the development of British institutions and empire and the great characters of English history are part of our own subconscious sense of what has gone before.

This comparison, too, will give us a much needed conception of the relation between Japan and China, and the tremendously different national experiences of the two great oriental nations. China and Japan are no more alike, no more one entity than England and the ancient civilizations of Greece or Egypt and Babylon are alike and the same. But as any Briton, despite his native reserve, will admit that western civilization took root in Babylon and Egypt, was fertilized in Greece, took stem in Rome, budded in medieval Europe, and came to full flower in England, thence pollinating the world through the empire on which the sun never set, so will any proud Japanese maintain that Japanese civilization rooted in ancient China, received its graft of virility from martial Japan and exhibits full flower in to-day's Nippon. There is to follow, Matsuoka tells us, a new and much needed pollination of the world with *Japanese* civilization.

A British member of Parliament who once lived in Japan writes: "The geographical position of the islands comprising Japan—their relations to the contiguous continent of Asia—is remarkably similar to that of England, Scotland, and Ireland in juxtaposition to the continent of Europe. The analogy can be carried further. Japan's people are a maritime, seafaring people. They face and overcome adversity. Japan has, moreover, a much smaller food-producing capacity than even we. The greater part of all her islands is uncultivable. Like ourselves, Japan has to rely on industrial development to enable her to produce goods to sell in return for raw materials, and to support an increasing population of virile, adventurous, resistant people. They rely upon adopted, adapted, and perfected modern material processes." [1]

II

Now let us take a brief painless course in Japanese anthropology and history, made vivid by comparison with English history.

The Japanese people, far from being a pure strain, are one of the

[1] W. Kirkpatrick, M. P., in the *English Review*, early in 1934.

world's outstanding examples of the melting pot. The historian San-
som says he finds the Japanese and British Isles alike in that "behind each lies a great and variously peopled continent. Beyond each
is an immense stretch of ocean. Each is a pocket in which immigrants driven by hunger or fear, or led by the spirit of adventure,
might assemble, and where, because they could go no further, they
had to diffuse or perish. The situation in both cases has led to a
feeling of solidarity and insularity."

The Japanese rightfully claim white blood. The earliest traceable
inhabitants of the islands were the Ainu, a white-skinned, dark,
bushy-haired, big-boned, amiable, fierce-fighting, dirty-habited people, who, up to the eighth century of our era, were still holding a
battle line in the northern part of the main island against the slant-
eyed invaders from the mainland of Asia. Only about a hundred and
fifty pure specimens of Ainu blood remain on a sort of "Indian res-
ervation" on the northern island, Hokkaido. A few members of this
almost extinct race, which may or may not be Caucasian, were
brought to the St. Louis exposition in 1900. They are apparently of
the same stock as Laplanders. Their blood is responsible for the
large, good-natured, steady type of Japanese one finds most frequently in northern Japan. We might compare the Ainus in Japan
to the indigenous Britons in England who were finally conquered by
the Angles and Jutes in the fifth century.

The dominant strain in Japan, paralleling the Anglo-Saxon in
England, is Mongoloid, or, as anthropologists call it, Tungusic, origi-
nating in the Asian mainland behind Korea. It is responsible for
Japan's country bumpkin type which, however, since the elevation
of the plebeians, has provided some of her greatest soldiers, statesmen, and millionaires. This broad-faced, heavy-lipped "Asiatic"
type Japanese may be regarded as the perpetuation of the prehistoric
Tungusic infusion—just as we think of the "stolid English" type as
the projection of the Anglo-Saxon.

Thirdly, Japan received a Pacific-island infusion related to the
populations of the Philippines, Celebes, Borneo, and Java. One
might compare this strain to the Celtic in Great Britain. It seems to
be responsible for the volatile, ordinarily happy, but quick-tempered
and fanatic mentality marked in the southern island, where so many

of Japan's history-making movements have originated. Along with this entered a small but persistent Negrito strain.

The language of Japan, if separated from Chinese elements that became so large a part of it after the fifth century, and from the English, German, and southern European words and American slang that have been absorbed during the last seventy years, is the polysyllabic, mellifluously voweled, staccato-consonanted speech common to both the aboriginal people of north Asia and the islands of the Pacific.

One more racial infusion—the dominating one during historical time—entered the Japanese islands. These long-faced invaders came from the mainlaind, as did the plebeian Asiatic strain, but were fine-boned and highly bred, known to the old historians as the "pure Chinese," rather than "primitive Mongol" type. They were very similar to the present southern Chinese who have not been mixed with Mongol nomads as have the northern Chinese. They became Japan's ruling aristocracy before the time of our Christ and continued so to the late nineteenth century. We find their parallel in England, although not chronologically, in the Norman conquerors. They brought with them enough Chinese civilization to enable them to conquer the earlier barbarian residents and to put forth a claim of heavenly origin and divine right to rule. Because their hatchetlike features designated aristocracy this characteristic became the criterion of pulchritude which Japanese wood-block artists love to depict in their color prints. This conception of beauty persisted until recent years when newspapers seeking large circulations and advertisers began exploiting the plebeian class by awarding prizes in their bathing-beauty contests to pansy-faced country girls.

Probably the superiority of the last infusion lay in its use of metals in warfare, which may account for the importance of the iron sword in myths regarding their conquests. The sword is the most significant of the three symbols of the Ruling House. The invaders, however, either did not bring with them or lost knowledge of writing which had been used in China at least since 3000 B.C. Japan's authentic history consequently does not begin until Chinese and Korean missionaries of the Buddhist religion arrived in the islands in the sixth century to teach their long-lost kinsmen their new faith. These learned aliens and their Japanese neophytes began recording the nation's annals in the classical Chinese language.

They were crossing the Straits of Tsushima between Korea and Japan in exactly the same years that Theodore of Tarsus, St. Augustine, and other pioneers of Christianity and western civilization were crossing the Straits of Dover and beginning to write down English history.

It is still possible to trace the dominant strains in Japan's melting pot on any village street of the empire. Among the nation's recent headliners, General Araki, for instance, is an example of the quick, sensitive, aristocratic type, even though sprung from the peasantry. Big, leisurely Admiral Saito had much of the Ainu in him. Admiral Okada, stop-gap premier after Saito, is decidedly the broad-boned, generally good-natured, yet ruthless Mongol type. Matsuoka seems to be mixed Ainu and Malay. The excitable Mr. Amau of the foreign office is typically the supersensitive Malay, and the kinks and curls in his hair disclose a strong Negrito infusion also.

III

By the time the Buddhist missionaries reached the shores of Japan's Inland Sea the true story of earlier contacts with China had been lost, just as all knowledge of Cæsar's conquest and Roman rule in England had been lost by the time the Christian monks reached Britain. Both Chinese Buddhists in Japan and Roman Christians in England founded cultural and religious movements as successful as any this world has known. Both, with that worldly wisdom characterizing men of God, concentrated their efforts on the outstanding native chieftains. Prince Shotoku became the first royal Japanese sponsor of the new religion and culture and began to rule A.D. 593, just four years earlier than the beginning of St. Augustine's mission at Canterbury under protection of King Ethelbert.

Prince Shotoku's tribe was already in control of the plain of Yamato, a triangular rice-marsh area sixty miles on a side lying between Lake Biwa, the foothills of Mt. Fuji, and the Inland Sea. This tribe had appropriated the name "the godly Yamato People." They claimed descent from a divine invader named Jimmu. The

Chinese and Korean missionaries found them worshiping spirits of beasts and practising ritual purifications including the burning of habitations defiled by death—as practised by early Zoroastrians and several African tribes. Their dwellings, consequently, were of primitive, temporary construction.

Vague traditions of continental origin may have inspired the tribe's quick responsiveness to the teachings of the priest-scholars from cultured Asia—or perhaps that responsiveness was just the first historical exemplification of the amazing Japanese trait of adaptability. Prince Shotoku and his court were quick to adopt the pompous Chinese rituals described by the missionaries—in fact, made them councilors of state to install a crude imitation of the hoary Chinese administrative set-up. The chieftain adopted the Chinese title "Son of Heaven," Tenshi, and "Divine Ruler," Tenno, which latter title is the proper designation of the Emperor of Japan, rather than Mikado,[2] "Great Portal." The claim involved in the term "Son of Heaven" was always limited in China by the humanism of the Chinese, which from the time of their first philosopher, Chou Kung (1000 B.C.), upheld the right of revolution and maintained that the "will of heaven is the will of the people," and that the "people are the foundation of the state." But the Japanese have always been literal-minded. They took the term literally, just as they later adopted and applied literally the code of instruction for females drawn up by the Chinese Imperial Consort, Lady Pan Chao, about A.D. 200. Chinese women never really conformed to this code, but when Japan got it centuries later, it was applied so thoroughly as to make high-class Japanese women the most docile and "finished" females on earth.

The Chinese "Son of Heaven" phraseology fitted well with the native myths of the supernatural origin of the tribe of Yamato. The frankly crude and vulgar, albeit sacred, stories of the incestuous gods Izanagi and Izanami and of their daughter Amaterasu, Goddess of the Sun, ancestress of the imperial lines, who sulked and hid in a cave, leaving the universe in darkness until the other gods enticed her out with a burlesque show, predate the arrival of civilization

[2] Popularized in the west by the Gilbert and Sullivan opera, rather than taken from Japanese usage.

from China, just as the Anglo-Saxon sagas of Widsith and Beowulf predate Christian civilization in England. For a western comparison to the Yamato chief's claim to godly blood we have to go back to the divine claims of ancient Greek rulers. Even Alexander the Great encouraged the scandalous gossip that his mother had played too near the slopes of Olympus.

As the old Anglo-Saxon tales were written down by the priests Bede, Alcuin, and others who diluted or censored their barbaric quality, so similarly were the prehistoric Japanese myths framed into scriptures, called the Nihongi and Kojiki. These books might be called the Old Testament of the Japanese to-day—save that the Japanese still believe their Bible and—since the nationalist revival of the eighteenth century—know what's in it. Out of Chinese historical incidents, hero stories, Mother Goose yarns and, Japanese King Arthur legends, scholars of the priestly Fujiwara family—still the highest nobility of Japan—framed her history previous to the eighth century A.D. Unquestioning acceptance of this "history" is taught every Japanese child at his mother's breast, his grandmother's knee, and in the public schools from kindergarten to college.

To give the reader an insight into the mentality of a nation of to-day, I should state here that such a résumé of historical research by scholars, native and foreign, as the preceding paragraphs, may be interpreted as lese-majesty, and its writer may be punished any time he gets within Japanese jurisdiction whether his statements be made in the boundaries of the empire or not! From 1920 to 1931 there was a short liberal interim when Japanese professors began to speak with a tinge of academic freedom. These unfortunate gentlemen are now either dead or discreetly silent. Academic censorship in Japan is one of those striking contrasts to the general parallel between Japan and England.

IV

The first permanent buildings in both island countries were the monasteries. In both some of the oldest of these original centers of culture and law survive. In England the monks built them in Gothic architecture of stone; in Japan the monks built them in Chinese architecture of the handy wood from the stately cryptomerias, relatives of California's redwoods, which still tower over Japan's shrines.

Horyu-ji, built by Prince Shotoku near Nara, the city which became Japan's first fixed capital, has survived 1,327 years of fire and earthquake, and is to-day the oldest wooden building in the world.

In both Japan and England a half century of the new civilization made codification of laws and fixing of social strata necessary. In England, slave traffic was discontinued, and the lot of the serfs improved. We find similar humane developments in Japan in the Taiho reforms of A.D. 646, which Japanese historians call the beginning of constitutionalism in their country. A striking difference between England and Japan was the luxury and sophistication assumed by the courtly and priestly families of the latter. For imperial China was nearby and enjoying under the elegant Tang dynasty its era of greatest wealth and most abandoned pursuit of pleasure. This "hothouse era" in Japan is graphically pictured in Lady Murasaki's *Tale of Genji* (A.D. 1000) one of the world's greatest—and longest—novels. The west's seat of pomp and power, on the other hand, was in Constantinople, far away from England, and magnificent Rome had long since been ravished and barbarized.

The great human figure of Japan's cultural dawn—her St. Augustine—is Kobo Daishi. St. Augustine, however, was of the common people, while Kobo Daishi sprang from the Fujiwara aristocracy, which was glad to build up prestige on his name. The date of the birth of Japan's first great native saint has been fairly well established as A.D. 774. As a youth he traveled about searching for more spiritual light among the none too well equipped Buddhist temple libraries of that time. In 805, when he was thirty-one years old, the opportunity of his life came to join a Japanese embassy to the court of the elegant Tang dynasty of China, whose glorious capital was in what is now the remote upper Yellow River valley—the true Old China.

Kobo Daishi's earnestness and spirituality made him greatly loved by his Chinese teachers. He was given access to the mystic sutras of Buddhism, learned Sanskrit, and became such a master of Chinese calligraphy that he was besought by great Chinese including the emperor for samples of his character writing. Returning to Japan, he became the greatest exponent not only of religion but of Chinese classical learning, painting, and poetry. To the present day many Japanese temples claim that their leading idols were carved or at least designed by Kobo Daishi. He also brought the Chinese science of medicine, which for that age had made truly remarkable development, and established hospitals.

Kobo Daishi is credited with giving religion in Japan its humanitarian flavor. This pioneer of Buddhism, like the present-day Kagawa, pioneer of social Christianity, took more interest in the cleanliness, prosperity, and happiness of people in this life than in their condition in the next. However, he maintained the true Buddhistic conception that this life—in fact, all sensuous existence—is an evanescent dream.

The school of Buddhism which this great character imported is called Shingon, which means "the true way." It comprised the first native reformation of the Buddhism called Tendai originally brought from China. Shingon is the only early Japanese sect which continues as a great church to-day. Kobo Daishi learned much about Christianity as brought to the Tang Court of China by the early Christian sects called Gnostics and Nestorians. He incorporated many teachings of the Indian Yoga school as taught by the Chinese. And his clean, realistic art shows strongly the influence of Greek classicism— which penetrated China at this period. The westward reach of Greek art was England, the eastward was Japan. Through the life of Kobo Daishi we see what a variety of world influences swept over Japan within a few centuries after her emergence from unlettered barbarism. Exactly parallel was England's experience.

Kobo Daishi, like Luther and John Knox, felt the great need of developing a vulgate literature for his people, particularly for religious instruction. To this end he invented the first Japanese alphabet, called hiragana. He took forty-eight phonetics, syllables rather than letters, from spoken Sanskrit, then tore to pieces Chinese ideographs, taking here a rib, there an arm, there a leg, so to speak, to get letters with which to write the Sanskrit syllables. Reverence for Chinese learning, perhaps, prevented him from adding Japan to the Sanskrit-alphabeted world—as Tibet and Mongolia were later added by Buddhist scholars.

Kobo Daishi fixed forever the order of the forty-eight syllables by arranging them in a beautiful Buddhist poem, which when Japanese children have memorized they have memorized the alphabet. Translated, the poem is: "Flowers, however fragrantly they bloom, are doomed to wither—who in this world can hope to be permanently living? When the last mountain pass is crossed I wake from my evanescent dream, subject no more to intoxication."

Typical of the succession of Japanese importers of foreign culture to come, Kobo Daishi sought to maintain Japanese racial consciousness by combining the prehistoric religious practices with the new borrowings. He proposed that the animal and hero spirits of the prehistoric religion were really primitive incarnations of the Buddha soul, and made possible that friendly intermingling of early worship and Buddhism which continued until sophisticated later times. The intolerant spirit of Christianity brought about opposite results in England, where Druidism was completely stamped out and lost.

Kobo Daishi established the earliest grade schools in Japan where he taught his vulgate alphabet, the Chinese classics, and for those who wished to go on, the Buddhist sutras. He built a sort of monastery-seminary on Mt. Koya near Nara, which has been the Mecca of Shingon believers for a thousand years, and draws crowds of a hundred thousand to its three-thousand-foot-high eminence on each anniversary of the great scholar's death. The Emperor changed the teacher-monk's humble name Kukai (Ocean of Emptiness) posthumously to Kobo Daishi (Law-spreading Great Master) by which succeeding generations have known him. This scholarly Emperor Saigo sent the monk a present of winter clothes accompanied by a poem which has become a classic in Japanese literature. More than a hundred years later the occupant of the Sacred Seat had a dream that Kobo Daishi was cold—that the robes Emperor Saigo had given him had worn out. Since that time it has been the custom of each succeeding emperor upon his coronation to send a complete new set of robes to Kobo Daishi's tomb.

v

Thus, in Japan and England alike, the native tongue was reduced to writing during the first two centuries of ecclesiastical culture.

Christian monks used the Latin alphabet to write English. In Japan the Chinese ideographs, all of which are monosyllabic, were first used to put down the polysyllabic native Japanese tongue, creating the world's clumsiest literary mess, with only one parallel in literary history—the writing of medieval Persian in Hebrew letters, which was called Pahlavi. Then Kobo Daishi helped with his hiragana alphabet. Later a yet more simplified alphabet made of short straight lines without flourishes was evolved, called katakana. It is regarded as either for use by children or for frankly "lowbrow" appeal, and is favored on the great perpendicular billboards and illuminated signs of modern Japan. A tabloid, newspaper, pamphlet, or ad directly appealing to the proletarian customer in Japan flaunts this fact by the use of katakana only.

The Japanese language to-day continues to be written in either of these alphabets, or in a combination of either one with Chinese characters. The Chinese ideographs, in turn, may be pronounced in either archaic or medieval Chinese, or, as the literary ear seems to dictate, in the native polysyllabic Japanese word for the thing. One often cannot know how to pronounce a gentleman's given name from his name card, always printed in Chinese characters, and must be told the preferred pronunciation. Several renderings of the name may become extant.

To this mélange was added about eighty years ago, the writing of Japanese in our Latin letters. Foreign words, freely adopted, were spelled either in our Latin letters or one of the Japanese alphabets.

The wave of Chinese culture brought by the Buddhist missionaries increased to a flood overwhelming the islands. Everything in Japan that we think of as distinctly Japanese to-day came from China: architecture and housing, cooking, dress, art, music, and sports. Accomplished Japanese traveled by the hundreds in China, and studied everything there from government to poetry. Most great Chinese teachers had Japanese students with whose earnestness they were much impressed. A devotion between the Chinese master and his Japanese disciple is immortalized in *The Song of the White Clouds,* by the greatest poet of China's history, Li Tai Po.

In Japan Buddhism was too deeply impregnated with the materialistic ethics of Confucius, and the quietist anarchy of Laotze and other Taoist philosophers, to turn into a state church with the emperor in the position, say, of the living Buddha of Tibet, or of Henry VIII in England. The prehistoric animistic and hero-worshiping cult of the islands was dubbed Shinto, a Chinese phrase meaning "way of the gods," and made the chief bolster of Emperor worship. Its shrines and deities were hospitably accommodated in the Buddhist temples and pantheon. Not until the era of sudden nationalism did it become, in our sense, Japan's state church.

VI

The rule of Japan's first cultured aristocracy, the Buddhist Fujiwara, was extraordinarily long. This clan, or rather collection of families claiming distant imperial connection or "god blood," controlled the court by providing imperial consorts, regents, and courtiers. But as the ecclesiastico-political set-up in England was disturbed by Norse invasions in the seventh and eighth centuries, so the Japanese set-up was disturbed by wars with the unsubjugated white Ainus of the north. These wars produced a fighting class who had little respect for the poetry-writing and incense-smelling of the imperial Court. The warriors intermarried with the conquered and built up remote baronies not subject to Fujiwara control. Thus began the rise of that unique warrior class called the samurai and of the feudalism in Japan which they dominated from the first century to the nineteenth.

This development ushered in the first period in which the experiences of Japan and England diverged completely. In England the chaos created by invading Danes ended with the conquest and strong-arm government of William the Conqueror in 1066. In Japan disruption came to a head but not to an end in a terrific struggle between two frontier warrior branches of the imperial house, which from 1156 to 1185 bathed the civilized portion of Japan along the Inland Sea in blood. The emperor became a pawn between the contending sides. Imperial dignity reached its lowest stage when two puppet claimants to the position of Arehito Tenno (God Living among Men) existed simultaneously in the rival camps.

These Wars of the Chrysanthemums—the Minamoto House used

the red and the Taira House the white—has often been compared to
the Wars of the Roses of the fifteenth century in England. They had
precisely antithetical results, although the incitement was the same
—a weak king and the desire of opposing great houses to establish
sole right to speak in the ruler's name. The York and Lancaster
nobles practically annihilated one another, ending the Norman
feudalism that never had flourished due to the independent merchant
and artisan classes of the growing towns. When Henry Tudor came
down from the Welsh border, cleaned up both sides, and took the
throne as Henry VII, the townsmen gave him that support which
kept the king absolute in England until democracy came.

In Japan the story was different. First, the Minamoto were so
nearly extinguished that the last heir of the house, the child Yoritomo, was preserved only through his beautiful mother's granting
her body to the victorious Taira lord who had slain her husband.
Yoritomo grew up incognito as a fisherman's son, learned his identity
by accident, rallied his clan, and exterminated the rival clan in a
series of combats that provided the greatest heroes of the Japanese
stage. The Taira warriors were drowned in the choppy waves of the
narrows of the inland sea, and their aristocratic women became the
traditional prostitute class of Shimonoseki, much diluted, I fear, in
seven intervening centuries, but still boasting the Taira headdress.
Left in undisputed control of the emperor's person, Yoritomo established him in Kyoto as a powerless figurehead and built a new capital, Kamakura, on a bay in the then northern frontier region.

From Kamakura, Yoritomo ruled a feudally organized kingdom,
while the old Fujiwara nobility fell into desuetude. The development
of arts and crafts took place under Yoritomo's shadow, and Kamakura became in his day the largest city in the world. To-day it is but
a quiet beach suburb of Tokyo retaining as monuments of its glory
the great outdoor Buddha of bronze and the museum-temple of
Hachiman, god of war.

VII

Warrior rule in Japan was paralleled on the Asian continent by
Kublai Khan's conquest of China, which completely cut off the
softening and pacifist influences of Chinese culture.

The Mongols became history's greatest conquerors, overrunning and ruling territory as extensive as the empires of Alexander, Cæsar, and Napoleon added together and multiplied by three. In 1274, and again in 1281, about the time that his cousins were pushing into Christendom as far as Vienna, Kublai launched his great armadas against Japan. The islanders proved to be the only people able to repel the persistent determination of the Mongols to conquer them.[3] Mongolian horseback warfare, and perhaps primitive firearms, were invincible in their land campaigning, but when they put to sea with hundreds of thousands of disgruntled Chinese and Korean conscripts, they were, to express it in current slang, "all wet."

Storms came up on both occasions to favor the Japanese and complete the destruction of the invaders; these provided the final conviction to the Japanese mind that their sacred islands were divinely protected. Their belief now is that the Son of Heaven must always win when every Japanese life stands behind him, and Japan must always win while the Divine One remains the core of the nation. The failure of the Mongol armadas against Japan is delightfully similar to that of the Spanish Armada against Elizabeth's England three centuries later. Both proved the disadvantage of a land power operating against islands before the day of air power.

The effect within Japan was disintegrative. Clansmen who had waded heroically into the sea and boarded the Mongol ships returned to demand special rewards from the decadent and impoverished successor of Yoritomo at Kamakura. The country's feudal lords engaged in a general scramble for spoils and honors which the Divine Person, under his leaky roof in Kyoto, writing verses to earn his rice, was powerless to stop. A nation which by this time numbered twenty million and stretched over the entirety of three principal islands was plunged into a welter of violence and valor destined to continue two and one-half centuries.

Then, in the late sixteenth century, came Japan's William the Conqueror in the combined persons of the most remarkable trio of Japanese who ever lived—three of the most spectacular characters this globe has produced.

[3] Unless one except also Java, where a rebel against the native dynasty welcomed the Mongols, used them, then turned on them and drove them out.

Chapter IV
Japan's Unifiers

KNOWN historically by what we call their first names, Nobunaga, Hideyoshi, and Ieyasu were born within eight years of one another in the first half of the sixteenth century. They were beginning the history-making careers which ended Japan's bloodiest era when England's consolidator, Queen Elizabeth, barely missing the headsman's block, acquired a throne. Typical products of their time, utterly different in character but soldiers all, a chain of events woven of courage, chicanery, and sheer luck made them, each in turn, supreme, and enabled the third (Ieyasu) to enforce the most protracted era of peace which history records outside of the Pax Romana upon a spirited and ruthless aristocracy to whom blood-letting had become the normal procedure in all controversies as well as justification of failure. Out of that era, in turn, grew the disci-plined, unified Japan which our world of to-day faces.

Nobunaga was a fighter pure and simple, loving the rage and risk of combat, given to violent tempers and lack of self-control. Hideyoshi, in addition to being a fighter, was a sublime psychologist and trick-ster. The modern psychographer would say that his ugly pockmarked face and bulging eyes, reminding one of a Chinese guardian of the gate (face and features which inspired ridicule among his contem-poraries until his sword or still sharper wit and courage replaced their contempt with surprised admiration), had as much to do with the unification of Japan as Napoleon's small anatomy with his con-quest of Europe. The Japanese, following their flair for nicknaming, called Hideyoshi "Monkey Face," but came to precede this with the appellation "Great." Since Hideyoshi's career, to be born with a simian face is to be a child of promise in Japan. To the character-

istics listed at the beginning of this paragraph, Hideyoshi added the
ability to withhold his thrust, that virility which inspires in men
intense personal devotion, and an unbounded ambition. Truly a
history maker had arrived in the world.

Hideyoshi had some characteristics which seem non-Japanese.
His family tree was plebeian, and might easily have included a foreign graft. The daring of his humor was positively Irish. His is the
most colorful personality in all Nippon's history. But his life work
would have left the world only a hero and not a nation if it had not
been for the third member of the triumvirate, Ieyasu, the aristocratic, cold-blooded, supreme watchful waiter.

Nobunaga, the first, the Julius Cæsar of the trio, was, in his
early twenties, left lord of a high-born provincial house in the foothills of Mt. Fuji. He was picked out for boss by the plebeian Hideyoshi, two years younger, who had already won local renown as a
fighter, witster, and adventurer. With Hideyoshi's help, Nobunaga
battled a great neighboring feudatory, killing one of its vassal lords.
The slain man's eighteen-year-old son had his sensibilities hurt because the old clan chief, mistrusting his youthfulness, hesitated to
place him in his father's shoes. The lad, young Tokugawa Ieyasu,
forthwith defected to join the two young attacking warriors who
had slain his father. Thus the notable triumvirate was formed.

In a typical youthful compact of the sort one finds over and over
in Japan, the three agreed to conquer Japan together. The difficult
point, inevitable with Japanese—which of the three should be supreme in the end—they agreed in unique Japanese fashion should be
settled as follows: When any one of the three would feel adequate
in his own heart to go to the Sacred Imperial Person and ask for the
supreme overlordship once held by the Shogun Yoritomo, he was to
do so without consulting his pals. The first to get the place would
be unquestioned—the other two would voluntarily become his vassals. The years were to see both Nobunaga and Hideyoshi trying
and failing in the face of the tremendous force of Japanese tradition. They were to see the more aristocratic Ieyasu succeed—after
waiting for his turn until he was an old man. Some Japanese wit put
descriptive epigrams in the mouths of the three. Nobunaga: "If the
cuckoo won't sing, I'll kill it"; Hideyoshi: "If the cuckoo won't sing,

I'll persuade it"; Ieyasu: "If the cuckoo won't sing, I'll wait until it does." The story shows him doing much while waiting.

II

These intransigent swashbucklers, carrying on from extreme youth into indomitable old age, made Japan a nation in the late sixteenth century. Men of the same pattern remade Japan in the middle of the nineteenth century—which lends significance to the young groups conspiring and assassinating in Japan to-day, and to Matsuoka's remark that if he knew the thirty youngsters who are to be Japan's future empire builders, he would turn Japan over to them.

Nobunaga as a youth ran true to pattern, showing so much indifference to his tutor's efforts that the loyal samurai committed hara-kiri in an ultimate and effective effort to reach the young man's conscience. Doubtless many a western teacher has been driven to the point of suicide by his pupils, but not quite in this sense.

Hideyoshi proved so unmanageable in adolescence that his family tucked him into a monastery where he made fun of the priests and organized amateur armies of the novices and generally kept the sacred precincts in turmoil until the men of God had to throw him out. An older cousin apprenticed him to various trades and professions, from which he got himself expelled thirty-seven times in succession.

Hideyoshi's family, finally seeing promise in the black sheep, fetched him home, but he was soon off on his own again, applying to a samurai for a position as page, which was curtly refused. He followed the samurai into battle in the guise of water boy, saved his life in a pinch, and attained at last the coveted foothold in the fighting profession ordinarily denied to one not born into the samurai caste.

Next, as mentioned above, he joined young Nobunaga by forcing, at the risk of his life, an interview with that hot-tempered lordling. Nobunaga was always, from Hideyoshi's viewpoint, overlooking him. He took to mounting guard at the castle gate an hour earlier than other soldiers; one dawn Nobunaga came out to enjoy a storm, and called angrily, "Is no one on duty?" Hideyoshi answered, "The only

one in your army that matters!" At a serious juncture in one of
Nobunaga's campaigns, a tempest tore down three hundred yards
of his castle wall. The official keeper in charge was very slow about
rebuilding, but only by Hideyoshi's keen eyes was seen in his true
light as a secret ally of the enemy. Hideyoshi made sarcastic remarks in the hearing of his young lord, until Nobunaga angrily
ordered him to rebuild the wall himself in the three days the young
critic had said ought to be sufficient. By bribing all the masons in
the region with fish, wine, money, and absurd promises of more
money, Hideyoshi accomplished this task. The surprised but not
pleased Nobunaga gave him a reward, which proved far from enough
to pay off his promises to the workmen. Hideyoshi tried to get out
of the dilemma then by telling them their lord had requisitioned the
balance of their wages for military purposes. The trick came to light,
of course, and Nobunaga, half admiring and half enraged, paid the
deficit. But he wouldn't allow Hideyoshi to speak to him.

Hideyoshi felt under desperate necessity to disclose privately to
his lord the treasonable plot of the castle keeper. He applied to the
castle priest to teach him the tea ceremony, although he despised
the priests and the tea ceremony equally. One afternoon he managed
to get permission to make his lord's tea, and bribed the cupbearer to
tell the lord, and also saw to it that gossip was spread through the
castle that he had sipped first from Nobunaga's cup—a deadly insult.
Nobunaga, in a towering rage, summoned the lad. Said Hideyoshi
coolly, "If it is your ambition to become the lord of all Japan, you
had best not be offended, for there is a purpose in my offense. But
if you are content to remain little lord of Owari, then here is my
head." Unable to restrain his curiosity Nobunaga listened to Hideyoshi's revelation. "But why bring me this problem," he asked, "if
you have no way of clearing it up? There is no use killing the petty
traitor in our own ranks unless we can destroy also the brains of the
plot in our rival's camp." "I have read a trick in the old Chinese
books. Let me try it here," replied Hideyoshi. Thereupon he had a
letter forged in the chief plotter's handwriting which threw such
slights upon his fellow plotters in the rival camp that they slew him
as a matter of honor.

Such anecdotes of Japan's greatest careerist may serve more than

heavy history to illuminate the Japanese character—indeed the most
serious Japanese historians regard them in this light.

III

From this time on, Nobunaga's affairs were more and more in the
hands of Hideyoshi, who did not fear his rages. Together they
pushed their conquest from this middle region of Japan westward
along the Inland Sea to the coast that looks towards China, while
young Ieyasu held the rear against the lords of the south and north.
Hideyoshi was in the process of subjugating the last clan that challenged their authority, laying siege to the great castle at Takamatsu,
when came the greatest crisis of his career. Through a quickness of
wit never surpassed by Napoleon, he cleared the way to supremacy.

This castle, whose ruins are a showplace of the Inland Sea to-day,
was one of the structures built by piling up Chinese architecture into
towers, and surrounding them with walls and moats, protected by
cannon and contraptions for pouring molten lead, which had been
built after descriptions of the castles of Europe brought by the
Portuguese mariners. The Europeans had arrived but a few decades
earlier. The amazing spread of castles over Japan at this time is the
most striking large-scale example of adopting European ideas—especially military. Within three months after seeing the first cannon,
Japanese metal workers had cast 700 of these weapons. The picturesque castles strengthened feudalism, being almost impossible for
an army of that day to reduce, and kept Japan disintegrated.

Hideyoshi had brought the occupants of the besieged castle to
that stage of starvation in which they were willing to talk terms, but
in which unreasonableness involving honor would have inspired a
prolonged and desperate resistance. A messenger brought Hideyoshi
news of the slaying of Nobunaga in Kyoto by another of his own
generals. The assassin anticipated that this news reaching the besieged clan would arouse them to keep Hideyoshi fully occupied
while the assassin was stepping into Nobunaga's boots. Hideyoshi
took every precaution to prevent the news leaking through into the
castle, but he could count on only a few hours to act. He knew that
if he left Shimizu, commandant of the castle, alive in his rear, he

was ruined. He offered terms which in one respect were generous, and in another bombastic and extreme; he demanded only the head of Shimizu. Shimizu's officers replied that they were willing to accept the terms as to themselves and men, but asked how they could be expected even to report to Shimizu the demand for his head.

"Ask Shimizu!" was Hideyoshi's cryptic reply, as he ordered a furious assault. Hideyoshi's whole future, and probably the unification of Japan, rested upon his guess as to the lord of the castle's psychology Shimizu made no reply to the officers who shamefacedly reported to him, but that night he committed hara-kiri. His officers thereupon surrendered the castle to Hideyoshi, who occupied it, declared amnesty, and ordered that Shimizu be buried honorably; that is, with his head still on his shoulders. Meanwhile he was ferrying his troops across the Inland Sea, for the march upon the capital, Kyoto. Shimizu's warriors went wild when they learned that Hideyoshi's own chief was all this time dead in Kyoto, and favored restarting the war again on his rear. Here enters a point of Japanese military honor, which, amid so much permitted chicanery, puzzles the westerner. Shimizu's noble relatives required the suicided lord's samurai to keep the armistice. In a whirlwind campaign on the main island Hideyoshi placed himself in the position of supremacy that had been enjoyed by Nobunaga. Meanwhile, Ieyasu looked on and waited. Perhaps he smiled satisfiedly when Hideyoshi asked for the title of shogun and was refused on the basis of his plebeian ancestry —to be given instead a specially created title, Taiko, "Great Prince."

Hideyoshi's campaign for supremacy following Nobunaga's death was full of the bloody incidents which go with Japanese warfare. Hideyoshi first compromised with one rival, then trapped him. The defeated chief staged a mass suicide including his wife and one hundred retainers.

IV

The campaigns conducted by Nobunaga and Hideyoshi had left Hideyoshi supreme and created Japanese military unity. At this point there appears, beginning with Hideyoshi, who like Napoleon, couldn't stop, the Japanese urge toward expansion and empire. A similar urge was stirring England at exactly the same time. Yet it is interesting to note that neither England under Elizabeth, nor Japan at the death of Nobunaga, owned an inch of soil outside of their own little islands. The history-making difference was that through two long reigns Henry VIII and Elizabeth had avoided war and conserved the wealth and man power of their country. After Elizabeth's death nothing could stop England. Hideyoshi, contrariwise, like Napoleon, started to build empire with a nation weakened by centuries of internal strife and bloodletting. Japan's empire building was doomed to be checked until Ieyasu and his dynasty should have accomplished for Japan such a work of discipline, conservation, and building of cultural superiority as the red-haired queen had presided over in England.

Before his death, Nobunaga had completed a struggle to end the power of religious elements to interfere in civil affairs which may be compared with Henry VIII's subordination in England of priestly influence. Buddhist monks had nested 3,000 fortlike monasteries under the great cryptomerias of picturesque Mt. Hiei, above Kyoto, which the tourist now ascends by cable car and between whose two peaks he swings in a cubicle suspended from a cable. These monks had so far forgotten the pacifist tenets of their faith as to have under arms at one time 30,000 men who sallied forth to raid the cities and interfere in the feudal warfare. Nobunaga finally burned the ancient buildings and put the monks to death. Another such center was the fortified monastery of Osaka, which it took ten years of desultory fighting and three vigorous sieges to reduce to ruin, and where 100,000 armed monks perished. After overwhelming the priesthood of the old religion, however, the unifiers of Japan had to deal with a new religion from the west, a problem which England was spared.

The conqueror Nobunaga was the first Japanese ruler to meet a European face to face. This white man was a Jesuit priest named Froez, who was granted an interview on the drawbridge of Nobunaga's castle in 1568, the year Nobunaga became supreme. The Jesuit and the warrior found themselves agreed in opinion regarding the Buddhist priesthood, with the result that the Christian was given a tour through the castle and received what was in effect official encouragement to introduce his religion.

Twenty-five years before this interview Europeans had first landed on the Japanese islands. The first arrivals were three Portuguese, blown off their course up the China coast by a typhoon. Their arquebuses were the first firearms that Japanese samurai had seen, but before they got away Japanese metal founders around Kagoshima were casting imitations.

Previous to the arrival of the shipwrecked Portuguese the white world's knowledge of Nippon had been limited to the reports of the Venetian trader, traveler, and administrator in China, Marco Polo. Marco Polo had transmitted what he had heard in the courts of the great Kublai Khan at Cambaluc—later Peking—about Zipangu, as he called it—properly Nippon-koku, "Sunrise Country." What most interested Europeans was his statement that gold was so abundant in Japan that it was used to cover houses. Kublai's informants must have confused the golden-colored lacquered surfaces of temples and lords' palaces with the precious metal. However, Marco was a reporter of Kublai's two failures to conquer Zipangu, and European adventurers had the healthy idea that any country too tough for the Mongols, who had overcome the Mohammedan world and as much of the Christian world as they wanted, was a good country to stay away from.

The Portuguese enjoyed a monopoly on European contacts with Japan until the early seventeenth century. Then rivalry grew up with Spain, which the Pope in 1493 had tried to forestall by drawing a line down the China coast, ordaining that all the world to the west including the Americas should belong to the king of Spain, and all the pagan world to the east to his other son, the king of Portugal. Imperialist geographers of the time never did settle which side of the line Japan was really on, but the great Japanese Hideyoshi eventually took action which made the question purely academic.

With the arrival, in 1549, of Francis Xavier, founder of Jesuit missions, the white peril dawned for Nippon. Xavier, himself a Spaniard, was under protection of the Portuguese king and was taken by Portuguese traders to Japan while waiting for permission (which never came) to enter China. He stayed but a short time, returning to the Portuguese settlement on the China coast, Macao, where he died while trying to get into the great empire where the older Catholic orders had pioneered under Kublai Khan three centuries before.

But Xavier left ardent brothers on the southern island of Japan who gradually penetrated to the main island and made contact with the chief lords of the nation. The progress of their evangelism was remarkable. The Japanese, an innately religious people in contrast to the Chinese, were ripe for a new religion. They were sick of half a millennium of fratricidal warfare and looting, and their previous religion of Buddhism fell into complete disrepute when its monks, sworn not to kill so much as an insect, took to arms and became the most predatory of all the gangs overrunning the land.

By 1582, the year of Nobunaga's death, the Jesuits had baptized upward of 200,000 communicants and erected more than 200 churches several monasteries and a number of schools, and had won the patronage of several lordly families. Before the beginning of the seventeenth century Loyola's Society boasted twice this number of communicants and a "plant" that was beginning to be one of the features of the empire. It looked like a duplication of the Buddhist conquest of the seventh century.

Shortly before Nobunaga's death the Jesuit Valegniani took the first Japanese mission to Europe, composed of four noble youths, to obtain the blessing of the Pope. Had the Roman Catholic penetration of Japan been carried out with a little more wisdom and less strife between the Christian elements, Japan might have become, following the Philippines, the second Asiatic Christian nation, and a base from which Christianity might have swept Asia as it had Europe. Certainly Japan would not then have been shut off for two and one-half centuries from the western world, but would have climbed step by step with rising European nations in political, scientific, and industrial development and in the construction of an empire on the Pacific, comparable to those built by the rising western nations. In that case, the world to-day would be an astonishingly different picture.

v

Hideyoshi, affected by his early contempt of the Buddhist priesthood, continued Nobunaga's policy of friendliness towards the Chris-

tian religion, even permitting his son Hideyori to marry into a
Christian family. Catholic missionaries claimed that Hideyori himself confessed the faith.

But it was not long before the narrow and controversial minds of
the European religieux came into conflict with the intense nationalism of Japan's unifiers. As early as 1565 and 1568 the Imperial Court
at Kyoto, sensing that Christianization of Japan would take from
the emperor the spiritual position which in that era was all he had,
issued anti-Christian edicts. These were ignored. Hideyoshi blew up
and gave the Jesuits twenty days to leave the country when he heard
that the priests were teaching that there was a law higher than himself. But his rage passed, and he did not enforce the order.

The position of the new faith was compromised when the Spaniards in the Philippines, jealous of the success of the Portuguese-
sponsored Jesuits, sent their Franciscan friars to begin a rival
evangelism, with a view to accomplishing in Japan what they had
already accomplished for the Spanish crown in the Philippines.
Hideyoshi quickly reacted, giving a historic initial expression to the
Japanese spirit of expansionism by sending a mission to Manila
(1591) summarily demanding that Spanish authorities there put
themselves under Japanese suzerainty. Hideyoshi could not forgive
himself that he had been born a half-century too late to beat Spain
to the annexation of the Philippine archipelago.

Philip II's sly governor-general in the Philippines, de Marinas,
seized Hideyoshi's demand as opportunity to send to Osaka a mission of negotiation composed of five Franciscans, who, in the Philippines, had been banned at the request of their fellow monks, the
Jesuits. After entering as diplomats, these men stayed as priests,
illegally founding several monastic institutions in Osaka which were
to have a tragic end for Christians and for European influence in
general, as well as for themselves personally.

For the time, Hideyoshi had turned his empire-building ambitions
in another direction, and had become fully occupied with his invasion of Korea. It was now Ieyasu's turn to play with the foreign
evangelists. In 1593, while Hideyoshi was in the heat of the Korean
campaign, Ieyasu in his castle at Nagoyu under Mt. Fuji was discussing Japanese rhetoric with the Jesuit Rodriguez, pitting him for

amusement against Buddhist and Confucian scholars. This ended with Rodriguez, under encouragement from Ieyasu, creating Japanese grammar. Before word-minded Europeans came to Pacific Asia neither Chinese nor Japanese literati had bothered with that pseudoscience.

Christianity had a unique place in Japan's first historical foreign campaigns. Hideyoshi's ablest general was a Christian lord. The Korean Admiral Yeh Sum-sin (Yi Sun-sin in Chinese), who defeated Hideyoshi's empire-building scheme with his metal-covered warship —the first in naval warfare—was also a Christian convert.

In 1590 Hideyoshi demanded of the Korean king aid against, or at least free passage through to attack, the empire of China, which he announced he was going to "roll up like a bamboo curtain." The Korean king replied that Hideyoshi's enterprise would be like sticking straws through a turtle's back, or scooping up the ocean with a clamshell, which are similes that must come unpleasantly to the minds of Japanese expansionists of to-day.

Hideyoshi required his feudal lords to provide between two hundred and three hundred ships manned with fishermen on which he transported upwards of 200,000 samurai to Korea. But the Korean admiral cut their communication with his ship, fashioned like a scoop, made of camphorwood covered with copper plates, and said to have had a deck covered with a metal dome. This, propelled by oarsmen, moved more rapidly than the Japanese boats, and belched fire at the enemy from a bronze rocket gun shaped like a dragon's head in the bow. Hideyoshi had to withdraw, but in the succeeding peace negotiations got insulted, and in 1597 again shipped over 150,000 invaders. These were the largest armies transported overseas between the fall of Rome and the Boer War. "Little" Japan, long before her modern imperial adventures, proved an amazing ability to maintain enormous forces overseas.

Hideyoshi's commanders had everything their own way until the Korean Christian admiral and his "turtle boat" were reinstated from retirement into which Korean court intrigue had forced them. This time the pioneer of metal fighting ships constructed several of these early monitors, but the Japanese had learned the game, too. Hideyoshi's Christian general turned admiral and took to sea in command of an opposition metal-covered fleet. The two oriental Christian commanders cancelled each other out in a sea engagement in which they both perished. Soon after (1598) Hideyoshi's forces won a decisive victory in northern Korea, taking 38,700 Chinese and Korean heads.

But Hideyoshi had died in bed in his castle in Osaka six weeks before that battle, begging that his braves be not left to become ghosts in a hostile land. No other Japanese had the will to go on and the policy of Ieyasu, who was now left dominant, soon proved to be the exact opposite of expansion on the continent. So the business of rolling up China like a curtain was suspended until the end of Ieyasu's dynasty, by which time the imperial west, particularly Great Britain and Russia, had taught Japan how to embroider conquest with diplomacy and had given her the more valid excuses for it of economic preservation and national prestige.

The Japanese victors could not conveniently bring home the heads of their victims so they cut off the noses and the left ears and shipped these over the Japan Sea in wooden sake tubs filled with brine. A tourist sight to-day is the Ear Mound near the image of the Great Buddha in Kyoto, where the gristly if not grisly trophies were finally hidden from sight and smell. The practice of head taking in Japan remained until 1877 one of the archipelago's connections with primitive South-Sea civilization, the last head officially taken by imperial order being that of Saigo, the hero-leader of the samurai rebellion of that year.

It is possible that Hideyoshi was pressed into his foreign campaigns by the necessity of keeping busy the hundreds of thousands of professional warriors who infested the land. He got rid of about 100,000 of them, but also dangerously impoverished the peasantry and cities which were the backbone of the nation. In addition to the treasure of the Ear Mound, Japan received from her first historical attempt to expand on the continent the secret of the ultradecorated porcelain which we know as Satsuma ware—for Satsuma warriors, returning to their homes in the southern tip of Japan, imitated and perfected the art. Aside from these things, the costly venture left Japan an ambition to try again and a tradition of the importance of a navy.

In all things personally dearest to his heart, the great Hideyoshi failed. He was all-powerful, but he never dared to assume the title of shogun. In restraining his vanity he was wiser, it seems, than Napoleon. Had he come into open conflict with the emperor, who would not give him a title forbidden to one of humble birth, but who otherwise ate out of the plebeian Hideyoshi's hand, his loyal but jealous supporter Ieyasu would have been privileged—nay obliged— to throw him over, and present-day Japan would curse instead of admire him. Hideyoshi hoped that his death might give him the honor he had to pass by in life. Not willing, however, to trust posterity to take the initiative, he built a gorgeous temple in which to enshrine his own spirit. But it never became sacred. The greatest historical character of the Land of the Gods remains a human being.

If he could not be shogun of Japan, thought Hideyoshi, he would conquer foreign lands and make himself *their* emperor. That failed. And his last intense desire to have his own flesh and blood succeed him in supreme power was destined to perfidious, tragic defeat. So much for human ambitions. Hideyoshi remains the inspirer of common Japanese. This man of the plebeians not even entitled to a surname, who had to adopt his name Toyotomi and his coat of arms, had grasped supreme power if not honor in the Empire of the Gods.

VI

Before embarking on his Korean campaigns, Hideyoshi had delegated to his old associate and vassal Ieyasu rule over the new and rough half of Japan north and east of the central mountains now called the Japanese Alps. Ieyasu had built a fortress on the marshes of Yedo (now Tokyo) Bay, giving, in his astute way, more attention to strength and spaciousness then to height and ornament. The moats of that castle encircle the sacred precincts of to-day's Son of Heaven, and the capital whose skyscrapers look into their placid waters is Tokyo, third largest city of the world.

On his deathbed Hideyoshi had summoned Ieyasu, who came expecting to be appointed successor to the supreme overlordship as his reward for a lifetime of patience and astute loyalty. But instead the dying unifier demanded that his old associate and survivor swear in

his own blood to place young Hideyori, Hideyoshi's son, over Japan's
214 feudatories. Knowing the jealousy of the lesser lords, Ieyasu
once more—for the last time—let policy check ambition. He was to
go to pains to explain, later, that he took the blood for his brush to
write this bedside oath not from his finger or gums, as the samurai
code stipulates, but from a scratch behind his ear, which he said
entitled him to regard it as not legally or morally binding. Lesser
instances of this sort of Japanese reasoning puzzle our own State
Department from time to time. Ieyasu also recalled that Hideyoshi
in a similar situation had given scant attention to the claims of
Nobunaga's heir.

Hideyoshi's son seemed very willing to leave authority to Uncle
Ieyasu who gave him his own daughter as an additional wife. He
grew into a likeable youth much under the influence of Roman
Catholic samurai, although Hideyoshi, late in life, had become
openly hostile to Christianity through one of those almost unbelievably stupid incidents that sprinkle history. A Spanish vessel, the
San Felipe, putting into the Third Island for repairs after a typhoon,
was highjacked by the always intransigent Tosa clansmen in this
fashion: They placed a pilot aboard to steer it to what they stated
was the proper place for ship repairing. The pilot ran the galley
aground and broke its back. Whereupon, quoting an old Japanese
law making a stranded ship the booty of its discoverers, they looted
it. The seizure being thus legal, Hideyoshi approved the clansmen's
action—another typical example of the Japanese idea of legality. It
was this sort of interpretation of law that eventually brought the
expeditions, first of the American Commodore Biddle and later of
Commodore Perry, to Japan's shores in the nineteenth century. Incidentally, one is reminded of more recent incidents, such as the
"punishment" consisting of a furlough and a trip around the world
meted out to the Japanese army officer who sold to the ex-bandit
Chinese ruler of Manchuria more than a million dollars' worth of
United States army materials fatuously left by Woodrow Wilson
under Japanese protection in Vladivostok.

The desperate Spanish pilot of the San Felipe tried bluffing, pointing out on a map of the world how much of it Spain owned, and
how dangerous it would be for Japan to insult his sovereign,

Philip II. The astute Tosa men asked how Spain got so much territory. The pilot naïvely replied that she first sent out priests to make converts in the nations she intended to conquer, then troops to combine with the new Christians against the native authority. The clansmen transmitted this testimony by fast courier to Hideyoshi, who, in one of the last of his history-making rages, ordered the Franciscans at Osaka, and some Jesuits and natives as well, forthwith crucified. The old Roman punishment of crucifixion was not native to Japan, but introduced by Hideyoshi as a fitting punishment for Christians who were always talking about the cross. The Japanese Cæsar, however, added the mercy of having the victim pierced through by two spears.

One hundred and thirty-seven churches around Nagasaki were destroyed in this first really serious outburst against Christians and Europeans, and all the Jesuits were assembled for deportation. At this moment Hideyoshi died. Ieyasu was hesitant. The Jesuits filtered back to their stations, eventually to suffer a still more horrible fate after this founder of the Tokugawa dynasty, in his deliberate manner, had convinced himself that he wanted none of them or their European civilization.

Ieyasu was getting old. Not much time remained for him to establish his dynasty and the unity of Japan. The new religion, and its distinguished patron, his son-in-law, residing in the great Osaka castle which Hideyoshi had endeavored to make the most self-sustaining and impregnable fortress in the world, were combining into an insufferable menace to his plans. Ieyasu exacted from an acquiescent emperor the title of shogun which both Nobunaga and Hideyoshi had failed to obtain, carrying the supreme military and civil authority given to Yoritomo in the twelfth century. At last the oath taken by the swashbuckling trio fifty years before had its completion! Ieyasu forthwith abdicated, passing the title to his grown son, Tokugawa Hidetada, whom he gave a stern training in the exercise of power.

In 1614 Ieyasu issued his final edict against Christianity. His tight-minded son was soon to follow with the most ruthless, and it must be admitted, successful persecution known to history. The Tokugawas felt insecure as long as Hideyoshi's family and castle at

Osaka remained. So father and son brought on a war with Hideyori's sympathizers, prosecuted it to the gates of the Osaka castle, and worked upon Hideyori's mother through that personage's younger sister who was bound to Ieyasu, for terms of peace permitting the filling up of the immense outer moat—too deep and wide and with too much water in its depths for any army of that day to cross. When time came for the filling, Ieyasu rushed in hundreds of thousands of workmen, carrying dirt with which to fill a section of the inner moat also.

The pact left Hideyori still alive, a situation that had to be corrected somehow. The opportunity came beautifully. The young man pathetically cast a fine bronze and gold bell to commemorate the clearing up of misunderstanding with the man who had been his father's retainer and who was his father's collaborator and his own father-in-law. You may see it in Kyoto to-day. Its principal Chinese inscription reads: "For the national family: peace and prosperity." The second and fourth ideographs are those used for the *Ie* and *Yasu* of Ieyasu, and the bell is so hung that the great cedar log used as clapper, Japanese style, swings against these characters. Insult! The bell also bears a lesser inscription taken from a Chinese classic: "East welcome bright moon, west convoy setting sun." One might think this was an allusion to the spread of Japanese empire, but to the Tokugawas it meant that they were to fade like the setting sun! But the depth of the irony—or treachery—is that probably the inscription which brought on the bloodiest campaign ever fought in Japan was supplied to naïve Hideyori by a Tokugawa!

Something like 100,000 samurai perished. With the aid of the fills unfairly made in the moat, Tokugawa's forces got near enough to the great Osaka castle to fire it. Hideyori disemboweled himself before perishing in the flames. Ieyasu proceeded to exterminate the entire family of his former comrade and master root and branch, male and female.

The amazing outer walls of the old castle and the unfilled portion of the chasmlike moat are still extant at Osaka to-day. Since 1933 a replica in concrete of the burned central tower, may be ascended in elevators. There are thousands of brown granite stones twenty feet long by ten feet wide in the walls. A few are thirty-five feet long, fourteen feet wide, and six or seven feet thick. Hideyoshi transported these from the Third Island across the Inland Sea. Nobody seems to have kept record of how they were moved and set up, but they are a far more impressive monument to his ingenuity and power than the Ear Mound of Kyoto.

Chapter V
The Hiatus

THE Tokugawa dynasty was supreme and Japan was unified. Ieyasu died a few months later. His remains (some say only one hair of his head) were eventually sepulchered in the most ornate group of mausoleum structures existing in the present world, stepping up a steep slope under the giant cryptomerias of his native mountains of Nikko. Chinese architects and artisans were imported to construct them. Summer tourists go to their cool precincts from the humid heat of Tokyo in four hours by fast electric train, and pay one yen to get into the inner sanctuary, and for a little extra see beautiful young nuns dance the sacred Shinto postures. Every tourist takes a snapshot of the famous woodcarvings of the sleeping cat and the three monkeys who "hear no evil, see no evil, speak no evil."

The first Tokugawa had not settled the problem of the Christian religion and European contacts. He himself had died without putting to death a single European. Although lacking Hideyoshi's lust for foreign conquest, he inherited his desire for trade, and sought earnestly to find a way of dealing with Europeans that would not subject his nation to their inextricably mixed religious and imperial ambitions. He left adequate instruction, however, as to what was to be done with the white bigots if a safe way of dealing with them could not be found.

Ieyasu had naturally turned to the Dutch and English who were not "in on" the church-blessed attempt of Spain and Portugal to divide the world, but were still in their humble beginnings. A Dutch ship had arrived at an opportune moment in 1600, bearing as its pilot a remarkable English seaman, Will Adams, possessed of little landlubber education but with a natural gift for statesmanship. The Jesuit fathers hastened to denounce the newcomers as pirates, which inspired Ieyasu to give Will Adams a favorable hearing. That historic interview resulted in the Englishman's remaining, partly under benevolent restraint, and partly because greater lands and honors came to him than could have come at home. The unlettered Englishman, Will Adams, was master shipbuilder and personal councilor to the cultured top lord of Japan until death.

This humble seaman occupied the first, and highest, advisory position ever granted to a white man in Japan. There is no indication that he was vindictive against the Catholics as most non-Roman Englishmen and Dutchmen were at the time. But when questioned by Ieyasu, Adams replied frankly. He gave Ieyasu to understand that there was a considerable part of the European world that had no more use for the ambitions of Spain and Portugal, and the means used to obtain them, than had the shogun of Japan. He described the savagery of sectarian disputes in the Christian world, which shocked Ieyasu, who was always inclined to tolerance unless imperiled.

Ieyasu sent a Japanese scholar, Nishi Soshin, all the way to Europe to verify Adams' reports, and Soshin ran smack into the horrors of Torquemada's inquisition. He was banqueted at the courts of kings and cardinals, but returned to help the mild Ieyasu's successors use every one of that Spanish torturer's refinements on the unfortunate Jesuits and their converts in Japan.

Ieyasu was further turned against Christianity by a conspiracy involving one of his own sons and a Christian official. Again, a Spanish mariner obtained through a priest the permission to survey the coast, and the couple went at it with such haste that Tokugawa's suspicion was aroused. On consulting Adams he was told that Christian nations considered surveying of their coasts by aliens a hostile act. The Portuguese and Spanish continued to get themselves in bad by importuning the shogun to expel the Dutch, offering to send ships to keep the merchantmen of the Dutch East India Company out of Japanese waters.

Their misjudgment of Japanese psychology was of a piece with that of courtiers and priests in Madrid, who openly talked of extending Spanish rule over Japan in the presence of a visiting Japanese Jesuit named Araki. Insulted by their presumption of his lack of national loyalty, the priest Araki returned to warn Ieyasu against his own fellow religionists, and in 1611 Ieyasu banished all Christians from his court forever. Three years later all priests, Japanese and European, were summarily shipped off to Macao. Churches were demolished and their congregations disbanded. Will Adams, despite his favored position, was compelled to renounce even his nonconformist type of Christianity.

The Dutch traders brought the final disgrace upon Europe by simpering talebearing on their fellow whites, and fawning willingness to undergo any humiliation and obey ordinances contravening their dignity as human beings and what might have been their consciences. They went so far as to curry favor by forging documents which sent Japanese Christians to torture and death.

The British were more upstanding, although scarcely admirable. No one to-day can laugh at the ship's log of jovial Captain Saris of the British East India Company, who recounts the fun he got out of inviting Japanese Christian ladies to his cabin and exposing to them a huge, very lewd painting of Venus, before which they knelt in puzzled reverence, taking it for some unknown representation of the Virgin Mary. At this time the British were too involved in India and China to follow the opportunity created for them by Ieyasu and Will Adams, while the Dutch, who were being crowded out of India and China by the British, were willing to sell their souls for a bit of that opportunity.

II

During the bloody century before Hideyoshi, Japanese were taking to the seas as pirates and freebooters just as were Englishmen at the same time. So terrible had become Japanese ravages on the Chinese coast that the Ming dynasty prohibited all intercourse with Japan after 1550, and the Manchu dynasty, after its establishment in 1644, felt compelled to remove every Chinese coastal habitation three miles inland.

The culmination of Japan's reaching out was a remarkable mission from east to west. Five years before the Pilgrim Fathers landed at Plymouth Rock, Tokugawa permitted his great and ambitious north-

ern vassal named Date (Masamune) to send sixty lordly Japanese
across the Pacific in a ship built under Will Adams' supervision.

The mission was under Date's retainer Hashikura and an intriguing Spanish monk named Sotelo whom Date had rescued from
martyrdom—evidently with the hope of starting a foreign trade to
rival that of his Tokugawa overlord. The ship put in at Acapulco,
Mexico, where the entire embassy, excepting Hashikura who was
saved for the honors in Rome, were baptized in Holy Week, 1614.
Here the embassy became guests of the king of Spain, and while its
ship waited, proceeded to Havana and across the Atlantic. It was
fêted and feasted in Seville and received by the Pope at the very
time all Christian missionaries in Japan were being herded into
Nagasaki for deportation!

In October, 1615, Hashikura delivered his letter to the Pope. Two
years later the embassy reached Acapulco again. A Spanish governor,
newly appointed to the Philippines, had chartered their Japanese
ship to sail to Manila, and the two parties went out together.

Hashikura and eleven Japanese, all that were left of the embassy
to the Pope, got home to Sendai in northern Japan in August, 1620.
Hashikura declared that Christianity was a "vain show" and Date's
associations with the Christians so little affected him that on his
deathbed he followed the barbaric oriental custom of junshi although
this had been condemned by the great Tokugawa himself—that is,
Date gave two of his retainers the privilege of committing hara-kiri
at his funeral so they could accompany him to the spirit world. Out
of loyalty, four samurai of one of these retainers gutted themselves
in turn. Ieyasu was dead and his successors were blindly shutting
out the world, while in the southern island a recanted Christian lord
played the part of Torquemada. This persecution was to lead up to
Japan's last civil war, which in turn was followed by the 230-year
period of Tokugawa peace of isolation, a complete isolation from
the western world during its eras of discovery and science, when it
moved perhaps faster than at any other time in history. Then, in
our day, Japan hustled faster than any western nation—to catch up,
and get ahead.

III

Tokugawa's first step toward isolation was a law forbidding Japanese Christians to go abroad, or engage in trade. All relations with the Spaniards in Manila were then broken off. It is worth noting, as light on the nationalistic Japanese mind, that first the "Christian" Date in the north and then Satsuma clansmen, seeing that Spain did not retaliate and seemed to be weak, revived Hideyoshi's plan to annex the Philippines. They sent spies and soldiers in disguise to Manila, but the ruling Tokugawa suppressed their scheme. In 1635 he issued a series of drastic edicts. Japanese vessels were limited to the measure of good-sized fishing boats. Eventually, to build a boat with a deck was made treason. Henceforth no Japanese might leave the shores of the islands. All men, women, and children in the realm were ordered to register at Buddhist temples, and secure certificates of non-Christianity. The ritual required trampling on the crucifix in the presence of the priests. Even the Dutch traders were put through this broad-minded little ceremony. It came to the point at which recanters, willing to trample on the cross, had in addition to sell themselves into servitude to get the bribes required by grafting Buddhist priests for the "certificate of non-Christianity" without which they were liable to be burned at the stake, sawn asunder with a bamboo saw, or hung by the feet over a pit until dead.

The desperate situation of the overtaxed, hounded, Christianity-permeated community of the southern island brought about the Shimabara insurrection of 1637. Despite the Tokugawa police system of installing an official spy in every five families and paying informers, 30,000 to 40,000 Christians and sympathizers, samurai, their women and serfs, fled on a pre-arranged date, with whatever weapons they could improvise, to a deserted castle on the coast near Nagasaki.

So valiantly did they fight that the overwhelming force sent by the shogun was making no headway when the Christian Dutch came to deliver the final blow to Christianity in Japan. Koeckebecker, head of the Dutch trading station at nearby Hirado, under orders from home to do anything to win official favor, moved his ships under the beleaguered castle and bombarded its helpless occupants

to death. In the massacre, completed by the shogun's soldiers, 37,000
perished. Before the final assault the women and children jumped
from the headland to death in the sea:

The Dutch were "rewarded" by being taken away from pleasant
Hirado and put behind a high board wall encircling the tiny island
of Deshima and by having their trade cut to two ships a year.

Not a Christian was left in the empire, so far as Tokugawa spies
could discover. But it takes longer to kill a religion than to plant it.
As late as 1650 we find the Tokugawa-sponsored Confucian scholar,
Hayashi, arguing against the "corrupt foreign faith." He says:
"Christianity is comparable to fox possession. It catches women by
pandering to their jealous instincts in inveighing against concubinage, and warriors by appealing to their miserliness in excusing them
from keeping more than one wife." Two and a half centuries after
Shimabara the second American minister to Japan, one of Abraham
Lincoln's generals, by sweet irony a Pennsylvania Dutchman named
van Valkenburgh, traveled in the southern island and spoke of religious freedom. Several hundred Japanese, mostly women, who had
received Christianity by word of mouth over seven generations and
secretly preserved its practices, met to worship the crucifix. They
were promptly arrested, but by the American minister's intercession
released. Thus began religious freedom again in Japan. It developed
into full liberty for missionary work, then the foreigner and his
schools were eliminated from Japanese Christianity. Imperial Japanese learned to make Christianity a prime pillar of its nationalism—
even as we do ourselves.

IV

The first half of the seventeenth century was a time of great
activity in the Pacific. The Russians reached the Pacific Ocean in
1636 and fought a boundary war with the Manchu dynasty of China
in 1680. Spanish galleons sailed regularly between Mexico and the
Philippines, which were part of the viceroyalty of Mexico. Portugal
was well planted on the China coast, and the British and Dutch
were steady callers.

Up to the time she isolated herself, Japan played the major rôle

in the activity of this abortive Pacific era. When the Spanish arrived
in the Philippines in 1565 they found Japanese ships trading there
and a Japanese colony intermarried with the natives. Japanese and
Chinese pirates, often in cahoots, frequently raided the islands.
Japanese vessels conducted a regular rice trade with Siam and ex-
plored the Pacific from the South Sea islands to the Aleutians.
Whether or not the Japanese crossed the Pacific and reached Mexico
before the time of Cortez is in doubt, but many visits by Japanese
traders occurred under the Spanish viceroyalty during the following
century. In 1602, before Will Adams fell into his lap, Ieyasu sent an
embassy to the Philippines to get ships' carpenters. Will Adams'
shipbuilding and coast-service work greatly stimulated Ieyasu's ambitions. By 1617 the shogun's merchant marine, flying the Tokugawa emblem of three leaves in a circle, and licensed for trade to
Korea, China, Australia, and (if we are to believe the documents)
Europe, consisted of 198 seagoing vessels. This fleet compared well
with those of the European maritime powers: Spain, Portugal, Holland, and England. The shogunal ships were called maru—a word
whose origin is lost but which is written with the Chinese character
for "tub" or "pill"—to the joy of wits who wish to find fault with a
Japanese vessel. "Maru" has come to be the equivalent of the western "S.S." although it is applied to anything afloat. Japan's seagoing
merchant marine was abolished in 1636, but as late as 1650 Japan
still had a thousand rice-carrying coast transports.

Japan's promising sea power at this time well bears comparison
with England's. After Edward III, 1350, England had claimed sovereignty of the "narrow seas." Japanese freebooters, whether claiming
it or not, actually dominated *her* "narrow seas" from the time of the
Mongol armada. In 1583 Elizabeth appointed her great admirals (or
pirates, as Spain viewed them) Drake, Frobisher, and Raleigh, to
look to England's sea power. They developed the galleon into the
decked warship. But five years later when the Spanish armada came,
England had only 200 deep-sea vessels, and many of them were not
in Hawkins' victorious fleet. The "felicissima armada" [1] of Spain
got only 120 ships to the Channel, half food and supply ships, in all

[1] To the Spaniards the "most blessed armada" rather than the "invincible
armada," since it was blessed by the Pope.

carrying 24,000 men, half of whom were ill. It was a picayunish affair compared to the Mongol armada of Kublai Khan.

In the normal course of development the center of the sixteenth- and seventeenth-century activity in the Pacific would have been a rapidly growing Japanese maritime empire embracing the islands of the south Pacific, the continent of Australia, and probably the American coast from Alaska to California. Instead, Japan legislated herself off the sea in 1635, and increasingly isolated herself until the middle of the eighteenth century. Two Dutch ships and ten Chinese junks per year became the sum total of her intercourse with the outside world. The head of the Dutch mission was allowed to cross the country and do obeisance at the shogun's court once in several years, and an edict stipulated that "there should not be two Chinese in any one fief at the same time."

The last attempt to break down this isolation until the end of the eighteenth century was a Portuguese mission of seventy persons headed by four venerables in 1640. All were put to death but the thirteen of lowest rank, who carried back the order: "For the future let none so long as the sun illumines the world presume to sail to Japan, not even in the quality of ambassador, and this declaration is never to be revoked on pain of death."

No other nation in history has known such isolation and self-sufficiency. When it was over, our Abraham Lincoln was to receive the first Japanese to come to the west officially for two and one half centuries—from a Japan that had remained culturally and mentally contemporary with Queen Elizabeth.

Thus the world's Pacific era was held back and destined to follow rather than coexist with the Atlantic era of world history. This setback weighs heavily on the Japanese mind. It is responsible for such a declaration as the following made by a Tokyo newspaper in 1921: "For two hundred and fifty years the Japanese slept at home while the European nations were busy making colonies and conquering territories. We were forbidden to go abroad. We were forbidden to build big ships. We were compelled to keep indoors, wasting our energies on such pastimes as versification and tea ceremony. The Tokugawa policy of seclusion enabled that government to remain on its legs in security and prosperity for two hundred and fifty years, but it prevented people from expanding abroad during that time, with the result that we are now suffering from overpopulation and racial discrimination. . . . We are now paying for the Tokugawa régime."

But Japan's nationalists of to-day have a new interpretation of the Tokugawa hiatus. They begin to divine heaven's will in the matter. As they now see it, the Tokugawas were fate's instruments for conserving the resources and bearing up the morale of Japan until the nongodly nations of the world should have hung themselves with their own rope. Japan, pristine, pure, and virile, may now proceed to do her duty in the world—collecting, as well, her deserved reward!

Chapter VI

The Genius That Disciplined Japan

A GREAT deal of light can be shed on this remarkable Tokugawa epoch as well as on the fascinating character of Ieyasu, the greatest administrative genius yet produced by his race, from a document known as the Legacy of Ieyasu,[1] treasured in the shogun's family. It seems to have been compiled during the three years following his death from notes of his conversations taken by intimate retainers—set down a little more accurately, perhaps, than the sayings of Christ and Mohammed. It had immense influence in governing the policy of his successors and shaping the Japanese people. In it Ieyasu recommends Confucian principles of government beginning with: "The people are the foundation of the Empire." He meant this benevolently, not democratically, but to-day it is regarded as rank heresy. The constitution of 1889 corrects it with the doctrine: "The Emperor is the head of the Empire, combining in himself the rights of sovereignty.... The Empire of Japan shall be reigned over and governed by a line of Emperors unbroken for ages eternal."

Although not so fantastic about it as the moderns, Ieyasu upholds the divine theory of Japan. "Since our bodies," says he in Article 72 of the Legacy, "are born into the Empire of the Gods, to adopt the teachings of other countries in toto would be to desert one's own master and forget the origin of one's own being. A clear decision should be arrived at as to what is proper to adopt, what to reject." Medieval Tokugawa is found here to be in perfect agreement with modern, Oregon-reared Matsuoka. Again Ieyasu, dependent as he was for his position on military power, warns against the empire's

---

[1] Translated and published by J. F. Lowder, H. B. M. Consul, Yokohama, 1874.

basing its prestige on this instead of on consciousness of the presence within it of the "Throne of Divine Blessing." If Japan's people become oblivious of the origin of the kingdom of their Gods, self-desire is apt to overflow. "Such a sin," says he, "is not a light one and will be punished in Heaven." Zealous as he was to protect himself and house with a spy system as good as Mussolini's or Stalin's in our time, he practically recognizes the "right of assassination" which remains a striking feature of Japanese politics. A superior who neglects to respect the dignity of his subjects may, he says, look forward to assassination.

The Legacy is an intriguing mixture of statecraft, personal apologia, national economics, and social organization. It is, the Legacy itself concludes, "an example which, although it may not hit the mark, will not go very far wide. ... I have exposed and laid bare the limited reflections of my breast. Let no future generation ridicule me as having the heart of an old grandmother. I have been a transmitter [this is lifted from Confucius], not a framer. I have not allowed myself to be in the slightest degree influenced by selfish motives."

Some of the testament is pure Marcus Aurelius moralizing: "Keep your heart pure, and be diligent in veneration to the gods. Apply the undivided attention of the mind to that which is naturally distasteful. Practice what you preach, though it grinds you down. Every man has his own use. Anything in heaven or earth or sea can be found out, save the thread of the heart of man. No wise ruler is ever cocksure. In hiring and dismissing officials, remember that the cold servant may be much better than the ardent."

Ieyasu's benevolent side is here: "Special commiseration for the widower, widowed, orphaned and lonely is the foundation of charitable government." He condemns gambling and drink but says offenders are not to be punished harshly. He bases his condemnation of junshi—going to the next world with one's lord—on Confucius, and ordains the most effective way to put an end to it, that of impoverishing the posterity of the too ardent vassal. (Yet a grandson of Ieyasu was to command two counselors of state to follow him to the Yellow Springs—the oriental Hades—and the custom persists to this day, the classical example of our generation being the self-im-

molation of General and Madame Nogi on the occasion of the
Meiji Emperor's funeral. Several patriots performed junshi when
Admiral Togo was buried.)

The harsh side of Ieyasu is expressed in his strictness regarding
class lines and requirement of absolute obedience. An "other than
expected fellow" (one who has forgotten to keep his place) may be
cut down without question, he says. To-day "other than expected
fellow" and baka ("fool") are the only real "cusswords" in the peculiarly curse-free Japanese language. The greatest crime, according to Ieyasu, is for a vassal to raise his hand against his lord, or a
lower class against a higher. He commands that the punishment for
this be the rooting out of every relative and companion of the guilty
person to the most distant, as well as his own death by torture. Next
to this supreme crime Ieyasu placed incendiarism, forgery, and poisoning. This harsh side of his administration increased after him,
until the principle of group responsibility made life for the Japanese
commoner a continual terror. Each group of five families came to be
held jointly guilty of any offense of guilt within it, except for such
members as might save themselves by reporting their fellows.

Ieyasu insists upon strictness and impartiality of courts and equal
care in meting out punishment and rewards. A high councilor and
frequently the shogun himself must from time to time sit behind the
screen and listen unseen to judges, plaintiffs, defendants, and wit-
nesses alike.

Punishments Ieyasu divides into nine classes beginning with
branding and going on through nose slitting, transportation, impris-
onment, decapitation without or with exposing of the head, crucifixion, burning, and boiling with oil. He does not include sawing,
breaking on the wheel, and burying alive, and expressly forbids
pulling a man in two between oxen, but both of these were used by
his descendants against insurrectionists, and, of course, anything
was allowable when unlucky Christians were concerned. The sawing
business consisted of tying the culprit to a pole on a public bridge.
A cut in the shoulder was started with a short, sharp bamboo saw,
which passersby might continue to drive through the man until he
was cut in twain. To the credit of Japanese pedestrians be it said
that the officials usually had to finish off the job by crucifying the

culprit on the second day. Legal tortures to extort evidence included pouring molten lead or copper in cuts and covering with plaster which dried and cracked the skin.

The Tokugawa punishments were not more cruel and probably on the whole were more just than those meted out in Christian Europe during the preceding century. Their variety was greatly enriched by importations from Christendom. While in fifteenth-century Europe nothing was thought of throwing Irish slave women overboard to lighten ship in a storm, and women prisoners seemed to be the special delight of torturers, a special code applied to women in Japan. For all crimes save murder, arson, and treason, for which they were decapitated, women suffered no more punishment than having their hair cut off, or being sold into bondage, where as a matter of fact they were already.

The Napoleonic code of law introduced in the Meiji era after 1870 was drastically to modify judicial punishment in Japan, perhaps even to err in the direction of leniency. Japan's present code is one of the most humane in existence. The Tokugawa punishment did not apply, of course, to the warrior caste, who, like the clergy of England with their "benefit," had their own laws. For minor infractions of their code or incurring the displeasure of their lords, samurai merely had their rank and yearly stipend of rice reduced. Beyond that there was only the "happy discharge" of hara-kiri for the men, and throat cutting for women. A woman, unless of such distinction that she bore the status of "honorary man," had no right to hara-kiri, nor, of course, did any plebeian—points regarding which little Madame Butterfly in the opera is just all wrong.

II

Land boundaries for the warrior class, says Ieyasu, are sacred. The proper judges should decide the boundaries and a man who whimpers over the decision should have his property confiscated. Ieyasu was lax about duels, hard on premeditated crime. He recognized the right of private vengeance, set forth in Confucius' dictum that one may not live under the same heaven with a man who has wronged his father. But the laws of Ieyasu required the avenger to announce to the court his intended victim, with evidence of the wrong, and to complete the vengeance within the number of days allowed by court order.

"Permit people," says Ieyasu, "to follow such religions as they please, save for that false and corrupt school," which meant Roman Catholicism. Mendicants, beggars, witches, and the outcasts (numbering about a million) were to be controlled through their own hereditary chiefs. The outcasts consisted of two groups, the Heimin, the "not people," and the Eta, the origin of whose degraded state is uncertain, but who under Buddhism were given those tasks, such as taking animal life, dealing with hides, etc., which made their souls ineligible to rebirth in human form. They lived in separate communities and even the length of roads that passed through their villages was deducted from reckoned mileage between points.

The official disability of the outcasts continued until the army and the public school system leveled all classes in Japan, seventy years ago. But there is still a king of the Eta who claims illegitimate descent from the great victor of the Wars of the Chrysanthemums, the first shogun, Yoritomo himself. A few Eta have risen in official and military life, a greater number in commercial life. The Christian social reformer Kagawa says that the Eta women are more beautiful than the average Japanese, and he believes that this is due to the fact that they have most frequently been given as mistresses to foreign visitors and residents, causing their class to benefit by miscegenation. Many of the present inmates of the cheaper houses of prostitution are of Eta origin.

Ieyasu claims that his own ancestry goes back into all of the "god houses," particularly through Yoritomo, the first shogun. He evinces the typical aristocratic interest in the welfare of the plebeian classes of peasants, artisans, and merchants, respected in the order named. The Buddhist priesthood constituted a fourth class. Tokugawa ranked his feudal lords, with the exception of the families personally attached to him as special guards, by their income in bushels of rice, but he says their real greatness is to be judged by the prosperity of their peasantry rather than of themselves—yet the Tokugawa era was one of steady decline in the condition of the farmers while merchants and artisans prospered, a condition repeating itself under modern industrialization.

Ieyasu emphasizes that men of ancient lineage and good repute among the plebeians are to be given every official support in building up local prestige, regardless of their wealth. The plebeian magistracies and tax-collectorships are to go to such men. Villages and guilds are to have the right of electing advisory elders to sit with the officials, and even the "groups of five" are to be allowed to elect their own head who is to be official spy on the rest for a year—showing, certainly, a large faith in popular support of the régime.

He lays down regulations for pruning trees, the protection of the peasants' rice crops, damage from shadows cast by buildings and hedges, and for fire protection in villages and cities.

Ieyasu's humanness is shown in his appointment of the petty lords who rallied to his banner before his doubtful Osaka campaign, to be "favored families" and shogunal bodyguard. They were able to lift up their heads in equality with the wealthiest feudatories of the realm. He says: "The fudai [2] great and small have shown the utmost fidelity, even suffering their bones to be ground to powder and their flesh to be chopped up for me. In what way soever their posterity may offend, short of actual treason, their estates may not be confiscated."

He confesses his own progress in theory of government: "In my youth, my sole aim was to conquer and subjugate hostile provinces and take revenge upon the enemies of my ancestors. The Chinese classics teach, however, 'that to assist the people is to give peace to the empire' and since I have come to understand that precept, I have undeviatingly followed it. Anyone turning his back upon it is no son of mine."

Ieyasu recounts that he has had ten thousand narrow escapes and eighty to ninety hand encounters in battle, and in thankfulness over his eighteen "close calls" he records that he has built eighteen temples in the neighborhood of Yedo.

[2] The Japanese word *fudai* resembles our "feudatory" in both sound and meaning. This happens to be true of quite a few words—for instance *ottsu* ("hot") —although there is no common etymological ancestry. Some Japanese words are adoptees from European languages.

III

In between multifarious regulations of ceremony, rank, protection of his palaces, of the emperor and the chief families of the kingdom, Ieyasu reveals many well-tempered views on life. Doctors, he says, are not to be allowed to become rich, lest they become indolent and reckless with lives, and they are to be "paid according to the shallowness or depth of their cure." He says that marriage is the greatest relation of mankind, and advises all young blades of sixteen to find a go-between to get them a wife. They should marry into a good family, and childless men should adopt an heir. In fact, a house that fails to provide itself a direct male heir by birth or adoption is to have its property confiscated regardless of other kin.

As Japan continued living entirely within herself, and the population grew from some 19,000,000 in the 1600's to 30,000,000 in 1850, this advice came to be disregarded, and it came to be shameful for a samurai to marry under thirty, and to have more than two children. Population was kept within bounds among plebeians by abortion and infanticide. But when Japan adopted western civilization after the middle of the last century and the Japanese leaders—even as European—wanted an unlimited supply of factory hands and gun fodder, these habits of population control had to be overcome by laws against infanticide, and encouragement such as state support to every sixth child. The result, abetted by sanitation, modernization of medicine and urban life, is that Japan's population leaped from 30,000,000 in 1850 to 75,000,000 in 1941, and is increasing at the rate of 1,000,000 a year—less war losses.

Ieyasu dictates that a cuckolded plebeian may kill his wife and her paramour, but if he spares one of them he is held to be equal in guilt—a shrewd deterrent to a husband merely seeking to get rid of his wife. As for the military class, he says they "know better than to disrupt society with such peccadillos," and the guilty among them, male and female, are to be promptly punished by their superiors. As a matter of fact they enjoyed a great many sex liberties prohibited among the proletariat.

Ieyasu shows great tolerance for homosexuals, stating that such cases are to be dealt with by judges only with great deliberation. As a matter of fact, pederasty among the samurai was a tolerated institution until very recent times, just as it has been among every warrior and esthetic caste in Europe. Everyone knows, the Legacy goes on, that there are twelve imperial concubines, and that princes may have eight mistresses, lords five mistresses, and samurai two handmaids in addition to a wife. "All below this," say Ieyasu, "are ordinary married men, but any samurai who will neglect his wife just because he loves his handmaid better should see in himself a very sunken and disreputable fellow." "Beware," says Ieyasu, "of the hen crowing at morn. Affairs of the household belong to the wife, and those of the lord to the samurai." "Poets and sages," he remarks, carefully exempting himself from suspicion of having done "social investigation," "say that prostitution is the worm-eaten part of society, but it is a necessary evil."

He ordains that roads, rivers, bridges, fords, etc., shall be kept up as "provincial thank tribute" and that lords committing indiscretions or becoming dangerously rich shall be given extra opportunity to show thankfulness by doing road work. He dictates the width of roads: the Tokaido, the great "Sea Road" forming the main artery of the nation between Yedo and Kyoto, thirty-six feet—or including trees and ditches on each side, 120 feet. The Tokaido is still the "main stem" and to-day consists of several tracks of railroad, an air route, and a concrete highway. Secondary roads were to be half this width and even footpaths to be six feet wide.

During the Tokugawa era Japan had the best roads of the time with strangely enough almost no wheel traffic. Lords and ladies were carried in palanquins with a definitely fixed number of bearers according to rank. Plebeians might not ride on horseback. Transportation was carried on by coolie guilds whose rate of pay, length of journey, work hours, and load for horse and man were fixed by law throughout the kingdom. Only official horse-post and military transport were exempted. To the present day this pertains in Japan, and the traveler who tries to over- or underpay a taxi driver or rickshaw coolie finds himself in trouble.

IV

Yedo was the unique city of the world. Seven out of ten of its population were of samurai caste living on the rest of the nation, and the remainder were menials, artists, or merchants serving them. The castles of the thirty-two great lords, built on the low hills, were the equals of most of the palaces of Europe, and there were five hundred lesser mansions. Avenues led through landscape gardens to lacquer-covered porticoes behind which were great halls covered with luxurious, thick, springy straw mats changed each year. Decorated sliding screen partitions separated the halls into rooms in which lords and ladies, swathed in yards of silk and brocade, knelt in the unique Japanese posture: buttocks against the heels, insteps against the floor.

On land reclaimed from the reedy bay were the crowded houses and tortuous lanes of the commercial section, and the flourishing Yoshiwara district where as many as fifteen thousand of the best trained and beautiful women of "the most ancient profession" worked and played. The whole town would turn out to see their street fêtes. They were gorgeously robed, daintily mannered, and their signs were a crooked obi sash and a red Japanese lantern. The canals had scores of arched bridges with heavy lacquered balustrades which were the public places for exposing criminals or making assignations.

The Tokugawa installed waterworks and subsidized volunteer fire brigades. In their medieval costumes, carrying their ladders and long-handled axes, these may still be seen in remote parts of the empire—although a modern motorized hook-and-ladder and chemical brigade will probably accompany them. The Tokugawas prohibited thatched roofs in Yedo. The city kept pace with London and Philadelphia in modernization up to 1850. In this as in other material respects Japan never got really more than fifty years behind the west in development.

Thousands of idle samurai from their lords' house- or bodyguards, and other thousands of ronin—literally "wave men," unattached knights whose lordly houses had been abolished or who had been dismissed—roamed the streets, looking for adventure or amusement.

The city became a nest of fraternities of samurai, clerks, artisans, and menials, who often degenerated to organized rowdyism. Wandering monks and nuns—the latter from all accounts comely, masculine young women not inhibited by modesty or humility—added color to the streets. The two Tokugawa mayors of the great city alternated every six months in number-one authority. They wisely erected gate barriers across the narrow streets which could be closed upon signal. Closing by frantic officials or hysterical keepers during the great fire of 1660, however, cost tens of thousands of lives. The street gates still survive around the Yoshiwara and in gay Akasuka.

Osaka at the other end of the empire on the Inland Sea was its busiest mart. The clan lords kept palaces at Yedo and warehouses and business agents, often with small garrisons, at Osaka. The Tokugawa government did not permit them to exchange goods directly between fiefs. Everything had to go through the great emporium of Osaka which was under the control of the shogun and his special guards. In Osaka merchants and money-changers first began to attain that wealth and dignity which was to permit them to supersede for a little while in our day the warrior caste as the aristocracy of the land.

Kyoto with the Imperial Court as its center was the Paris of the empire. Here artists and literati congregated and fashions originated in dress, sports, and literature.

v

Historians have taken a large interest in Ieyasu's control of his feudal lords, much more systematically worked out than in European feudalism. The daimyo or head lord of every fief was required to spend six months of each year in official residence in Yedo where the Tokugawa shogun could get hands on him at any moment. He was required to keep his chief ladies there all the time and, during his six months of absence on his fief, his heir or chief counselor also. Sixteen barriers in the highway system were placed under Tokugawa guards and every passing lord or coolie had to submit to minute search and account for his movements. The guards particularly watched for feudatories trying to make direct contact with the

Emperor, or great clan ladies sneaking off home from their Yedo residences. At the premier barrier of Hakone thousands of feet up on the shoulder of Mt. Fuji women were usually required to tear down their mountainous oiled headdresses to show whether any papers were hidden inside—which made the hairdressers' guild of that barrier town one of the richest in the kingdom.

In his testament Ieyasu gives the total revenue of his empire as some 30,000,000 koku (one koku being 4.96 bushels of rice). The present relative value would be somewhere between three hundred million and a half billion United States dollars—no mean revenue for a state in the seventeenth century. Of this he designates 20,000,-000 to his feudatories great and small and the remaining 8,000,000 or 10,000,000 for the government, which meant the Tokugawa family, its castles, armies, and special police, and the upkeep of the emperor. The Divine Person and his court actually came off with about the same amount as the pettiest lords in the kingdom, and less than some of the big farmers or goshi, the kulaks of Japan—half samurai, half plebs. In 1871, at the close of the Tokugawa era, the lords and samurai were entirely dispossessed but the goshi were allowed to retain their lands. Their heirs formed the landed class of the 1920's and 1930's who struggled to keep up appearances in the provincial cities while tenants refused to pay rent, and Japan's small modern banks, dependent for funds on the deposits of this landed gentry, went broke.

Ieyasu obviously liked to hunt, hawk, and fish with "diving birds" (cormorants), and didn't hold with those moralists of his time who condemned such sports on the part of samurai. He wanted them carried on without damage to the peasantry and fishermen. They provide in times of peace, says he, desirable approaches to the excitation of war. There is something British about him here. On the other hand neither did he hold with those swashbucklers who condemned pursuit of the gentle arts by warriors. Music, says he, is a very proper avocation for soldiers. He was himself a devotee. One of the rarest things that I have been privileged to see is a play bill of the classical posture drama called No, of date about 1580, showing Nobunaga, Hideyoshi, and Ieyasu taking leading parts in the same performance. Yet Iesayu was no milk-and-water fighter. Later generations in the era of peace which he established were to become such. Then the fighting spirit was to be brought back by the civil strife of the middle nineteenth century and Japan's foreign struggles.

Ieyasu recommended military colleges as well as Confucian learning to his samurai. His testament contains the famous phrase quoted by General Araki and others of to-day's superpatriots: "The girded sword is the living soul of the samurai." For a samurai who forgot his sword or was caught without it, Ieyasu decrees softly: "The lapse may not be overlooked," which means hara-kiri.

It will be seen that there was a great deal more to the Tokugawa régime than blind following of precedent. Yet conservatism was its keynote. Says Ieyasu in the testament: "In the absence of precedent, forbid the framing of any new measures whatever. Disturbances always arise from innovations. If a faulty regulation has been allowed to remain in force for fifty years let it stand. . . . I once," he confesses, "made an innovation, about a Buddhist sect. Don't do this." This hide-bound phase of the Tokugawa rule drove seething young patriots of 1850 to go chopping heads with their swords.

Chapter VII
Japan Comes Out

THROUGH Ieyasu's remarkable testament we get a very human picture of the rule which gave one of the longest stretches of peace in history to a nation that had been torn by the worst forms of civil war for five hundred years. Under the Tokugawa dynasty Japan was one of the quietest, most cultured, and prosperous countries of the seventeenth, eighteenth, and nineteenth centuries, and the only one in the world living in unbroken peace. England was the only other community not experiencing great civil strife during this period. Both missed it narrowly perhaps. Yedo had a gunpowder plot for burning the city. Yet during this period Japan fell behind the bloodletting white nations materially and morally. Here is an argument for the Nietzsches and Hitlers!

England went straight out of internal solidarity into commercial and political expansion. Japan built a wall of isolation around her solidarity. Once she hurdled that wall the parallels between British and Japanese development became again very striking.

Let us sum up what went on within that wall. From 1650 to 1860 Japan was a ponderous pyramid in set layers: twenty-odd million peasants, artisans, and merchants (eighty per cent on the land), and topping them a million-odd warriors and nobles in subdivided strata, with a million or so Confucian scholars and Buddhist and Shinto priests, nuns, and temple attendants as sort of filler, and the Tokugawa tyranny at the apex. Everything became hereditary, from the regency (in the event of a shogun being in minority) to the plebeian magistracies—filled by daikwan, each of whom was god and government for 20,000 to 50,000 peasants. The population was kept to the capacity of the rice land to feed it. This society was stable enough to survive a score of great famines due to flood and drought, many disastrous earthquakes and typhoons, and a combined fire and winter storm (1657) which destroyed the greatest city, Yedo, at the cost of 100,000 lives, the shogun's castle, 500 lordly mansions, 300 temples and shrines, and 9,000 warehouses. Yet the Tokugawa government was able to feed the refugees from its storehouses, and advance credit for the rebuilding of the city.

The great fire of London described in Pepys' diary, which, nine years later, burned public buildings, 13,000 private houses, and took six lives, was a bonfire in comparison. Nor could London provide, even in the person of Samuel Johnson, a parallel to the Confucian scholar Hayashi, who had to be carried out of his burning house in his chair—still reading his book. No greater disaster ever overtook a city until the earthquake and fire of 1923 destroyed the same one again, at the cost again of 100,000 lives.

In addition to surmounting these "acts of God" the Tokugawa Japan was able to support a nonproductive warrior class numbering five to seven per cent of its population and to muster armies of a size unknown in Europe. In 1634 the shogun made a visit to the emperor at the head of 307,000 armed men. No western nation at this time moved armies larger than 60,000 men nor was one able to put a force overseas as large as Hideyoshi's Korean expeditions until England's Boer War of 1900. "Little Japan" in historical comparison with the powers of the west never has been little, either in military strength or national revenue. Japan in all ages has been a first-class power.

But by 1800 the tyranny that had held together this solid structure had become financially and morally bankrupt. The descendants of Ieyasu had become nonentities who spent their time on dogs or esoteric studies, and their counselors had become corrupt and vicious. The reductio ad absurdum was reached in one of the sakai (hereditary regents) who pandered to his egotism and perhaps his effeminacy by issuing official stamped permits to seek the favors of the ladies of the court—or perhaps he was a pioneer in eugenics! The great feudal houses and governments had experienced the same degeneracy, and among the increasing number of unattached warriors, the schoolmen, and their pupils, criticism became outspoken.

After the suppression of foreign relations, England had been busy with India and China, and Russia with the settlement of Siberia, while Spain and Portugal had faded from the picture. Now the foreign push began again led by the Russians and British and brought to a climax by a new nation, the United States of America. The Russians stepped on Japan's northernmost island and on the disputed long slender island of Sakhalin, north of that again. Rezanov, who died in 1807 in Siberia en route home from California, created under charter from Queen Catherine the Russian-American Company, which he intended should exploit the entire north Pacific. A dozen or so times between 1792 and 1807 Russian fleets poked their noses into Japanese ports. The Tokugawa were powerless to punish these infractions of their drastic law.

In 1813 Sir Stamford Raffles, who had established British power at Singapore, made an effort to open relations with Japan, and in 1846 the American Commodore Biddle with two gunboats put into the port of Uraga to return some Japanese fishermen who had drifted across the Pacific and to make friends.

At first the Japanese declined to receive the letters which Biddle carried from President Polk. Finally they received them and in return gave him orders to depart. He was asked to receive this communication on a Japanese boat. While he was passing to it he was pushed over by a Japanese. As he had instructions not "to excite a hostile feeling or distrust of the United States," he accepted the apology tendered. He later made speeches in the United States recommending conquest of the exclusive islanders and conversion of Japan into a base for American empire in the Orient. A year later a shipwrecked American sailor threatened his jailers with vengeance from American ships of war but they said they had no fears since a common soldier had knocked down an American commander and no notice had been taken of it. Which reminds one of the Japanese reaction to President Franklin D. Roosevelt's temporary withdrawal of the American fleet from the Pacific. Japanese psychology did not change between 1846 and 1934.

In 1853 came Perry's fleet of steam war vessels which broke

Japan's pretense of seclusion and brought about within fourteen years the end of the Tokugawa régime.

Japanese officials watched, characteristically, like foxes from their lairs. The Dutch supplied the Yedo government with annual digests of current world news and European journals. The foreign offices of the west, on the other hand, did not know that there was a ruler in Japan other than the shogun. Perry who came addressing him as "Emperor" was astonished at the knowledge of the Japanese concerning contemporary politics in the outside world. The first British ambassador, Sir Harry Parkes, coming from adventures in China where he had grown up, discovered the true status of the Yedo government.

Coming like chickens to the feed, nineteen nations including Peru and the kingdom of Hawaii applied for and got treaties of intercourse following the initial one made with the United States. Mr. Townsend Harris who negotiated that treaty was a high protectionist Republican. To him tariffs were a moral principle. So was prohibition. Harris introduced the Tokugawa officials to customs duties and drew up for them their first schedule, prohibitively high on liquors. His making of tariff schedules a part of treaties was to prove an infinite nuisance to Japan. The selfishness of the western powers became undisguised. Each endeavored to beat down Japan's import duties on such articles as it had to sell her. For instance the British were constantly beating down piece-goods duties. Later the picture existed exactly in reverse: Great Britain putting up tariff walls on non-empire piece goods, and Japan doing everything to beat them down. Japan did not succeed in throwing off foreign interference with her customs duties until 1911.

II

Strength of character prevented Japan from becoming a victim of the British-Yankee opium ring as had China. Another battle with western cupidity was over the export of Japanese gold and silver coins. Not only was gold coin drained practically clean (the ratio of gold to silver was much lower than in the west, giving opportunity for immense profit) but silver also was disappearing in

return for the foreigners' outrageously priced nicknacks. Patriotic
assassinations (in characteristic fashion) called repeated attention
to this evil. Officials at the reluctant advice of the Dutch who had
to assure them that such an act could not be made a cause for war,
instituted Japan's first bullion embargo in 1866. In return for this
favor Dutchmen in Japan were excused from the necessity of trampling upon Christian images.

The "reverse English" on this draining of gold from Japan came
in the 1930's when (as a depression measure) the United States
Treasury bought all gold offered at an artificial price—to bury it in
a Kentucky vault—and Japan gladly sold out clean in return for
steel and oil and rubber and airplane parts.

The naïve Tokugawa officials had also accepted the principle of
extraterritoriality previously applied to China and Siam, and it was
not until after Japan's defeat of China and demonstration of sea
power that she got free of this infringement of sovereignty.[1]
Wounded Japanese pride is never very discriminating and seven attacks on foreigners plus the burning of both British and American
legations were carried out during the first few months of Japan's
treaty relations by samurai who hardly knew what extraterritoriality
or customs duties were but didn't like the "fish eyes" of the red-
nosed barbarians looking over their country and western "elephant
feet" stamping about over the sacred islands. Foreign powers made
strict demands for punishment of attackers. The Tokugawa government paid the indemnities but seldom was able to punish the
samurai attackers, who were heroes to their own clans.

The statesmen who had to take over when the Tokugawa régime
collapsed suffered deaths and losses of legs for "allowing" the nation's "shame" to continue. Never before was it made so clear that
high Japanese officials are always in the position of commanders
sniped at from behind for not leading their men into danger fast
enough. After the assassinations of 1931-1934 an irate M.P. remarked
that more civil leaders had died of guns and bombs than had gen-

---

[1] Great Britain, chief "clinger-on," agreed in 1894, about the time Togo sank
Chinese troop transports, to a treaty to go into universal effect in May, 1899.
England gave in when she saw that the United States was not going to intervene
on China's side against Japan. This marked the turn in British policy leading up
to the Anglo-Japanese alliance—made to hold Russia down.

erals on the battlefield! In her long fight for national equality,
Japan had the constant sympathy of the United States, who, however, agreed to give up special privileges in China only when all
other powers would do likewise. Japan obtained her first treaty on
a basis of full equality from Mexico in 1888. From that time until
the great Pacific War an official friendship existed between Japan
and Mexico on which, however, the Kaiser presumed too heavily in
ordering his foreign minister Zimmerman to propose to Mexico, in
early 1917, that she get Japan to change sides and join in partition-
ing the United States. This piece of German asininity, cleverly inter-
cepted and gleefully transmitted by the British secret service,[2]
enraged Woodrow Wilson even more than the submarine sinkings.

Japan's sufferance of an inferior status among nations was a false
interlude in her history, and more for being trapped into it than for
anything else the Tokugawa were hated—as the Ashikaga house had
been hated in the fourteenth century for sending "courtesy" tribute
to China. Shortly before its overthrow the Tokugawa house received
a typical Japanese warning in the action of a samurai patriot who
beheaded with his good sword the twelve wooden effigies of the
Ashikaga in Kyoto. To show how past and present history dovetail
in Japan: the downfall of the 1934 Saito cabinet was hastened by
attacks from patriots and press who raked up an essay by its home
minister satirizing this beheading of the wooden statues. The official
had written it in his early journalistic days, and had never dreamt
that a contrary opinion regarding a medieval incident could end a
modern career.

III

All through the troublous times of 1854-1889 the American official
attitude, laid down by Daniel Webster and followed by John Hay,
who got his first personal contact with Japanese when he received
the samurai embassy of 1860 in President Lincoln's office, was to
protect the independence of Nippon. This was an extension to Japan
of the White House policy toward China, in effecting which the
United States had stood up against Great Britain and France. Lord

---

[2] See Lloyd George's *Memoirs of the World War*. Wilson felt toward Mexico
a good deal the way Japan felt toward China between 1915 and 1936.

Palmerston, premier in London, was also very generous, but his ministers and admirals in the far east repeatedly took a strong hand despite his instructions. After an allied fleet had bombarded Choshu and exacted an indemnity of $3,000,000 gold Congress remitted the American share, a precedent followed much later with China in regard to the Boxer indemnity. Japan used the returned American money to build a breakwater in Yokohama Harbor, where visitors meet the inquisition of the water police.

It took two bloody civil wars, one in 1867-1868, and another in 1874, to end the old era, and it took a number of convincing foreign military and naval demonstrations to wring from the emperor the laconic recognition of foreign relationships entered into by the tottering Tokugawas. The change of Japan's attitude is expressed in the memorial of the emperor's councilors: "Let the foolish grouping: 'foreigners, dogs, goats and barbarians' be abandoned forever, and the court usages imitated from exclusive China be reformed. And let the foreign representatives be bidden to court in manner prescribed by rules current among nations."

IV

When Japan began catching up in the modern world of industrialism and militarism, Britain, with her usual practical reaction to world developments, thought to "use" Japan! It appears now how thoroughly Japan used England—something no white nation ever accomplished. The astute British met their match.

Toward the close of the last century, Great Britain's prime fear was of "the bear that walked like a man"—Russia might become dominant in Asia and threaten Great Britain as chief imperial power in the largest continent. Britain's secondary fear, or to put it in a more British way, dislike, was of Germany's political expansion in the Pacific, seizures on the coast of China, and growing trade. And her third bugbear was Yankee competition which even then threatened British trade on the Pacific. Faced with all these difficulties British statesmen thought it clever to encourage the rise of an ambitious little Asiatic sea power off the coast of Asia—a power that could check Russia and Germany and cool the American im-

perialism and dollar diplomacy of McKinley, Roosevelt, and Taft—
but which, as God and every Briton knew, could never, being non-
British and of an inferior race, become a real rival to Britannia, the
queen of the ocean! So the British advanced money (at interest as
high as 10 per cent) to the young statesmen around Emperor
Mutsuhito, first ruler of modern Japan after the overthrow of the
Tokugawas, for surveying and distributing the land, paying off the
very depreciated pension bonds of the dispossessed feudal lords and
samurai, and building the Japanese navy (for which the British took
the contracts, providing themselves a second profit).

When it came to Japan's war with China (1894) the *London
Times* freely predicted that little Japan had walked into the jaws of
the dragon, and some gloom was felt among British money lenders,
who, however, relied on their government's ability to protect their
loans even if China were victorious. The Japanese showed unsuspected capacity in the science of organized killing. Machine-guns,
naval artillery, and steel ships—the west's improvements during
Japan's isolation—received their first real tryout, paradoxically
enough, in this war between oriental nations. The Manchu throne of
China proved that it "ruled a rich empire always ready to pay but
never ready to fight."

Britain's statesmen granted the newcomer a formal alliance in
time to bolster her against Russia and forestall the scheme of Emperor Mutsuhito's Prince Ito to split Asia between Russia and Japan.
The Anglo-Japanese alliance in its original form had little meaning
other than as a means of keeping the new Asiatic power from swinging into some rival's orbit. For shrewd Japan it meant eventually all
of Pacific Asia instead of half, and was the security offered international bankers, chiefly British, for funds to fight the czar. The Russian court had interpreted Japan's defeat of China as an obstacle
removed on their Pacific front; with French money they had begun
railroads and naval bases in the now humbled and reasonable
Chinese throne's Manchurian viceroyalty, and were even feeling for
the hegemony of Korea.

After Japan had checked Russia, drawing in Theodore Roosevelt
as sponsor of her victory and humbling Russia more perhaps than
British statesmen had wished, the British found themselves under

the necessity of greatly increasing the scope of the Anglo-Japanese alliance. Again, in the midst of the 1914-1918 World War, Japan procured a renewal of this valuable alliance with the world's greatest maritime and industrial power. England found herself getting into a false position, both as concerned her own selfish interests in Asia and as concerned rising sentiment against Japanese imperialism and diplomatic chicanery among the sister Anglo-Saxon peoples of the United States, Canada, and Australia. She was glad indeed, at the Washington conference of 1922, to get out of an open two-power alliance with a nation which was now more her rival than her protégé.

Through this alliance with England Japan gained her sinews of war. Besides enabling Japan to defeat Russia the alliance softened American resentments against her infringements on China and her crude and flagrant annexation of Korea, whose independence the United States had in a treaty promised to make "a matter of grave concern." The alliance provided the glorious excuse for the "meddling" prophesied by the diplomat Prince Hayashi. To "help her ally" Japan entered the World War, taking German islands in the Pacific and seizing Germany's armed port and railway in Shantung province of China. In doing the latter Japan aggressed upon China sufficiently to arouse Chinese protests; this in turn gave the excuse for Japan's "Twenty-one Demands," intended to convert China into a dependency.

After the main fighting between the white nations was over Japan made her obligation to her European ally the diplomatic background for invasion of Siberia. Woodrow Wilson tried to dilute the Japanese expedition to innocuity by sending along 10,000 Americans. He pledged Japan to send no more, whereupon she sent 100,000; but Russian winter and Russian bolsheviks rendered this endeavor to annex Pacific Siberia a failure. If the Japanese army in 1921 had been equipped for fighting at forty below zero, as it is now—thanks to the Manchurian campaigns—there would be no Russo-Japanese question to-day between Lake Baikal and the Japan Sea. Russia would already be eliminated as a Pacific and far eastern power, and imperial Japan would be able to give full attention to eliminating the American obstacle to her progress in the Pacific.[3]

[3] As written in 1934.

Chapter VIII

Japan and Britain to Their War

T̶HE Tokugawa era (1603-1867) was Japan's belated Elizabethan era.[1] It was the period of ascent of law and order, of the establishment of supreme central authority, of the beginnings of foreign trade, and the rise of a middle class soon to be augmented by the introduction of the machine. At the time of Henry VIII England fought her wars outside only. Because the disorders preceding Japan's age of unification were more prolonged and intense and because her era of unification took on an extreme tinge of isolation and lasted a century and a half longer than necessary, degenerating at last into a period of stultification, Japan got behind England a matter of some two centuries in the parallel paths of progress followed by the island kingdoms from the dawn of history.

When Queen Elizabeth died in 1603 and Ieyasu in 1616, neither Japan nor England owned an inch of land outside its archipelago. The military concerns of their rulers were with recalcitrant underelements: the Japanese shogun with the Ainu in the north island of Yezo, now Hokkaido, and the British crown with Scotch and Irish clansmen. But England upon the death of Elizabeth was ready to blossom in the most amazing imperial expansion the world has yet known. Her Drakes and Hawkinses were already sailing the far oceans. The British East India Company was founded a year before Elizabeth's death; the African and Hudson's Bay companies were soon to be born. Elizabeth's Sir Walter Raleighs and John Smiths were preparing to hoist the British flag over a new continent.

---

[1] That is, the period to be compared to the combined reigns of the many-wived English Henry VIII and his virgin daughter, if we may combine them without taking cognizance of the interval between "Bloody" Mary and Edward VI.

Japan upon the death of Ieyasu was oppositely going into her long
hibernation, and this was to last until less than a century ago, when
her young patriots, already restless, were douched wide awake by
the rising white tide which all but submerged their nation. They
took charge and set about to make up the lost ground of two centuries. In a century they did so as far the material side goes—and
more, until Japan saw herself oustripping the western world, particularly her contemporary island nation, England, even as she had
been temporarily outstripped.

II

Many are the parallels in English and Japanese development during the Elizabethan and Tokugawa periods. Both nations rose from
crude backwoods culture to high elegance accompanied by the
growth of a superiority complex, manifested in the plays of Shakespeare to whom England was the only civilized nation on earth and
the writings of the Japanese neo-Confucianists who saw in themselves the flower of all Chinese classical learning. Ieyasu found his
samurai ninety per cent illiterate. He wanted them cultured. Also
he wanted them interested in something other than warfare, since he
was establishing an era of peace, and he wanted a learning that
would fortify them against both the Christian teaching and the
Buddhist influences with which he and his predecessors had tussled.
He began the official sponsorship of the Chinese classics which
eventually made the chief Chinese scholar in Yedo a Richelieu of the
empire. Experiment proved that nothing is so good to cool the fev-
ered blood of warriors as Confucius, although the ancient sage's
common sense and peaceful ethics were preferred in versions that
had sprung up in the fourteenth and fifteenth centuries in China,
which recognized "direct action" and were tinged with a pragmatism
that makes them logical forerunners of Henry James and John
Dewey.

By the middle of the eighteenth century it was as desirable for a
samurai to have a smattering of Chinese learning, know the tea
ceremony and be able to designate two hundred odors by their
proper names, and to exchange political hints, insults, or coquetry

in verse, as it was desirable for the courtiers of Louis XV to know how to dance the minuet.

Another importation from China, brought in person by its Chinese exponent Gem Bin, was judo, commonly called jiu-jutsu, which the officials were glad to encourage as a means of expending energy otherwise than in sword swinging.

As the beginnings of popular education—for the upper class—were made under Elizabeth in England, so public schools for sons of the warriors started in Japan in 1666. Scholars began to turn out great patriotic histories. The schools and the histories bred the spirit destined to overthrow their Tokugawa sponsors.

The Tokugawa administration brought to Japan what the Elizabethan period climaxed in England: the supremacy of law over individual power and whims. There is a difference, of course. To the British mind the law, based on precedent and the lessons of the past, is above the sovereign, and in theory applies equally to all classes. In Japan until the fall of the Tokugawas, law differed for the various classes and the emphasis was upon a rule of order rather than the typically British rule of law. However, Ieyasu in his testament made it plain enough that for even the highest lords there was law from which their position and power could not exempt them.

England's superior morale—that which has given England stability over her sister nations and sustained her force in dealing with them—is in the subconscious acceptance of the law by her people. Japan's morale and driving strength lie in her rule of order. The difference in the two peoples is that the Japanese, haunted by divinity within them, allow the individual conscience to place itself above the law, provided only its possessor be willing to give up his own life as a mark of his sincerity. In England law is higher than the fluids of the gods within men. Both Japan and England have a certain basic conservatism and awe of precedent which provide the steel ribbing within their concrete national structures, but as Viscount Kato, one of Japan's greatest statesmen and diplomats, put it, "Japanese people tend to go ahead too rapidly. We have no such repugnance to change as English people."

Under the Tokugawas, as under the English Tudors, nationalism came into existence. People in the next town came to be fellow subjects instead of foreigners. There went into Japanese nationalism, however, a fanatic loyalty and love of sacrificing life for a master which contrasts strangely with the purely practical courage of the British. The latter is stubborn courage, the former is frenzied courage. To put it again, the fundamental difference between the two maritime nations is that the British are materialists, turning God into a common-sense, well-behaved presiding officer of the universe, a sort of heavenly King George, whereas the Japanese are still on edge with spiritual urges.

Both peoples, of course, have God mixed up with national needs and ambitions. But the emphasis is different. Compare Kipling's "white man's burden" with Matsuoka's "divine mission" and you have it. England never really felt a divine mission to conquer the world. She did feel herself the possessor of a sublime permit to exploit as much of it as convenient. The British took their paramountcy as their due—God handing the world to the best man, so to speak, and expecting him to keep it decent out of respect for himself. But the British never got themselves identified with God. He was in His heaven and they on their earth. The Japanese, on the other hand, think of themselves as part of God—as His arm intervening in earthly chaos. Their history, instead of merely doing Him honor, as in the case of the British, becomes to them the direct outworking of His will.

I like the opinion of the British historian who has helped me with the comparison: "If it had not been for the humbling effect of Christianity, the British would have developed the same complex as the Japanese. The particular British type of egotism represents their compromise with their religion—a sublimation of sublime self-conceit into a sincere desire to see peace on earth, without assuming the full responsibility for establishing it."

England, coming along late in comparison with Spain, Portugal, and Holland, stumbled into empire. The British never knew exactly where their feet would light, as when they lost the major part of North America and gained India and Malaya instead (the same Lord Cornwallis who surrendered at Yorktown is honored by a statue in Penang), or when they made the frightfully bad trade to Holland of Malacca for the Dutch East Indies. But where the

British foot was once planted the British head showed amazing stubbornness and devilish guile in keeping it placed. Only where empire definitely becomes a losing business proposition—as is the trend in India—does England willingly ease the weight of her foot.

Destiny to the Englishman was being on hand to gather in the clams when the tide went out. He tried to have his muscle hard for the digging—although he usually had to improvise his shovel. Japan, on the other hand, like Rome, is an empire builder by conviction. The gods came down and pushed back the sea to make the Japanese archipelago, and left their divine progeny thereon to continue the work of spreading order in a maudlin world. Therefore Japan must stay even where it does not pay to stay, as indeed it has not yet paid in Formosa, Korea, or Manchuria. Destiny to the Nippon man is sweeping back the ocean to farm the shellfish.

III

Japan climbed to the rank of first-class power through her political relations with England. Even more significant are her industrial gains through the contact. They would make a book—they have already made thousands of folders of confidential reports in Mr. Hugh Dalton's Board of Trade Offices in London. Since I have quite enough book here already, I will give only one anecdote which interprets the whole development. In September of 1933, Manchester textile manufacturers, desperate over their inability to compete with Japanese products, so far overcame their belief in British superiority as to order from Japan two hundred improved Osaka looms. But Japan's supreme trade board took possession of these looms as they lay crated for shipment on the wharf at Osaka. Japanese machinery manufacturers were forbidden to sell or divulge to the world Japanese improvements upon equipment, although the western world had supplied Japan all the fundamentals. Japan had outdone England in the first important product of machinery, textile manufacturing, which was the foundation of England's wealth and world trade supremacy.

The industrial parallel between Great Britain and Japan is now the pertinent one. Back in 1576 the old Britisher Hakluyt, recorder of pioneer voyages, wrote: "Our chief desire is to find out ample vent of our woolen cloth, the natural commodity of this our realm. The fittest place which in all my readings and observations I find for that purpose is the manifold islands of Japan and the northern parts of China, and the regions of the Tartars next adjoining." The English historian Trevelyan comments: "Not lust of conquest but vent of merchandise first drew our countrymen." One might compare the British desire at the end of the sixteenth century to break into the Pacific-Asian market with her woolen goods to the twentieth-century Japanese cotton-goods drive on the United Kingdom and the British colonies—which inspired M.P.'s from Manchester to hold up before the House of Commons pairs of Japanese woven drawers bought under the shadow of their idle factories and frantically to demand protection against articles selling for less than the overhead cost of the same goods made in their mills.

It turned out to be cotton goods made by machine in imitation of the handwoven product of India (to the ruination of the Indian weavers) rather than Hakluyt's woolen goods that took England around the world. In turn, Japan's superiority in the manufacture of cotton goods built her trade empire and underwrote her political empire. Asian industrialism, like European, begins with cotton. This is true in China and India as well as Japan. Japan does not propose to let a still newer rival outdo her, however, as she outdid England. Hence the bombing of every Chinese cotton factory not under Japanese control. To-day the three great cotton-goods centers of the world are the Inland Sea of Japan, the lower Yangtze River of China, and Manchester. Japan controls the first two.

Abundant good coal enabled England to build supremacy with the machine. It made her the world's factory of the nineteenth century and the necessity for bringing raw products from all over the world and shipping back the finished goods made her its merchant and banking nation.

Japan possesses the exact corollary to England's coal in her enormous supply of easily harnessed water power. Most of Japan stands on end; her prevailing winds are from the warm Japan current on her eastern shore to the arctic current on her western. Moisture-laden clouds condense against her serried mountain ranges, sending steady torrents to the sea. Japan's industrial pioneers, the Mitsuis and Mitsubishis, began thirty years ago staking out water-power sites and to-day are able to supply their multifarious factories from their own properties at the cheapest power costs in the world. The American, British, and German electrical trusts that helped them start are to-day trying to hold at least their home market against electric goods ranging from bulbs to dynamos, made with this power.

In 1932 Japan had 5,000,000,000 yen of sound earning investment in water power. She had 850 distributing power plants operating, among other things, 6,000 kilometers of electrified railway; in addition were 7,000 power plants chiefly used for individual factories. A total electric power capacity at the end of that year was about 6,000,000 kilowatts completed and under construction.

Hydro-electric power made Japan the cheap-goods factory of the world, particularly of Asia, South America, and Africa. White capital and labor managed to bar her goods from Europe and America, and to an extent from other parts of the world where western imperialism still had leverage. Thus the western competitive system was forced to traduce its own philosophy of free competition and survival of the fittest.

IV

England in the days of her expansion enjoyed the advantage over her rivals of internal solidarity and peace. After the time of Henry VIII—save for the brief, short struggles attending the rise, and again the fall, of the Cromwells—she has fought all her wars on other people's territory. Internal solidarity and prosperity were the endowment enabling her to take fullest advantage of her primacy in the machine and steam power. Japan, over the same space of time, had to fight a few sharp, bloody, internal wars before being ready to confront the world. But since 1894 Japan has also fought all her wars on other people's soil. The analogy goes further. England was able to build empire while her continental rivals cut one another's throats. Japan plans to build empire while the white and Christian nations bleed and suffocate one another to death.

England had the field first, but Japan was luckier than England. She was luckier in her continental neighbors. Save for Russia, whose heart is six thousand miles away, she had no first-class military rivals on the continent. In this there was temptation, and Japan might have been wiser to adopt the British policy of meddling but never owning on the continent. However, Japan had no such mare's nest in her rear as England has had for five hundred years. Behind her Japan had people in a much more primitive stage of material power than herself, and the military advantage of a mechanized nation over industrially undeveloped peoples was never so great.

Again, Japan is geographically better placed than her rival island empire. The bleak Atlantic holds no such nugget pockets as Formosa, the Philippines, Borneo with its oil, the Celebes, Java, and Australasia. England had to cross wide oceans to find great wheat valleys like those of the Nonni, Amur, and Sungari which lie in Manchuria and over its Russian border in Siberia. England had no opportunity to keep the mineral resources, communications, banking and industry of Europe in her grasp, but those of Asia lie in the lap of Japan to-day. England did make full use of the sympathy of European Protestant countries such as Holland and Scandinavia and as their potential defender brought them within her trade empire. Yet her opportunity here was not as great as the parallel one which turned Buddhist Siam, Mongolia, and Tibet in the direction of Japan, the world's one first-class Buddhist power. Nor did England ever have in Europe a cause for winning underpeoples to her brood, such as the general revolt against white dominance sweeping China, India, Burma, Java, and the Philippines. Even the peoples of the east coast of Africa whispered of an intense interest in rising Nippon.

To-day's Japan is the center of the prettiest picture the world has ever seen for the building of modern industrial power and empire.[2] Here it is: the agricultural regions of Pacific Siberia and Manchuria; the fur and cattle country of Mongolia; the fishing waters of the northwest Pacific (the most productive in the world); the water power of Japan; the mineral resources of China and Manchuria; the oil of Sakhalin and Borneo; the tropical products (necessary to modern industry) of the Philippines and the South Sea islands; the docile, low-standard laboring population of Korea and

[2] Map: inside rear cover. Bear in mind that this and the following paragraphs were published in 1935. They are history in 1942.

China; the disciplined people of Japan, eminently fitted to be straw bosses; the easily monopolized, potentially great market of China; the markets of the Dutch East Indies, India, Africa, and Latin America—avid for cheap goods—and beyond them the lands of the hitherto dominant peoples of the world, outclassed in their own game of industrial competition.

Nippon has made mistakes, but thus far has missed no chances nor failed to exploit any opportunity. Hope that Japan will not realize to the full the advantages of her geographic and historic position can lie only in two possibilities. One is that such power as still resides in the west will combine and bear down upon her while she is still vulnerable. The other is that she will overplay her hand. The first, not too likely, boils down to a combination against her of Russia and the United States, with the reluctant addition of Great Britain. The second possibility the reader may prognosticate for himself after having sketched with me individual lives which give the best criteria for judging a nation. Personally, I find that for every Japanese zealot there is a Japanese conservative, for every reckless trait, an offset of caution and great ability to bide the time. Nor do I find that through the delicate years of Japan's participation in the world poker game thus far she has committed any ruinous error.

Let me conclude this survey of Japanese-British relations prior to 1941 with verbatim quotation of a few paragraphs written in 1934. I shall not clutter up the page with quotation marks since I am quoting myself, and I rely upon the reader to change the tense to past—since Pearl Harbor:

The British are the world's greatest realists in international politics. Better than any other nation they appreciate Japan's innate strength, the advantages of her position and the difficulty and cost of dislodging or overwhelming her. Perhaps the parallel of their own national and industrial growth gives them a better sense of Japan than is possessed by other contemporaries. There exists in England of the 30's no heart for squarely opposing Japan. England has an instinct (which she calls common sense) for compromise with political developments which cannot be blocked.

When Japan cuts squarely into the British markets, takes dividends from her upper class, and throws her workers on the dole, Britain's gorge rises, of course. She tries little trade wars and prohibitive customs tariffs and embargoes, as recently in India, where Japan made up her losses in the Chinese boycott of 1931-33 and found a traders' happy hunting ground. But Britain's trade wars always end in compromise.

The same is true in the political and naval spheres so far as Japan is concerned. Great Britain above all will never repeat Russia's mistake of sailing a navy five thousand miles into the arms of an enemy.[3] She builds up the strength of Hongkong with new guns, galleries bored through its rock cliffs, and mines in its harbor entrance. She feverishly completes her $50,000,000 naval and refitting base behind Singapore Island. These are her first and second trenches to be held as long as profitable, but she recognizes that their value is more moral than real. In war it would be almost as impossible for her to maintain communications with them as it was for Russia to keep open her sea route to Port Arthur. And, as for the trade war, Hongkong and Singapore will become expensive ornaments quite useless to the practical British mind when Japan possesses herself of the trade of South China, India, and the Philippine Islands. Periodically Japan takes up the "Kra canal" project with the amenable Siamese government: a sea-level water passage through the Malay peninsula to be created by twenty miles of dredging which would shorten the route from Tokyo to Bombay or Europe by a thousand miles, put Bangkok near a sea lane and leave Singapore isolated six hundred miles to the south. Fortification of the canal would largely nullify the strategy of the Singapore naval base. Nature is with Japan—some time the canal will be built.

Great Britain used the situation—the fright of the helpless Dutch —to establish a tacit protectorate for the time being over the Dutch East Indies. This cost the Dutch certain commercial concessions and cost the British nothing. Great Britain did not carry it far enough to make it an open challenge to Japan. When General Allenby of Palestine fame went out to Singapore to confer on this matter with

---

[3] Britain did not attempt a fleet action against Japan's navy. But she did (December, 1941) expose two of her best vessels to Japanese air attack near Singapore and got them forthwith sunk.

the high naval officers there and (according to oriental newspapers) it was learned that Japanese patriots had planned to assassinate him, the British spirited him out to sea and hushed the matter up.

England followed the same wait-for-the-cat-to-jump policy in China. Should Japan get into mortal combat with the United States or Russia or both, Great Britain would be in a position to exact many favors from the oriental empire—as well as from the other side—and should Japan be crushed, China and the South Seas, including the Philippines, would plump into Britannia's patient, copious lap—it was thought. The head of the British propaganda bureau in India said to me ten [now eighteen] years ago, "We will get out of India when it no longer pays to stay. But God is always good to the English. We still have Africa, the world's greatest unexploited continent. That is where the British Empire of the twenty-first century will be built."

I have an idea that he was wrong about that—that there will be no empire in the twenty-first century, an idea bolstered by the refusal of so-called British colonies in Africa to restrict the import of cheap Japanese goods just to support Manchester. Also there are developments in New Zealand, Australia, even Canada which would entitle a pessimist about the British Empire such as the late Dean Inge to predict the splitting of the British Empire wide open over policy toward Japan's rise.

But the Indian bureau chief was right about British policy. Such being its essence, the Tories of the London *Morning Post* and *Daily Telegraph* and Lord Rothermere advocated a renewal of the Anglo-Japanese alliance and the recognition of Manchukuo—just as Rothermere supported Sir Oswald Mosley as long as there was no likelihood of British fascists coming into power. Oppositely, Jack Mills, labor leader, demanded that labor "hammer" from the British government "the declaration that there shall not, in event of war, be any assistance, financial or physical, from Great Britain to the state which has outlawed itself in the eyes of the civilized world" [Japan, after its attack on China]; and can place a resolution before the British labor party that "every trade represented here is slowly being battered out of existence by the slave conditions in the Japanese industrial world." Great Britain will feel her way and make no commitments while Tories growl their admiration of the Japanese strong arm, while laborites and idealists denounce, or while the even fewer and less vocal Americanophiles assure Americans that our cousins will always be found at our sides. English statesmen have no doubt that a great war will be fought on the Pacific, but they do not propose to fight it. To paraphrase an old gibe, England can best benefit from such a war by permitting every American and Russian to do his duty.[4]

Reports of British-Japanese alliance coming out of Moscow, the Hague, and Nanking, and flying thicker and faster as the naval controversy grows more acute between Japan on the one side and the United States and Great Britain on the other, may be regarded in the light of the above. So may British good-will and trade missions to Manchukuo. Understandings between Japan and England unquestionably exist; regional and ephemeral, such as during the Japanese war in Shanghai and the armed occupation since; or such as Japanese military occupation and control of the British coal-concession area where the Great Wall meets the sea. The former largely kept the Chinese government in Nanking from aiding the resistance of its local Shanghai troops to an extent which would have brought declared war and an offensive against all China by Japan; the second enabled the British coal administration to get its product to market at prices noncompetitive with Japanese coal and to industries in Shanghai and elsewhere willing to accept Japanese dictation. But these are just little practical understandings to meet temporary situations.[5] They are not alliances. In the nature of human affairs alliances do not take place between the world's two most fundamental rivals.

[4] This and following paragraph are as published in 1935.
[5] The last was the closing of the Burma Road, August, 1941.

MEN AND EMPIRE

Chapter IX
Japan's Face Sets

W ITH the collapse of the Tokugawa in 1867, Japan went into a state of flux. Twenty years later it had set into the empire we face now. Authority was in the hands of Prince Sanjo of the Imperial House, regent for the unusually intelligent, vigorous, fourteen-year-old Emperor Mutsuhito. Sanjo was a remarkably adaptable character to have come out of the world's oldest court. He and his clansmen advisers, Okubo, Itagaki, and Saigo, were willing to place the initiative in the hands of youngsters like Ito, Yamagata, Takahashi, Katsu, and Inouye, who had gained a few months' first-hand experience of the west by knocking about London or San Francisco and by being shanghaied into western ships' crews.

One would not expect benefits to come out of the experiences of these youths. Yet their policies as statesmen toward the west, which had maltreated, ignored, or patronized them as stranger youths, prove the discriminative sense of the Japanese mind. At the crucial time, they were the only persons of their race who had any knowledge whatsoever of the world Japan had to face, and these youngsters went about the complete reshaping of their nation as a military genius would revamp an army to meet enemy formations and tactics never before experienced.

They experimented widely. It was the age in the west of adulation of the god Democracy and the establishment of constitutional monarchies, and the young statesmen first worked in the belief that introduction of something democratic and constitutional in Japan would raise her prestige and magically increase her power and prosperity. The institution of Emperor, which for seven centuries had increasingly faded from importance in Japan's political life, was at this time amenable to development either in the direction of constitutional monarchy or the opposite one of absolutism.

The young sovereign Mutsuhito came very near to becoming a human being, and from reports of the time now suppressed, he liked it. The idea of the young fellows returned from abroad was, first, to have him cancel the imperial delegation of authority to the Tokugawa shogun, and then to make him a constitutional monarch after the type of Henry VIII of England or Frederick the Great of Prussia. Mutsuhito was taken in 1868 before an assemblage of feudal lords in Kyoto to swear the following "charter oath": "The practice of discussion and debate shall be universally adopted, and all measures shall be decided by public argument. High and low shall be of one mind, and social order shall thereby be perfectly maintained. It is necessary that the civil and military rights of all classes be assured, and the national mind be completely satisfied.

"The uncivilized customs of former times shall be broken through, and the impartiality and justice displayed in the working of nature shall be adopted as a basis of action. Intellect and learning shall be sought for throughout the world, in order to establish the foundations of the Empire." [1]

"Ozoro ni"—"Dare to climb"—was the keynote of the intelligent young Emperor, and the opening words of one of his many short poems.

He was transferred at the head of a great procession to Yedo, which was renamed Tokyo (eastern capital) and made the titular as well as actual capital of the nation in place of Kyoto, which had held the title, only, for the last six and one-half centuries. Emperor Mutsuhito went about to openings of harbor works and railroads in great flowing yellow Chinese robes and samurai topknot to the delight of the common people, who not since the early days of Japanese culture had looked upon a Tenno. He even insisted upon reading the newspapers. (To-day, however, the Tenno hears his news orally from an Imperial Court reporter.) On the occasion of the Emperor's opening of the new Yokohama station it was transformed into one of the world's finest chrysanthemum shows. The crowds were prostrate on their hands and knees but were not compelled to keep their eyes on

[1] MacLaren, *Political History of Japan*, pages 63-64.

the ground, nor were the windows of upper stories shut as at the present time. Even much later this human Son of Heaven permitted Prince Ito to come to his waiting room with his hat on and a cigar going full blast, and on the great night of the fall of the Russians at Port Arthur in night kimono—the equivalent of a nightshirt.

II

Whether Japan would remain Japanese at all came to be a question. Prussian court dress was adopted and has stuck to this day. Captain Brinkley, an artillery instructor, later to become the writer of six-foot shelves on Japan, relates how Count Todo of Ise gave him £5,000 (face value) worth of the bonds issued to feudatories in lieu of their estates, as an expression of gratitude for the loan of a British officer's uniform in which to appear before the Emperor. While the Captain's British cannon were en route, his pupils practised with batteries made of wood. After the real cannon arrived, Captain Binkley had difficulty getting the samurai to dispense with low ceremonial bows to one another on the touching off of each shot.

A fad sprang up for the writing of the Japanese language in Roman letters, instead of the usual mixture of Chinese ideographs and one or another of two Japanese alphabets. Words were introduced by the hundreds from European languages, especially English. For a time it was even proposed to adopt English as the official language of the Empire, and the wearing of European clothes (atrociously fitted) became the fashion in the capital. Inouye as minister of finance even sponsored European ball-room dancing as a means of impressing the west with Japan's up-to-dateness, and Nipponese gentlemen and ladies were hopping up and down in the salons of Tokyo on bandy legs that came from sitting on mats.

Soon the superpatriots put a stop to all this with a few well-directed murderous attacks. At times of high fervor such as the present, mixed dancing has an unpatriotic and immoral flavor in Japan. After 1934 it was prohibited by the police in all private homes and permitted in a few of the best hotels one day a week from eight to ten-thirty P.M. The cabarets which superseded the old-fashioned yoshiwara [2] as Japan's licensed houses of joy, and where it is recognized that people go only in order to indulge low-mindedness anyhow, through certain political hookups got exemption—up till twelve-thirty o'clock or so.

In 1935 there were eight licensed dance halls and about a hundred and fifty dance studios in Tokyo, and dance fans dared to say that the introduction of western dancing added much to the grace and poise of the youth of Japan. However the patriots kept close eye on them. Girls must dance, not talk or drink, with customers, and were forbidden to "partner with" students. An American Broadway revue doing a scene called "La Vie Paris" was broken up by members of the National Foundation Society, who took the stage, berated the audience, and scattered hand-bills reading, "With a war with Russia imminent, love or erotic revue is ruinous to the Japanese spirit." The patrons were ostensibly arrested and the American actors failed to get their visas extended and had to close the show.

By the time of the end of the foreign craze in the eighties, the general fear and terror of white men that greeted Perry's arrival had given place to respect and even affection, because of the high personal quality and kindliness of physicians, teachers, and even traders who represented the west in Japan during the early period. After Japan's successful war against China in 1894, the general resentment against the white man in the orient vanished, but in its place came the attempt to demonstrate equality or superiority by treating him brusquely. Gradually this has become the common attitude of Japanese in contact with whites.

Along with the phenomena of unbalance evident in Japan from 1870 to 1890, measures of amazingly definite statecraft were executed. In 1871 the feudal system was abolished and the country nobility removed to towns on pensions. By 1874 the land had been distributed to the peasants after one of the greatest surveying jobs ever carried through, the peasantry had been entirely freed from attachment to the land, and a money land-tax substituted for rice croppage.

Japan did not run wild on the mechanical side of western civiliza-

---

[2] The Yedo precinct name has come to be used for gay quarters (yukwaku) generally.

tion and neglect its less gaudy aspects, as other oriental nations have done. By 1882 the islands had only seventy-eight miles of railways and a hundred-odd steel vessels, but during the same ten years 30,000 American-style public schools—for commoners as well as aristocrats—averaging 100 students each had been established.

The extension of military service and public-school privileges to plebeians and outcasts blotted out class lines. Disorderliness of samurai and resentment of the rising plebs soon brought about the prohibition of sword wearing. Within a few years men who had cut commoners in two to test their swords were acting as doorkeepers for commoners in banks and offices or even wielding shoe-brushes instead of swords.

III

In the unbalanced seventies and eighties were shaped the three dominating features of the Nippon we face. All three began as reactions against the non-Japanese softness of the transition era. The first is the god-position of the emperor; the second, Japan's superiority complex towards her cultural forebears Korea and China; the third, the Japanese conviction of the nation's divine mission in the world.

The same emperor who was started off in his boyhood as a popular constitutional monarch was made in his manhood, by the constitution of 1889, "heaven-descended, divine, and sacred, preëminent above all his subjects, reverenced and inviolate.... The law has no power to hold him accountable to it. There shall be no irreverence for the Emperor's person. He shall not be made a topic of derogatory comment, nor one of discussion."[3] For Ieyasu's "the people are the foundation of a nation" the constitution substituted "the Emperor is the foundation of the nation."[4]

What the framers of Japan's constitution found in Bismarck's Prussia greatly bolstered the position given the Emperor. They felt that Japan needed something as useful as the state church in European nations. And so the cult known as Shinto, which Buddhism

[3] *Commentaries on the Constitution,* by Prince Ito, its framer and official commentator.
[4] The opening phrase of the constitution.

had hospitably adopted and housed in little shrines to the fox spirit, rabbit spirit, etc., in its great temple grounds, was transformed by edict into a national cult under a government bureau, and its priests were entrusted with care of the shrines of the Imperial Ancestors and national heroes, conduct of state and military funerals, national triumphs, etc. Every village was obliged to erect a Shinto shrine—in the plain, thatched, prehistoric Japanese architecture—fronted by an avenue of torii. The larger of these invariably have a captured cannon or some symbol of military victory, as well as survivals of animism like the sacred white cock or horse, and the purifying ropes of woven straw with paper streamers suspended. Outside the gate is the beautiful and simple symbol of the crystal-pure fountain with its flat bamboo dippers, from which visitors wet tongue and fingers. Japanese soldiers, preparing for an attack in which they expect to give up their lives, drink a cup of pure water.

A delegation of the Young Men's Buddhist Association of Hawaii, American citizens of Japanese ancestry, visiting in 1933 the shrine of Ise particularly dedicated to the Sacred Mirror, were told that 6,000,000 persons had made pilgrimages to that shrine within the year. Australia's trade commissioner, Mr. John Latham, recently visiting Japan to further business diplomacy, presented the shrine of Ise with two dozen Australian white leghorn cocks and hens. The common folk of Japan rest in the assurance that the spirits of the great men of the past are housed in the Shinto shrines and from these vantage points watch over the welfare of the nation. (The sacred fowl are luckier than the priests, who are required to keep their mistresses off the grounds!)

The Imperial birthdays and other great patriotic festivals of the year, very numerous in Japan, were made one of the cares of Shinto priests. The most interesting of these days is the boys' festival falling on May 5th. Boys are treated to displays of dolls representing heroes of history and this is a prize occasion for instilling the martial and stoical spirit into lads who are then sent out to fly kites made to imitate black and red carp which are symbols of long life and virility. Failure to observe the boys' festival and wish the sons of the house health, success, and happiness is considered exceedingly bad luck in a Japanese household. Recently the baby Crown Prince celebrated his first boys' festival, the occasion of great ceremony in court, noble, and political circles. The infant heir to the throne was presented with a fine woodcarving of the awe-inspiring ninth-century conqueror of the Ainu on the northern island, the hero Tamuramaru. Girls have a lesser festival on March 3rd, when dolls exhibiting all the graces of womankind are displayed for the delight and instruction of the little women.

Shinto is not a very live thing in Japan to-day, but it is a capable housekeeper for the very live spirit of patriotism. Already it has begun acting as keeper for the trophies of the Manchurian and China operations. These are housed in a shrine in one of the gardens of the Imperial Palace itself which was opened with a ceremony of purification by the Shinto priests.

One evangelical sect calling itself Tenrikiyo Shinto, does exist, and celebrated its 113th anniversary in 1938 by completion of a great temple upon which its followers worked in squads of thousands, called their holy labor for God. This sect is really the Japanese indigenous "Christian Science" founded by a sort of Japanese Mary Baker Eddy (died 1887), whose holy psalms regarding the "buoyant life without concern" (yoki gwashi) comprise its public service. The foundress, "priest-god" for her religion, which she called "the last teaching of the world," catalogues all disease as the result of eight kinds of mental dust: coveting, grudging, passion, hatred, enmity, fury, greed, and haughtiness. The present patriarch, a descendant of the foundress, is a splendid-appearing gentleman of much influence in Japan. His religion is no mean thing, claiming 11,000 temples in Japan, sixty on the mainland of Asia and thirty-four in America. The sect operates along ultramodern lines, placing exceedingly clever and attractive illustrated full-page ads in Japanese and English leading newspapers.

There survives also, of course, in the most ancient temples, the pure witchcraft which calls itself Shinto. A vivid description of this spirit possession occurs in a recent book by a mountain-climbing missionary.[5] On the sacred peak of Ontake, "the god came down" and a girl of about twenty, "of singularly sweet face, particularly susceptible to the influence of the gods," took part in a rite in which

[5] *Scrambles in Japan and Formosa* by W. H. Murray Walton.

she passed into a state of possession. She held in her hand a divine gohei rod. Five men who attended her knelt before her and chanted prayers, thus bringing the girl into their power. Then: "Suddenly she turned round and faced them. . . . As they continued she swayed slowly from side to side, now and then shaking as if in convulsion.

"After a short period she gradually raised her head. All the beauty had gone—instead every feature was strained. The pilgrims were silent now, for the god was descending. Then her eyes opened, but not to see: they were as those of one blind. In a moment the men in front of her burst out once again into gestures and shouts and waved their gohei violently before her. Then suddenly she spoke, but it was not her voice; it was something unnatural, awful, devilish. She announced that she was the voice of Hachidai Gongen, and as such was prepared to unfold the mysteries to her worshipers. Questions were asked. . . . Then the members of the band came forward one by one and knelt before the insensate girl. A wave from the attendant priest and in a moment she was all action, brushing, poking, striking, thrusting the figure before her; then with a click, like soldiers at drill, she was back once more in her original position, her rigid arms supporting the gohei in front of her face. Again the performance was repeated over another worshiper; even the children had to be treated.

"Finally all were satisfied and steps were taken to bring her back to her normal condition."

But all this has no more to do with official Shinto in Japan than the Oxford Movement has to do with the Established Church in England.

IV

Regarding her oriental neighbors, Japan had the choice of setting herself up as their champion against the buccaneering white nations or joining the latter in their looting game. Both material necessities and psychology drove Japan to join the looters—the psychology even more than the material pressure. The development of the steel navy had temporarily put Japan in a position of relative weakness toward the western powers. Until this could be evened up her statesmen hesitated to oppose the predatory nations. It seemed wiser to encourage their cupidity in the direction of China—but to join in, to prevent them from making China a base against Japan. And if Japan were to rival them in resources and markets it must be at the expense of her fellow orientals.

But the decisive factor was the vanity of the Japanese people. Japan ached to exact indemnities from some weaker nation, just as England and America had exacted them from her, and to force her Asiatic neighbors to exempt Japanese from their laws, just as the westerners enforced extraterritoriality on Japan. And what a boost to the pride of a brand new manufacturing nation to tell some people still more backward than her own how much customs duties they might impose on goods she proposed to ship in and sell to them!

Japan was like the small boy on the block, who joins in the gang's depredations to prove that he is a regular guy. In a little while Japan was to grow big enough to take the cream of the loot. As she makes herself master of the area she begins to find the conduct of her fellow gangsters exceedingly reprehensible. She adopts the rôle of Asia's protector against them. In 1901 Japan got the privilege of having soldiers play around in China the same as the big white boys. That was a great moral victory. But to-day Japan holds half of Asia "in the interest of peace and order," and bombs cities and villages "to encourage peace and order" among the startled and frightened citizens!

Japan has put every screw on her oriental neighbors that the western powers ever put on her. The U.S.S. *Wyoming* sailed in 1863 into the Straits of Shimonoseki, sank several of the Choshu clan lord's ships, silenced his land guns, and then assessed an indemnity on him several times greater than the damage he had done the American firm whose ships he had whimsically fired upon. Japan has lost no opportunity of applying this precedent in China.

In the eighteen-sixties London lent Japan money to pay off a British-levied indemnity at the gentle interest of ten per cent. England thus benefited twice. Japan in turn exacted from China in 1895 a war indemnity which forced that ancient nation to acquire for the first time a national debt. In 1917 Japan lent, against the protest of the Chinese people at large 600,000,000 yen to Chinese officials—which they appropriated as pay for signing away their nation's rights. She then threatened to occupy China because China was remiss in payment of this "debt." Every trick that England ever used in Europe or Asia, Theodore Roosevelt's original method of procuring the American Canal Zone, every stunt of American government-backed high and rotten finance in Latin America, has been studied and analyzed by Japan and applied appropriately in her relations with those neighbors for whose peace and prosperity she now proclaims herself solely responsible.

Korea's rulers, remembering Hideyoshi, had no cause to be surprised at Japan's reaction towards mainland Asia, but her decision to outdo white aggressors at their game was a shock to China. Sun Yat-sen at the time of his death in 1925 still hoped that Japan might right-about face and become the honest shepherd of the Asiatic flock against the white wolves. Present China has given up that fatuous hope, although Indian revolutionaries and Siamese princes, whose sentiment is made possible by remoteness, entertain it. If one seeks the wellspring of Chinese hatred of Japan he will find it not so much in the defeats and punishments, more or less deserved, that Japan has administered to her big neighbor, not so much in all the inexcusable incidents of military frightfulness and interference, but in the feeling that Japan betrayed older fellow racials who taught her culture and entered upon aggression which was, after all, a confession of inferiority complex toward the west such as China herself has never felt. Had Japan chosen the other way— of making herself leader rather than master of Asia—history would be writing a vastly different chapter to-day.

v

The development of the third phase of Japan can be followed, simply, through the telling statements of a few spokesmen. I think they have never before been put in sequence. I begin with the memorial offered by Lord Hotta in 1858 before the overthrow of the Tokugawas, truly a remarkable document to be written in a Japan that had entered upon relations with the west only four years before:

"No unity exists among states of the world.... Rival chiefs assume titles of king or emperor. Each aims to gain supremacy over the other.... The countries of the world are so related that the action of any one involves others.... The statesman must have his calculations based not on the strength of any single country, but on general conditions.... These rivalries will never cease till someone possessed of extraordinary power shall assume the hegemony that will unite all others under his sole authority.... It is entirely against reason and also against the principle of nature to convert into formidable enemies the nations which we could in time use to our advantage.... The present condition of the world shows it lacking in a ruler sufficiently powerful and virtuous under whom all countries could be united. Among the world's rulers (aside from Japan) there is none noble and industrious enough to command universal vassalage. To have such a ruler over the whole world is doubtless the will of Heaven. Before the countries of the west can be unified under such a ruler it is necessary for us to establish relations, form alliances and conclude treaties.... Where other nations intervene we should do the same.... *The objects should always be kept in view of laying the foundation for securing hegemony over all nations.*[6] For this purpose shipping and trade should be developed. Where foreigners excel us we should remedy our defects.... The national resources should be developed in military preparation vigorously carried out. When our power and national standing have come to be recognized we should take the lead in punishing the nations which may act contrary to the principle of international interests. We should declare our protection over harmless but powerful nations. *Such a policy could be nothing else but enforcement of the power and authority deputed to us by the Spirit of Heaven. Our national prestige and position thus ensured, the nations of the world will come to look up to our Emperor as the Great Ruler of all the nations, and they will come to follow our policy and submit to our judgment.*[6] This ideal realized, the Ruler of Japan will have accomplished a deed commensurate with the great responsibilities he owes to Heaven and the Earth. Our land of the Gods is ruled by Heavenly Rulers of one unbroken lineage since the beginning of time; and

6 Italics the author's.

the relations between the Ruler and the subjects are correctly established, while the fundamental institutions are clearly set forth. Japan
is beyond comparison with other countries where ruling dynasties
and national institutions have suffered frequent changes. With us,
the Heavenly Descendants of one unbroken lineage have always sat
on the Throne, and our country occupies the foremost rank as the
oldest among nations. Our territory is not extensive, but we surpass
other countries in the fertility of the soil and also in population.
Moreover our people are brave and loyal, which will commend them
to the special favour of the Spirit of Heaven. We can safely trust
to the protection of the Great Ruler of the Universe. Now is the
opportune moment offered us by the changed condition of the world
of old to make a united national effort to seize the opportunity for
realizing the great destiny awaiting our country, as stated above.
For this purpose, speedy permission is respectfully and humbly
solicited for opening intercourse with foreign countries." [7]

It may open the reader's eyes to something fundamental about
Japan to learn that the official who first urged the establishment of
ordinary diplomatic relations upon a Son of Heaven established but
a few months as actual ruler of Japan, gave as his reason that the
opening of relations with western powers could be regarded as the
first step to making the Sacred Person the ruler of the world, and
saw Japan's cautious entry into world affairs culminating in Japanese world hegemony. I doubt if even the state built on the seven
hills of Rome launched into the affairs of the Mediterranean basin
with such amazing egotism and faith in its destiny. The lineal heir
of that Lord Hotta who wrote the first memorial in modern times
about Japan's divine mission to conquer the world, is the present
diplomat Hotta who made Japan's deal with Mussolini and after
"Pearl Harbor" became Japan's ambassador to Hitler.

The Japanese are sincere—their faith in themselves is naïve and
implicit. The astigmatism of the race causes them to regard as
reasonable and self-evident the claims made for the nation of the
gods and its Ruler. When other nations of Asia or we of the west
fail to look upon Japan as the world's ultimate lawgiver and estab-

[7] See full translation of this long document, remarkable for its time, in *Lord
Hotta* by Henry Satoh, pages 73-79.

lisher of order, the Japanese are genuinely surprised and pained. They sincerely credit our failure to agree as pathetic ignorance or wilful obstruction of heaven's way.

Now let us—twenty years after the Hotta memorial, listen to Viscount Tani upon his return from the west just in time (1888) to help draft Japan's constitution: "Make our country secure by military preparation.... Encourage and protect the people at home, and then wait for the time of the confusion of Europe which must come eventually sooner or later   Such an event will agitate the nations of the orient as well, and we will then become the chief nation of the orient."

Next read Count Hayashi's comment upon the interference of Germany, Russia, and France to rob Japan of the fruits of her victory over China, in 1895:[8] "Japan must keep quiet and lull suspicions and wait her day—then not only put the meddling powers out, but meddle herself."

Chronologically follows the declaration of the Black Dragon Society upon the outbreak of the World War (1914): "We must skilfully avail ourselves of the world's general trend of affairs ... bring to realization our great imperial policy.... This is the opportune moment for Japan quickly to solve the Chinese question. Such an opportunity will not occur for hundreds of years to come.... Present conditions in China favor execution.... It is Japan's divine duty to act now."

A few months after this Japan's war premier, Marquis Okuma, who had been close to Hayashi back in 1905, stated: "Those who are superior will govern. We must prepare ourselves for being a governing nation—we need more force to back diplomatic dealings." Okuma's diplomats illustrated the last idea by delivering the notorious "Twenty-one Demands" to China's president on war-office paper watermarked with guns and battleships. Then Okuma used his vast prestige and hearty reputation with Americans to mislead them with three messages through a Japanese news service: "Japan acts with a clear conscience in conformity with justice, and in perfect accord with her allies. Japan has no territorial ambitions.... The imperial government will take no such action as to give to a third

[8] Count Hayashi, *Secret Memoirs.*

party any cause for anxiety regarding the safety of territories or possessions.... As premier of Japan I now state again that Japan has no ulterior motive, no desire to secure more territory, no thought of depriving China or other people of anything that they now possess. My government and my people have given their word and their pledge, which will be as honorably kept as Japan always keeps promises." By that time Japan's troops were marching across Chinese territory. Later exhibitions of such honorable keeping of promises were the seizure of Manchuria and annexation of the mandated islands, and the conquests of 1941-1942.

Japan's enhanced relative position among the world powers, due to the assiduous effort of the Christian nations to exterminate one another, logically justifies the progress of the divine philosophy to the point expressed by Major General Nonaka (Shomei) in 1918: "Peace that every man wants will not come until the world is under one central authority. Two new tendencies will follow the World War: a great race in military preparations and a strong denunciation of war. But what can bring about a universal peace when every condition is adverse to its realization? Judicial authority which has not the official power to enforce its verdict is worse than useless. Besides, standards of fairness and codes of honor of different nations vary. The theory of restriction of armaments is impracticable. What standard shall be used in limitation for the different nations? There is no power in the world to prevent mobilization in times of emergency. The peoples of the world may be inspired with the ideals of peace, but so long as material problems of self-preservation exist, so long as population increases, so long will social and political conditions favor war.

"Peace will come when the whole world is under one government. The world tends toward this at present. Each existing nation was produced by the conquest of many tribes, and when its central power is strong peace prevails within it. In Japan this is true. The ultimate conclusion of politics is the conquest of the world by one imperial power. Which nation is likely to be the conqueror of the world? That nation which is strongly united in patriotism, has unquenchable imperial ambitions and willingness to make every sacrifice for the ultimate goal. In the present contest for world power,

Japan cannot afford to indulge in temporary dreams of prosperity. The Japanese nation, in view of her glorious history and position, should brace herself to fill her destined rôle." [9]

Much has been said by Chinese and "anti-Japanese" Americans about a certain Tanaka memorial presented to the Emperor in the late nineteen-twenties by the inconsequential, amiable General Baron Tanaka, who through his hookup with the Seiyukai party contrived to occupy the position of premier of the nation for a little while, then got into scandals over red light districts and ended his life in the house of his geisha mistress. This document, the text of which the Chinese claim to have obtained for us through a Korean clerk, purports to contain the scheme for seizure of Manchuria, domination of China, appropriation of the mandated islands, conquest of Russia, and defeat of the United States Navy, now apparently in effect. The author published the Tanaka Memorial in 1934 (Columbia Press, Seattle, Washington) with a history of the document—as nearly as he could verify it. But we do not have to speculate over the authenticity of such a document. We will do better to pay attention to such unquestioned passages of instruction as Lord Hotta, Viscount Tani, Premier Okuma, and the Black Dragon Society have supplied us. Americans think the Tanaka thing is shocking or striking because they are so ignorant of what went before it.

Western arrogance and aggression have acted as acids to resolve the chemical bases of Japanese pride and material dearth into a dynamite that threatens to blow the human race off this planet. Let me conclude this chapter with the words of the 1934 edition, unrevised. The reader will relate them to the events they predicted. So here they are, as they stood, and their application is not all past:

The thing that observers must know, that they must not allow to throw them off guard, is that despite the ebullience within her, Japan, having purpose and plan, can wait. Let those who say, "Well, the war was going to break out this spring, and now it's winter and all is pacific," remember that every cause for Japan's war with China was present in 1884, but Japan waited till 1894 to open it.

[9] Magazine *Taiyo*, April, 1918, translated in Japan *Advertiser*.

Let those who say, "The clash of interests can be peacefully compromised," remember that Japan knew she must fight Russia six months after her war with China was over in 1895. No European nation in those circumstances could have held back more than two years, but Japan waited nine. Let those who say, "The crisis has been definitely averted," read the newspapers of the winter of 1903 and the spring of 1904, when London editorial writers remarked, "There was no justification for all the excitement. Japan and Russia will not fight. Neither one is in a position to carry on a war." Let them read that the Russian armies got off their toes, Russian transport across the continent of Asia became laggard, and Japan talked conciliation. And let them read on, to the spring morning when Togo pounced upon Russian ships that had been playing too far away from home base. Let those who say, "Japan has wisely turned her energies to development of the territory she already has," and "The military element is submerged now," remember that the Japanese armies were all set to take possession of Manchuria in 1928 after the Black Dragon Society had engineered the assassination of the Chinese governor. But in 1931 when the world believed imperialism was dead in Japan, her armies took Manchuria.

History and the gentlemen quoted above tell what to expect from Nippon to those who want to know. Soviet Russia, at least, has read. Hence the "less warlike" the situation becomes on the Siberian border, the more armies and supplies Moscow puts there.[10]

It is time to examine a few Japanese lives in order to get a conception of the human stuff which Nippon is able to put into her drive for empire.

[10] All of the above was "pre-Pearl Harbor" admonition.

Chapter X
Yellow Mettle

<hr/>

IF in the days of the rise of the British Empire one were to have asked, "What is England, and what may be expected of her?" the best answer would have been: King Ethelbert, William the Conqueror, Shakespeare, Elizabeth, Clive, Vancouver, and Lord Nelson, and enough about these and connecting lives to make a tapestry. Through them the confident, order-loving, travailing, dominant spirit of the English race had spoken.

Said Yosuke Matsuoka regarding Nippon: "The Meiji Restoration was brought about by men in their twenties and thirties. The present emergency is infested by old men. If only thirty or forty young men equal to the occasion should make their appearance, a man aged like myself had better promptly withdraw." [1]

Matsuoka was middle-aged, and some of the most indomitable characters to whom he referred, like Saionji, Takahashi, and Saito, were seventy. Before "Pearl Harbor," Saionji, mouthpiece of the emperor, and Saito, great proconsul of Chosen (Korea), died, and Takahashi, romantic financial genius, was removed by assassination. But Matsuoka's remark about the young men who remade Japan a half century ago gives us a good introduction to the characters who stand second row back in the picture that is Japan. It is not possible for Matsuoka or any one to-day to pick out the thirty youths who, a half century from now, will join the pantheon with Kido, Okubo, Itagaki, Saigo, Fukuzawa, Yamagata, Ito, Katsu, Okuma, Nogi, and Togo of a half century ago. But those heroes, statesmen, and remarkable adventurers once looked not greatly different from the fanatic young cadets and superpatriots who have

[1] *Asahi Weekly,* January 31, 1934.

recently stood trial for purging Japan by assassination and terror.

To sketch one of the lives of the Meiji group is to learn much about the making of a feudal archipelago into one of the world's first-class powers. The most significantly typical of these lives, I think, are Katsu, Yamagata, Ito, and Admiral Togo. In another book [2] I have sketched Yamagata and Ito—the reader who has time and interest will look them up. Other readers will get quite a pertinent idea of what Japanese of that generation were like from a brief digest of Katsu's life.

Katsu (Rintaro or Awa), a count when he died, began as the desperately poor grandson of a blind beggar in a period when class lines were almost as rigid in Japan as castes in India. Frail and effeminate in appearance—perhaps the result of the terrible injury suffered at the age of twelve from a mad dog—yet he was one of the most dangerous swordsmen in an empire full of sword swingers. He was the father of the Japanese navy, the first man of his race to command a steamship across the Pacific. Gaining his education by browsing in book stores, he became a great scholar in the classical Chinese, and, in addition, became one of the first Japanese proficient in European literature.

His blind grandfather had crossed from bleak Echigo on the Japan Sea to the capital of the Tokugawas, now Tokyo, and with the coins thrown to him had begun financing the penny-ante gambling of samurai around the castle gates for fifty per cent of the winnings. He could not see his clients, but must have had some blind man's instinct for picking winners, for he ended with a fortune sufficient to buy for his son the position of heir and son-in-law in a samurai family. The Japanese custom, pertaining to this day among families who have a daughter but no sons, is to adopt a son-in-law who takes the father-in-law's name. An amazing slant on this is the comment of the protesting midwives' union of Tokyo against recent medical laws: "You pick on us because we are neither pretty enough to marry into another family nor rich enough to entice a man to marry into ours." The only practicable way for an outsider to become a Japanese subject is to become a son-in-law. It was used by Lafcadio Hearn.

[2] *Eminent Asians* (D. Appleton-Century Company), 1929.

The first Katsu to enjoy, by purchase and marriage, the samurai name, lived as a soldier and scholar, and had nothing left to give his young son Rintaro save a remarkably Spartan training. A dog had torn the lad's testicles nearly off. His will to live was fanned by his father's telling him that no *man* would consent to die from such a shameful injury—inflicted by so low a beast. But only the most painful sewing could repair him, and in those days there were no anesthetics in Japan. The father placed the point of his sword at the child's nose. "If you utter one cry," he said, "you will die in a way that at least will not be shameful!" After the operation the father became the most tender nurse and devoted himself to bringing the lad through alive.

To make up for this adolescent misfortune, Rintaro determined to be the best swordsman in Japan. To prove himself worthy of one of Tokyo's great fencing masters, he went to an abandoned temple night after night alternately to practise with his wooden sword and meditate until dawn. Then he would go and take his lesson, and proceed to his day's work. Samurai fencing was a mental as well as physical training. The self-hypnotism and projection of the thought stream along predetermined channels was as much part of it as the marvelously placed and powerful strokes. It is this mental training that present-day Hayashi and Araki brought back along with the long swords into Japan's army officer's education. To see a Japanese slip from hysterical anger into the state of cool frenzy in which the ordinary human inhibition of fear is completely eliminated is an awesome thing. The nearest that we know to it is the "killer" frenzy of the desperado, but that is a crude and untrained thing. The Japanese cult gives its practitioner a deep, philosophical control the while he becomes as dangerous as a stalking tiger.

The poverty of the Katsu family reached the final depths where there were no copper coins for the special cakes to celebrate the new year, which even a beggar family is ashamed to lack. A relative in a distant suburb offered some. The lad walked across the city to fetch them. After midnight, dead tired, nearly frozen, tortured by the shadows visible through the paper walls of happy family groups eating and drinking to the year's gala festival, the boy Katsu reached the bridge over the canal near his home. Katsu, as count and great man, used to recall as the blackest moment of his life that time when the coarse, handmade paper wrapped about his precious cakes burst and they rolled off the high-arched bridge into the dirty water. To keep himself humble in his great days, Katsu used to go and stand on that bridge.

He was hungry for learning and fascinated by books, and formed a habit of loitering in a certain book store to gaze at the titles. A merchant, Shibuta by name, a bookworm who frequented the place, understood. Still, it was long before the book-loving merchant made bold to speak to the lad who, in spite of coarse cotton gown and pinched face, bore the two swords of the samurai which his grandfather had bought the right to wear. In those days the wealthiest merchant did not speak to the poorest samurai unless he were spoken to first—or craved to be cut in two. The book dealer contrived to get the shy boy to address the merchant first. Whereupon the merchant was able to make known his desire to supply paper and books to the youth. It would be his contribution, he said, to the nation's greatness. Katsu was enabled to begin keeping a diary and notebook, and at the top of every page he wrote, "Thank you, Shibuta."

But Katsu wasn't satisfied with Japanese and Chinese books. He had seen the strange left-to-right printing of some clumsy, and I am afraid very stupid, Dutch tomes, but this had opened the entire outside world to his imagination. For two hundred years since the Tokugawa edict destroying deep-sea shipping, Japan's only contact with Europe had been through the one or two small Dutch ships per year allowed to load and unload in the little harbor of Nagasaki nearest to Shanghai, and the score of Dutch supercargoes and merchants permitted to reside in semi-imprisonment on the tiny islet called Deshima—now part of the foreshore.

The Dutch merchants were mostly an uncultured lot, content to spend their constricted residence in drinking and playing with the doll-like outcast women of the Tairas (see p. 28) whom the authorities—very human in regard to sex—permitted to visit them freely. When Japanese gentlemen, despite the official ban on social intercourse, did talk with the Dutchmen, the latter used the opportunity chiefly to run down their fellow whites, the Portuguese, Spaniards, and other Roman Catholics. But shortly before and during Katsu's childhood some superior men among the Dutch, coming out as physicians to the settlement, were granted more freedom than the merchants, and began to exert a revolutionary influence. Young men of the eastern and southern clans were beginning to envisage the possibility of successful rebellion against Tokugawa tyranny. They wanted to learn any secrets of power which the west might know. Young fellows about the Tokugawa capital such as Katsu, were likewise interested.

As early as 1771, two young samurai had won a tremendous, though perilous, prestige for western learning by demonstrating to intellectual warriors on the cadaver of an outcast that the accepted Chinese anatomy, while correct in regard to blood circulation long before its discovery in Europe, was decidedly wrong in its general "geography" and the Oranda (Holland) books were right. On the pretext of studying medicine some samurai procured a negative sort of permission to study the Dutch language and got the Hollanders to supply books. A surprising number of the books on medicine dealt, inside the covers, with military tactics, ordnance, and such matters —the heavy military science of the German school current in Europe after the Napoleonic wars.

Young Katsu presented himself before the most noted Japanese scholar of the Dutch language in the great city Yedo, which Katsu was later to help transform into Tokyo. "But you are an Edokko [sort of equivalent to being a New Yorker, and commonly translated to-day, 'Tokyo kid']," said the sarcastic scholar to the avid young man. "You've got their impatience. I can see it on your face. No Edokko has the patience to learn the barbarian's language. Get out!" He would not even give the tearful young man time to say that he was only two generations from Echigo, which, according to oriental ways of speaking, made him still an Echigoese.

But Katsu found another teacher and, before he was twenty, took away from the teacher who refused him, laurels as first Dutch scholar in the empire. He soon needed a Dutch dictionary. There was not one on sale in the empire. He made two complete longhand copies of his teacher's dictionary and sold one for enough to buy his other study books. Just then there appeared in a book store a Dutch volume on military tactics, priced at 50 ryo, the equivalent, roughly, of 3,000 yen or normally, U. S. $1,500.[3] Katsu's wealth didn't total fifteen hundred cents. He made a deal to pay 10 ryo (on time) for a year's lease of the book. He took it home and started copying it.

When he turned sixteen, his father nonchalantly retired to a monastery and appointed the son responsible head of the house. The custom of retirement of pater familias to write poetry and study beauty and religion—still met with in Japan—strikes one as excellent when the son is left something to go on with. Here is the pathetic yet significant note in Katsu's handwriting at the foot of the last page of his year's work of copying, a feat comparable in the west only to the prodigious labors of our medieval scribes: "No mosquito net in summer—no blanket in winter—stuck to desk— better to keep awake and write with frozen hands than go to sleep and freeze—tore boards off veranda to heat my fingertips and to keep warm sick mother and sister who lack enough rice to resist cold." Under this he writes the Chinese character for finis, and under this again, very small: "But ah, the ultimate success—it is still beyond my reach. It may not be expected!"

In this ambitious melancholia, plus the fact that when Katsu wrote the last phrase he did expect the ultimate success and continued to work for it, lies the whole Japanese mentality.

This was not the intrepid young scholar's last adventure as a scrivener. Another Dutch book on military tactics appeared in the store—as stupid, we may be sure, as the first, but it was from that strange continent Europe, and it was the golden book to Katsu. The price was 60 ryo, say 3,600 yen. This time the indigent scholar begged small sums from every relative and equal whom he dared approach until the amount was made up. Then he ceremonially bathed, girded on his best starched kimono and swords, and marched to the book store with this fortune which would have set him up

---

[3] Henry Satoh, contemporary English diplomat in Japan, says that 3½ ryo were exchanged for an English pound in 1858—showing how Japan was mulcted of her metal money. Rice sold for about two koku (approximately 10 bushels) per ryo (varying to one in time of scarcity), making 35 bushels for £1! The ryo had, of course, varied greatly since the time of Ieyasu.

Rice was worth, just previously to the world war of 1939, in Japan about ￥30, about £2 or $10, per koku—$2.00 per bushel, or 2½ bushels for £1. Obviously the commodity dollar is the only unit of comparative value the historian may use. Using rice as Japan's real criterion of values, Katsu's book was priced at $1,000!

in any business—only to find that the book had been sold a few
hours before.

By persuasion and threats the young samurai finally induced the
apprehensive book dealer to tell him the purchaser. Katsu walked
across Yedo into the wealthy young samurai's house. "Will you
sell?" he asked that surprised individual. "No," was the answer.
"Then will you lease?" asked Katsu. "No." "Will you then—I only
ask because you refuse the other two—lend?" "I need the book all
the time," was the curt reply. "Do you sleep?" asked Katsu. "Yes,
at night." "I don't," said Katsu. "Will you let me come and get the
book at your bedtime, and bring it back at dawn, keeping this
money as security?" "I won't let the book go out of the house!"
replied the more and more annoyed purchaser. Katsu's hand went
to his sword. It came near being a point of honor involving some-
body's elimination. "Then," said Katsu, "will you let me come and
read it here while you sleep?"

The young owner collapsed and assented, but, very likely on
purpose, neglected to inform his gatekeeper of Katsu's nightly mission. Katsu came the three miles each evening, however, and stood
until the gate functionary's resistance broke down. In six months he
had read and made a complete copy of the eight volumes. When the
rich young owner saw this he changed his attitude toward Katsu and
presented him with the printed work, insisting that he had earned it
fairly. Katsu sold it for 30 ryo and started a school of tactics and
gun designing. Soon he was turning out ordnance for lords in all
parts of the empire.

Japanese metal workers had begun imitating the first Portuguese
arquebuses they had seen, in 1643, but it remained for Katsu and
his fellows to catch up with the European progress in firearms of
the eighteenth and nineteenth centuries.

The splendid Japanese foundrymen, whose superiority can be
seen in the images and bells of Japanese temples, sent Katsu the
usual designer's percentage. To their amazement Katsu returned the
money with instructions to put it into making better guns.

Okubo, imperious high clansman of Satsuma, the powerful south-
ernmost clan, who was becoming the John Adams of the revolution
that was brewing, looked up the self-reliant young Katsu and in-

troduced him to Lord Abe, the most forward-minded of high Tokugawa officials. From that time on Katsu was a major figure in affairs. Katsu's acquaintanceship with the Dutch turned him toward navigation and sea power as well as ordnance. In the fall of 1853 high Tokugawa officials and populace alike received a shock in the appearance of the American Commodore Matthew Perry with a steam squadron in what is now Tokyo Bay. According to a contemporary the "hairy barbarians" caused more panic than the pest that swept the country twenty years later. Old people, women, and children fled from Yedo. What we call the white race were known variously as "pink-nosed," "fish-eyed," or "hairy barbarians," contact with whom would be a contamination.

At the present day there are still old folk in Japan who think foreigners are innately immoral, do not take baths, sleep with their boots on, and otherwise show that they are nearer the animal category than to the divine race of Nippon. All this Katsu, who had a correct estimate of the white pioneers, had to face. Out of it he at least got permission, the same year Perry landed, to establish Japan's first naval school at Nagasaki with Dutch instructors. The king of Holland presented the Japanese fleet a 150-horsepower gunboat which, commanded by Katsu for the Tokugawa government, may be called the foundation of the Japanese navy, although the eastern clan lords had before this time procured little steam vessels.

For the next few years Katsu's amazing adventures were chiefly at sea. Once he steamed into a back-country inlet and was casting anchor when he saw two rustic samurai behind a screen of trained cucumber vines light the fuses of a pair of cannon pointed straight at his ship, ten paces away. The policy of these bumpkins, apparently, was not to fire until they saw the whites of the eyes and then to let go everything without questions. Taking a mighty leap from deck to bank and bounding past the gun muzzles, the slight Katsu struck out the fuses.

He had too many shipwrecks to record. Once, in a freezing sea, he had himself tied to the mast in order that he might remain on the wave-swept deck to give orders. The mast snapped over his head; the rope eventually broke. The numbed Katsu recovered just enough use of his limbs to grasp the gunwale as he was being washed over.

Such of the crew as remained gave up and sought refuge below, but Katsu, although to go on was now a pure, useless exhibition of the Japanese spirit, crawled back and retied himself to the mast, remaining there until the storm abated.

II

In 1860 the first treaties made between Japan and a western government had been concluded by the combined firmness of Commodore Perry and the diplomacy of Townsend Harris, first American plenipotentiary to China. Katsu was delighted when Okubo accepted this then bizarre suggestion that Japan ask for exchange of ratifications to be made in the capital of the United States, by an embassy led by Lord Hotta himself. What a chance, thought Katsu and his fellows, to see the insides of a western power! They were not aware, as Japanese diplomats and military men are fully aware now, that this particular power lives in a glass house which even magnifies for the convenience of rivals and potential enemies who want to inspect the works. But Katsu could not bear the slur on Japan's pride involved in the acceptance by the noble-born Japanese ambassadors of passage on the American warship U.S.S. *Powhatan* which was offered them by Townsend Harris.

Katsu couldn't get any formal hearing but procured the understanding Okubo's semiofficial permission to escort the United States warship in his 100-ton flagship. He was ill of a fever, vomiting blood, on the secret sailing date. "But," said he to his friend Fukuzawa, "rather death at sea than meaningless death on the mats." His wife was entirely unaware of his plans. "I'm going across the bay [to the new foreign settlement of Yokohama] to get coal and a little foreign medicine. I'll be all well when I come back," he assured her. His sailors didn't know their destination any more than did his wife. Fukuzawa, who was to become Japan's most prominent Christian and founder of her journalism, went with him.

The U.S.S. *Powhatan* soon left its escort hopelessly behind. Whereupon Katsu and his seamen and ship, none of which had ever before been out in the real ocean, took the northern, stormy, dangerous, then untraveled but short great-circle route for the Golden Gate.

The hundred-tonner was waiting for the embassy when the *Powhatan* steamed into the Golden Gate. She was the first vessel to fly the rising-sun flag in American waters—the first Japanese war vessel to cross the Pacific, the first Japanese ship seen in a port of the United States. The frail Katsu thus became the pioneer of the second largest ocean-going merchant marine in the world and one of the three largest navies, and the end is not yet.

He and Fukuzawa had been deathly seasick all the way across. The frontier population of San Francisco gave a tremendous wild-western ovation to this first Japanese naval hero, who in his kimono looked to them like a fine-boned woman instead of the traditional seadog, but whose sword was quick as lightning.

When he had got this far the Japanese spirit of adventure overcame him and he was hell-bent for exploring the coast of South America and impressing Japanese prestige upon Peru, but the chief of his embassy stepped on his plans. The embassy traversed the continent to the White House, where its members were received by President Lincoln in the midst of Civil War excitement. They were in medieval Japanese costume. Lately their impressions of America have been published in English.[4] They stated that they had never conceived there could be so much land nor that there could be a human being like Abraham Lincoln or women like the hoop-skirted, dancing ladies of Washington.

Katsu sailed his ship home although most of the sailors died of cholera en route, and he was made chief of the navy—actually the first Japanese minister of the navy. Yet he was not one of the Satsuma nobles who regarded the navy as their own, but a poor lad of beggar descent from the stunted pines of Echigo. He began the education of Togo and the Satsuma men who were to be Japan's sea hierarchy.

Events became dangerous for him after his return. He was attached to the Tokugawas, who before long were being overthrown by a ruthless campaign of assassination and the arms of the great clans of the south. His personal bravery and impeccable honesty

---

[4] By the Townsend Harris Foundation of the Japan Society, New York. America's impressions of them—and treatment of them as if they were cute, educated Negroes, were reproduced in *Life* Magazine of February—1942.

and quick sword brought him through that storm of 1867-1868. In Kyoto he was attacked by assassins. A samurai, walking the streets and seeing the unfair advantage taken against him, cut an assassin in two just as the fellow's sword was reaching for Katsu's heart. The revolutionary eccentric Sakamoto (Ruima), greatest swordsman of the empire, came, sworn to kill Katsu for championing foreign influences and upholding the right of foreigners to enter Japan. Katsu talked the hero out of drawing his sword and into being his pupil. Sakamoto continued a supporter to the time of his dramatic assassination—a favorite theme of the Japanese stage and screen. It took several score of swordsmen to down him.

Strong prejudice against the navy still prevailed. The Tokugawa shogun was summoned for the first time in two and one-half centuries to the emperor's court in Kyoto. (For that long the Tokugawas rather than the emperor had been in the "summoning" status). Katsu offered the "navy" his one little ship, to take the shogun around to Osaka to save him the conventional land progress down the island. Though a terrific storm was experienced, Katsu persuaded his kingly guest to stay aboard. It was a telling victory for the navy party!

The weakened shogun's visit to the emperor in Kyoto failed to stem the rising tide of Tokugawa doom. The royalist guards of the Choshu clan had taken matters in their own hands. Waiting off Osaka, seaport of Kyoto, Katsu saw that ancient capital forty miles away break into flames. Alone he left his ship to investigate. He saw three samurai swirl down the river in a small boat and jump ashore, saw two of them commit mutual suicide by sinking their daggers in each other's hearts, and saw the third cut his throat. The fact that they had no time for ceremonial disembowelment was proof of the desperateness of the situation. A lone warrior floating down in another boat was suddenly crumpled by a hail of bullets from the shore. Katsu got some through his hat.

Katsu was at least able to dissuade the royalists from their intent to burn the great city of Osaka, mart of the Tokugawas. This brought suspicion of sympathy with the losing side, and Katsu was dismissed from office and confined to his house. This was the conventional prelude to an invitation to commit hara-kiri. Okubo advised his young friend to take the injustice casually. By some miracle the usual sealed letter with its significant past-tense encomium which spelled fate never arrived.

Katsu went out in the white cotton clothes of the dead to plead with the warring elements for peace. In a little hotel in Choshu territory he was spied on and fired at. In suspicion the Japanese are quite impartial, treating fellow countrymen no better than aliens. Women and children had fled this area and Katsu worked the only old slavey left in the hotel nearly to death making him a new suit of cotton underwear and dressing his hair each day. When she made bold to question the guest lord over his eccentric habit, he told her that a man must have garments and hairdress ready for death, which did not reassure her but which she took pride later in repeating to her grandchildren.

Because Katsu outranked in imperial honors the clan nobles who came to deal with him, the latter sat, clad in their silks, on the veranda of a temple while Katsu in his cotton squatted in the main hall. They would quite gladly have caught and put to the sword the whole Tokugawa officialdom which Katsu represented, but their code required conventional deference in formal meeting. Laughing, Katsu arose. "Since you won't come in to me," he said, "I will go out to you." He went out, squatted on the veranda; then all arose and went in.

The most intelligent man in the delegation was the youngster Inouye (Haruki, still in his teens). He had got back with his comrade Ito from London upon hearing of the danger hanging over their clan, only to be attacked by fellow clansmen for breaking the prohibition against going abroad. Inouye still had a plaster over the wound on his face. He was to survive to become the establisher of Japan's state finance.

Katsu told the Choshu clansmen that with the Europeans, Americans, and Russians pressing in, this was no time for fratricidal strife, and they agreed—too well. Katsu couldn't argue them out of their logic that the thing for the government to do was to join them in a coöperative general massacre of the foreigners.

Then Katsu went back to learn that his superior in the shogun's capital, the Tokugawa lord Keiki, after letting him risk his life, had found it good policy to forget that he had authorized the mission. In the orient every negotiator has to get used to this sort of thing. But Katsu, feeling that honor required that he save his lord's face rather than his own, destroyed all the documents and took the blame. When the shogun's place was suddenly left open by death, it was Katsu who simply assumed the privilege of nominating this Keiki, the lord who had let him down, for the supreme rulership, because no member of the Tokugawa family itself dared suggest it. The stupefied house council ratified the nomination. But Keiki's rule was to be short, the last of the Tokugawa line and of the feudal era.

III

The hostility between the Tokugawa government and the Choshu clan dragged on until Satsuma and Tosa openly, and many other clans passively, joined Choshu and brought the two-and-one-half-century dynasty and the whole structure of feudalism crashing to the ground.

When the combined British, America, and Dutch fleet organized to blast the Choshu clan off the earth for five incidents of firing on foreign vessels around the straits of Shimonoseki, Katsu was the man to persuade the foreign admirals to grant six months' respite. But the incidents between Choshu and "pink-haired barbarians" continued until an allied fleet did open fire on Choshu's capital and punished it. The clansmen were glad to accept the self-initiated mediation of young Inouye and Ito. To Ito, then, remained the delicate task of bringing the victorious clansmen whose war cry had been "Exterminate the foreigners!" into politic friendliness with the white world. This twenty-year-old lad established the foreign relationships of the new empire—became, in effect, its first minister of foreign affairs, and grew up to become the first elder statesman and write the constitution.

Younger men were coming up to take the burden off Katsu's generation. By this time Togo was graduating from Katsu's naval school. There were a few delicate situations, however, for Katsu to save before he was launched upon the placid waters of his later career.

Back in Tokyo Katsu found a knock-down-drag-out fight going on between British naval instructors who had been invited out by the Tokugawa government and Dutch instructors whom a Japanese had brought back with him on a warship sent out by the Dutch government. One can almost hear the rivals agreeing on *one* thing: "These natives will never get anywhere by themselves. Directed by us, if they will give us sufficient authority and obey us, they might keep their end up." It is exactly the same language that vain Japanese of 1936 used so smugly about China. All of Katsu's early associations had been with the Dutch. Yet he chose to build Japan's navy under British rather than Dutch instruction. With some difficulty he raked up three years' advance salaries for the importunate Dutchmen, gave them an additional bonus and grand farewell banquet, and shipped them home.

Thus this frail swordsman of the old Japan was responsible for establishing that relationship between the world's two maritime empires which was to provide the eastern one with all the naval experience of the western one, provide capital from the older for carrying on the wars and building up the industry of the newer, turn Japan against Russia, bring about the Anglo-Japanese alliance, and eventually put Japan in a position to challenge her own teacher's position as ruler of the waves and boss of the world's trade and industry.

Loyal to the Tokugawas as he was, Katsu nevertheless prevented them in their last hours from borrowing 200,000,000 francs from France to fight the clansmen. Katsu knew that if the Tokugawas did this England would oppositely finance the clansmen and Japan, as a result, would suffer the fate of India, whose princes, ranging themselves with France against a British supported raj, or emperor, soon lost all Indian independence. Delicately, Katsu suggested abdication to Lord Keiki, and the disappearance not only of Tokugawa paramountcy but of the entire institution of the shogunate and the era of feudalism. He had proved his loyalty and was one of the few on the inside who could execute this delicate mission. "But," protested the lord, "the Tokugawa position is established by three centuries of history!"

Katsu's answer is very pertinent to the Japan of to-day—in fact, to the whole world of to-day: "The history and traditions of three centuries, if incompatible with the spirit of the age, count very little. A statesman should note first the general tendency of the times."

Under the new empire and constitution Katsu became successively admiral, minister of the navy, member of the house of peers, and count. He sent his son to Annapolis, as one of the first oriental students there, received the young graduate back proudly in 1887 and took stoically the young man's death from a riding accident soon afterwards. In 1899, Katsu died, full of honors, his indomitable will having driven on for seventy-seven years his sickly and damaged body. Two days before he died he adopted as his heir and bearer of the once humble name of Katsu a son of his old master, the near-divine Lord Keiki, last of the shoguns.

While Nippon produces men like Katsu, Nippon will make history.

Chapter XI
Contrasting Characters

OUT of two contrasting characters of the restoration period flowed the two streams that became the dominant features of modern Japan. From the swashbuckling, fanatical, albeit heroic and self-sacrificing Saigo (Takamori) flowed Toyama, Togo, Araki, Suetsugu, Matsouka, and Tojo, the Black Dragon Society, the spirit of the Japanese army and navy, and the divine-mission expansionists. From the worldly-wise success-worshiping, suave, money-loving Fukuzawa (Yukichi) flowed the modern industrialists and new "robber barons" of the machine who succeeded the warrior caste for a time (1874-1931) as lappers-up of the cream. Also from Fukuzawa, a sort of Japanese Benjamin Franklin, flowed the line of astute diplomats whose job it is to hold up before the world's eyes a false front of unity and mirage of cherry blossoms waving under Mt. Fuji. In 1934-1935 came the attempt to unite these two divergent streams into one flood for swamping the world with Japanese goods backed by soldiers and ships.

More than one hundred biographies have been written about Saigo. He lived and died a fighter, he possessed the stubbornness of a great bear, and evidenced a slowness in mental reactions that went with his giant physique, huge head, beetling brows, and the large penetrating eyes that lit his otherwise heavy face. Although born in Satsuma at the extreme tip of the southern island, he might be called a good example of the aboriginal northern Ainu type of Japanese.

Satsuma had always been the chief "thorn in the flesh" of the Tokugawa dynasty. It was the Sparta of Japan, and was often as much trouble to Yedo as was the Grecian Sparta to Athens. Satsuma was constantly running the embargo laid down by the Tokugawa on foreign intercourse. It was the first part of Japan to become acquainted with Europeans who manufactured firearms in the sixteenth century. Again in 1858 its feudal lord (Nariakira), cast about eight hundred cannon after a modern Prussian model while intriguing for the final downfall of the Tokugawa overlord.

Into this atmosphere of rebellion Saigo and his younger brother— a much more tactful person—were born in the Street of the Blacksmiths in the seaport of Kagoshima, sons of a clerk who barely managed to rate membership in the samurai caste. Saigo's stepmother was his first teacher and best friend, and he went from her instruction into the clan school for samurai boys. At the age of thirteen, being ridiculed for his failing to keep up with their sallies of wit, he drew the sword worn after the age of twelve, and engaged in a duel which left him wounded and muscle-bound for the rest of his life. Thus prevented from attaining first rank as a swordsman, he turned to the Chinese classics, Zenism, and the study of military theory to attain preëminence. He became a true exponent of the doctrine based on Zen, that if the inner emotional life were kept properly tuned to receive those heavenly impulses specially granted to the Japanese race it was unnecessary to acquire a wide knowledge of contemporary events of the nation and the world. This was the exact opposite, you note, of Katsu's philosophy and from each Japan derived strength. Saigo's rival, named Okubo, was growing up in the same clan—destined to be protector of the Katsu type.

From 1828 Saigo pegged away as a clerk in the clan government. In 1850, on the charge of poaching on his lord's game preserves, he was banished to the famous little island of Oshima, where women own and till the land while their men fish. He got back in time to accompany his feudal lord to Yedo the year following Perry's visit. For the Tokugawa regent had summoned his greatest vassals to counsel with him about how to handle the arriving foreign barbarians. Additionally, he wished to keep an eye on his vassals to see that they were not illicitly getting into touch with the barbarians, or, on the other hand, stirring up revolution against a shogun who appeared too weak to keep barbarians off.

On the long journey to Yedo the Satsuma lord became fascinated with Hercules-statured Saigo, and, on arrival at his mansion in the shogun's capital, made the warrior his chief gardener so that long talks between two persons of such different rank would not excite suspicion. The Satsuma lord eventually got away from Yedo, stopped in Kyoto to make an effective understanding with the emperor aiming at overthrow of the Tokugawas, reached his home fief and began mobilizing his troops. Then he suddenly died, leaving the clan in the hands of weak men who sought reconciliation with Yedo.

Saigo was left in the most exposed position in Yedo, and first thought of disemboweling himself. Restrained from this by a friend, he made his way to Kyoto where he further endangered himself by becoming the champion bodyguard of the chief priest of a Kyoto temple named Gessho, whose death was at this time desired by the Tokugawas for plotting their overthrow. Saigo and Gessho became the David and Jonathan of the period, and it seems that the big warrior became lover to the priest as well. Homosexuality was frequent in both priestly and warrior circles, particularly in Spartan Satsuma where it is said still to persist.

The pursued couple fled from point to point along the Inland Sea and down the coast of the southern island. Eventually they hid in the very shadow of the clan government of Satsuma. They were found out and Saigo was ordered by his own lord to escort his bosom friend out of the clan territory into the hands of the shogun's waiting executioners. Instead, they fled from Kagoshima on a Chinese junk, taking along the makings of a splendid feast. Safely out at sea, they ate and drank to the full, went to the prow, bade ceremonious farewell to one another and jumped in. Gessho was drowned, but his body was fished out and on it was found the poem: "This unclouded heart like the moon, falls among the waves of Satsuma." On the rescued Saigo's person was found his death poem: "Adrift on the sea of destiny— Let the wind blow and the waves rise."

Gessho's death saved Saigo, his friends in the clan government giving out that both had perished. Then they smuggled him into exile once more in Oshima. He went protesting, tears rolling down his face for his lost friend. On Oshima the magistrate became so impressed with his prisoner that he gave him his own daughter as concubine and housewife. Eventually news came of the assassination by royalists of the Tokugawa regent. Saigo put on a big feast and went out in the garden and did a sword dance in celebration.

Saigo's clan lord fetched him back to Kagoshima, exiled him once more, and fetched him back yet again to become commander of the clan army. He was told to lead it north and to make contact on the main island with another great clan, also disaffected, the Choshu, and wait there for the arrival of his clan lord. Determined to pre-cipitate open rebellion against the Tokugawas, Saigo pushed on to Osaka, looking for fight. His clan lord was frightened and furious, demoted him and sent him to a desolate isle where he was kept in solitary confinement.

In 1863 a British squadron sailed into Kagoshima, sank the Sat-sumas' gunboats,[1] and burned the city as punishment for the killing near Yedo of a member of the British legation who had failed to dismount from his horse as the previous clan lord had passed by. In consternation the clan leaders brought Saigo back and made him virtual head of the clan. Okubo, Katsu and others persuaded the shogun to abdicate, and when the new imperial government was formed they made Saigo minister of war, then commander-in-chief of the national imperial forces. He had suffered enough at the hands of his own clan lords to throw his weight heartily with the move-ment for the abolition of the fiefs. The feudal system was ended by the decree of August, 1871, and no lord of the time cared to dispute it by challenging Saigo's army.

But Saigo, swashbuckler at heart, insisted that the reorganized Japan should immediately set out to build empire, taking up where Hideyoshi left off 225 years earlier. Ordinary samurai began to suf-fer a great deal as their lords retired to vast estates as country gentlemen. Saigo demanded a war as occupation for them. He was allowed to lead the expedition against Formosan aborigines (1873) which, however, got Japan into difficulties with China. Great Britain smoothed out the affair profitably. Saigo then demanded that his warriors be sent against Korea. His fellow clansman Okubo, real-izing that Japan had a long way to go before launching upon for-eign expansion, got imperial veto of Saigo's imperialist scheme. Saigo resigned from the new government at Tokyo, returned to

[1] Most of Japan's present high naval officers are Satsuma men.

Kagoshima, and pledged the unemployed warriors that they should have their war.

In Satsuma he established a school, branches of which sprang up all over the island, each a political hotbed for rebellion. Particularly were the samurai angered over the creation by young Yamagata, an erstwhile pupil of Saigo, of a modern plebeian army, clad in khaki, drilled in the goose step, and recruited from the new common schools. The sword-swinging, mail-coated, peacock-feathered warrior caste scoffed bitterly at the idea that plebeians could fight even though armed with Mauser rifles. In January, 1874, some young samurai hot-heads seized the new Kagoshima arsenal from the imperial war office and began making powder for their own forces. Their act, one repeated over and over in Japanese history to the present day, forced their leader, Saigo, either to repudiate his own followers or to lead an open rebellion. Their pretense, of course, was that they wished to rescue the emperor from the dilettantes who had him in their possession at Tokyo.

Okubo, left as chief figure of the infant régime at Tokyo, made a typically Japanese effort at a short cut to eliminate the danger. He knew how great was the hold of Saigo on the imagination of the country and how dangerous would be a general open rebellion of the warrior caste which had dominated Japan for centuries. He sent nineteen youths secretly to Satsuma with instructions to assassinate his old pal Saigo the moment the hero should take up arms. One of the youths came under suspicion, was tortured, and confessed the plot. Copies of his confession sent over the province served as a general call to samurai to rise against the new order. Okubo was read out of the clan.

Word came to Okubo in Kyoto. He dismissed the other imperial counselors without a word, giving the impression that he would try conciliation. Had he called the cabinet together, hesitation among them would have appeared and everything might have been lost. Okubo calmly went to a geisha dinner that evening, and in the night he procured the stamping of the sacred imperial seal below proclamations ordering young Yamagata's new army to get the head of Saigo and exterminate the rebels. Japan was breathless with consternation, but the position of the Sacred Person was now pledged.

The issue was the tremendous prestige of the samurai caste versus loyalty to the emperor, and the result, after a bitterly fought campaign costing some 70,000 lives, was the end of the samurai caste. It was proved once and for all that a proletarian with a gun is better than an aristocrat with a sword, and Japan still remembers the lesson. As the samurai went down, Japan's plebeians came at last into their own. Dyspeptic young Yamagata, still in his twenties, became Japan's empire builder. He was to remain so till he was eighty-five.

Saigo's men fought like tigers, but the big fellow's heart was not in the war. He did not resent the imperial order to take his head, remarking that with his heart already torn in two his head mattered little. His own young brother fought against him, and it was with tears that the ordinarily ruthless young Yamagata ordered the decapitation of Saigo's body after it was found in a haystack. Admiral Kawamura, a relative, who had fought against him, took up the bleeding head, washed it and gave it formal samurai burial.

Saigo has become as much of a hero to imperial Japan as the American rebel Robert E. Lee to Americans. He is honored as one of the founders of modern Japan, and as the true incarnation of the spirit still pervading the islands, which acts out of the loyalties and impulses of the heart rather than the knowledge and caution of the head.

II

The totally different personality and mentality of Fukuzawa aid in understanding Japan's resources in men at this crucial period. Fukuzawa was the friend of Katsu who dared to cross with that pioneer on the first voyage of a Japanese steamship across the Pacific Ocean. From childhood he showed that practical combination of idealism and worldly wisdom which the American colonies produced in Benjamin Franklin. Asked as a lad by his brother, a Confucian moralist, if he had settled his aim in life, he replied, "Yes, to become the richest man in Japan."

When he was twelve or thirteen his brother scolded him one day for stepping on a paper on which was written the name of the clan lord. This aroused rebellion in the lad, who wondered, "What would happen if I stepped on the name of a god?" So he tried it and heaven failed to strike. Then, to make a final and complete test, he took a piece of paper on which appeared a sacred name and subjected it to the most debasing uses which his boyish mind could conceive. He confesses that he was scared to death as he went through with the trial. Again, he took the image from the shrine of the fox god, popularly dreaded for spirit possession throughout the orient, and substituted a stone. With great glee he saw his neighbors come and worship, unwittingly, before this pebble. From then on, even after his conversion to Christianity, Fukuzawa was at heart a rationalist. This experience has a counterpart in the early life of Sun Yat-sen, founder of new China, also Christian and also rationalist, who tested his boyish iconoclasm by upsetting all the idols in the village temple.

Fukuzawa made himself one of the first English translators in the empire, studying English while his friend Katsu studied Dutch. When the Tokugawa government appointed him to accompany the mission to the United States and Europe he sailed abroad on Katsu's ship. For this service he received an advance of $400, $100 of which he remitted to his aged mother in Choshu. The remainder he carried intact to London to purchase English books. He records that the members of the mission supposed they would not be able to eat the western barbarians' food and took with them a huge supply of rice. Also they had lanterns and candles, thinking these would be needed in western inns. They dressed in Japanese kimono with the elaborate slit overskirt, had their hair done in samurai topknot and carried the samurai's two swords.

On his return in 1864, Fukuzawa visited his home town, Nakatsu, to persuade some of his fellows to take up western studies. He found soldiers equipped variously with guns and swords marching about the streets declaiming against foreign devils, and children singing songs and playing at exterminating barbarians. The barber who was shaving him said he would like to cut the throat of any Japanese who had anything to do with the blue-eyed devils. Fukuzawa kept very still, indeed. Two attempts were made on his life, one by his own cousin and boyhood playmate, who stood outside Fukuzawa's house all night watching through the rice-paper panes, waiting for a guest of the family to leave so that the private little intrafamily murder should take place without offending a stranger. The guest seems to have got drunk on sake and remained all night. The young patriot skulking outside got tired and went home. Again, an innkeeper, where Fukuzawa stayed with his mother the night before he was to take a boat out of his inhospitable home district, betrayed him to several young patriots, who rushed into the inn, but suddenly got into an altercation as to who would have the honor of dispatching the traitor. Daybreak and the boat came before they made a choice.

III

Fukuzawa, like Benjamin Franklin, was a man of unending curiosity and amazing variety of interests. Everything that came to him he tried to apply to his changing nation. He is known for getting Protestant Christianity off to a fine start by becoming its first prominent Japanese convert, for introducing the art of public speaking into Nippon, and for founding Keio University, which, with the support of Mitsui money, furnished so many of Japan's early diplomats that the foreign office was referred to as a "department of Keio." Fukuzawa's influence was so strong in the ministry of education that it was sarcastically called another branch of Fukuzawa's school, and he introduced athletics to replace swordplay in the education of Japanese youth. He founded the first political party modeled after American patterns, the Seiyukai, and used it to force the promulgation of a written constitution; he founded and edited the first great newspaper in Japan, pioneered in cotton spinning, hydro-electric power, and many other industries, and accumulated his boyishly desired million yen several times over. And he transmitted to new Japan the practical western ethics of success: gogettism and taking care of Number One.

Japan, where to-day political orators regale their audiences for six hours at a stretch, where parliamentary debate bites, fumes, and drools, where students hold public-speaking contests in both Japanese and English,[2] where labor agitators orate from soap boxes and patriots stir their hearers to tears and murders, where reformers such as Kagawa hold audiences spellbound and the radio broadcasts

[2] Since 1939, in German instead of English.

dozens of speeches a day, where luncheon and dinner-club speaking goes to greater lengths than in any other country in the world and every welcome of a visiting diplomat or school teacher is made the occasion for interminable orations—this Japan, for better or worse, knew no public speaking before 1873. The reader will hardly be able to believe this, but it is true. The Tokugawa police system could not have been friendly to the spread of ideas by oratory. But also it was the general belief of literary Japanese that their language, while excellent for instruction of disciples by master, was not suitable for public declamation. The imperial "charter oath" of 1868 had legalized discussion and debate but no medium for them existed. Whether Fukazawa did his people a service or a cruelty is beside the point, but he certainly loosed a new force in their national life when in 1873 he translated Robert's *Rules of Order* into Japanese. He had to invent parliamentary terms and found difficulty in rendering even the words *speech, premise,* and *conclusion.*

Fukuzawa organized a little public-speaking club, and brought in for its edification the troubadour story-tellers of the street and tea houses, who alone, he said, possessed a native art of declamation. Even Fukuzawa's great friend, the educational pioneer Mori, ventured before a society of scholars that a public oration on a serious subject could not be understood. Whereupon Fukuzawa arose and said, "Gentlemen, give me a moment to tell you something." He launched into an oration on the Formosan expedition, the burning question of the moment. After an hour, finding that all ears were still waiting upon his words, he suddenly asked his auditors if they had understood. They nodded. "Well," said Fukuzawa, "that was a speech, and it was in Japanese." Within fifteen years Fukuzawa had developed public and parliamentary speaking sufficiently for a parliament to function, which, since its inception in 1889, has never seemed to lack for words.

"Money," Fukuzawa taught his people, setting aside the sayings of his Christian Bible regarding "the root of all evil," "is mightier than anything else. My countrymen, you must exert yourselves with all your strength to make money. For thus may the fountain of national power be deepened." Strange teaching for a people who

had always been taught that money making, and particularly merchandising, was the mark of a low-class person, and where the aristocratic warrior class had for centuries been forbidden to engage in
money-making enterprises! It caught on quickly enough, however,
and Fukuzawa was one of the leaders in a battle to teach the new
Japanese business man that ethical business is the best policy and
that petty frauds are inexcusable.

When business instead of warfare became the main interest of
ambitious Japanese, such crude and deplorable breaches of commercial honesty commonly occurred that the Japanese received a stigma
throughout the world, which accepted as an axiom the statement
that "Japanese are so dishonest they have to employ Chinese tellers
in their banks." This historical canard arose from some tourists'
having seen Chinese clerks in a newly opened branch of a Hongkong
British bank in Japan. The difference between the reputation of the
Chinese merchant of old guild days whose "word was as good as his
bond" and "the dishonest Japanese" was due to the fact that in
China for millenniums merchandising had been an honorable business and merchants a highly respected and organized class whose
guilds held their members to strict honesty for the honor of the
trade; whereas in Japan the merchant, save of a few old houses like
Mitsui was, until the restoration, a pariah. During the first few
decades after that he was usually a declassed samurai who knew
nothing whatsoever about business and was at the mercy of his one-
time servant. To-day, when the Japanese government exerts the
strictest supervision over business practices for the sake of further-
ing Japan's trade invasion of the world, and when at the same time
the magnificent old Chinese guilds are breaking down under the
impact of political confusion and western industrialism, the prover-
bial estimate of the comparative honesty of Chinese and Japanese
merchants bids fair to be reversed.

Fukuzawa was a hearty believer in the right of capital to take its
profit. He could be quoted in justification by the Mitsui bank as it
made 100,000,000 yen profit at the expense of the nation when it
went off gold in 1932.

In his early years Fukuzawa was known as an iconoclast, and
was called Japan's Rousseau and Voltaire. He indulged in scathing

sarcasm about the deeds of the superpatriots and drew word pictures of samurai which a newspaperman compared with the gargoyles of the roof of Notre Dame. Few men in Japan have survived that sort of thing to die in bed. Fukuzawa is perhaps the only great Japanese of whom it can be said that his pen proved sharper than the sword. Japan greatly needs to-day another iconoclastic worldly wise, idealistic, emotionally balanced, selfish, and humanitarian Fukuzawa.

Chapter XII
Patriotic Supergangster

THE existence of a national supergangster like Toyama (Mitsuru) in the apparently orderly society of Japan is astounding to those who know that nation only in its outward aspect of a highly regulated people, unfailingly obedient and respectful to their officials and aristocrats. The truth is that a whole substratum of Japanese psychology protrudes itself in the interference with government policies of this dominant character, this now almost ninety-year-old patriarch, erect, with high arching brows, long white beard, and the face of an angel. He is the surviving link between feudal and imperio-industrial Japan, a national hero who has attained the status of a god among the thousands who celebrate his birthday or come kneeling to his house. A Japanese journalist calls him the only truly Homeric figure in the modern world and the term seems to fit.

This writer in 1924 stated that several thousand persons would offer their lives at any time for the sake of Toyama. During the great earthquake and fire of the previous year a crowd of Japanese and even some Koreans, forgetful of their persons, families, and property, dashed through the flames to Toyama's home to save him and his family. Years later, Toyama goes where and does what he pleases, laughing at official condemnation of his instigation of the youths who plan and commit political assassinations against such men as Prince Saionji, Premier Saito, Lord High Chamberlain Makino, American diplomatic and consular representatives, and others. And never were both this modern Old Man of the Mountain's power and influence greater. The former resides in his dictatorship over the Black Dragon Society (Kokuryukai) and its many affiliates, which number such respectable organizations as the Jimmu Society, the National Foundation Society (Kokuhon-sha) the Spirited World Society (Genyosha), the Retired Officers' Association, the Veterans' Association, and a group of superfascist millionaires clustered around the dour intriguer Baron Hiranuma. These societies live on funds extorted from rich men, donated by demagogues for political ends, or slipped secretly to them out of army, navy, or foreign propaganda budgets. They are even reported to have blackmailed Japan's two greatest newspapers.

Through Hiranuma—a poor boy who became first an attorney, then procurator, and in this position learned and remembered so much about leading personalities that he was knighted and made a member of the emperor's privy council—Toyama's arm reached into the sacred precincts of the imperial throne itself. Later this Hira-numa became premier, then one of the inner clique who plotted Pearl Harbor—probably at the order of Toyama.

No one knows the combined membership of the various police-listed societies of which Toyama is high priest, but it reaches mil-lions. These organizations are the continuations of the swash-buckling warrior groups who at the middle of the last century first attacked foreigners and then overthrew the isolation régime that had ruled for two and one-half centuries. Through those restoration-time cabals the present brotherhoods connect with a medieval an-cestry of blood and terror. They persist in military circles and among the impoverished peasants much as the Ku Klux Klan and its related movements persist among the poor whites of the south-ern United States; at times they spread over the nation and domi-nate its politics and schools, as the Ku Klux Klan did in America during the 1920's. Also like America's Ku Klux Klan in its flourish-ing days, the Japanese societies include many unsuspected leaders of the political and industrial worlds.

A staff writer of the then American newspaper in Tokyo, the *Japan Advertiser,* had the courage to interview several of the pa-triotic gangster chiefs. "I warn you first of all," said a metropolitan police official to him, "to be very careful what you write about these societies. A laudatory report will elate them and make them rampant, but even a slight offense to their pride will cause trouble. Remember what happened to the two big newspapers!

"They're all rogues and bravadoes and spend their days in gambling or other unproductive pursuits. Their rule of life is the relation of oyabun-kobun [boss and followers]. Their bosses are in most cases building contractors. [Which lends color to the situation in Hawaii, where contracting is in the hands of Japanese almost entirely, and the contractors are the racially arrogant portion of the Japanese community. Contractors find it easy to possess explosives and keep tools usable as weapons.] [1] The police consider it wiser to allow a latitude. It would not help to scatter these bravadoes through the country. Their actions really depend upon wirepullers behind the scene."

The newspaperman found the headquarters of the Great Culture Society to be a house of five rooms with a hall for practising judo (jiu-jutsu) and fencing. The leader told him that it was not wise to tell foreigners the intimate details of Japan's domestic politics. "The people are like so many blind men and must needs be guided by some trustworthy hand," he said. "We, the patriotic youth of the empire, have combined to carry out that mission. We rely more upon a small body of youths well trained for quick action than upon great numbers. We have no definite programs as regards political affairs, but we will sally forth at every call of justice—led by the sense of justice that is inherent in the Japanese soul, which must not be confused with foreign-made ideas of justice. *We feel ourselves to be kin with the fascist movement in Italy*. None can tell what the result of our actions will be once our blood is stirred."

At the Great Action Society the newspaperman found a chief dressed as a Shinto priest. "We move along the Great Road in the Middle," he orated, "believing both the Left and the Right to be wrong. We are united in the firm conviction and the profound spirit of Dai Nihon shugi [Greater Japan tradition]. We intend to arouse present-day society from its idle slumber. At present, action is the most effective means for obtaining this end. We have taken upon our shoulders the difficult task and the responsibility of casting the

---

[1] This was written in 1934. It "concretely" accounts for the Hawaii "Fifth Column" of December 1941.

first stone into the surface of the dull waters. Now is the time for action for present-day society has become impervious to opinions expressed through speech or the printed word. As typical examples of our spirit and activities I mention: (1) the assault upon the dance at the Imperial Hotel, (2) the opposition voiced at the birthday celebration of rich Okura [the sentimental baron's wind funeral rehearsal] and (3) opposition to universal manhood suffrage. We feel at one with the fascisti of Italy. Society is like a triangle controlled by one pin in one angle."

At the Black Dragon Society the newspaperman found much business going on. Mr. Uchida, the ostensible head, told him, "Our society is concerned mainly with the foreign relations of Japan. But it is inevitable that domestic affairs should also come into consideration. In both fields we uphold and adhere to Yamato damashii, 'YAMATO RACE, SECOND TO NONE.' We have not yet adopted any definite attitude toward the disputes between labor and capital, but are eagerly investigating the causes for such disputes. We operate one rooming house for three hundred laborers." (In this rooming house was found an American flag ripped from the flagstaff of the American embassy.)

Next the interviewer went to the Anti-Red Society. "Although we still retain the name of Sekkaboshi-dan, nowadays our sole aim is not merely to defend this country and people from bolshevist influence. We are the mentors of society: nothing more! We have organized the Japanese Industrial Army, a nationalist trade union which will be in accord with the spirit of unity between emperor and nation, and the upholding of Imperial prerogative over industry and expansion of the empire."

At the National Essence Society, Kokusui-kai, the questioner was told that "Political party leaders are like merchants who sell to the highest bidder." A proletariat governed by conservative ideas will be created to stand by Japan's old traditions, in opposition to the liberal attempts of *haikara* men like you," pleasantly laughed the retired major general in command. Haikara is the Japanese appropriation of our slang term "high collar," so much used in I.W.W. days.

Hirota, Minister of Foreign Affairs when the conquest of China

was undertaken, was Toyama's disciple and a member of his Black
Dragon Society from childhood, was educated by the Society and
owes Toyama his personal loyalty. Warlord Tojo, who opened up on
America and Britain, is a Toyama man. Japan's insolently smiling Old Man of the Mountain has many other "boys" in the cabinet
and the general staffs of the army and navy.

Toyama is not the only phenomenon of his kind in present Japan.
There are the Buddhist priest Inouye (Nissbo or Akira) and several
loccor gangster-patriot chiefs, and Tachibana, founder of the "Love
of Country" school in Mito, breeding ground of direct-action patriots and connecting link between farmers and army. But Inouye's
Blood Brotherhood is neither so old nor so entrenched as the
Black Dragon Society. So priest Inouye sat in jail, charged with the
murder of the finance minister of the same name as himself, Inouye,
and of the Mitsui millionaire, Baron Dan, and further with inciting the East Asia Supremacy Society to plot the murder of the
premier. And Tachibana began a life sentence for implication in the
murder of "Old Fox" Inukai. But while they were incarcerated their
organizations drifted more directly under control of chief dragon
Toyama, whom the police never dared to jail.

II

Toyama, born in the provincial-minded and frenzy-inclined southern island some ten or fifteen years later than Katsu and Fukuzawa,
came early under the spell of the Samson-like Saigo. He received his
education under strict Spartan discipline in the "school of heroes"
conducted by Miss Takaba (Ran or Osamu), a unique female disci-
plinarian and intriguer whose sex alone kept her from being one of
the foremost swashbucklers of the period. She rose to influence in
that Spartan portion of Japan where women were most subordinated
and ignored, and where even in matters of love they were frequently
made secondary, as in the Greece of Plato's time. She never married
but kept open house for statesmen who came to consult her. Says her
biographer, "Miss Takaba was born a woman by mistake, and all
through life resented and loathed the trick nature had played upon
her. She was never seen in woman's dress, and allusion to her as a

woman would bring the quick blow of her small hard fist to the speaker's cheek. She even wore the two swords of the samurai. Although this was strictly against law and custom, none said her nay." Judging from the truculent Toyama, who always speaks of her with gratitude, there was nothing effeminating about her influence. For a boyhood model Toyama took the great conqueror Hideyoshi. Later in life he became a passionate admirer of Napoleon.

We are here treated to an example of the amazing spread of influence of the world's Napoleonic characters. Alexander the Great inspired men of Europe down to medieval times, and it seems very likely that the conqueror of India, Asoka, and the conqueror and unifier of China and builder of the Great Wall, the great Chin, were both moved in the third century before Christ by the Alexander saga which had percolated west over Asia. Cæsar in our day has been the directly credited inspiration of Mussolini and Mustapha Kemal. And Napoleon's influence in our world embraces Mussolini and Hitler in Europe and Toyama in Japan.

In his youth he emulated the youthful Hideyoshi by studied evasion of all apprenticeships. He was once signed by his family to a potato vendor. In the middle of the night he began shouting at the top of his voice, "Potatoes for sale! Who will buy potatoes?" When told to keep still he remonstrated that he was practising his newly assigned profession and certainly ought not to be interfered with, unless the family were willing he should give it up. Next they apprenticed him as clerk to a shop selling geta—the Japanese wooden clogs. One day the proprietor returned to his shop to find a crowd purchasing as rapidly as they could get to the counter, and his stock almost cleaned out. He was congratulating himself that in spite of indications he had found a genius of a young salesman—till he discovered that Toyama was selling the clogs for five sen a pair and had almost ruined the store.

Thereafter Toyama wandered about the country free to emulate his model, climbing mountains, sleeping in temples, now and then executing some bold act of derring-do or eccentricity which got him talked about throughout the land. Once he risked his life to save a comrade from drowning in a pool. Again, he turned up road-stained at the swankiest inn in Nagasaki. "Toyama wants a room," he said. He was informed with supercilious politeness that the inn was full. "Then," he said threateningly, "may I beg a cup of tea at your honorable hostelry?" (Tea is served without formal charge.) The head clerk was glad to compromise on this. The tea sipped, Toyama laid a ten yen bill on the tray. "Water money" (tip), said Toyama. The inn found a room for him. In the morning Toyama hung up a scroll on which he renamed the inn the "Ten Yen Restaurant." The inn was ridiculed at first and then ridicule changed to fame; to-day the Ju Yen Ro of Nagasaki flourishes because of its contact with Toyama.

Toyama happened into a backward region where a robber chief had looted the homes of the poor. Toyama went to his lair, sat down and simply stared at the chief until he bowed, offered apologies, and handed the loot to Toyama to return to its owners. The bandit then took an oath that he would never again rob poor or weak persons, which is pretty much Toyama's own code—as long as the poor and weak are sons of the "divine race."

III

The existence of the Black Dragon Society became generally known in the years preceding the war with China (1894), when its head Toyama, then in his forties, made two implacable public demands upon Japan's officialdom:

First: For the summary ending of Japan's inferior status internationally, created by the treaties granting foreign governments a veto power over increases in her customs tariffs and authority within her boundaries over their subjects and citizens.

Second: That Japan should make war upon China to acquire Korea, and perhaps Manchuria, before Russia could establish herself impregnably in those neighboring mainland regions. For emphasis on this second aim the Society adopted its present name, Black Dragon—the Chinese name of the Amur River between Manchuria and Siberia.

The Machiavellian Marquis Okuma, founder of Waseda University, who had pushed Saigo's warriors into rebellion by cutting off samurai pensions in 1877, and had forced the granting of the consti-

tution in 1899 by getting the goods on high officials engaged in a
great land scandal in Hokkaido, was the great statesman and politician of the time. He was successively minister of finance, minister
of foreign affairs, and premier. Japan's greatest conversationalist, he
kept open house always and boasted that he never touched a pen.
Nothing but a few signatures, immensely valuable to collectors, exist
in his handwriting. Toyama became his devil. As far back as 1871
he had called Okuma a traitor for borrowing money from England
to build Japan's first railroad. Okuma, it is reported, offered him
a quarter of a million yen bribe to leave Japan forever. "I'll take
the money but no boat," was Toyama's reply.

In 1892 Okuma secretly negotiated agreements with foreign countries providing for the *gradual* abolition of the foreign privileges
injurious to Japan's sovereign rights and dignity. The London *Times*
revealed what he had done and it was cabled back to Toyama, who
sent a disciple to throw a bomb at Okuma's carriage, taking off one
of the statesman's legs. Okuma narrowly escaped bleeding to death.
The bomb thrower committed suicide on the spot, and there was no
proof by which Toyama could be convicted. He was caught in
Osaka but laughed at the police who grilled him, and soon they
and the department of justice were receiving so many threats that
they were glad to announce his release. Since then he has been practically above justice. Toyama later called on Okuma, who received
him in a sardonic vein, asking him if he had come to bring back
his leg. Amiably smiling, Toyama opined that any high official
should be willing to donate a leg for the sake of emperor and nation.
Okuma confessed that he saw much to admire in the buccaneer!

Toyama called at the home of Prince Matsukata, head of one
of the five godly families. He found an equipage waiting at the door
and was told that the prince could receive no one since he was just
setting off on a journey. Insolently, Toyama told the servant to go
back and ask the prince if he felt quite sure he would arrive at his
destination. Toyama was received and the journey was postponed.

Toyama paid one of his famous visits to Count Soejima, whose
acquisition of wealth had created some talk among patriots. "What,"
asked the count of Toyama, trying to throw him off the scent, "do
you think is the most urgent financial need of the nation?" "For me

to become a millionaire!" replied Toyama, eyeing the count. Toyama forthwith went out and borrowed money from Tokyo usurers and set himself up as the latest nouveau riche. The time came when the usurers insisted upon payment. Toyama invited them and various high personages to an elegant restaurant, entertained the party lavishly with food and geisha, and then invited all to spend the night at his expense, promising that if they would do so he would bring payment in full before they would feel ready for business on the morrow.

He left, returning the next morning with money for all debts and a number of largesses for friends and acquaintances known to be in distress. In the interim he had gone out and sold to Mitsui title to coal mines in Hokkaido which he had obtained by political pressure. It was a Gargantuan parable acted publicly to show the nation how corrupt was politics and how easily riches were obtained. At the end of it Toyama emerged the poor man he has always been, although he could probably levy several million yen in a few hours. No needy suppliant has ever been turned away empty from his rough board home between Tokyo and Yokohama, which is the headquarters of the most dreaded power in Pacific Asia. He has been seen to take off one of his garments to give to a needy visitor.

Toyama is deaf alike to praise and criticism. Time and again officials have tried to draw his fangs by nominating or appointing him to office—to no avail. He prefers to crack the unanswerable whip of assassination from behind the scenes. Says a writer of 1933, "Toyama has made assassination a respectable political weapon in Japan." The Japanese attitude toward assassination growing out of their fatalistically light regard for life, is simply the Greek ostracism carried one degree further. It is felt that the victim should leave this earth for the good of the nation and race—this is not necessarily a stigma upon him personally or even politically. Says the reverend Mr. Yamamoto in defending his brother priest Inouye, with a sophistry which makes Buddhism—that forbids the killing of an ant—subscribe to this attitude: "Because Buddhism has as its main objective human peace, the removal from life of any one who does harm to the welfare of mankind (mankind = divine

Japan?) may not be considered a crime in the light of Buddhism."

A recently published book of patriotic anecdotes bearing the benediction of the Black Dragon Society relates how the notoriously corrupt party leader Hoshi, who was probably under Toyama's influence, held up the old militarist and dictator Yamagata, Japan's Bismarck, for a straight bribe of 300,000 yen in return for the votes of the Seiyukai members of Parliament. Yamagata would have gained his purpose anyway, but he had reasons worth more to him than the 300,000 yen for wanting the budget passed smoothly and without delay. He and a friend dug up the money from their private purses. The dyspeptic war lord, who never forgot anything, eventually took his revenge on Hoshi, who committed suicide after entanglement with a French girl. But Toyama implies that Hoshi's means of obtaining the 300,000 yen, which became the revolving campaign fund of the Seiyukai party, was a patriotic act.

IV

Most of the interventions of this amazing man in the course of Japanese history since the restoration naturally will not come to light until after the death of himself and the men he bullies. A leading Japanese magazine tells his most amazing piece of effrontery thus far revealed.[2] The significant thing to us is that its publication caused only a higher lift of the eyebrows on the face of the ancient chief dragon, and seemed to be generally approved by the magazine's vast reading audience as a good example for present times.

Toyama, it is related, awakened from his nap to see one of his pupils stealing off. Reading the black looks on the lad's face, Toyama said, "You are going to kill some one. Tell me. I won't prevent you." "I am," confessed the lad, "but please don't ask whom." "All right," said Japan's Old Man of the Mountain, "just so you don't kill Ito." "Oh!" wailed the boy, "you exempt the very man I am after! It is Ito alone who prevents our national development, who is faithless to the emperor. He is the big chief of the anti-war group. Now is the time to go to war with Russia. Shall we lose our chance

[2] "Ito and Toyama" by Nomura Koto in *Hinode*, July, 1934.

to defeat her? Ito, able to block us because he is foreign minister and intimate of the Tenno, must be killed."

"Now listen!" said Toyama, doubtless congratulating himself on the way his instruction had taken hold of these youngsters, "sit down and compose yourself. Ito has too much sense to block us. He is merely too slow and cautious. You know he tells you himself he is acting for the sake of his country."

In typical Japanese hysteria of frustration, the lad burst into tears. "Now," soothed the old master, "suppose we change Ito's mind?" "But," protested the lad, "every big man of our opinion has pleaded with him in vain." "*Toyama* hasn't yet called on him," was the reply. "Hold your sword until I see him."

This was in July, 1903, when the czar's agents were pushing down into Korea, and Russia was building an army base on the Manchurian prairies that was to grow into the city of Harbin. Patriots were much concerned over a pacifist movement headed by the socialist Katayama (Sen), which was conducting great demonstrations in protest against the war spirit. The first statesman of the empire, Ito himself, favored a bargain with Russia dividing China and Korea between Japanese and Russian influence.

A Japanese conclave, says the relater of the story, composed of the captain of Japan's largest battleship, several army officers, and several members of the ministry of foreign affairs, decided on a quick undeclared war on Russia. "We will have to carry Ito along," they concluded, "or kill him." But the man who should normally have been their go-between with Ito seemed to be disqualified inasmuch as a short while previously he had got drunk and publicly stated that Ito should not be allowed to live a day longer. Toyama took over the problem. "You boys go back to your ships, troops, and dossiers," he commanded. "I'm seeing to Ito."

A few days later, accompanied by four friends, one of whom was Kono, president of the House of Commons, he approached Ito's official residence. Ito was just seeing off the previous foreign minister, Aoki. "Good! Now he can't say he is out!" exclaimed one of the approaching party. Aoki, passing Toyama on the steps, addressed the chief dragon in alarm: "You are not going to hit Minister Ito?" "I don't know," growled Toyama, and pushed in with his friends.

Ito overheard this exchange. Toyama had not bothered to put on the dress of ordinary respect. Under the circumstances, Ito had no great inclination to cordiality, and yet, with these five surrounding him, he knew that refusal to parley would mean his death on the spot. He remembered the fate of his predecessor Okuma. So he took them into his reception room.

Kono made a speech of seven thousand words about the inevitability of fighting Russia sooner or later and the evidence that this was the time indicated by heaven. Ito listened coldly. Suddenly Toyama broke in: "Kono, desist! A man of Marquis Ito's intelligence already knows these things better than you do. Mr. Ito, I won't try to force reasons on you. Statesman Ito, whom do you consider the greatest person in Japan?" "Whom do you?" countered Ito. "His Majesty, the Tenno," replied Toyama. They all bowed their heads. "Yes," said Ito, "no dispute about that." "Then," pursued Toyama, "who is the greatest man among his subjects?" "Well—" stalled the veteran statesman. Toyama looked him in the eye ."Ito," he said, "do *you* want to be Japan's greatest statesman?" "—or a dead dog?" was implied. Slowly Ito, the writer of the nation's constitution, rose and gave his hand to this superblackmailer and threatener. "Toyama-san, I understand," he said gruffly. "It's for the sake of the country," remarked Toyama, rising. "*Now* we are a united nation, and we will win." He signaled to his fellow gangsters to leave.

Such is the inside story of the making of the decision by Japan's officialdom which took the nation into its greatest war before 1941. A few months after the Toyama-Ito interview, rising young Captain Togo, one of Toyama's disciples from his home district in the southern island, opened hostilities, after which Ito's foreign ministry issued the formal declaration of war on the Czar. It was all dress parade, in a way, for December 1941, and Pearl Harbor.

v

Toyama's amazing influence has not been confined to the violent enterprises of his own nation, but has reached out into revolutions in China and in India. When, in the first decade of the twentieth century, Sun Yat-sen, Chinese surgeon, visionary, and revolutionist, fled to Japan from the tortures prepared for him by the Manchu empress-dowager in Peking, it was the already venerable Toyama who gave Sun refuge from both the Chinese and his own Japanese officials, and protection from the tong assassins hired by the Empress. Under Toyama's roof Sun Yat-sen revamped his revolutionary plans, created his great revolutionary party, the Tung Min Hwei, and from Toyama he received the encouragement and a share of the funds to go back and succeed. At this time Inukai was a member of Toyama's inner coterie and also Sun Yat-sen's friend and protector. Inukai, who was to become the old fox in Japanese politics, once showed me a scroll written for him in Toyama's house by Sun Yat-sen, whose writing to-day is among the most prized in the world. Amazingly enough, another member of their coterie was Dr. Hoshino, who became the famous scholar of the Tokyo Imperial University and an inspirer of radicalism. That Toyama plays no favorites and is able to handle heterodoxy in his own family is shown by the fact that in 1932 he sent his own youngsters to assassinate Inukai, then premier, and he caused Hoshino to be shut up in his own house until he died.

Perhaps still more amazing in view of Japan's aggression upon nationalist China to-day is Toyama's friendship with the generalissimo and dictator, Chiang Kai-shek. The ancient chief dragon and the young dictator were sworn in the oath of blood brotherhood, which means much to orientals. Chiang Kai-shek, a graduate of Japan's Imperial War College, became amanuensis to Sun Yat-sen, later organized the Chinese Nationalist army, and upon Sun's death became its generalissimo. With the aid of Borodin and the bolshevik officers whom Sun Yat-sen had borrowed from Moscow, Chiang fought his way from Canton diagonally across China to Hankow, then down the Yangtze River to Nanking. At this point he broke with his Russian and Pro-Russian collaborators. By quick, ruthless strokes he established his supremacy, only to be forced out in 1927 by fellows who feared his dictatorship. It was generally understood that he thereupon retired to his native province, Fukien. Actually, he went also to Yokohama secretly to receive encouragement from the same old chief dragon who had inspirited his dead master, Sun

Yat-sen. In 1928 he returned from Toyama's bosom to Nanking to become again the dominant figure of new China, and the following year he gave the Japanese Toyama a state reception in Nanking. Perhaps this explains what the puzzled American and European reporters could not explain when, in the autumn of 1931, the Chinese nationalist chief Chiang Kai-shek failed to render material support to his viceroy Chang Hsueh-liang, being driven out of Manchuria by the old chief dragon's disciples in the Japanese army—again when, in the spring of 1932, the Chinese generalissimo and president evaded open military support of the Chinese Nineteenth Route Army, heroically resisting overwhelming Japanese forces in the streets of Shanghai. But from 1936 on, after being kidnapped by the same Chang Hsueh-liang whom he had let down, and after giving a pledge to fight Japan to his kidnapper, Chiang Kai-shek became the indomitable leader of unending resistance to old Toyama's empire-builders.

The British Empire as well as China has felt Toyama's influence. In 1915, after Japan joined her ally in the Great War, England demanded the arrest of two Indian revolutionaries operating in Japan and China. Toyama, through his Black Dragons, stirred up a furore of protest in Japan. England's pressure was, nevertheless, so great that the Japanese police came for the Indian intriguers. They had disappeared. The police made a point of not looking in Toyama's house. Even Japanese police know where valor should end and discretion begin. The ambassador fulminated, but when it had all blown over the Indians emerged, now full-fledged Japanese subjects, and as such they became most useful in stirring up disaffection in India when England raised too high the barriers against Japanese goods in her Indian empire. After Japan broke with Britain, at the end of 1941, these Indians led a delegation pledging India to the Mikado.

Toyama's "mob" had much to do with railroading Japan into the 1915 campaign in China which was to take advantage of the World War. Again, the prelude to the conquest of Manchuria and the war on China (undeclared throughout) was very similar to the prelude to that with Russia except that the foreign minister in 1931, Baron Shidehara, did not assent as did Ito. So the army ignored him and proceeded anyhow, and when popular feeling had reached a high pitch Toyama's patriots drove Shidehara from office. In all these great events Japan's venerable prophet of violence took a decisive hand. What we learn from Toyama is that such a character can be counted upon to overcome the checks official prudence or conscience may put upon Nippon's mailed fist whenever that fist feels fully ready to strike. Old Saigo failed to take his nation into war in 1874 but his pupil Toyama perfected the procedure, and, being less of a gentleman than Saigo has carried it out ruthlessly and flawlessly.

Toyama's chief aide in the Manchurian expansion was Komei (Tokuzo), forty-eight years of age and in line for the chieftancy of the Black Dragon Society. He set the stage for the military leap and was rewarded by being made the leading official of the new empire of Manchukuo, but he proved to be of too adventurous a disposition to get along in official life. After all, there must be some calm in the midst of every storm. So Komei went disgruntled into retirement in Japan and took revenge on "softies" by publishing an exceedingly frank autobiography which proved to be very embarrassing to Japan's diplomatic front. The book has been suppressed and Komei officially branded a liar in regard to the facts of his own life— nevertheless he has made a small fortune out of them already.

Komei was born in a village on fresh-water Lake Biwa which stretches like a sausage for sixty miles north of Kyoto, parallel to the Japan Sea. From childhood he called himself the China ronin—a ronin or "wave man" being an unattached samurai or knight errant. After ten years on the South Manchurian Railroad Komei resigned to roam about China and Manchuria gathering information. Ultimately he was made a counselor to the Asiatic bureau of the foreign office by Yoshizawa, a rising young bureau chief; he returned the favor in 1931 by helping to make this Yoshizawa Japan's chief delegate to Geneva and Japan's foreign minister.

Komei boastfully tells how he cooked up the revolt in 1925 against the immensely wealthy and elegant little ex-bandit satrap of Manchuria, Chang Tso-lin. He bitterly complained that if the Japanese money interests which control the South Manchurian Railroad had not given support to the Chinese Chang, Manchuria would have been brought under Japanese control then. Angrily, Komei withdrew from official intrigue, but when the military were planning their outburst of 1931 they called him to become their chief adviser. He states that the seizure of Mukden in September, 1931, the overthrow of the young Marshal Chang, son of the assassinated ex-bandit ruler, and the seizure of the government banks in Manchuria were his contribution to the increase of the Japanese Empire, followed to the letter by Japanese War Minister Minami (Minami was front for Araki, who later stepped from behind the scenes).

Komei implies that Major Dohihara under his instructions kidnapped the young scion of the abdicated Manchu ruling family of China from his hideout in the Japanese concession in Tientsin, and forcibly brought to Dairen this heir, who called himself Henry Pu Yi, while Komei up at Mukden organized the dummy committee of Chinese which declared the secession of Manchuria from China and asked Pu Yi to take the throne. Komei was perfectly frank with Lord Lytton, head of the League of Nations' investigating committee. He told Lytton that Manchuria was the doorstep on which Japan must plant her foot in entering China's household to run it for the welfare of Japan and the world.

One of Komei's best agents is Ohashi (Chuiji) whose one-time friendship with the author changed to a determination to keep him out of Manchukuo. Ohashi is a sort of dual personality: a little Teddy Roosevelt when in western coat and pants, and a suave little Dr. Nitobe of the orient when in kimono. Not many years ago he was Japanese consul in Seattle, where it was the writer's opportunity to insist that he be given adequate protection from American hoodlums trying to keep him from living in what local people regarded as the swank part of town. Later he became consul general in Los Angeles and so influenced that previously anti-Japanese community by a combination of American forthrightness and oriental finesse that through years of Japan's attack on China the sympathies of the southern California metropolis remained with Japan. Los Angeles' Japanese population, called by its community newspaper "little Nippon" was the largest outside of Pacific Asia or Hawaii.

Ohashi was consul general at Harbin in North Manchuria when the Japanese army leaped, September 18, 1931. Ohashi (the word means "chop-sticks") took care of the Russian angle, tactfully giving Soviet officers sufficient advance notice of the coup to prevent

Russia's becoming embroiled. When the Japanese army reached Harbin Ohashi became "little king" of the Russo-Chinese community, and was later made head of Manchukuo's foreign office. He negotiated the purchase of the Northern Manchuria Railway from Soviet Russia, and under Matsuoka, who likewise had American experience, he became acting head of Tokyo's foreign office.

Thus do the wheels within wheels of the complicated machine which is Japan move her forward in the path of her divine mission.

Chapter XIII
Japan's Lord Nelson

T̲HE Samson-like Saigo brought us down to 1874, his disciple, diminutive Togo,[1] to 1934. One demanded the beginning of his country's expansion on the Asiatic mainland and found himself in rebellion against his government (though never, from his viewpoint, against his emperor) for being ahead of his time. The other established his nation's naval preëminence in the eastern hemisphere, made the building of Asiatic empire possible, and placed Nippon in the position of challenger of the white world.

Togo was born, in 1847, into a family of even lower rank than Saigo's. His father was a petty county officer. It seems a question whether or not the boy was properly entitled to carry the swords of samurai rank. But his application to studies in Saigo's school attracted the big patriot, who used to put his arm about Togo affectionately and introduce him as that "tiny fool, Togo."

While Saigo was in banishment, Togo, at the age of sixteen, helped try to resist the disastrous British bombardment of Kagoshima of June 1863 which brought Saigo back. The lesson of trying to resist modern methods and equipment was plain. Saigo sent his bright pupil to study at Katsu's new naval academy near Kobe. From there Katsu sent him as one of fourteen graduates to study at the Thames Nautical College, London, and he filled out his cadet-

---

[1] "Seagoing" Togo of a generation ago—not to be confused with diplomat Togo, foreign minister at the time of Pearl Harbor. They are of the same clan (Satsuma).
A voluminous new biography of Admiral Togo in English (Tokyo, 1934) has been published by the son of his contemporary and previous biographer, Admiral Ogasiwara.

ship on board His Britannic Majesty's gunboat *Worcester*, 1871-1878.

Meanwhile the fighting members of Togo's family had been almost wiped out in Saigo's rebellion. The sheer luck that he was a student in England at that time saved him to become Japan's Lord Nelson. At the close of his cadetship he was commanded to supervise the construction of the warship *Hiei* being built in England. Togo returned with this prize of the Japanese fleet and took up a routine naval career. At the age of thirty-four he married the daughter of one of Japan's new viscounts.

His character was a compound of quick assimilativeness and stubbornness. Admiral Yamamoto (Gambei) recalls that when both were junior officers on the flagship *Fuso,* Yamamoto challenged little Togo to race up the rigging. He beat Togo twice over, but Togo would not confess defeat, claiming that he had torn his trousers and pride compelled him to take one rung at a time. Truth was, a different kind of pride prevented him from admitting defeat.

Another instance of his stubbornness was his point-blank refusal to obey the navy order in regard to a salute due a foreign celebrity on a visiting battleship. Togo, mistaking, it seems, the rank of the celebrity, first gave him a salute which was several guns short of his due. The celebrity protested to the government, which ordered Togo to take his ship and make the proper salute. Togo sailed out and fired merely the number of guns required to make up the difference. More guns he absolutely declined to fire even at peril of demotion.

II

Togo first came into newspaper prominence when he was dispatched as the captain of the *Naniwa* in 1893 to make a display of force off the kingdom of Hawaii in view of the rumors that that little island kingdom was about to be annexed to the United States. His next great publicity came when he precipitated the war with China in 1894. This war had been decided upon by Toyama's Black Dragons, although they knew the secret agreement between the czar and China's administrative viceroy, Li Hung-chang. What held Japan back was not fear of Russia but the fact that England also was pro-Chinese at the time, her motivation being the purely non-altruistic one that she was in the process of selling China a good-sized navy and getting a strangle hold on the commerce of the Yangtze Valley.

Togo's orders were to see that no more Chinese troops were transported to Korea. Sailing about the Gulf of Chihli which cuts in from the Yellow Sea almost to Peking, Captain Togo encountered the British vessel *Kowshing,* transporting eleven hundred Chinese troops. He ordered the vessel to heave to, which the British captain was prevented from doing by the officers of the Chinese infantry, whereupon Togo sank the ship and almost every one on it. The war with China was on—without declaration—and for a time it looked as if there would be complications with England. Togo returned home to report to Admiral Yamamoto, commander of the navy. He later confessed that he feared a reprimand. But Yamamoto told him to sit down and called for champagne and two glasses, whereby Togo knew that his action was approved. He was sent out again onto the high seas and, after several successful encounters, led a midnight attack on the Chinese navy in the harbor of Weihaiwei, in Shantung, which practically destroyed the Chinese battle fleet, at that time actually superior to the Japanese. Ting, the Chinese admiral in command, committed suicide rather than surrender.

Togo became rear admiral and commander of the battle fleet in 1898. He got additional prominence in the Chinese Boxer affair, when he reduced and held the Taku forts at the mouth of the river passage to Peking as prelude to the allied expedition to rescue the European and Japanese besieged in the British legation quarter in the Chinese capital.

Togo's great opportunity came four years later in the war with Russia. He was appointed commander of the united squadron as the situation grew tense. Passing by Tokyo, he paid a brief visit to his wife and two sons and daughter who were attending the peers' schools. Although weak from a cold and suffering from bronchial complications, he hastened on to his flagship, the *Mikasa,* saying, "I always get well at sea." He sent back word to his family not to distract him by writing. His oldest son used to bicycle down to the naval office daily to learn the news of pater familias. During the entire campaign he wrote no letter home. On board his *Mikasa* the swarthy Imperial Prince Higashi Fushimi acted as drillmaster, willingly placing himself under the command of the commoner Togo, although in later years when Togo was at the height of his glory he was to be but an attaché of the Prince's party.

III

In characteristic fashion Togo opened the war previous to declaration with a night attack on the Russian base of Port Arthur, very like the attack on Weihaiwei. With small torpedo destroyers he sallied through the narrow gateway of the harbor, which is protected by sheer hills all around. Several Russian capital ships were put out of commission before the Russian commander, Makaroff, knew what was happening. Togo completed the raid by sinking one of his own vessels in the narrow passageway, bottling up the large Russian ships. Several, however, had run the gantlet into the open sea. Togo pursued and sank them one by one, as well as several cruisers from Vladivostok that tried to join forces with them.

The Russians had believed that their sea power concentrated at the two Pacific naval bases of Port Arthur and Vladivostok was sufficient to prevent the Japanese from landing troops on the Asian mainland, but Togo quickly wiped the Russians off the Pacific. General Nogi was enabled to transport a couple of hundred thousand men to Manchuria, beat the Russians back out of Korea, defeat them at Mukden, and invest the hilltop forts protecting Port Arthur where a goodly proportion of Russia's carefully prepared battle strength lay helpless.

World famous for his spectacular destruction of the czar's Baltic fleet, Togo nevertheless maintained that his surprise destruction of Russia's small Pacific fleet was the more important. "For," said he, "it was necessary to eliminate this equal force without serious loss to ourselves. But when the Baltic fleet came, I could have afforded to have sacrificed the entire Japanese navy in destroying it." After Togo's death a copy of his Russian rival Makaroff's book on naval tactics, thumbed and marginally noted before 1904, was found among his possessions. Togo knew his rival commander

through the book. No one knew Togo's mind. It has happened again
—since.

The last chapter of the history of the great sea power which had
been founded by Peter the Great is perhaps the most dramatic in
the annals of naval warfare. The outcome, which seems to have
depended so largely on the character and strategy of the one man
Togo, initiated the era of the decline of western prestige and power
which we are only now beginning to appreciate. Reluctantly the
czar allowed himself to be persuaded to dispatch Russia's great
Baltic fleet to Pacific Asia, a stroke which could result only in
complete victory or final disaster for Russia.

Under the command of Admiral Rozhesjenski the fleet left Libau
in the Baltic on October 15, 1904, and steamed down the North Sea.
So suspicious were the Russians of British connections with the
Japanese that they expected to be attacked by torpedo boats in the
North Sea and in their nervousness actually opened fire on British
fishing trawlers off the Dogger Bank, killing several fishermen and
almost precipitating war with Great Britain. A British fleet shadowed the Russians until they had reached the open Atlantic. Passing
through the British-controlled Suez Canal was now out of the question, and the Russians steamed the record-breaking distance for a
modern navy around the Cape of Good Hope. Putting in at Mada-
gascar they learned that Port Arthur had fallen and the only base
left to them in the north Pacific would be Vladivostok.

Meanwhile, Nogi had sacrificed thirty thousand men to capture
a few hilltops commanding Port Arthur and had turned the captured guns away from his waves of advancing soldiers against the
neighboring hill forts and the Russian ships in their own harbor. A
stir rose in Russia to call the fleet back, but the czar was persuaded
against it largely to save Rozhesjenski's personal vanity. Instead,
Russia's last few ships were sent under Rear Admiral Nebogatov
to bolster the armada. This time the Russians bought their way
through the Suez Canal and the two fleets joined in the harbor of
Camrangh Bay, French Cochin China, in the spring of 1905. The
French, financial allies of the Russians and friendly to the fleet,
allowed it to outfit as best it could there and proceed north. Camrangh Bay, finest naval base site on the China Sea, thus attracted

the attention of Japan's naval experts. In 1941, after France gave up to Hitler these Japanese experts made Camrangh their chief new base for the conquest of Malaya and the Dutch East Indies.

But to go back to the spring of 1905: a high council of Japan's naval officials was held in the presence of the emperor himself, and it was decided to choose a supreme commander for the fleet on merit alone. The choice fell to Togo. The dispute regarding strategy between him and the naval office, however, was not settled. The ministry wished to take the part of caution and wage a war of attrition against the great armada coming towards Japan. Togo, on the other hand, wanted to risk everything to accomplish its sudden and complete destruction.

IV

Obviously the Russians would try to reach their Vladivostok base either from the open Pacific to the north of Japan, or from the China Sea into the Japan Sea through the Straits of Tsushima, two hundred miles wide, separating Japan and Korea. Togo never had a doubt in his own mind as to which route the lazy Rozhesjenski would choose. The navy office had kept most of the Japanese force around the northern entrance, but Togo, confirmed in his hunch by reports that the Russian fleet was steaming too close to the China coast to swing out into the wide Pacific, took everything into his own hands and ordered the concentration of Japan's entire naval strength at the double island of Tsushima lying midway of the Straits. The story is unofficially told that he called his under-admirals aboard his flagship and said to them in his quiet way, "I have decided to risk everything; if you are with me, we will take oath together here that in event I have guessed wrong, we will all commit hara-kiri; if I have guessed correctly, and we destroy the Russian fleet, we will offer ourselves to the Emperor for punishment or reward, as the Sacred One may see fit."

To encourage Rozhesjenski in his course, Togo issued a communiqué that his own flagship was damaged and incapacitated for action. He had already lost two of his six capital ships and eight ships in all, by typical Japanese daring and his own disregard of technical limitations. The Russians were superior in capital ships and inferior in cruisers. Also their cruisers were hampered by the necessity of protecting their flotilla of supply ships, colliers, hospital ships, and the like. The Russian guns outranged the Japanese, but Togo told his commanders that range does not matter when fleets close, and that Japanese always close.

Togo did not depend alone on his hunch and the willingness of the officers and men to risk their lives. Although Japan had been the latest nation to learn western science, Togo's navy was the first to take battle advantage of its most wonderful invention, wireless. Some ten years earlier Marconi had announced his unbelievable invention to the world. The young Italian inventor had tried to demonstrate it to the United States navy by means of wireless dispatches from a small boat off the Jersey coast to New York during the triumphal return of Admiral Dewey from Manila in 1899. Listening New York could not make out his signals and western navies had paid little more attention to developments in wireless. But Togo had got hold of a number of little wireless instruments, installed them in Japanese fishing boats and scattered them with navy operators over the sea in the direction from which the Russians must come. Each outfit could relay a mile or two.

In spite of all this the Russian fleet nearly slipped past Togo. One of Togo's vessels spied it in the two-hundred-mile-wide passage between Japan's main island and Korea, on the morning of May 27. Ten minutes later the Russians would have been safely over the horizon. Leaping from behind the double island, Togo's ships surrounded the armada. To all his commanders he flashed his paraphrase of Lord Nelson's command at Trafalgar. It took the impersonal form demanded by the Japanese language: "The rise or fall of the Empire depends on this battle. All must exert their utmost efforts."

The Russians began firing, but Togo had them from broadside. Their ships were rolling and their marksmanship proved abominable. Togo ordered his fire withheld until a distance of six thousand meters. The strategy was one of the most perfectly executed in the history of large fleet actions. The Japanese coördination was perfect, gunnery deadly. As Togo's battleships blocked the armada, his cruisers, faster than the Russians', ran rings around it and made destructive sallies from the flanks and rear. At nightfall, with a marvelous piece of imagination, Togo called off all his big ships and threw in his torpedo destroyers to torpedo without hesitation anything that looked like a big ship. Explosion after explosion punctuated the night, and the battle fleet sailed back and finished up Russia's sea power in the morning. Some ships surrendered and were incorporated in the Japanese fleet. Rozhesjenski, wounded, chose to go down with his flagship. Only two or three Russian vessels escaped destruction or capture and raced up the Japan Sea to the Golden Horn of Vladivostok. Overnight an oriental nation had become one of the world's greatest sea powers.

Togo's communiqué of the victory to the Japanese people began: "Thanks to the virtue of the Tenno, and the benevolence of Heaven..." He went direct from the battle to the shrine of the Sun Goddess at Ise to announce the victory to the progenitress of the race.

v

Possibly no great fleet will again be able to act with such central coördination. In 1914-18, at least, the battles between the British and German fleets were disordered by enemy jamming of the radio and conflict of each side's own short waves, while flag and mirror signals were rendered vague by smoke screens. Probably no fleet will ever again hope to win over a great enemy by sailing into his arms. Therefore, Great Britain planned her Singapore naval base, and the United States, Pearl Harbor, remembering well the lesson Togo taught at Tsushima, and Japan remained unchallenged in the seas between these two outposts of white power.

Togo always believed in the surprise attack. As to national policy his idea was to have definitely in mind whom his country must fight next, prepare with both diligence and caution, and when the clash became inevitable, leap first.[2]

The Japanese nation went mad over Togo's victory and he became, in their minds, even more god than hero. A Togo Society

[2] Men whose business it was to be prepared had this book in their study courses. It was used at both army and navy officers' schools, and its author lectured before the officers at Bremerton, Fort Lewis, Pearl Harbor, Newport, Leavenworth and elsewhere.

was formed. Togo had drunk from a well in Kobe, which was forthwith labeled with tablets written by two admirals. He came to be called Japan's highest personage outside the emperor, although for political reasons he was never given the highest formal honors. This adulation moved him not at all. He was quite truly a selfless man who saw himself as an instrument of the state. The little Japanese Nelson who attended American Ambassador Griscome's state dinner in a vice admiral's uniform after his great victory, because he simply hadn't had time to pose for the tailor to make an admiral's outfit, would have drawn his mouth tighter in his typical grimace had he been able to hear the order that his state funeral be attended only by men in evening dress and silk toppers and women in the abominable Victorian dress of the Japanese court.

Since Togo's victory, the Japanese navy has been a law unto itself. It was politically interfered with only once, at the time of the London conference of 1930 when the liberal Premier Hamaguchi dared to accept a foreign pact unratified by the navy. In 1922, at the Washington conference, ratio limitation was good strategy for Togo's navy, but by 1930 the Japanese navy saw a clear road to equality with Great Britain and America, and bitterly resented restriction.

Old Togo, long in retirement, took a definite position against the treaty which he said was the defeat of the three cardinal demands of the Japanese navy. Having taken a stand, he maintained it with his characteristic stubbornness, so that when the navy chiefs who had sought his aid against the treaty tried to get him to relent, being compelled under political pressure to accept its terms for the time, he refused to do so. They had to have the emperor fetch Togo's old associate Saito from Korea to come and talk the old admiral out of his stubbornness, for they dared not proceed over his head—he was too great an idol with the populace. Nevertheless the liberal papers of 1930 took humorous shots at the old seadog fighting on dry land. That was before the patriots "purged" the country and started to build empire again. When Togo died, May 30, 1934, at the age of eighty-seven, not a newspaper dared to recall the genial criticism once directed at him.

Togo enjoyed a world tour of triumph following the coronation of King George V, in 1911, which he attended as a member of the suite of Prince Higashi Fushimi, who in war time had been under him as drillmaster. The other great hero of the Russian war, General Nogi, also was a member. The English public began a lionization of Togo which increased in volume on the continent of Europe and in the United States. He was cheered by crowds in London, and the British papers editorialized on England's pride in having helped to turn out such a figure. He addressed the cadets at his old school, Thames Nautical College, visited the tomb of Captain Smith, its commander in his day, and took presents to the captain's widow. His address at Thames College, given in English, is so far as I can discover, the only formal speech Togo ever made in any language during his life.

He dined with Asquith, Roberts, Kitchener, and Shackleton, and actually said so many words at table that Asquith warned him he was in danger of losing his sobriquet, "the silent admiral." He re-established it with a vengeance when he came to America. General Verbeck, on behalf of the governor of New York, met his ship, took him aboard a launch, and for one hour showed him New York harbor. The American general, who was born in Japan of a pioneer missionary father, explained the sights in Japanese. Newspapermen noted that Togo, who knew English as well as anybody, answered not one word. He may have been amazed at Verbeck's Japanese. He may have resented the appearance of patronizing him, or he may have been silent out of sheer humility. Who ever knows with a Japanese? His silence continued through the reception at City Hall given him by Mayor Gaynor, to the great embarrassment of this talkative politician and his suite.

This manner of response to an uproarious American welcome did not, however, kill Togo's popularity in the United States. He was received on the floor of the Senate, and Congress passed a special bill for the expenses of his welcome, a unique honor previously reserved for such heroes as Lafayette. The high point of his tour was his visit to Theodore Roosevelt, in retirement at his rambling Sagamore Hill house on Oyster Bay. Said the hospitable Teddy as he rushed out to greet the little admiral, "Sagamore Hill has never before welcomed such a great man as Admiral Togo, and never will again." Roosevelt may have been right. The less than five-foot Togo may have started something that will affect the life and destiny of this nation as much as a nation can ever be affected by a life outside of it.

Togo's diminutive stature, his close-cropped head, his restraint of speech, combined, however, with great personal kindliness and democracy of action, and the wry twist of his mouth, captured the American public from the Atlantic to the Pacific coast. He was sketched, photographed, and editorialized upon as "our Togo." He became the only Japanese ever generally known to the American public. For a time Americans showed their hero worship by naming small pet dogs "Togo." All that, however, was before the Great War. Postwar Americans forgot the only Japanese they ever knew— so much so that when he died nothing appeared about him beyond the obituary stuff of newspaper morgues, and our greatest newspapers and magazines applied the stock editorial formula that "we never publish articles on a dead man."

The American public never knew that the apparently wry twist to Togo's mouth was the result of pain that had gripped him most of his life, and which increased in intensity until his death. He was a sufferer from bladder stones, throat cancer, and bronchial trouble. On his return from his triumphal tour he settled down in a humble unpainted frame house on a hill in the center of residential Tokyo, a home half western style, half floored with Japanese mats, such as most middle-class Japanese maintain to-day. Unknown to most people, Togo was called upon to be private tutor to the Crown Prince, now Emperor, which accounts for the navy-mindedness of the Imperial Court at present—an angle which American Admiral Standley called attention to in his world-wide encomium upon the occasion of Togo's death.

He became almost a legendary figure, appearing publicly on the anniversaries of his great victory, but he was god to the young officers in the navy. Naval Minister Osumi was more than glad to get his statement, "All officers in the Imperial navy must be prudent in speech and action," at the time of the trial of navy cadets for the Inukai assassination.

VI

The Japanese people learned that their hero was near death while they were in the midst of the most fervent celebration (the twenty-ninth) of his victory ever held—under the stimulus of the new naval competition between Japan, America, and England, and the general talk of the great naval crisis coming in 1935. They learned that he had been receiving treatment with radium supplied by Japanese hospitals and the navy at a cost of 350,000 yen, and that he had hastened his death by rising from bed to practice the bow he wished to make towards the palace when the Emperor would leave it to attend the commemoration of his victory.

Representatives of the army and navy and the foreign embassies began to call at the modest wooden home. The Empress sent him a basket of fruit, and six hundred school children selected from all the schools about Tokyo came to his courtyard, bowed and prayed. Finally the Emperor sent him the rank of marquis (which many a rich industrialist had been able to obtain), the junior grade of first court rank, sanction for a state funeral, and a dozen bottles of wine —the last an honor reserved until all hope is gone. Togo called for his formal dress to be laid across his bed, to receive with thanks the gift which we westerners would regard as too much like a death sentence. Immediately after receiving the Emperor's emissary, he fell into his death coma. His wife, who had been bedridden for six years in a nearby room, rose and sat on the mats near his low wooden bedstead during his last hours. The room where he died was only eight mats large, and bare save for a painting of Mt. Fuji.

Togo's state funeral was the grandest of the eleven that have taken place during the sixty-six years since the restoration. Japanese papers boast that no state funeral in the world's history has been attended by so many contingents from foreign navies. Admiral Kanji Kato, jingoist of the Japanese navy who turned Togo against the London treaty, was chief ritualist—clad not in admiral's uniform but in the elaborate white robes of a Shinto high priest. All the immediately following high dignitaries were clad in Shinto costume, but at the grave the western custom of each mourner's throwing in one shovelful of earth was followed.

Every ship of the Japanese navy, wherever located, and American, British, French, and Italian gunboats in Japanese waters simultaneously fired a salute of twenty-one guns. In the grave was buried a flat stone two feet square, its face carved with five hundred Chinese characters reporting the career of the admiral, and protected by another flat stone bolted to it, which Japanese papers remark will be a historical relic when dug up a thousand years hence. Twelve sailors who fought under Togo on his flagship *Mikasa* at the battle of Tsushima were appointed in two shifts to keep two lanterns burning for fifty days and nights. Floral wreaths were delivered from the heads of every great government and from naval heroes from Jellicoe down.

China came back as a naval power at the funeral of the man who wiped her out as a naval power by sending the cruiser *Ninghai*, built in Japan a year earlier, with a complement of 365 officers and men—the first Chinese warship to visit Japan in twenty-two years. This ship had been delivered to the Chinese while Japanese gunboats were bombarding Woosung, the port of Shanghai. The Japanese attackers had ceased fire to dip their colors during the process! Other Japanese built cruisers are following the *Ninghai*—in fact China is getting a navy built, trained—and *controlled*—by Japan.[3] The Chinese marines sent to Togo's funeral arrived late for the full parade. By the perhaps significant courtesy of the American marines who led the foreign detachments, the Chinese fell in behind the stars and stripes, the French, British, and Italians following. The Russians were conspicuous by absence.

When the formal funeral was over, the informally dressed public was allowed to approach and bow before the great black and white funeral pavilion in Hibiya Park opposite the Imperial Hotel. They were led by the eighty-nine-year-old Mrs. Akimoto, who founded a boy scout organization in Japan. Many fainted, and one man died in the waiting, rain-drenched crowd. An international radio hook-up was arranged between Japan, America, England, and Manila. American Admiral William H. Standley, chief of naval operations, gave a radio eulogy in which he said that the deceased "combined tactical and strategical wisdom with character and leadership"; then

[3] This in 1935.

Radio City's orchestra cut in with a Japanese tune orchestrated by Tin Pan Alley which they thought would be "atmosphere." Japan was scandalized. The tune is a popular drinking song of the Japanese gay quarters. Japanese station JOAK had to apologize to the nation for bringing it in, and one of Radio City's very serious board meetings was held the next day under Vice President John Royal!

With the death of Togo, Japan's army and navy lost their last super-rank officer risen from the ranks. The three remaining field marshals and fleet admirals are all princes of the Imperial blood— emphasizing the connection of the services with the Imperial House.

While some papers said that there was danger of too much deifying of Togo, a seventeen-year-old youth bringing fifty-five sen to the police on his bicycle (which was faithfully delivered to the Togo residence) started a movement for turning the Togo home into a shrine ranking with that where General Nogi and his wife committed hara-kiri. Togo Square is to become the Trafalgar Square of Tokyo. The imperial rescript to the spirit of Togo reads in translation: "Communing with the ancestral gods in spirit of sincerity, and forestalling the foe with the common presence of your mind, you decided the fate of the nation...while we were the Crown Prince, you extended your wise aid to us and lent us your support. Under three régimes have you served as a most faithful subject. You won the respect of the entire nation, and your fame extended to the ends of the earth." A leading newspaper started a movement to have the inscription on monuments to heroes, beginning with Togo, written in vernacular instead of classical Chinese.

War Minister Hayashi said: "With the nation facing a crisis, we have lost our naval hero and our saint." The deposed liberal premier, Wakatsuki, whom Togo helped ruin by fighting the London pact, spoke: "Admiral Togo did a great service to the nation in unifying the imperial navy."

The navy's hour had come in Japan's history. An admiral, one of Togo's "boys," a sublieutenant on his flagship *Naniwa*, was made premier in order that the entire resources of the nation might be directed toward Nippon's domination of the western Pacific. The publicity gained by the navy through the death of Togo strengthened this national conviction. Togo had eliminated Russia as a rival on the sea. His successors were expected by their nation to overcome either by diplomacy or war the superiority of America, which stands in the way of Japan's completion of her "divine" mission.

Said the New York *Times*, commenting on Togo's place in history: "That naval skirmish of forty years ago in the Yellow Sea was the curtain raiser in a drama in which Manchukuo is the latest episode. Japan's rise to power has been felt directly or indirectly in every corner of the earth. Japan's defeat of Russia imparted a shock to the Czarist system from which it never recovered. At Port Arthur and Mukden in 1905 the fate of the Romanoffs was really sealed.

"Few persons now living have escaped the influence of events in Russia since March, 1917. The Soviet experiment had its first rehearsal in the winter of 1905-6 when the government of Nicholas II was reeling under the shame and loss of the Japanese adventure."

Here and there human touches show through the exhibition of perfervid nationalism attending Togo's death. Says his disciple and friend, Admiral Okada, who took over the premiership from Togo's old service mate, Admiral Saito, a few days after the hero's death: "I never heard Togo laugh aloud, or utter a reprimand with a raised voice. He accomplished his purpose without noise."

Save, one notes, the noise of well-timed explosions of warships caught off guard.

Chapter XIV
Adventurer and King of Finance

Now for another side of Japan. In contrast to Togo of the sea, take a character whose personal story is the whole history of Japanese banking. Takahashi (Korekiyo), repeatedly imperial minister of finance, with a laugh, carries on his eighty-year-old, still erect shoulders the weight of a national budget fifty per cent unbalanced. In more ways than one, Takahashi was the counterpart in life of the hoary Japanese god Daruma, who has a rounded bottom. You tip him over only to have him rise of his own equilibrium and rock back and forth with a smile.

Also, Takahashi connected the swashbucklers of 1854 with those of 1934. No more fascinating life could be recorded. Takahashi really lived two lives. He was a boyish hanger-on of that amazing group who overthrew feudal authority and then went, dressed in get-ups that might be worn by a Congo African going to town to-day, to mid-nineteenth-century America and Great Britain to find out how the west did things. He saw his financial and political fortunes ruined several times. Assassins shot three chiefs from over him, so to speak. He could coöperate heartily toward the divine mission about which the young fellows were so serious, smiling the while at their intensity.

He was the only man of high finance and great wealth in Japan who dared to tell the military that they were bankrupting the nation. So, in the patriotic purge engineered by Hideki Tojo in 1939, which went into the record as a mutiny but received little punishment, Takahashi was assassinated.

II

He was born in 1854,[1] the year Commodore Perry brought contempt upon the Tokugawa tyranny in Japan by sailing into a harbor against its laws with a fleet too big for it to drive off. He was the eldest son of a man with the rank of orderly—really servant to the warrior class.

Like many history makers of Japan, he was reared by a Spartan grandmother, who kept a tiny courtyard for the two in the capital so that the boy could grow up under the shadow of the tremendous events changing Japan's world. Her first idea of giving him the means of raising himself in the world was to teach him the Confucian classics.

At ten years of age he was making bamboo screens. Then like Samuel of old he became a temple page. A northern lord coming to worship and play chess with the priests, fancying the lad, sent him to the "foreigners' port," Yokohama, to study English and foreign learnings; his first teacher in these was the wife of an American missionary. Later he and a pal became office boys to a British merchant, and in 1867, when he was fourteen according to oriental reckoning, his clan raised money to send the two, and a third boy, to America.

Parting was not easy, especially for the old grandmother, who nevertheless insisted that, to be of use to his country, he go to a land as far and strange to her as Mars. Her parting gift to her grandson was a sharp sword, accompanied by instructions never to pick a fight but never to let an insult go unavenged—which reminds one of the letter written to Andrew Jackson at the same age by his mother when she was about to undertake the fatal task of nursing yellow-fever patients in Charleston, South Carolina.

The future premier and minister of finance, a future admiral, and a future governor of the Bank of Japan, crossed the Pacific in the steerage of an eight-hundred-ton steamer in company with seven hundred Chinese coolies en route to build Mr. Harriman's railroad. These boys, accustomed to daily hot baths and meticulous Japanese cleanliness, recorded that the American crew burned cayenne pepper

---

[1] Serial biography, Tokyo *Nichi-Nichi*, 1924, anonymous.

in the steerage quarters to force the coolies out on the decks for cleaning of the quarters.

The lads landed in San Francisco in 1867, in what they imagined was proper foreign regalia—frock coats with the tails cut off, and women's shoes—the only leather shoes they could get to fit their small Japanese feet. In characteristic Japanese fashion, they were too impatient to wait for their friends in the Japanese community to come down to the ship, and set off to find fellow clansmen supposed to be studying at the college in Berkeley only to get completely lost. They climbed to the peak of one of San Francisco's convenient hills and, looking over the harbor, were transported to see a rising sun flag. The ship's interpreter knew enough English to help them find their friends.

Many of the aristocratic boys who pioneered in America and England in the middle of the last century had astonishing experiences that reflect upon our own civilization, but none more amazing than fifteen-year-old Takahashi. The money for the American stay of himself and mate had been placed in the hands of an American trader in Yokohama, who directed them to his father near San Francisco. The boys, who had learned to swing swords in Japan and regarded men who swung hoes as meat on which a samurai might at will test his blade, found themselves in free America, bound out in servitude, compelled to weed cabbages on the truck farm of this old miser in return for crusts of bread and cots to sleep on.

Takahashi's comrade made the best of it, hoping some one would come along and save them, but Takahashi turned sullen and wouldn't work in spite of deprivation of food, whereupon the shrewd American persuaded him and an older clansman living in San Francisco, whom he secured as a witness, to sign a document which the two Japanese thought was an arrangement for Takahashi's schooling. It was actually a sale into apprenticeship to the family of an early American politician living in Oakland, a man later to become American minister to Peking. Thus it was that Takahashi often said that he was sold into slavery in America.

By his own statement the lad was treated more as a member of the family and companion of the children than as a servant, and

it was here that he learned the idiomatic Americanese and knowledge of the American psychology and many of the frontier American
mannerisms that later showed under his kimono. But when Takahashi was scolded for quarreling with a Chinese cook, and then got
his face slapped by the young master for impudence, he went to his
room and started polishing the sword that his grandmother had
provided.

He determined that the young wife should be compelled to witness the slashing—first of the Chinese cook and then of her husband. *She* was then to die, after which Takahashi would cut out his
own bowels. When she came in and found him at work on the
sword he informed her of the decision. She managed to argue him
out of it by getting her husband to apologize for the slap. But
young Takahashi still felt that his face had not been entirely saved
and he quit the Oakland home to lead a life of near-starvation on
the San Francisco waterfront.

He finally ran into an American merchant who was honorary consul for Japan and with whom he placed his claim against the truck-
raising father of the American trader who took his money in Japan.
This merely resulted in the old miser's establishing claims for passage, food, and clothing, which left Takahashi and his comrade fifty
dollars in debt! To get the two of them clear, Takahashi had to
borrow from a wealthier Japanese student passing through San
Francisco.

Just at this time the independent existence of the clans, one of
which had sent the young man to America, was ended by imperial
edict. Left with neither moral nor financial backing, the boys shipped
back to Japan in company with a stranded Japanese adventurer,
who cheated the boys out of their meager possessions.

On arrival in Yokohama two years after leaving it they pretended
they were Americans, being guided by the older adventurer, since
Japanese students were still subject to death for stealing abroad—
and daring to return. Takahashi relates how, their hair really standing on end underneath their hats, they jabbered unconnected English words, repeated the multiplication table, and said anything else
they could think of to one another as they walked past the harbor
police and officials—which shows how little Japanese authorities

knew about westerners just a short time ago, as well as how lax were their regulations.

Takahashi and his friend thought the safest place to hide for the time being would be a classroom; also they had got no schooling in America, so they registered in the forerunner of the Tokyo Imperial University, which had started out under Mori (Arimori), founder of Japan's great educational system. The boys (Takahashi was now seventeen with no formal education) were immediately jerked out of the class and made teachers, so rare were men who had any knowledge of English or the outside world at all.

The life of a young professor, thought Takahashi, needed a little brightening up with the most popular geisha of the city. When he lost his job over her, he proposed that she should support him until he could find other work, and went to live with her. Shortly after, a group down in the southern island who wanted so ardently to learn English that they didn't care who taught it invited Takahashi to teach down there.

The pioneer educationalist Mori remembered Takahashi when in 1873 he was able to bring the American professor Morley to advise the new ministry of education. The pioneer minister of education summoned young Takahashi back to be Morley's Japanese secretary and go-between.

Takahashi's connection with the commercial world, which occupied the second half of his life, grew in a strangely indirect way out of his educational connection. Morley's friend, the American missionary Hepburn, had compiled the first Japanese dictionary. The missionary privately printed his work in two volumes only to discover that every little Japanese printing house was pirating it— a situation not much improved at the present time. But Morley spoke to Takahashi on copyright and patent customs in western lands and put him in touch with sources which made him Japan's first authority on such things.

Meanwhile, Takahashi had been offered what he later described as "a swell job" as principal of the education ministry's new college at Osaka. He apparently felt for once in his life a slight lack of confidence in his qualifications. His mind turned to a teaching fellow, Ichijo, who to his disgust had renounced the ambitions of this life and gone in for an intense experience in a Buddhist monastery. He betook himself to the monastery to show Ichijo what a coward and egotist he was for running away from the world at this very exciting and crucial time. Ichijo retorted in affectionate fashion by pointing out in scathing language how totally unfit Takahashi was to assume the position of college president, or in fact any position whatsoever.

Then occurred an incident which probably could take place only in Japan or academic Germany. The two agreed to have a formal debate on the active versus the retired life. Whichever one lost was to espouse the life of the winner, regardless of cost. Takahashi had to agree with the judges that the philosopher-quoting Ichijo had tied him up in knots, even though Takahashi had resorted to the arguments of Christianity, in which he never had the slightest actual interest.

So Takahashi, with tears in his eyes, resigned the "swell job" before he started it, thereby outraging the men who had given it to him and putting an end to his career as an educationalist. He stuck to Ichijo and the monastery seven months—seven months which made this zestful adventurer into a great man. Through introspection and study of Chinese ethics, Takahashi attained the sense of values and philosophy of life to which he rightly credited the success of his late-built career. One of the most formative portions of this education was his careful refusal of Ichijo's Zen philosophy that a man is justified in pursuing any course of action provided only that he has no selfish purpose. Takahashi concluded that control of impulses, no matter how noble, is necessary, and that deeds are to be judged by their fruits, rather than by their motives. With superheated patriots shouting and shooting around him, Takahashi became Japan's Gibraltar of the commonsense viewpoint. "Pure intentions" continue to be the plea of the Zen-impregnated warrior class and that portion of the population which Theodore Roosevelt might have described as the "lunatic fringe," which in Japan is at times almost the whole cloth.

In 1899 Toyama's young swashbucklers invaded Mori's house, where Takahashi was living as an understudy, and slew Japan's Horace Mann for "dangerous thought" and for carrying a walking stick in the shrine of the imperial ancestress of Ise. Forty years later (1939) Takahashi suffered a similar fate. "Dangerous thoughts" in 1899 consisted in the advocacy of the abolition of sword wearing and preferring riding in a carriage to be carried in a palanquin; but they bear an exact analogy to the accusations brought to-day against assassinated leaders by the self-constituted protectors of Japan's purity. Always the immediate excuse is some sort of disrespect to the Divine Family. In an essay written, significantly, shortly before the 1932 epidemic of assassinations that took the head of his official family, Takahashi said the accusation against Mori of carrying a walking stick in the sacred grounds was trumped up.

Even to-day the privilege of carrying a cane in the grounds of sacred shrines and imperial palaces is a high honor granted only by special imperial edict and certified to the vigilant police with documents. The late Admiral Togo boasted the honor—had it put in his official obituary—and Prince Saionji, the last of the elder statesmen, cabinet creator and voice of the emperor, carried his six-foot black staff as an Italian general would carry his decorations. American tourists to Japan wonder why they must lay down umbrellas or swagger sticks at the gateways of the holy places, and continually try to slip them past the guards! Remembering the reason given for killing Mori, I still shudder at an experience in the same grounds of the holy of holies at Ise, the oldest shrine of the Divine Family.

In this southern shrine is kept the Imperial heirloom of divine authority, Amaterasu's mirror. In the park among the thousand-year-old sacred cryptomeria trees, on the bank of a stream so sacred that Japanese dip its water to rinse their mouths only after it has flowed past the shrine, a quick-eyed Japanese friend and I barely prevented a bibulous American gentleman from relieving himself. The time was just following the Shanghai war when feeling against Americans was on the edge of violent expression throughout the Empire. Had that fellow's fingers been less fumbly, the world might have been treated to the spectacle of a national and racial struggle set off by an incident surpassing the imagination of H. G. Wells, who in *The Shape of Things to Come* had the final world war begin when a German Jew tried to relieve the pressure of a seed under his false teeth and at the same time salute a Polish fascist officer.

When a Japanese department of industry and commerce was established in 1884, Takahashi, as Japan's only trade mark authority, was appointed to establish and head a division of patents based on the French department. It must be said that Takahashi's patent office has been chiefly interested in encouraging and protecting Japanese inventiveness rather than giving protection to foreign products, but Japan isn't the only nation guilty of this sort of thing.

With the encouragement of superiors, who even at this early date wanted Japan to have a hand in international exploitation, Takahashi resigned his position to head a scheme for development of gold mines and farming in Peru. It had been cooked up by one of the world's most colorful international swindlers, a German consul who had married the Peruvian president's daughter. Going to investigate the layout, Takahashi found that his agents had been sold mines that were either inaccessible or worked out by the Incas. He found on his hands in Peru the persons of several thousand Japanese farmers, artisans, and miners, and at home the claims of holders of a half million dollars' worth of worthless shares. It is significant to note that this first Japanese attempt at foreign exploitation took place in Latin America.

Takahashi sold his Tokyo home to get money to repatriate the Japanese workmen who had gone to Peru. After a few months of retirement, during which his life was threatened by the angry shareholders—who seemed to be not as docile as Wall Street's victims—Takahashi found employment as a simple clerk in the new Bank of Japan.

He was now thirty-five years old, with enough flamboyant adventures behind him to fill several ordinary lives, but his real career was still ahead of him. After his greatest débâcle, his luck turned and wealth and position literally plumped into his lap. In three years he rose from clerk to head of the Imperial Bank of Japan. Then he was transferred to help organize the official exchange organ, the Yokohama Specie Bank, of which he was soon vice president. Following the war with China, he went to Europe and floated Japan's first foreign-subscribed loan. This made him vice governor of the Bank of Japan, and he became the good financial servant of Prince

Yamagata, Japan's Bismarck, who was engaged in squelching democratic tendencies and setting Japan's feet on the path of continental
empire.

Came the war with Russia, and it was smiling Takahashi who
went to England and raised the huge British loans, also an American
loan (with the aid of Jacob Schiff) with which Japan whipped the
czar. Takahashi became successively president of the Yokohama
Specie Bank and governor of the Bank of Japan, was made baron,
and then viscount.

III

He sat upon these heights for twenty-five years. When a cabinet
could not be organized for lack of a financial man, Takahashi was
drafted. He knew more about banking and business than any other
man in the empire. He knew politics, too, having (more for fun than
anything else) financed and become boss of the majority party after
the cabinet overturned in 1914.

Takahashi helped elect the first proletarian premier of Japan,
Mr. Hara, and became his finance minister. He took over the
premiership when Hara was assassinated for endorsing the Washington treaties of 1922 respecting Chinese sovereignty and the world
naval ratio. It was nothing new to him, therefore, when another
premier to whom he was finance minister, "Old Fox" Inukai, was
shot in 1932. The next cabinet, headed by Admiral Saito, thrust
upon the military patriots by the Elder Statesman Saionji, relied
upon Takahashi and his mastery of finance. The Saito cabinet fell in
1934 over financial scandal in Takahashi's own ministry. One vice
minister went to jail and the other took the ministership off his old
chief's shoulders but the "god of finance" still smiled.

The remainder of this story of Takahashi, the author begs leave
to quote just as it appeared in the printing of 1934. He confesses
himself stumped over how to "bring it up to date." Perhaps it is
more valuable as it stood:

Takahashi is fearless. He tells protesting taxpayers that their
taxes must be increased, and then he uses every ruse possible to
delay increasing them. He tells his fellow millionaires that they
have got to buy another billion yen of treasury bonds to supply

army and navy demands, or he will turn them over to the mercy of General Araki. He tells General Araki that he is a fool and that the military socialists would make Japan the laughing stock of the world in six months. He tells foreign minister Hirota that Japan's foreign relations must be predicated upon national give-and-take rather than the fulfilment of Nippon's divine mission in the world.

Yet with his hard-boiled way of looking at things as they are he expresses better than Hirota the concrete basis of Japan's diplomacy: "Economic conflicts are particularly fierce and all nations intend to repress Japan. Thus there is a sort of economic war. This economic battle is more dangerous than warships. Diplomatic operations only succeed by sufficient military strength. The years 1935 and 1936 are a dangerous period for the nation. We must be fully prepared for those years. Military equipment exists to perfect diplomatic operations."

This is the Japanese version of the European doctrine popular from Machiavelli to Bismarck: that war takes up where diplomacy leaves off. When Ramsay MacDonald the pacifist is through announcing Great Britain's intention to build more navy, Takahashi the realist rises to promise 200,000,000 yen additional to Japan's navy to meet the crisis of 1935 and 1936. Since human beings must play the international farce, he gets his cue in it gaily and, perhaps, with more knowledge than any other actor involved. Great Britain and the United States, no longer restrained by the doctrine of thrift since they are trying to save themselves by spending anyhow, propose to bankrupt Japan with a building race. And Japan, capturing the world's trade by leaps and bounds, accepts the challenge. It becomes a race as to whether the Anglo-Saxons can spin out of their own vitals faster and longer than Japan can draw off the seven seas.

Because Takahashi takes neither himself nor the universe nor Japan's divine mission with complete seriousness, he is more modern and civilized than the other seventy million Japanese. But he will go along as far as they need him. And when they need him no longer, he will remain a most valuable window through which we may glimpse the Japanese soul.

"They needed" this eighty-year-old man of vision and wisdom no longer after 1939—they assassinated him.

When that which Takahashi upholds goes, with him will go the entire individualist-capitalist system of Japan—a Frankenstein monster, built, turned loose for an amazing run, and violently stopped all within one human lifetime. He personifies the industrial system as Japan has known it. If success in building world empire is hers, Japan will keep that system until it breaks of its own weight, as in the west. If Japan's present method of empire building gets stopped, a new kind of empire, a sort of imperial state socialism, will be attempted. Takahashi is, one may say, the key figure of Nippon.

Chapter XV

Liberal, Saint, Scientist

H̲ᴀꜱ Japan, thus far, produced any lives guided by a truly international philosophy? Let us look at the men among Japanese who have lived nearest to an ideal of world-love, rather than Nippon-love.

The most beautiful figure of Japan, who illumined his country for a long generation as Tagore did India, was Dr. Nitobe (Inazo), whom this writer revered as a master and a saint. His inner impulses were always towards the most idealistic utterances of Jesus Christ. In his boyhood Nitobe became one of Japan's pioneer Christians, then no easy step for a high-caste Japanese. He immediately found himself in conflict with the sectarian-minded missionaries. To get a church into which he could invite a fellow Christian of any denomination, he and his youthful fellows had to build one out of their own slender resources.

Nitobe's international and interracial marriage is best described in his own words: "A son of the most conservative clan of the most provincial part of Japan, taking back to his island a daughter of the most conservative religion [Quaker] of the most conservative city of America [Philadelphia]." When it came to religion, or something so sacredly personal to a Japanese as marriage, Nitobe was willing to fly in the face of his clan and race—a defiance that means even more to a Japanese than to a westerner, and which half a century ago meant more to both than we of to-day can well understand.

Nitobe became a synonym for internationalism, one of the originators of the League of Nations' idea, and was for twelve years a member of the high secretariat in Geneva. He wrote books in beautiful Japanese, and in English, whose vast vocabulary he mastered to a greater extent than any writer I know born to the language. These books seem to hold the essence of world outlook and ultramodern idealism. Indeed, Nitobe came to be an object of such suspicion to the patriotic societies and jingo militarists that they sufficiently overcame the Japanese awe of a scholar to threaten him with death —even to manhandle him. Nitobe became a teacher of the world with Japan as his base, very much as Tagore was a world teacher with India as a base. He adopted the gentle Quaker religion of his wife. It was the author's privilege over a span of years to take hundreds of Americans, old and young, across the widest ocean to the feet of this beautiful sage who illuminated, as a candle does a shrine, the household amid the Japanese Alps, meticulously managed by his indomitable American wife.

The wound to his national pride caused by the discrimination of the American immigration act of 1924 marked the turning point in Nitobe's life. He loved America and Americans. I never saw any man suffer more because of racial discrimination as evidenced in our immigration act. He could not quite say, "Father, forgive them for they know not what they do." If it had been an injury to himself— yes, easily. But it was an injury to his nation, to the basic pride of Japanese manhood, to the divinity of the race of Nippon, to the Divine Person, the Emperor, the Son of Heaven. And Nitobe, who with his loyal wife had sworn never to set foot again on the shores of his "second motherland," as he used to call the United States, and who had risked his life to criticize his own country's militarism, became General Araki's apologist for the undeclared war upon China to any audience that would listen to him in America. His last words to me in a New York hotel were, "Why didn't they call me, Josef? Each morning I awake in greater blackness!" And one of the last things he wrote in his column in the Osaka *Mainichi* was a weird interview between himself and the spirits of fellows who had gone before, put into the mouth and vocabulary of his faithful and puzzled old housekeeper. "The master goes about lately muttering to himself, 'Tired ... and sight so dim ... coming soon now ... please wait a little while ... and send samurai, real samurai, whose spirit is pure!'"

Throughout, Nitobe's life was an effort to harmonize the intense self-sacrificing, self-centered spirit of Japan, in which he saw great nobility, with the larger vision which came from outside. His tragedy was born of the impossibility of harmonizing incompatible concepts. Nitobe could no more make his Japan world-minded than could Christ so make his Judea.

Nitobe endeavored to make out of the cult of the Japanese warrior a creed of nobility that would command the respect of and inspire the world. He named it bushido, or the way of bushi—not a fortunate title in view of the habits of the swashbucklers who bore that name in Japan in feudal times, but perhaps, also, our western knighthood wasn't so noble to those who had to wine it, dine it, bed it, and curry its horses.

Bushido with its emphasis upon loyalty and austerity does command our respect. But it is no inspiration to the elimination of those things which threaten human destruction. Nitobe, its idealist creator, dying in Vancouver, B. C., in the fall of 1933 of a broken heart more than of pneumonia, realized this and chose to die a loyal Japanese. He definitely placed his spirit in the care of the Japanese kami, the gods of nationalism, since he could effect no compromise between them and the gods of his ideals. After his death his adopted son, American-educated editor of the English-language voice of the foreign office, the *Japan Times,* revealed that it was the internationalist, Inazo Nitobe, called upon by the victors over Russia in 1905 for suggestions about Manchuria, who told them to make the captured Manchurian railway "Japan's East India Company."

II

Left alone to uphold the banner of anti-jingoism, first by Nitobe's compromise, then by his death, was the aged yet doughty Ozaki (Yukio). The two men, independent in their careers, were drawn together through their families who lived as summer neighbors and intimate friends for years. The half-Japanese (her mother was English) supersensitive, literary Mme. Ozaki was always more strange in Japan than the entirely American, capable, grand lady from Philadelphia who was Mrs. Nitobe, and whose motherliness constantly and confidently went out to timid and lonely souls.

Ozaki, because of his independence, perversity, and eccentric venerableness, might be called the George Bernard Shaw of Japan. In politics he was called Japan's Senator Borah, but this went only for Borah's independence, oratory, and unsparing denunciations always embarrassing his own party—not for Borah's inconsistency. A conservative little man, hunter and alpinist in spite of his diminutive size (Japanese cartoonists used to love to show him and his rifle quite ambushed behind his huge flaring mustaches), elected to Parliament continuously by his faithful home district ever after he stood for office in 1878 at the age of nineteen, dubbed "god of constitutionalism" since he became one of the few sincere Japanese believers in a representative form of government, but beginning in his seventies to show traces of disillusionment, Ozaki was a lone eagle through two generations of politics.

In the early 1900's Ozaki gained fame as Tokyo's first "reform" mayor and also as Japan's most prominent celibate official. As mayor of Tokyo he presented to its sister capital, Washington, the beautiful cherry trees which each spring blossom about Potomac Basin. Hiroshi Saito, Japanese minister to the United States, followed Ozaki's example by donating cherry trees to Central Park, New York. Letters for another Ozaki coming by mistake to the Tokyo mayor piqued his interest. He found the real addressee to be the daughter by an English lady of a Japanese ambassador to England. This ethereal, high-strung Miss Ozaki had been secretary in Italy to Marie Corelli, and had come to Japan to begin a literary career of writing Japanese folk tales and fairy lore for children. The two Ozaki's met and married. The two daughters of this union reacted from the unearthliness of their mother and the moral conservatism of their father by bicycle riding, jazz dancing, going about without chaperons, and otherwise meriting the title of Japan's outstanding moga—a slang contraction from the English "modern girl," which has as its complement, mobo—"modern boy."

The sincere Ozaki and the turncoat Inukai were both protégés of Okuma, a politician with the force of Theodore Roosevelt. Ozaki was made minister of justice under Okuma in Japan's first political party cabinet (1898), and dedicated himself to making the cabinet in Japan as powerful and important as it is in England. This was something that Japan's Bismarck, Yamagata, who had built Japan's army and suppressed her internal dissension and was laying the foundations of her continental empire, could not permit. He and Toyama's Dragons set their men to watch upon Ozaki, and they heard him make a speech scolding an audience of constituents in which he used a hypothetical parallel: "Why do you vote for the richest men? If Japan were a republic, you people would elect the richest man in the land to the presidency!" The newspapers yelled "Lese majesty!" from one end of the country to the other. Not only Ozaki but the whole cabinet fell.

For years Ozaki was cursed when he appeared in public. A Japanese banker in Seattle who dared to sympathize with him lost his depositors and was ruined. What particularly wounded Ozaki was that he would at any time have laid down his life for his emperor. He began to write books to prove the compatibility of democracy and the imperial system. The militarists have alternately scorned him and respected him for his intrepid spirit. At three different periods their jingoes have made attempts on his life. Once he owed his escape to his active youngest daughter, who threw her maiden's kimono around the little statesman, who just fitted it, and faced the assassins in a simulated fury of indignation at their invasion of a room occupied by ladies only.

Ozaki has stirred up plenty of trouble for politicians and corrupt nobles. In 1907, with his fiery oratory, he pushed the impeachment of Premier Katsura until that prince and general fled from office, but only once since his short term in cabinet office has Ozaki been something more than leader of a parliamentary opposition and embodiment of the irreconcilable trait in the Japanese makeup. This instance greatly concerns the United States.

In 1921, as naval rivalry between Japan and the United States was getting into full swing, Ozaki submitted a resolution in Parliament for a naval limitations conference, which got 38 votes out of 323. So the little orator took the issue to the people. His success proved the fallacy of his own theories that elected representatives represent. In all cities of Japan he addressed mass meetings handing out postcards addressed to the premier, demanding army and navy cuts and asking the Japanese government to approach President

Harding and Lord Balfour for a naval agreement. The high officials who had made quips at his expense were soon deluged with post-cards. Ozaki's was the first popular movement anywhere in the world for the theory of voluntary limitation of death-dealing power by nations, and it is worth while to note that it took place in Japan. The Japanese jingoes finally got alarmed over Ozaki's campaign and followed him with cinema shows on the horrors of unpreparedness. This propaganda back-fired and ninety-eight per cent of his hearers sent in the postcards. The mention by the Japanese ambassador in Washington to Secretary of State Hughes of this postcard deluge actually opened the way for the 1922 conference and the first naval limitation agreement.

This idealist, grown deaf and old but still vigorous and graceful of gesture, did not hide his feelings when in 1931 the military clique overthrew his work and took Japan out of the ranks of peace-seek-ing nations into those of believers in force. He was in the United States, accompanied by his lively but devoted daughters, to visit his frail wife in a sanitarium here. While his old neighbor Nitobe was offering elaborate apologia and saying to westerners: "You have done the same things yourself," before the Japan Society in New York's Hotel Astor, Ozaki in my studio was describing the Japanese war lord in terms that even the press had to modify for print.

Mrs. Ozaki died in America. The bereaved old man went to Lon-don, where he received a challenge from a veterans' organization in Japan, daring him to come back and be assassinated for his state-ments. He took the first boat for Japan, daring them to assassinate him! The world watched with interest as his ship touched its first Japanese port. But at the orders of the war lord Araki himself, who appreciates this kind of spirit, the police scooped up the assassins on the wharf, and during succeeding years all shots at Ozaki went wild. He moved as freely about Japan as his stiffening joints per-mitted.

Of course, if this courageous spirit had offered a real threat to the control of military power instead of an opportunity for it to show chivalry to a defeated foe, the story would be different. Big army and navy men can afford to be generous with an idealist who used to go about telling the public (because he believed it) that press

stories of western nations increasing their forces against one another
were just propaganda from the Japanese war office!

But old Ozaki was indomitable. He formed a "Blue Cross Society"
including Kagawa (Toyohiko), Abe (Iso), the "father of baseball
and socialism in Japan" whose many socialist parties have gone the
way of liberal socialism elsewhere, and Noguchi (Yone), once noted,
"Japanese poet in English," protégé of Joaquin Miller, lion of Fifth
Avenue drawing-rooms and friend of Sarojini Naidu of India and
London. Noguchi married a New York woman of rare quality and
returned with her to Japan, to revert to Japanese culture and the
Japanese language as a medium and settle down as a professor in
Japanese universities. He also took a Japanese wife and had a second
family, leaving his gifted "American" wife to rear in brave fight
against terrible poverty his gifted children (one is the sculptor,
Isamo Noguchi). Never, however, would she permit a word to be
spoken against him—which estranged her from the indignant Mrs.
Nitobe, who bristled at mention of the name of Yone Noguchi. This
Americanized Japanese, who was once famous for his poem, "Yosem-
ite," became the literary champion of "Asia for Asiatics." He was
host to Tagore of India in Japan—and in 1941, the recipient of
Tagore's corrosive deathbed exposé of the Japanese imperialist
hypocrisy proclaiming a "War of Emancipation" for China and
India. Meanwhile, Yone's son Isamo, an American citizen born of
his American mother in the United States, drew posters for China
War Relief.

Such are the men, representing diverse elements of Japanese
idealism, who announced as the world stood upon the verge of the
abyss of 1939, that they would coöperate with Romain Rolland,
H. G. Wells, and professional good-will organizations of New York,
Paris, and Rome in one more effort to save the world.

III

One Japanese, and one only, can be said to have transcended
Japanese nationalism,[1] and that is Kagawa (Toyohiko), who comes

---

[1] After Nitobe passed, internationalism was supported only by international merchants whose motive was obviously selfish. All the more did the "samurai" despise
internationalism.

near to being Japan's (and the whole world's) one practising as well
as professing Christian. He is often called the Mahatma Gandhi of
Japan, and in mysticism, absolute fearlessness, total disregard of
possessions and physical comfort, he parallels the mahatma. It may
be that Gandhi loves the sense of power—at least he has become
very accustomed to it—and if this be true the twenty-five year-
younger Kagawa is a truer saint. Kagawa's love for mankind seems
to be for *persons*—seems to be less inclined to sacrifice individuals
to a cause—but this may be because in Japan human suffering does
not loom so tremendously as something to overcome, as in India,
and because Japan's Buddhism was combined with the stand-on-
your-own-feet teaching of old Confucius, and always laid emphasis
on individual purpose and action in contradistinction to the Hindu
concept of impersonal evolution working ponderously through the
mass. Or the greatest difference between the saints may exist simply
because Kagawa is younger, with the personal affections attendant
upon virility, or because people whom he tries to help have not yet
put him in jail so many times.

For the application of the philosophy of love Kagawa, although
perfectly happy himself in a dollar-and-a-half suit, would make use
of all the abundance of the earth and man's modern facility in exploiting it. He would distribute the world's goods as evenly as Marx.
Mahatma Gandhi is a combination of Jesus, Tolstoy, and Thoreau,
the discovery of whom, one after the other, shaped his mind. Kagawa,
who has the practical as well as the mystical Japanese mind, might
be described as a combination of Jesus, Karl Marx, and Henry Ford.
His preachment is that ministers should stop trying to satisfy miser-
able people in this life with promises of gold-paved streets and fruit
off the twelve-cropping tree of life in the world to come. Kagawa
took Christian propaganda, not only in Japan but throughout Pacific
Asia, right out of the hands of British and American missionaries.

Kagawa, like Matsuoka, owes much of his mentality to his American associations. Whereas these gave Matsuoka the punch behind a
confirmed and aggravated nationalism, they worked in Kagawa's
sweet soul to develop his understanding of the needs of the whole
human race, yellow, white, and black.

In boyhood he was morbid over the unhappiness of the mother

whom he loved, who was the proud but neglected concubine of a spirited, reckless man of warrior caste. The father turned pioneer entrepreneur, helped found the great Osaka Shosen Kaisha (one of Japan's two world-wide shipping firms) and died a bankrupt. The sensitive boy was on the point of committing suicide when handed the *Gospel of John* by a street-preaching American missionary named Myers. Here was an idealism which satisfied the craving, which became an absolute necessity to the young Japanese, for something to work, sacrifice, and die for, bigger than himself and more important than personal comfort.

Kagawa put into a literal living of Christ's teachings what the average Japanese usually puts into national and personal ambitions. Being expelled from a missionary theological dormitory because he brought there first, stray dogs and next, abandoned infants; being allowed to faint for lack of food while butlering in an American home to earn tuition for a graduate course in Princeton—in fact, learning what Christianity is like among Christians—was no discouragement to him. To-day, through an application of Christian principles to society, which takes the form of fostering labor unions, peasants' unions, coöperative organizations, and a lay order called the Friends of Jesus, Kagawa has become a prophet of economic democracy throughout the east.

His fight against the new industrial plutocracy and his championship of the peasants by no means displease the military groups— they feel a kinship in this fervor. A large number of the most nationalistic spirits of Japan, such as Matsuoka, are nominal Christians who, like the good Christians that built the British Empire or exterminated the American Indian, have merged their Christian fervor with a more primitive nationalist creed.

Because of points of sympathy and because of his tremendous hold upon the imagination of the peasants, who are their foundation and from whom they spring, the military in Japan tolerated Kagawa's occasional denunciations of force and patriotism, and permitted him to return to Japan unmolested after trips to China, the Philippines, and America to apologize for what Japanese armies did abroad. In Japan they keep him muffled by surrounding him with police "for the sake of protection from fanatic patriots" or by packing his halls with their own crowd.

Kagawa is important—in the eye of time, perhaps the most important thing in Japan or Pacific Asia or the world—but he could no more save the course of history in his generation than Jesus, not even mentioned by contemporary historians, did in His.

So much for the hopes of American missionary societies whose representatives once looked askance at Kagawa but in the 30's made him their pet and cited him as proof that we need not be disturbed over Japan. Kagawa had a few loyal disciples. But they were not destined to stop the nationalist tide sweeping Japan into world empire or defeat such as befell Germany, and Kagawa himself felt compelled to resign from every peace society of foreign origin, "for fear of being misunderstood by his people." Kagawa *has* interpreted the "mission of Japan" on a spiritual plane as did Christ the mission of Israel. A Nippon disillusioned of its national egotism may through him become in a future century a teacher to the world.

Meanwhile, Japan's warlords may let him speak to feel the reaction—as he did speak on his arrival home from America in November, 1941—on the last boat back (which Japanese authorities told him to take), and as he spoke again about the time of the first United States bombing of Tokyo. A defeated or frightened Japan will need its Kagawa, and try to use him. Maybe it will even understand and appreciate him!

The tragedy of the beautiful human being Nitobe was evidence that one might not expect true internationalism in Japan in this half-century. There is distant promise in the remarks of the sophisticated and quite unascetic Count Futara (Yoshinori) in the recent session of the Diet: "One may doubt whether the so-called Nippon spirit is the *true* spirit of Nippon fostered for thousands of years. The true Nippon spirit is international and lies in conquering without fighting, and I believe confidence in victory grows out of this spirit. To return to this ideal of the national establishment is the right step toward meeting Japan's international emergency."

Two men of Japan, Kagawa and Ozaki, unreservedly and openly condemned the superpatriots and their actions. But Kagawa alone is supernationalist. Kagawa has not the slightest inclination to speak slightingly of the emperor, but his thought soars higher than the Sacred Precincts in Tokyo. To him the American exclusion act is wrong because it is antisocial and un-Christian, and I think he resents its application to Japanese no more than he would to Chinese or Patagonians. Ozaki resented that act as a Japanese, and, standing on the lawn of his alpine home where Colonel and Anne Lindbergh rested, he so told a group of us in language that would have been an insult from any other Japanese. Then one of his beautiful daughters served us delicious tea and cakes.

IV

It is well here to take an example of the Japanese spirit outside of military, government, and social reform circles. I choose a pioneer in medical science.

I know of no more typical example of the indomitable, sensitive, touchy, determined, persistent, and rash Japanese mind than Noguchi (Hideyo),[2] whose character was made in Nippon and his fame in America, whose most spectacular work was done in South America, and who met death off the Gold Coast of Africa. Noguchi's career is an answer to those who question whether the sons of Nippon have the capacity for organization as well as imitation.

He was born (1876) in a little clump of thatch-roofed, mud-floored huts in the Third Island, Shikoku, regarded as the poorest part of Japan. When Noguchi's father knew there would be another mouth to feed he deserted the family—a not uncommon situation in Japan, and one effectively used by Japanese novelists and dramatists. The baby was put under the care of his sister, but at a moment when the girl had unsaddled him from her back to help her mother work their acre or so of land the infant Noguchi toddled into the hibachi (floor brazier). His left hand was burned to a deformed stump. Only the tearful care of the sister and the will and work of his mother saved anything of his right hand. Fearful scars were left on other parts of his body.

[2] I am indebted to Gustave Eckstein's splendid biography (Harper & Brothers, 1931).

When the lad entered village school his classmates increased his sensitiveness by shunning or reviling him, as boys will do, for his deformity and poverty and the shame of his father's flight. As he was brooding over means of suicide, a Japanese surgeon, one of the earliest introducers of western science to his people—for this was only fifteen years after the overthrow of feudalism—happened to visit the village. He tried out his new profession on the sensitive crippled boy, with the good result of restoring the use of one hand. In a surge of gratitude and devotion, Noguchi, who like all Japanese boys and despite his handicap dreamt of being a soldier, dedicated his life to the art of healing instead of to that of destroying. The pioneer surgeon was so impressed that he gave of his slender earnings to start the lad's education.

But there was a side to Noguchi other than the philanthropic— the boundless ambition common to his race. Since he was going to be a medical scientist, he would be the greatest in the world. As the adolescent expressed it, "I will be a Napoleon to save instead of to kill—I can already get along on four hours of sleep at night!" He coolly announced, "I will be a physician to the Tenno (Emperor)." He did not pause to consider that the crippled and deformed are not admitted to the Heavenly One's precincts. In fact, through his life, when his ambition was high, he never thought of his deformity at all—not even when he was making love to a girl of another race.

The nearest he could get to western medicine was the frontier drug shop opened by a couple named Kobayashi, where he got a job as roustabout. He picked up materia medica and persuaded the druggist and his wife to advance him money to go to medical school. A nearby peasant, likewise, he talked into investing in his ambitions. Noguchi had the typical winsomeness of the Japanese artist type. He never failed to get what he wanted from people of any race if he wanted it badly enough, and sometimes he made the most sudden and astounding demands.

His internship was spent as one of Japan's first quarantine officers. He "passed" two American army physicians on their way to the Philippine Islands to trace to its source the yellow fever that scourged American cities during the nineteenth century. They aroused his interest both in epidemics and in America. Regarding the latter he got the idea that "freedom reigns and a man can push his way through to eminence." After a brief interval of experience in China he determined that it was time for him to go to America and that his friends must send him, even though one of them had to sell his wife's bridal kimono to provide passage money.

Here the pompous, improvident, bohemian side of Noguchi appears. The departure for the west of the one who was to become the world's greatest medico must be duly celebrated. Noguchi gave a banquet for himself. When the food and geisha had been paid for the passage money was gone. After everybody had sobered up his friends sold some more stuff. This time *they* bought the ticket—in steerage.

Noguchi turned up in Philadelphia before one of the United States army doctors he knew, without warning, with the bland statement that he had come to learn and work and all he would need from this friend would be living expenses. He got them.

The year Noguchi arrived, Dr. Walter Reed proved, through his experiment on two United States army privates in Havana who volunteered themselves as feeders for infected mosquitoes, that yellow fever was transmitted to human beings by mosquito bites. It remained for the Japanese boy, handling his tubes and microscopes with his one hand, to discover the germ.

In the laboratory he would work, as did Edison, for twenty, thirty or forty hours at a stretch. Then he would turn lazy as a turtle, and eventually come out of this to throw about all the money he could find or borrow. He nearly married a Japanese girl, then had an emotional flirtation with a Danish girl, and finally was married to an American girl from New York, who effaced herself and mothered him and his manuscripts and let him live according to his bents. No one, of course, could have done anything else with him. This woman, being wise, did not try.

Noguchi was working on snake-bite serums when, to the relief of his self-chosen patron the Rockefeller Medical Research Foundation took over his support. The old keeper of reptiles at the Philadelphia Zoo, if still alive, will hold you for hours telling stories of the quirks of "that funny Jap."

Noguchi's accomplishments in medicine include contributory work in infantile paralysis, snake-poison serum, and trachoma. It was he

who first procured a pure culture of the spirochete of syphilis and
determined the syphilitic nature of paresis (general paralysis) and
tabes dorsalis (locomotor ataxia). In 1918 he discovered the yellow
fever parasite and the newspapers discovered him. He developed a
prophylactic vaccine and curative serum for that dreaded plague,
which, along with mosquito elimination, abolished one of the greatest scourges of mankind.

The question remained as to whether the yellow fever of South
America and Africa was caused by the same or a slightly different
spirochete. Noguchi was the one to follow through and find out.

Before he began his investigations in dangerous portions of the
world, he went back to Japan to visit his mother. Japanese papers
tell how on September 8, 1915, he detrained at the new railway station in his little native hamlet to be met by its mayor and all the
dignitaries of the prefecture, dressed in celluloid wing collars and
the local version of frock coats. His clothing awry and unpressed as
usual, the scientist stepped to the platform, passed them, and bowed
before a wrinkled old peasant woman in worn but clean starched
kimono.

"Mother, I am Seisaku [his childhood name]," he repeated until
at last she recognized him. The tears coursed from her eyes but she
insisted that he go and be properly received by the official delegation
who had come to do him honor, before giving his attention to her.
The officials had been thrown off by hearing the man call himself
Seisaku, for they knew him as Hideyo. But the latter name, meaning
"great manner of the world," had been adopted by the young egotist
after he left his mother's side.

Noguchi took his mother and the old druggist pair who had been
his second parents, the Kobayashis, across the Inland Sea to the
great geisha dinner tendered him by Japan's notables in Osaka, the
New York of the empire. Much copy was furnished to the sentimental Japanese reporters by his attention to his mother and the
aged village drug-shop proprietor. The most popular geisha of the
city increased her publicity by weeping at the sight. Noguchi could
not persuade the humble old peasant, who had staked him, to come
to the great function. So before leaving his native village, he who
could be the most arrogant of human beings went to the peasant's

hut and against the protests of the overwhelmed old farmer knelt
and touched his forehead to the ground.

Noguchi's work in South America resulted in the isolation of the
parasite and germ of two of that continent's dread diseases. In 1928,
at the age of fifty-two, against the earnest protest of his wife and the
Rockefeller Institute staff, for he was already an advanced case of
diabetes, he organized with Stokes of America his expedition to the
infested Gold Coast of West Africa. "What does the persistence of
the fever there matter in comparison with your importance in the
world of medical science?" they asked him. It was his Japanese
pride, as well as the scientific mania, that took Noguchi to his death.
"They have suggested that I have jumped to conclusions," he replied. "If Noguchi is mistaken, Noguchi will be the one to prove it."

On the coast, at Acera, Stokes, first, placed the yellow fever mosquito on his wrist. The curative serum that worked on the American
continent did not save him. Soon afterward Noguchi was carried
aboard ship in a delirium. He died, muttering, "Funny Noguchi!"
Probably he thought it was an immense joke upon himself, or maybe
upon the world. He always dramatized himself. He had made ex-
periments of great importance but in his secretive Japanese manner
he would confide in no one until absolutely sure he could stand
against attack, and the knowledge gained at the cost of his life
perished with him.

V

Japan has already produced a goodly quota of men of science, the
best known of whom, aside from Noguchi, is Takamine, discoverer
of insulin and extender of the alphabet among the vitamins, who
also married a western woman. Takamine's work and name were
commercialized by a big New York firm. Another is Dr. Kitazato,
famous for pneumonic plague research although the culminating
work in this was done by the Chinese doctor Wu Lien-teh. Dr. Kitazato proved the tetanus infection to be the cause of lockjaw, and his
work led to the discovery of diphtheria antitoxin. He founded an
Imperial Serum Institute which discovered at least one of the dysen-
tery bacilli and made the first good serum. In 1925 Dr. Kitazato resigned from the deanship of Keio University Medical College be-

cause of a feeling of disgrace over the attempted suicide of his son, who had become involved with a geisha girl. The students themselves persuaded him to return. He is a great character. But Hideyo Noguchi, with his improvident, supersensitive, demanding, alternately gay and sullen temperament, his supreme egotism, and belief that he might more likely be right than the whole world, is overwhelmingly typical of the Japanese artist and esthetic type—as truly Nipponese as the warrior type. Many a top-flight American medico and scientist will never forget him.

Appropriately, the splendid biography of Noguchi was done by a German fellow scientist. In ambition, egotism, devotion to abstract ideals, ruthlessness in pursuit of an end, and fatalism, on the one hand; with an emotional and sometimes esthetic sentimentality that approaches the maudlin on the other, the Japanese and German minds show a marked similarity. The fineness of a Goethe is, I should say, more frequent among the Japanese. Alike, Japanese and Germans make indomitable warriors, persistent scientists, and emotional poets. The literal-mindedness, theoreticism and ignoring of human values that have brought down Germany from her high estate will also ruin Japan.[3] Time and place may have a great deal to do with it, and Japan's opportunity is more like ancient Rome's than that which confronted the Kaiser's Germany. Japan is still too new in this modern world for us to judge.

[3] As written in 1934.

Chapter XVI
Diplomats and Administrators

GROWING out of that over-rich mold of past Japan is another group of men, sometimes called liberals, who are no more liberal than Sir John Simon and make no boast of their idealism but merely profess a hard-boiled practicality and a certain gentlemen's pride of avoiding extremes. They have no directing but a certain tempering influence on events. They are the sort chiefly appointed to make contact with us and from whom we were all too apt to get our conception of Japan. They are not exciting or exhilarating as are Japan's gangsters, warriors, and saints. But they have played their part in the Pacific era of world history, and copy-desk men will need "morgue stuff" on them.

The first to deserve mention among them is old Prince Tokugawa (Iesato), not son by blood, but direct heir of the line which ruled Japan with absolute power from 1606 to 1867, and was then overthrown with some bloodshed. After a short period of penance the wealthy Tokugawa family was given top place in non-imperial blood nobility, with hereditary title of prince. For thirty-five years one present suave, luxury-loving, hospitable head of the house of Tokugawa was president of the house of peers.

As sponsor and national president of Rotary International in the Japanese Empire this aristocrat occupied a unique position as a good-will emissary, particularly to the United States. He was chosen to broadcast the first trans-Pacific Fourth of July message to the people of America (1934). He was the exponent of the patronizing philosophy of not getting excited.

Tokugawa was head of the Japanese delegation to the Washington Conference of 1922, lending weight rather than slant. The Prince was governor of the Japanese League of Nations Association until (on the occasion of Matsuoka's walking out of the Glass-House in Geneva) his organization opportunistically transmuted itself into the Japan International Society for the propagation abroad of the Japanese viewpoint. This is a sincere Japanese conception of the true function of an international society.

On his recent tour of the west the Prince, although growing pompous with age, distinguished himself at deck golf. He was a fan of the Japanese No drama, the lengthy, slow-moving pantomime of conventionalized and de-emotionalized passion, and a performing patron of one of its sects—who are in bitter controversy over the right way to sing it: whether by sputtering it through the nose or honking it from the back of the throat, etc. His other passion was for Japanese wrestling, which is a belly-pushing match between 350-pounders on a sand-sprinkled earthen dome.

The prince made some good hits on American public opinion. He pointed out the complementary nature of Japanese-American trade. "So far," he said, "we find ourselves rivals in only a very few things, such as piece goods, rayon, canned fish, rubber goods, electric-light bulbs, and light machinery." He neglected to say we would be rivals in every other manufactured product just as rapidly as Japan gets around to imitating it. He pointed out that Japan alone of great nations had not defaulted on an American loan. "Remember," said the Prince, "that we Japanese have been through a long period of anxiety over and proximity to two of the world's worst upheavals—the Chinese and Russian revolutions."

In southern United States he suggested that the maintenance of oriental relations and trade representation in China was a bothersome business, which we Americans don't understand anyhow, and which was apt to get us mixed up in international complications. Why not turn all this over to Japan? She would buy the cotton here, pay for it on the spot, and attend to export and manufacture through all of Asia—in fact, given a little time, the whole world. Some southern editors thought this an excellent idea. But the state and commerce departments in Washington felt that Americans were capable of maintaining direct contact with their own markets. Meanwhile, Japan plants cotton in North China and encourages the growth of long staple in the Argentine and near east.

The Prince's last action in the United States was a ceremonial inspection of the new Japanese culture center in Columbia University, where he exchanged complimentary speeches with President Nicholas Murray Butler. That Don Quixote of democracy should have recalled the Prince's famous gibe at democracy: "Are President Wilson and his chauffeur equals?" At any rate, the Japanese culture center seems to be demoted to just the plain—and exceedingly useful —Japanese room of the Columbia University library since Americans failed to provide funds matching the value of the Japanese-donated books.

II

Less aristocratic in type than the Prince were two liberals who graduated from Japan's army and navy to become Japan's great colonial administrators. They were Admiral Saito and General Ugaki.

Saito (Makoto) reminded one strongly of old Hindenburg of Germany. He was the only pilot who could steady Japan's helm following the epidemic of assassinations in 1932. For two years Saito kept the flame of patriotism within bounds. He said to the Japanese Parliament: "There is an abyss before us, but we must not face it with fear and unrest. It is necessary at this time to have a further faith in the nation. For this a conscience is needed."

Saito was described by a Japanese journalist as being "unstampedable as a mountain—a non-Japanese type winning by Fabian tactics." The Japanese phrase for Fabianism is "masterly irresolution," which the journalist thinks is rare among the hasty-tempered Nipponese. Any one who has tried to commit Japanese to this or that definite decision is inclined to feel that a maddening "masterly irresolution" is one quality of Japanese from bean-curd peddlers to premiers. Old Saito's nickname was Lord Dawn, an allusion to his predilection for sitting up over drinks and conversation till morning. Like Matsudaira and Konoye, he is a big man physically and the Japanese adage seems to hold good that bigness and amiability go together. Possibly in Japan this is a racial matter, where the large stature is credited back to the white Ainu aborigines, who in historical times populated the north—a genial people, in a bear-like way.

Saito began as a midshipman. He was from the north of Japan and the navy is run by and gives its promotions to Satsuma men from the extreme south, but the handsome Saito was able to repair this disability by marrying the daughter of the navy favorite, Admiral Nire, thus becoming a Satsuma by the familiar Japanese procedure of adoption. His promotion was rapid.

Saito became one of Prince Saionji's "boys," taking the post of premier when the political parties needed disciplining. But Saito's great job, and one that makes his personality an essential part of Japan's empire, was the pacification of Japan's first great imperial conquest, Korea. After an era of violence in Korea, including Japan's war with China in 1894-1895, her war with Russia in 1904-1905, and a Japanese-engineered assassination of the last Korean queen, the Tenno annexed Korea in 1911.

Incipient rebellion culminated in the black spring of 1919 when the Japanese army determined to down independence movements once and for all, and went to the length of crucifying Korean Christians and burying women agitators alive. The sympathizing American missionaries of Korea could not at that time be ignored or deported as they were later, and they bolstered up Korean hopes and gave Japan a black name throughout the world the while they offered Koreans the solace of Christianity. The amazing result was to make Christianity the favored religion of the people of this backward Asiatic land—a situation which militant Japanese Buddhists are now out to change.

Defending Japanese actions in Korea, Matsuoka flung a gibe at an American audience—that the Japanese, after all, killed fewer people in Korea than General Funston did in the Philippines, and Funston's water cure was perhaps no more pleasant than some punishments meted out to Koreans. However, the mess in Korea (renamed Cho-sen) needed cleaning up. Saionji sent Saito to do it, and his success is one of the best pieces of colonial administration in the history of imperialism. He was greeted with an explosion as he rode into Seoul on the governor-general's train. A piece of dynamite fell into his lap. He tossed it out the window without a quiver, nor did this expression of Korean hospitality influence his reconciliation policy. Saito's policy was one of enlightened paternalism, described by the Koreans as "the velvet paw of a cat." He yielded in no whit to the Woodrow Wilson doctrine of democracy and self-determination prevalent at Versailles and mouthed by Korean intellectuals trained in American-staffed Christian schools. His was the opposite and Japanese doctrine: "Maintenance of law, order, justice and material well-being are, more than is liberty, the bases of modern civilized society."

Thus Saito speaking in 1918, anticipated Mussolini in succinct statement of fascist philosophy. He did not neglect practical considerations. Japanese soldiers were ordered to hide their hatred of the missionaries behind unfailing courtesy, and the governor-general invited them to his teas and requested their advice in shaping the country's educational system. He compromised their opposition to Japanese rule by appointing a number of Japanese Christians as underadministrators. Saito quieted the young Korean intellectuals, although one can hardly say he won them over, by giving a certain number of them innocuous jobs with good salaries and letting them run newspapers, under careful censorship, of course.

To the Japanese, Saito said, "My most important service in Korea is to make the Koreans think and feel like the rest of us Japanese. There is still in Korea a combination superiority and inferiority complex which must be overcome." One wonders if there wasn't something like that in Japan also.

Practically, Saito's ten-year rule of Korea and his successor Ugaki's continuing velvet-paw administration worked out in the gradual replacing of Koreans by Japanese farmers on the rich rice lands of this picturesque peninsula, and in the creation of a delanded Korean proletariat which was pushed out on the Manchurian plains as pawns of Japan in that new vassal state, or made into a low-waged laboring class for the great Japanese war factories established on the Asian mainland. A million and a half of the 13,000,000 Koreans are already residents of the puppet kingdom of Manchu Tikuo (Manchukuo), but remain under direct Japanese authority.

A remarkable amount of highly scientific reclamation and flood prevention has been accomplished in Korea, but this benefits the Japanese settlers, and through them the big Japanese financiers, rather than Koreans.

The Koreans, and the Burmese at the other end of the Mongolian racial spread, are the true philosopher peoples of the yellow race. Japanese and British overlords have had difficulty converting them to ideas of work and thrift. An American friend operating a gold mine in Korea before the complete closure of the "open door" in the peninsula, made a good strike and, to share his fortune, doubled the hourly wages of his miners. The Chinese among them immediately came to ask if they couldn't work overtime, whereas the Koreans decided they could live by coming to work only every other day. Yet Koreans make more docile workmen and sturdier workmen than people of Japan or China, and under Japanese straw bosses enable Japan's industrialists to make goods even cheaper than they can be made in Japan.

The communist agitator replaced the Christian missionary as the messianic prophet to disgruntled Koreans. Problems too modern and complicated for Japan's Victorian type of administrator, Admiral Baron Saito, fell to the warlord Araki and fascist Matsuoka. Araki's first interest in Korea was the construction of one of the world's greatest plants for producing munitions and poison gas, an area fenced off behind thirty miles of electrified wire on the west coast of the peninsula, and connected by new railroads and freshly driven tunnels with the great basin of the Amur-Sungari river system of north Manchukuo and Siberia.

Placid Saito's favorite phrases were "exaltation of universal justice" and "progress of the nation's destiny." "When," said he, "the Empire is celebrating the arrival of the Crown Prince, the people of the nation whose central structure is the Imperial Household will strive for a regeneration of the national spirit, realization of the nation's ideals and fulfilment of the Empire's mission; but let them abide by the rescript 'to embrace the golden mean.' Our big defense budget is due to world conditions. We still have many problems and are still in a state of emergency. Japan at this time is being put to the test, but let us regard the emergency as a to-be-expected phase of national progress." Saito is father of the tactics described by

Ariyoshi (Akira), hearty minister to China, as the "duck method"; looking as placid as a picture above water while paddling furiously underneath.

In spite of militarists, naval building races, imperial progress on the continent, and a budget fifty per cent unbalanced, old statesman Saito had time to consider the education of primary-school children. Following the resignation of his young minister of education, caught in the sort of textbook graft frequently winked at in the United States, Saito himself headed a committee to draft a new educational system, with a complete revision of textbooks "for the inculcation of morals instead of personal ambition." Morals in Japan means primarily loyalty of the sort Araki and Matsuoka talk about. But Saito tried to combine with them the Confucian balance and sense of proportion, "the golden mean" which was the core of his own life. He devoted the last years of his weighty life to building little children into a generation to survive, and succeed, the Matsuokas and the Arakis.

III

Ugaki (Kazunari, also called Issei) is a type of Japanese in whom the scientific viewpoint takes precedence. He drew up and put through the plans for the complete mechanization of the army by late 1935. Substituting mechanical and scientific efficiency for numbers and tradition, he cut the army by four divisions and eliminated many officers. Naturally he wasn't popular. It was a relief in all quarters when he was given Korea to boss.

In Korea, Ugaki continued Saito's velvet-paw colonial policy with the greatest success. I have never seen a finer group of young administrators than Japanese department heads under Saito and Ugaki, some of them trained in America. Ugaki is very popular with the peasants, toward whose interests he inclines by natural bent, and was asked at one time to organize a peasants' party. But for us his chief importance is that he mechanized the army.

But the industrial and export crowd centering in Osaka (Japan's New York and Chicago combined), whose suspicion of Tokyo officials is analogous to that which New York interests feel toward Washington, invited Ugaki to come and put himself in the spotlight for premier. His journey might have had policy-affecting results had his influence not been killed by an incident which sheds light on petty political and social customs in Japan. His small ship stopped at the sacred island of Miyajima for a visit to the great shrine and torii which at high tide stands out in the sea. As he was descending his gangplank two geishas suddenly appeared. As the press photographers touched off their bulbs, one was hanging from either arm of the great military reformer and administrator.

The next morning General Araki, hero of the super-patriots, who takes pride in his virtue, and on whom no one ever "got anything," lectured through the Japanese press to 50,000,000 interested readers on the impropriety of frivolity on the part of high political aspirants at this moment of national crisis. This message appeared alongside the flashlight photos of Ugaki and geishas. There was nothing to be done about it. The tourist trade of the beautiful sacred island where no vehicle is allowed, not even a rickshaw, but where geishas abound, has not since suffered. A serious reverberation of this incident was the conspiracy among university students to assassinate General Ugaki on the occasion of Admiral Togo's state funeral.

As to availability to head the cabinet in a future crisis Ugaki speaks in parables: "When we have headaches we call a doctor. When a garden has dandelions, we get a gardener." He can never, however, be more than a stopgap in the trend toward the extreme expression of Japan's divine mission.

General Ugaki's human and artistic side was shown when he posed for a struggling young artist whose painting was thrown out of an exhibit because one uniform was inaccurate. This fine, handsome man with his wide brow and intelligent, responsive face will be remembered more for mechanizing the army for its nationalistic job, than for keeping that nationalism within bounds.[1]

IV

Some of Japan's diplomats are striking fellows for looks. One such is high-born Matsudaira, long at Washington and the court of St. James, 180-pound outdoor man and music lover of dashing

[1] These two paragraphs as written, 1934.

appearance who held swimming records when a student, and whose Washington-educated daughter became consort of the Emperor's westernized younger brother, Prince Chichibu. This freedom-loving Chichibu (revised spelling "Titibu"!) was an unhopeful Crown Prince. The superpatriots were not more relieved than himself by the birth of a male child to the Imperial Couple.

It is the job of Japanese diplomats to preserve the outer aspect of Japanese unity and the illusion of Japanese adherence to treaties and observance of international good form. They do it remarkably well, considering what they are up against. Viscount Ishii reports the chronic complaint of the Japanese embassy in London before the war, that navy men backed by the navy influence at home constantly interfered with foreign-office orders and embassy business. The embassy in Berlin registered a complaint of the same nature against the army and Japan's minister to Peking said that military officers constantly overrode with haughty arrogance the diplomacy of his ministry.

But the diplomatic mind is important and interesting only when motivated by deeper interests than a distinguished career, as in the case of the divine-mission impulse in Hirota or with the veteran Viscount Ishii (Kikujiro), in whom we find the polished diplomatic mind allied, as Japan's older diplomacy has chiefly been, with industrial interests.

Ishii is a suave gentleman, well known to program committees of the American chambers of commerce. He is the high confessor of Japan's inner clique of plutocrats. He toured America to advise a "business man's common-sense settlement" of difficulties on the Pacific. He put before the ex-statesmen, financiers, and lady members of the Japan Society at the inevitable banquet in New York the proposition that the Kellogg pact should be revised to include outlawry of boycotts as well as war, and was on the point of carrying this to President Roosevelt when the merchants of Osaka decided to boycott Indian cotton growers until Great Britain should release a larger share of India's piece-goods market. Japanese talk about the immorality of boycotts and their equivalency to war, which had been taken up by American pacifists and Senator Borah, stopped forthwith.

Ishii returned to Japan to inform his people that both Franklin Roosevelt and Ramsay MacDonald asked him not about Japanese armies in Manchuria but about rubber-soled shoes in the United States and the British Isles. He was astonished, he said, by their interest in such small matters, but considered it significant. Japanese industrialists required something more vigorous than Ishii diplomacy. They were preparing for trade war with no quarter given and none asked. Diplomatic kidding had had its day. Ishii was temporarily successful with it when times were more favorable. He induced Wilson's Secretary of State Lansing to sign an executive understanding (without treaty status under the American constitution) recognizing Japan's "paramount interest due to propinquity" in Manchuria. The question soon arose as to whether interest means curiosity or privilege or right. For instance, any young man has an interest due to propinquity, in the young ladies about him, but possessive assertions must be based on more than proximity.

When the United States state department was given to understand the Japanese definition, "Ishii's Lansing agreement" quickly went into the wastebasket. It was a Japanese diplomatic stunt. The most spectacular stunt perpetrated by a high Japanese diplomat on American officialdom and public was in 1915. The Associated Press man in Peking, Frederick Moore, cabled a scoop on the Twenty-one Demands made by Japan, written by the very Hirota who is now foreign minister. The demands were, in sum, that the Chinese President Yuan Shih-kai, who was then plotting to make himself emperor, sign over to Japan control of China's army, navy, treasury, police, concessions in Manchuria, and a few minor items of sovereignty. This was so that Japan could protect China from the kaiser. Yuan took the risk of the threatened Japanese invasion and personal assassination in disclosing these demands to the American newspapers. He wanted to discover whether China could count on help from Woodrow Wilson. So astounding was the news that it went up to Melville Stone, president of the Associated Press, who took it to Secretary of State William Jennings Bryan.

The two called on the suave Chinda, then ambassador at Washington, to ask him if the report wasn't utterly impossible. And Chinda gave them the assurance expected and some tea, where-

upon Frederick Moore was told to take a vacation for his nerves
and cable no more rumors at forty cents a word. In disgust, Moore
went to the Japanese legation in Peking and impressed upon them
his value, which later resulted in a five-year connection with the
propaganda department of Japan's foreign office. When Secretary
Bryan asked Ambassador Chinda why he lied, the Ambassador
replied that he was obeying instructions, and furthermore, what
would Mr. Bryan expect?

Yet, counting on our short memories, Japanese diplomats come
regularly to instruct Americans. In Ishii's memoirs he attributes
his influence in signing up Lansing to the good audiences and press
that followed his dinner speeches in New York. The same tactics
didn't work with Franklin Roosevelt and Secretary of State Hull.
Ishii and his type then gave way to Amau and Kurusu. Then Tojo
dispensed with all diplomats.

Ishii's sly advice to his own people that "no policy is wiser for
Japan than to uphold the theory of open competition, for Japan
is endowed with all factors to outdo foreigners in Manchuria and
all of China," appealed no longer to the new militarists, statesmen,
and industrialists. They were more and more inclined to an open
showdown with the west. Their substitute for Ishii's old-fashioned
diplomacy was Amau's manifesto.

v

The last great liberal statesman of Japan was Baron Shidehara
(Kijuro). Like Ishii connected with Japanese big business, married
into the Iwasaki family (the second richest in the empire) he
graduated from the big-business attitude into as fine a sense of international fair play as has been seen in a modern world statesman.

Shidehara, self-possessed, democratic in manner, who could make
as delightful a ten-minute English speech as I have ever heard,
served as vice-minister under five cabinets, then became minister,
when "Old Lion" Hamaguchi, last of Japan's great party chiefs, was
shot by a superpatriot. Shidehara had to take the active leadership
of Japanese "good neighborism." Hamaguchi lingered on for a year.
Then the patriots demanded his presence, according to custom,

wound or no wound, in the Diet. Hamaguchi went against doctor's orders and died. And the patriots' hatred henceforth centered upon Shidehara, who had promoted the Washington Conference, upheld the London Agreements, and insisted that foreign policy should respect the lawful rights and interests of other countries as well as the protection of Japan's own.

The patriots called him weak-hearted and fawning and nonresistant. They frothed at the mouth when a Japanese adventurer disappeared in China or a Chinese loan was defaulted and Shidehara held them back from using the army. Chinese diplomats, pretty helpless themselves, hastened his downfall by their slowness in conducting reasonable negotiations with him. Coincident with the leap of the Japanese army in Manchuria, the mob at home set upon Shidehara, yelling for his blood for the crime of putting the rights of other nations on a plane with those of Japan and hesitating to flout treaty commitments. His subordinates, men he had given appointments, publicly cursed him from their security under the wing of the army. The mild-mannered, fearless diplomat was saved from assassination such as overtook lesser figures only by the bursting of a blood vessel in his brain. For months he lay at the point of death in his castle-like home near the sea, which is encircled by steep hills like a wall and reached through a private tunnel.

Hirota, a very different man actuated by a very different philosophy, then sat at the chief desk of the foreign office, but the superpatriots recognized that Shidehara's detailed knowledge was vastly greater than theirs and permitted him to come and advise them, when he was able to get to the capital with the aid of canes. They permitted him to proceed with his great work on the diplomatic history of Japan, which the Emperor has underwritten.

One of his last acts was to defend the right of Japan's friends to maintain mental independence, and the writer owes to Shidehara's intervention the fact that he was not expelled from the Japanese islands in spite of newspaper attacks, fuming patriots, and his "deportation"—by airplane—from Manchukuo. There are those who say Japan will again need and call on Shidehara. I agree with the first part of this.

Chapter XVII

Gods in Politics

W̅E̅ H̅A̅V̅E̅ had a glimpse of the charming liberals whose job was to dress Japan for western eyes, and cover by diplomatic front the advancing bayonets. We have to be introduced to one more type of man before we know the entire Japanese political family.

The Japanese sort of "gods in politics" existed nowhere else in the modern world. They were not deified heads of revolutions such as Lenin and Hitler. Five families in Japan are called kami-no, or "godly," because by tradition they have the same divine ancestry as the Son of Heaven himself. The imperial consort must come from among the women of these five families. Japanese "gods in politics" are members of these five Sacred Families who are called to mundane political and official work. Their status protects them from ordinary political blame and defamation, and protects the régime which uses them from being overthrown by ordinary political methods and by the equally ordinary—in Japan—method of assassination. You can see how important are these moderators and conservators.

Perhaps the type disappeared, its usefulness over forever, when Saionji died and Konoye passed the premiership to warlord Tojo in the fateful summer of 1941. Perhaps it will be used again, to great effect, by a Japan that must placate victors or get on with rivals. In any case the kami in politics is an important and unique feature of the face of Japan which we must know to see Japan as she was when she engulfed the western hemisphere and the Pacific—three-fourths of the world—in war.

The author wrote of Saionji in 1934:

"Prince Saionji (Kimochi), ninety-five years of age—officially—last of the genro or elder statesmen, voice of the Divine Person, walks with his shepherd's staff amid hysteria, assassination, and dissimulation.

"Anything may happen upon the taking away of this fragile life, unless Saionji can build younger men into an equal position of prestige. He alone has prevented militarists or fascists from taking supreme and open control."

"The military," said the newspaper *Yomiuri*, "feel it essential that the nation assume a policy of expanding armaments. No time can be lost. Vast sums of money must be spent to meet the situation. The present political system cannot be relied upon. It follows according to the military that what our country needs is one big party to give expression to the will of all classes. There appears no reason to believe that the military leaders will not have their way unless Prince Saionji is able to save the constitution again."

About a century before William the Conqueror founded English Norman nobility the House of Saionji was established by the Emperor Murakami. Every one who has been in Kyoto has visited the Kinkokuji, the Golden Shrine—built by a Saionji in the twelfth century, on one of the great bronze bells of which may be read the dedication by the elder statesman's ancestors.

Prince Saionji was not born a Saionji—no Saionji ever is. For this branch of the Fujiwaras carries to extreme the Japanese custom of acquiring heirs by adoption rather than birth. The virility and mentality of Japanese houses from the most noble down to those of small business has been preserved by the intelligent, but to us not exactly affectionate, preference of a bright younger son of some poor relative or friend over a stupid or spoiled offspring. This is a phase of the still prevalent custom of exchanging sons for rearing. The custom existed in Sparta, medieval France and England, and modern research in the anti-social effects of parental spoliation might well bring it back in the west, unless it is precluded by the new Russian system of communal child-rearing.

So long ago that the true reason is lost in the mists, a Saionji pledged all succeeding bearers of the name against marriage. One version has it that this Saionji's pet deity was Benten, the virgin goddess of beauty and talent. Benten, being a jealous little snip, will not permit herself to be worshiped by married people. Her jealous curse was heavy on this early Saionji's unfortunate wife and in sympathetic distress he decreed that no Saionji henceforth should have a wife. Another story is that the family totem, a white snake, which can be found in the ancient shrine in Kyoto, would become incarnated in any woman who might marry the head of the house —sufficient reason to confirm any family chief in bachelordom.

The most likely explanation of the Saionji custom is that the early Saionjis, much influenced by Buddhism as were all the Fujiwaras, took the vow of celibacy in some priestly connection and this became a tradition. In any case this family preserves as much family solidarity as in any family of which mother and child are the core, and gains in addition a unique position in the minds of the eccentricity-loving Japanese people. Of course, the absence of wives and mothers in the Saionji family does not rob its men of the comfort of women. The Saionjis may take concubines, and are considered exempt from the not very seriously enforced modern Japanese law against secondary wives. Their natural sons, however, may not become heirs to the name and estate.

The present Saionji was born a Mori, and the Moris were the lords of Choshu who ruled the end of the main island near the Asiatic continent till the end of feudalism in 1869. Choshu has since produced ninety per cent of the high officers of the Japanese army. Prince Saionji, of divine blood by adoption—a hurdle easy for the Japanese mind—yet has blood ties with most of the Japanese army commanders. Another Mori by birth was adopted as heir by the great General Nogi. In 1934 he turned back his inherited peerage to the Emperor and his name to the Nogi family, saying he was unworthy of them—an exhibition of humility without parallel in the west.

II

Saionji was made a boy courtier at the age of four, that he might be playmate of the Crown Prince—who was to become in youth the Emperor of the restoration, Mutsuhito, the only Emperor of modern times to take a personal active leadership in the state.

Thus Saionji bore the prestige of having been youthful mate and manhood friend to the Emperor worshiped after his death, under the posthumous title of Meiji, as an equal of Jimmu Tenno, founder of the "divine" line. Vast, beautiful, and costly shrines and sacred parks to Meiji in Tokyo, Keijo (Seoul, capital of Korea), and elsewhere outdo, I think, anything ever built in the world, ancient or modern, in so short a time, to honor man become god. Saionji's blood brother was adopted into the Sumitomo family of financiers, and became the head of Japan's second largest bank and money king of Osaka, Japan's New York.

The old statesman was well entrenched, you see. Yet so were the Tokugawas, eighty years ago; and when the youngsters of the peasantry wrote oaths in their own blood to assassinate him and overthrow the dominance over the Imperial Person of new lords of wealth and industry, Saionji saw only too clearly the parallel to the group that overturned entrenched wealth and authority in his youth, whom he then had ebulliently joined.

In his teens he had returned from Paris full of Rousseauism, and founded a newspaper, *The Oriental Free Press,* actually advocating a republic. His idea was that a Japanese republic could still retain the Divine Emperor. The young noble further scandalized exclusive Japan by giving dinners in honor of authors and actors à la Paris. A commoner or petty aristocrat doing such things would have been promptly trundled off to jail, but there was no way to stop the young Fujiwara nobleman until the Divine Person himself, Saionji's ex-playmate, in gracious words requested the discontinuance of the publishing venture. Since then no member of the high nobility has ventured into journalism. It was therefore natural that Saionji, grown old, could understand and lovingly correct Prince Konoye, when this young fellow-clansman, after reading Tolstoy and Kropotkin, scandalized his family by requesting permission to resign all titles to the nobility.

During Saionji's middle career he held many high offices, including the premiership, and acted as plenipotentiary at several European capitals. After his return from the Versailles Peace Conference he was a maker of officials, rather than an officeholder. In 1920, against general aristocratic and military opposition, he asked the Emperor to appoint for the first time a non-noble, non-uniformed political party chief to the premiership in the person of the commoner Hara. Hara was assassinated, but every following chief of the Japanese government had to have his name offered to the Emperor by Prince Saionji.

Saionji was the sole survivor of the inner group of adventurous youngsters under Saigo, Katsu, and their generation, who transformed Japan from medievalism into one of the world's great powers. This group at one-third the age were as revolutionary in their time as the Matsuokas of to-day. Yet they grew up to become the Tenno's elder statesmen. The first to receive this honor was Ito, drafter of the constitution; the second Yamagata, organizer of Japan's modern army; the third Inouye, Ito's comrade and establisher of Japan's monetary system; the fourth Kiyotaka; the fifth Kuroda of Russo-Japanese War fame; the sixth the younger Saigo; the seventh Matsukata; and the eighth, last, and youngest, Prince Saionji. The contumacy of this group while still young was not dangerous to the world at large, as is Japanese impatience to-day. In their youth the older industrial and maritime powers of the west were flattered at young Japan's imitation. Other nations were patronizing and helpful and Saionji and his associates developed a trustful friendliness toward the western powers not present in to-day's revolutionaries. The young restoration Emperor, Mutsuhito, held the reins on the fiery young steeds who pulled Japan along while they nipped at one another. He knew just when to slacken on one and pull in on another. Saionji, ten years younger than the other members of the group, was taken into it because of his savoir faire, independence of spirit, and intimacy with the Tenno. He lied about his age, boosting it from fifteen to twenty-one. Right willingly would he have deducted the extra six years from the official year book later—but the reckoning, being official, stood.

This inner group ruled Japan under the emperor throughout the violent and crucial twenty years between the fall of the Tokugawa feudal régime in 1869 and the promulgation of the constitution drafted by the intrepid Ito (of the group) with advice given in Prussia by Prince von Bismarck (taken down by the youthful Saionji acting as Ito's clerk). After 1889 parliamentary forms existed. But the already veteran group went right on doing the ruling. Saionji was its last surviving member.

The new constitution provided for the emperor's voice to be expressed and parliament to be mentored by a privy council of some thirty tried statesmen appointed by the emperor upon the nomination of the cabinet head. The eight veterans became the inner clique of that privy council, each bearing the title, not provided for constitutionally, of genro (g as in "go")—"elders." In time all its members save its youngest died full of honor and years and received state funerals. Then in 1927 Saionji procured the emperor's promise that their vacant seats would not be filled—but that he might go down in history as the "last of the genro." He was the last of more than that.

Saionji's idea seemed to be that the minister of the Imperial Household, the lord high chamberlain of the court, and the president of the privy council, and any living ex-premiers should succeed to the job of sitting on the lid in Japan. But the military blew it off.

Saionji's capacity for acting as combined lid-sitter and safety valve in the right proportion enabled Japan for long to follow a grand *weltpolitik* of getting what she wanted without actually clashing irreparably with her displeased neighbors. When in 1933 the young crowd took the bit in their teeth and were obviously going to quit the League of Nations, Saionji had the Emperor issue an edict endorsing in conservative language what was being done, while cautioning that nothing exciting was to grow out of it. Before Matsuoka could get back to Tokyo from Geneva, Saionji had arranged that the most outspoken expansionists would hold no place in high office. The ninety-year-old statesman, although he did not visit Tokyo for two years, was on the job!

When the Saito cabinet fell he surprised Japan and Admiral Okada, whom he had not seen for five years, by placing that fairly conservative navy officer in the premiership and through him laying squarely on the complaining navy full responsibility to prepare to battle the United States and to do it in a way not ruinous to the nation.

During the decade between Hara and the military revolution of 1931, Saionji consistently nominated majority party heads for the premiership. After the military outburst accompanying the seizure of Manchuria this was out of the question. In his great old age, Saionji, like Hindenburg of Germany, was forced to give way to new forces.

Amid the flames, Saionji's aristocratic leisureliness of mind preserved him. A member of the Japanese House of Peers writing in English said that the secret of Saionji's life was the three "ins"; intelligence, indifference, indolence. His contemporary, the strenuous Okuma, called him a cool but breezy poet in politics. He passed his time reading novels, writing verse, and playing on the biwa, the Japanese banjo which is a traditional hobby in his noted family.

Saionji's restraining and humanizing influence on the fulfilment of Japan's divine mission on the Asiatic continent can be deduced from an incident which took place on his tour of Manchuria following the Russo-Japanese war. At a military banquet he heard a high Japanese officer speak superciliously to a Chinese general, invited for the sake of form rather than his importance. The ever-mild civilian, Saionji, personally rebuked the army officer on the spot, and required of him an apology which he dared not refuse. If Japan ever wins China over, it will be because she has Saionjis as well as Arakis.

Japan, essentially a medieval-minded nation, basically unneighborly, attained such neighborly standing as she possessed in the world because of her Saionjis. They alone have that larger sense of humor which is the sense of proportion. Nippon's great good luck is that her godly ones do not take themselves too seriously. This preserves her, while the fact that her people take her gods most seriously gave her a tremendous advantage in a sophisticated milk-and-water world of moderns who had nothing to fight for—only everything to whimper against.

Saionji spent in all nearly twenty years of his life abroad. Prince Otto von Bismarck commented upon Saionji's brilliant powers of conversation when he was Japanese minister to the imperial Prussian court. It is interesting to compare the influence of western residence upon Saionji and upon men of the later generation, like Matsuoka and Hirota. When the trend in the west was liberal and international it was liberal and international in Japan—even among persons born under feudalism and part of an aristocracy claiming divine descent. When the west became nationalistic, militaristic, and petty, Japan outdid all the western nations in these tendencies. Japan is the world's barometer—the Japanese are the most sensitive to world currents of any people on earth.

With political parties dead before they reached maturity, Japan was a ship going full steam ahead, driven by fascist-minded super-patriots. The ship rushed on in a zigzag course. When the hand of the impatient young element became temporarily uncertain on the wheel, the hand of the cautious older element, strengthened by the imperial touch, bore back. But there was no reversal of the course— the resultant direction is implacably forward, and probably a lot of rocks were missed by the zigzagging before the final head-on clash.

III

From aged Prince Saionji, the most important personage in the empire, who has never been interviewed or permitted a direct quotation of his words although once he ran a newspaper, we pass to younger Prince Konoye, a favorite of the Japanese press and interviewed by reporters all over America.

Imagine a six-footer, bland, handsome, democratic-mannered— who in the firm belief of 70,000,000 people is a descendant of the gods and whom even we must accept as the head of the oldest noble family in the world. This prince, Konoye (Fumimaro), trained at the knee of an aristocrat of his own clan, Saionji, was the last hope of representative government in Nippon! In his youth he had what Japan considers radical tendencies, but this only endeared him to old Saionji, who had similar youthful enthusiasms and knew how to handle them. At forty-four years of age, Konoye was considered very young for high office (the average age of high office holders in Japan is about sixty-five) but he became head of the most sublime of the Five Sacred Houses, and soon afterward, premier. The Imperial House which has no name, or a name which, like the Hebrews' Jahweh, must not be spoken, stems directly from the Goddess of the Sun; whereas the Five Sublime Houses, from which the emperor must take his consort, stem from the related gods who accompanied the grandson of the Goddess of Light in an emigration to the Japanese archipelago. Here the gods found barbarians whom they reduced to submission and into whom they infused divine blood— thus founding the Japanese nation.

The democratic-mannered Prince Konoye, as every Japanese schoolchild is taught, is the descendant of the highest ranking of the original group of godly adventurers, the god Koyane-no-Mikoto (*no* means what *de* does in French or *von* in German). His is the head house of the clan of Fujiwara. For twenty-one generations, according to official Japanese history, the descendants of Koyane occupied the high place of priestly mediators before the emperor. The twenty-first of the priestly line (about A.D. 625, near the beginning of authentic history) turned warrior-avenger against the Soga clan, who revolted and, for the one time in Japanese annals, dared to kill a god-emperor. The Sogas had been the first adopters of Buddhism in Japan and wanted to keep control of it in their own hands.

They were exterminated, and the Koyane high priest was given the family name of Fujiwara (meaning "wisteria plain"), the greatest name in Japanese history. For half a millennium, through its superiority in Chinese culture, through its patronage of Buddhism which swept the land, and through its women and regents in the Imperial Court, the Fujiwaras were the voice of the Emperor and the land's wealthiest lords. An outsider is inclined to ask, indeed, how much of the blood of the Goddess of the Sun still persists in the male head of the Divine House, and whether, with one Emperor after another for scores of generations taking a Fujiwara woman as consort, the Imperial Family itself is not overwhelmingly Fujiwara.

Thus the newest comer in Japanese politics ties up this twentieth-century empire of submarines and piece-goods yardage with the age of the gods. Yet the nearer one gets to the Holy of Holies in Japan, the less mysticism he is likely to encounter, and whereas Matsuoka and Araki talk "divine mission," Prince Konoye talks in language understood by Americans.

IV

Konoye's aristocracy is so unimpeachable that he can afford to be democratic, and he backed his younger brother's decision to follow a public musical career, which scandalized many Japanese commoners. The younger Konoye, after studying in Europe, founded and conducts the Tokyo Symphony Orchestra. To see a descendant of the gods swinging a baton, leading Japanese musicians in Ravel or Gershwin, is one of the sights of paradoxical Japan. In 1934, at the invitation of the American maestro, Henry Hadley (whom the author of this book had previously taken to Japan), musician Konoye came on a guest-conducting tour of the west.

Prince Konoye visiting America to see his son graduate from a prep school for Princeton, said that the constant thought in his mind was of the eight millions added to Japan's population in the last ten years. He believed that such increase, taking place at a million a year, could be cared for only by industrialization. Where get the raw materials and sell the finished goods in sufficient quantities? The principal answer as he saw it was "China," although the industrialists themselves expanded that to "the world." He feared that Russia would get the lead in China through communist indoctrination; should that take place Japan would suffocate. He did not think Japan needed to come into clash with the Anglo-Saxon world, he didn't like big navy budgets, he preferred increased taxes to bond issues.

When he took his seat in the House of Peers he dared to go against the old aristocrats—including his father—on the matter of support of political party rule. For this Prince Saionji, the imperial voice, made Konoye, one of the youngest peers, president of the House in the stead of pompous old Prince Tokugawa. In a pinch, as last ditch against the peasant-born militarists, Saionji let his protégé enter the arena of politics.

A cabinet head who could see the Imperial Person at any time without intermediaries or formalities was a powerful figure. But when Tojo was ready, Konoye stepped aside, assuming blame before a dummy parliament for not "completing the China incident," with tears coursing down his aristocratic face. Now the warrior Tojo, with no Saionji to stand between, sees the weak young Emperor at will.

We of the west must not think the Konoye democracy of manner implies any lessening of fidelity to the imperial tradition. The liberal prince's statement upon the coronation of the puppet emperor of Manchukuo was sufficiently revealing: "The fulfilment of a destiny anticipated for decades." In the minds of Japan's aristocrats, the rest of China also earnestly anticipated a similar glorious destiny!

JAPAN AGAINST THE WORLD

Chapter XVIII
Modern Samurai

JAPAN was an auger for boring deep. Conservators like Saionji provided its solid shank. Such diplomats, official and unofficial, as suave, aristocratic Tokugawa and dissimulating Ishii were the oil for cooling the friction of its progressive penetration. The blood brotherhoods were its drive. It is now time for us to look at the lively military and naval figures who are its pointed bit and the fiery or sullen demagogues and spokesmen who are its screw bevel for holding gains.

The most self-explanatory and spectacular character of the warrior class is the five-foot-two General Araki (Sadao), who can be a covered brazier as well as a firebrand. Counting on murder-minded cadets and starving peasants whipped to the verge of action by Toyama's "mob" to force the civil government into line, this "twentieth-century samurai" took the army and proceeded to conquer Manchuria in defiance of the world. He was ready to move farther —on against Russia—when the noble lid-sitters, aided by an influenza epidemic that gripped Araki's diminutive body, prevailed upon him to take a vacation.

Sitting on his feet on tatami mats, dressed in formal kimono, the low-voiced, mild-spoken, actively gesturing little general wrote rousing statements for the press which forced elder statesmen, politicians, diplomats, and industrial barons into line. By way of relaxation he wrote hokku—seventeen-syllable poem-epigrams—on the Japanese spirit, or on cherry blossoms. The cherry falling to the ground in all its blooming promise is the literary symbol of the divine selflessness of the race—much found in its poets, warriors, and ladies of the demi-monde.

"We shall have a new samurai class," says Araki, "who, like our medieval warriors, will live simply, and only for the Emperor." Araki is the most striking phenomenon of the combination of western instruments and medieval mind—modern Japan. He is a Moses shooting his way out of Egypt in an armored car, insisting the while upon literal observance of the ten commandments and the feast of the passover. When Araki proposes that the two major and one minor political parties of Japan dissolve themselves by general acclamation, to be replaced by government by direct imperial rule, backed by a single party comprised of representatives of all classes and all organizations, it is not taken as theory. The political bosses and their plutocratic connections don't talk back. They just hope that their keeping still will lead the doughty little warrior and his crowd to focus on something else for a while.

The economic and financial systems of the country built on western competitive philosophy are all wrong, Araki says. He urges wholesale rejection of western thought which must be prevented from contaminating the country. "To know oneself and the enemy is the secret of victory.... For the Japanese successfully to cut a way through the heaps of difficulties there is only one method and that is the thorough realization that they are Japanese.... We who believe in the Japanese tradition and feel the pressing power of the Nippon spirit sincerely hope that every member of the nation, without a single exception, will awake from his nightmare and that all the people will unite in carrying out the heavenly way." The communism of Russia and the individualism of America are equally vicious to Araki. The educational system which teaches individual ambition and the false worship of success must be revised completely. "All ideas in conflict with the Japanese spirit must be barred."

Araki of the impoverished Southern Island peasantry, self-disciplined after the Spartan code of the feudal samurai, who gave a lesson to wriggling, noisy members of Parliament by sitting on his feet without moving for six hours in the balcony of the lower house, is haunted by the same idealism that moved the radical wing of the German Nazis. Like them, he finds his proletarianism swamped. The empire, three times as large as Japan proper, that he carved out of China to relieve pressure upon Japanese peasant and laborer, is turned into a potato patch for the Mitsuis and the Iwasakis whom he had promised to squeeze dry.

Araki found that these Japanese J. P. Morgans and Andrew Mellons were the only persons who could buy the bonds and manufacture the equipment to keep 800,000 of his Japanese troops and Manchurian legions overseas and make Japan supreme in the Pacific. And, a true military man, he must put money and supplies for his forces before economic reform. Yet Japan's best military mind alarmed the plutocrats by wandering to the distress of old neighbors bending their backs to plant rice and hatching cocoons with the heat of their own bodies, while having neither rice to eat nor silk to wear. Typically, he saw a military solution of it all, and said, "Soldiers have always saved Japan. To our soldiers shall fall the grave responsibility for quieting unrest in our agrarian communities—both material and spiritual unrest." [1]

II

As to Japan's diplomacy, Araki put the words into the mouth of his foreign minister, Hirota, "All are eager to fulfil the mission of our nation. Withdrawal from the League was due to its views fundamentally differing from our intention of maintaining permanent peace in the orient as the heavenly mission of Japan. The Manchurian incident has made us realize our destiny and duty. It was nothing but an international application of the national spirit. In time this spirit will be recognized by the world."

The miniature, redoubtable General Araki was not ambiguous as to the foreign obstacles that Japan might have to sweep aside. Araki once said to an American (the foreign office asked the interviewer not to publish it): "If the Soviet does not cease to annoy us, I shall have to purge Siberia as one cleans a room of flies."

To the newspapers he explained: "Since every nation conducts war preparations with its neighbors as the objectives, it is natural that the U.S.S.R. is the hypothetical objective of our army, and the United States navy the hypothetical objective of our navy." Araki

[1] Newspapers of November 1, 1933.

was conducting at the moment the most elaborate army manœuvers in Japan's history in the presence of the Son of Heaven himself, directly opposite Russia's port at Vladivostok, and at about the same time his brother officers of the navy were winding up grand manœuvers of 138 vessels of the Japanese fleet between the Philippine Islands and Nippon. However, "preparedness," stipulated Araki, "doesn't mean rash action."

Araki was the show piece at the mammoth mass meeting[2] of young men's organizations at which Matsuoka and the ministers of education and agriculture proposed the pan-Asia doctrine to delegations that had either come from, or been drafted to represent, India, China, Turkey, Persia, Afghanistan, Siam, Malaya and the Philippines. A program was submitted for the "emancipation of Asia" from white domination under the lead of Japan. Pan-Asianism has had greater psychological influence on the people of Japan than material results among the varied peoples of Asia proper. Yet its influence is not lost upon Indian revolutionists and the intelligentsia of all dark populations. China and Korea, of course, got the real flavor of Japan's type of "emancipation." But no such tough tradition of resistance to a unity imposed from above exists among the Asian peoples as that which made failures of the attempts of Charlemagne, Napoleon, and Kaiser Wilhelm II to unify Europe. Indian revolutionaries, who have their largest "cell" in Osaka, enjoy the kudos given them in Japan, make good use of Japanese contributions, and publish "dangerous thoughts" freely so long as they circulate them only in "white" empires. Dealers in "freedom" and narcotics are alike required to confine their trade to Japan's neighbors.

Japan's ultimate success with her brand of Japan-Asianism depended upon her political and military success against Russia and the United States, and her commercial success against Great Britain. Asia waited to see—and less and less skeptically of late.

The temporary heroes of Araki's undeclared war on China of 1931-1933 suffered a strange mortality. Generals Taman and Honjo, who marched their men thousands of miles over frozen plains of north and south Manchuria, succumbed soon afterward to illness. General

[2] Hibiya Park, December 16, 1933.

Muto, Japan's first Manchurian commissioner—the supreme power in the "independent" state of Manchukuo—died with suspicion-arousing suddenness from what seems to have been cancer. An attendant at Japan's victory celebration at Shanghai suddenly walked forward and placed a bomb on the rostrum. Japanese police stated that he was a Korean communist—who hasn't been heard of since—but persistent rumor says he was a Japanese superpatriot out to punish his country's high officials for victory so delayed that it was a national loss of face. He killed the chief representative of Japan's business imperialism in China, took the leg off the jingoistic chief diplomat in China, Shigemitsu, and an eye out of the commanding admiral, six-foot Nomura, graduate of Annapolis, friend of Franklin D. Roosevelt, who was to turn diplomat and become Japan's "front" in Washington while his navy buddy Yamamoto planned the attack on Pearl Harbor.

III

General Araki traded posts with the silent, long-mustached General Hayashi (Senjuro), then doffed uniform for kimono and tabi [3] to allow the curative waters of Japan's hot springs to heal his influenza-racked body, and perhaps also, to allow the diplomat Hirota to attempt to heal the uneasiness caused by his frank speeches. Previous to his appointment as Japan's supreme war lord, Hayashi was chief of army education, which it is worth while to note is one of the highest positions in the Japanese army. It actually means control of morale and general theory, and of the military police who can be used almost as the G.P.U. in Russia or the fascist police in Italy. Into this key post Araki soon put his single-minded pupil, Tojo (Eiki or Hideki).

Araki and Hayashi had been brought together by their mutual hobby—old swords. Miniature Araki revived the custom among Japenese warriors of wearing the long two-handed samurai sword, which, with a correct stroke, is a weapon that will cut a man from neck on one side to thigh on the other. In the 1932 Shanghai scrimmage a Japanese lieutenant cut with his sword through the barrel

[3] Split-toe Japanese socks, worn with the wooden clogs.

and waterjacket of a modern machine-gun. It fell to Hayashi, a connoisseur who delighted Japanese by coining the epithet "steel bible" for the sword, to make the old sword "regulation" in place of the "tin" appendage copied from western armies, thus reviving Japan's unique sword-beating industry. Many an officer's family went on short rations to pay for one of these weapons, which take months to turn out and cost from 2,000 yen [4] up.

Hayashi echoed Araki's warning to the American state department and the League of Nations that any attempt to destroy the accomplished facts of Japan's "peace" work in Pacific Asia would lead to just the world war which western idealist statesmen wished to avert. Leave it all to Japan and she would accomplish the peace they craved. Hayashi is a German scholar, and loves to identify the *ewige Frieden* or "eternal peace" of Kant with Nippon's divine mission. "The proclamation of a monarchy in Manchuria," says Hayashi, "clearly proves that Japan has no material ambitions on the continent. It ought to satisfy all those western statesmen who doubt Japan." Pu Yi may be set up and Pu Yi may be set aside. All is well, according to the Araki-Hayashi philosophy, as long as whatever is set up comes under the supreme ordinance of the Son of Heaven. The League of Nations would become a virtuous institution if it would put *itself* under the imperial guidance.

This Hayashi took the office of minister of war at the age of fifty-eight, which places him among the younger mature set in Japan. He is five feet six, four inches taller than his teammate Araki, as reticent as Araki is talkative, boasts that he hasn't seen a doctor for twenty-five years, and pets his Kaiser Wilhelm mustaches that reach almost to his flaring ears—the bushy sort of mustaches that Japanese cultivate to show how much more virility (and white blood) they have than their Mongoloid Chinese neighbors. Hayashi's stern but not unkindly face can break at wide intervals into a broad smile. He says "Araki is no saber rattler and I am no weak-kneed pacifist. I don't talk about what I can't do, and if I can do it there is no need talking about it."

However, he very significantly talked about "the stabilization of Japan's military plan to bear the shock of the 1935-1936 emer-

[4] The yen has varied from a half to a fifth of the United States dollar.

gency." [5] He intimated that he had prepared a secret national defense scheme of large proportions and sweeping scope covering political, economic, and social as well as military fields. It was based on
his predecessor's, Araki's, methods, the special cost to appear, he
considerately stated, in the next budget.

Hayashi retained the support of peasants and laborers, although
his aid to their problems went little beyond providing work in the
overtime-working munitions industries. A brother adopted into another family and therefore bearing a different name—from the Japanese viewpoint actually no longer considered a relative—got tainted
in a Tokyo municipal scandal. Hayashi resigned as minister of war
in shame for his family—or, it might be more accurate to say, in
pride. It took the lid-sitter of the army general staff, Prince-of-the-
blood General Kanin, to keep him in the cabinet.

To an American newspaper woman Hayashi remarked dryly that
Americans may fail to understand Japan's actions in Manchuria
because they do not appreciate that Japan was thinking about Manchuria for several years before the 1931 conquest!

Hayashi has shown evidence of possessing the empire-building
mind exemplified in Admiral Togo—the combining of meticulous-
ness with timely individual initiative. In 1931, when Araki's cohorts
under General Honjo broke out in Manchuria, Hayashi was commander of the Japanese forces in Korea. In direct disobedience to
cabinet orders from Tokyo, he took a division across the Yalu River
(the border between Korea and Manchuria), inspiring Honjo to
proceed with the conquest despite the frowns of the world and the
resistance of Chinese guerrillas. Hayashi was a hero before this. In
1905 with seventy men—sole survivors of two regiments—he carried
by assault one of the hilltop fortresses at Port Arthur.

IV

Hayashi knows Russia and speaks Russian. He was military observer on the Austrian front during the last war, but he was swept

[5] Japanese leaders thought Germany would "begin" on Russia, in 1935-36. They
had to revise their schedule when Hitler made a deal with Stalin in 1939 and began
on Poland.

back into Moscow in the débâcle and experienced the first stages of the great revolution. Japan's armies have an experienced elder-statesman general for dealing with Russia.

War Minister Hayashi's press-bureau head, Major General Tojo, soon to be "army education" chief, then, in 1941, lord of the Pacific War, blurted to Japanese reporters, who excel in the journalistic art of putting their victim's foot in his mouth for him, the war department's outlook and objective: "Japan's neighbors, the United States, Russia, and China, knowing that Japan is likely to be confronted with various international difficulties in November, 1935, are steadily preparing for war.... Japan's desire for expansion on the eastern Asiatic continent, manifested in her Manchurian policy, has been her unalterable policy since her foundation.... Japan should maintain strong pressure on the continent. Only thus can she keep at bay the Soviet's attempt to advance in the Orient." [6]

The Japanese army, having learned from its Manchurian campaigns how to exist in subzero weather and having developed great mobility over roadless plains, feels capable of proceeding at any time with the Russian part of the divine mission. That job is sooner or later to eliminate Russia from Pacific Asian affairs and establish the boundary of Japan's directly ruled empire 1,400 miles back from the sea; from the Arctic south to Lake Baikal; along the lake, longest in the world, flanked by 17,000-foot-high mountains; and across 200 miles of rough but passable country to the Gobi Desert and China.

No modernly equipped army of any size can to-day pass north of the lake or south through the desert, and Hayashi's strategic railroads and tank trails have the passable stretch at their mercy. If the Trans-Siberian Railway is cut here (and it is most difficult to prevent the cutting of a thousand-mile stretch of track in lonely country) Vladivostok is isolated from Moscow—hence Russia's effort to put a self-sufficient force east of Lake Baikal. Unless that force could quickly capture Manchuria it would starve. Russia's railway isn't able to do much more than feed it now and the civilian population of 600,000 is always on the border of starvation. If America would feed it from the sea (Russia is stocking American flour) it

[6] *Time Magazine*, February 19, 1934.

would continue to fight and be very difficult to dislodge indeed—but how would American warships capture and hold the northern straits of Tsugaru and La Perouse which Rozhesjensky did not even try— unless by air offensive along the Aleutian chain? Russia talks of a new railway through the mountains and over tundras north of Lake Baikal—will it ever be built? When Hitler invaded Poland the Trans-Siberian proper was not yet entirely double tracked, save in optimistic Soviet newspaper reports, and her Amur railway was rotting.

Japan has built a great munitions center on the west coast of Korea, has tunneled through the border mountains and built its new strategic railway into the heart of Manchuria, has taken over the Russo-Chinese line in Manchuria, giving Russia a price which is more than it is worth and which still is an insult, and is all set to sever the none too good all-Russian track along the north bank of the Amur River to Vladivostok.

Shared by all Japanese from diplomats to clerks is the army's confidence that Russia is at its mercy and that, had the Russian problem stood alone, it would long since have received a simple and drastic settlement. Japan has no intention of sharing with Russia the destiny predicted by Oswald Spengler: that "Russia and Japan will have command of the world by means of Asianism." Had Spengler said "Japan or Russia," he would have spoken more truly.

The Japanese army knows that the Soviet power of to-day is not the czar's Russia of 1904—no other nation has so much intelligence of Russia. It also knows that Japan of to-day is even more not the Japan of 1904. Russia is still in industrial youth, Japan is reaching maturity. In 1904 Togo had to conquer the seas before she could land armies on the continent. Then Nogi had to spend six months and 30,000 lives to reduce Port Arthur, and Oyama had to build a military railroad the length of Korea, from Fusan to Mukden, and fight his way into the mainland. But in 1934 Japan's railways were built, her supplies already transported, and her troops already quartered on Russia's front and flank.

Under the circumstances General Araki was entitled to feel confident that he could "purge" Siberia, and the Japanese belief that Moscow would squeal but not fight by herself seemed justified. Some fear of Russian baby submarines fabricated at Vladivostok existed, and a real anxiety over the basing of several hundred Russian planes, mostly antiquated models, within six hours' flying distance of Japan's paper and matchwood cities.

The army set about to nullify these menaces in the usual stubborn, methodical Japanese way. The populations of great centers were put through air-attack drills costing millions of yen and absorbing the existence of the community for two weeks at a time. The 1934 air maneuvers postponed a strike at Osaka, and continued in complete darkness at Tokyo, despite a severe earthquake shock and torrential rain. Five hundred thousand members of the volunteer civilian defense corps performed their duties under the slogan, "Defend our skies." "As sirens announced the approach of enemy squadrons, volunteers wearing gas masks rushed about the streets laying down smoke screens, extinguishing fires caused by imaginary bombs and hustling theoretically wounded on stretchers to emergency stations.

"The firing of antiaircraft guns on the roofs of large office buildings, the staccato of machine guns and the clamor of fire engines racing through the streets made the raids as noisy as they were spectacular. As the raids got under way in the afternoon volunteers laid down smoke screens which blanketed the downtown district and caused pedestrians to go about holding their noses and choking.

"Three cities were in complete darkness, all lights being extinguished except those in factories and newspaper shops, where the work went on behind windows covered with dark shades. Traffic was at a virtual standstill, with street cars stopped and automobiles traveling slowly with headlights off or dimmed.

"The lights were even extinguished in the Imperial Palace and 600 policemen and 500 soldiers of the imperial bodyguard division, under Prince Yasuhiko, were guarding the palace. Emperor Hirohito, however, is absent from the city, summering at Hayama." [7]

Campaigns are pushed for rebuilding Japanese cities in concrete. Aircraft are increased in number to several thousand, a squadron of attack pilots are trained to the exalted tactics of flying into their targets with a load of high explosive on board—a life for a sure hit—

[7] New York *Herald-Tribune*, September 1, 1934.

and aircraft detectors and antiaircraft protection are developed to the highest degree.

The Japanese people are taught to be as ready for war as Adventists for the second coming of Christ. When Russia is welcomed into the League of Nations, the *Japan Times* writes: "We must be thoroughly prepared for all possibilities." A try-out war mobilization of industry was recently ordered, in which every factory actually had to suspend making its old product and start full blast to make the product assigned and specified by the general-staff mobilization plan on outbreak of war. The army, on the whole, is ready to go. It is waiting on the navy. The position of the United States of America in and toward Pacific Asia—the imperial navy's problem—complicates and slows up indefinitely Japan's execution of her divine mission in Pacific Asia, particularly its Russian portion.

On December 7, 1941, after trying to talk us out of blocking her, Japan took action to remove us as an obstacle.[8]

[8] The above paragraphs, save the last, are as published in 1934.

Chapter XIX
Men, Boats, and Naval Ratios

Vice Admiral Suetsugu (Nobuharu), commander of the Imperial combined fleet, openly established navy control of Japan's international policy in 1934. He electrified the country by presenting over the heads of navy minister, premier, army, privy council, and elder statesman a demand [1] signed by the sixty commanders of his fighting vessels for a government that would stand by the navy in the ratio controversy with the United States and Great Britain. The best that lid-sitter Saionji, elder statesman, could do in the interests of conservatism was to place Suetsugu's friend and senior of less fiery temper, Admiral Okada (Keisuke), at the head of the new cabinet.

Fire-eating Vice Admiral Suetsugu was accused of giving away strategic secrets of the Japanese navy in his refutation of American Admiral Pratt's argument against submarines at the London Conference in 1930. He has been compared to the retired American admiral in his unconventionality of opinion, bluntness, and recklessness of statement. The difference in conditions governing the United States and Japanese navies is shown by the fact that, whereas Pratt retired under the suspicion and opposition of his fellows, Suetsugu, always a kicker against the pricks, became the most powerful personality in the Japanese imperial navy. Only when his navy was ready to strike, in the late 1941, did he retire from fleet command, leaving the younger Yamamoto (Isoroku), his aide in the naval conferences, to be the Togo of Japan's greatest naval

[1] In official language, and especially when made, as this one, direct to the emperor, a "memorial."

war. If Japan's navy wins it, she will need no more Togos. She will rule the seven seas.

Japan's constitution, it is to be remembered, provides that the civil government has no authority over either the navy or army, but makes cabinet, army, and navy each individually responsible to the Emperor only. In other words the premier of Japan (custom has given him this title; constitutionally, Japan has no premier, but only a president of the cabinet) has no control over his own ministers of war and navy whom he must appoint upon the nomination of the army and navy general staffs, whereas on the other hand these ministers, who must be a ranking general and admiral, can wreck his cabinet at any time by resigning. Or if army or navy wishes to prevent an appointee to the premiership from forming a cabinet, it will simply refuse to relieve a high officer to accept the position of minister. It is as if the admirals of the American navy could tell an American president-elect whether he might form his cabinet or not, and what he must take for his naval policy.

Around Suetsugu crystallized Japanese resentment against the inferior ratio given Japan at the Washington and London Conferences of 1922 and 1930. At the time of the London confab, Suetsugu was commander of Japan's submarine fleet. He is also credited with the severe discipline and gunnery practice which has brought up the marksmanship of the Japanese navy in recent years. At London he went against the whole limitation theory. The only way the British and American delegates could prevent him from bringing it to naught was by giving him equality of submarine flotilla, which they did under the formula that the submarine is purely a defensive weapon.

Suetsugu showed his contempt by returning home and launching several submarines, the world's largest, with cruising radius great enough to take them from Japan into Los Angeles harbor and back, carrying a little knock-down plane or two. I wrote in 1934: "America has no such ships—would need two years to build them. In view of this, American officers, at Pearl Harbor in the Hawaiian Islands and at the small American bases from San Diego to Bremerton on the Pacific coast of the United States, remember that Togo crippled China's fleet in 1894 by an unexpected raid into its base,

Weihaiwei, and sank Chinese troop transports before declaration of war, and that Russia's Pacific fleet was bottled up in Port Arthur before declaration of war in 1904. They should remember in this connection, and while Japan officially is pleading that the submarine be classified as a purely defensive weapon, the calculating Suetsugu's fighting dictum: 'There is no demarcation between attack and defense.' "

II

Suetsugu, as commander-in-chief of all Japan's floating fighting power, and director of the greatest naval display and mimic warfare ever held in Asiatic waters, which lasted from July to October, 1934, demanded the same equality in all branches that he won for his submarine arm. He made the American headlines by writing a prefatory chapter to a fictionized description of the coming war of the Pacific, followed by an interview [2] to the effect that Russia and America would encircle Japan, that Charles and Anne Lindbergh flew to Japan in 1931 for the purpose of spying, and that Japan was preparing for war with the United States. When there was a fuss, he replied that he never reads interviews attributed to him or criticisms about him.

The result, of course, was a great boost to the American big-navy program in Congress, which in turn was just the boost required to put over in the Japanese Diet the largest naval budget in Japan's history. Some members of Parliament, allowed to speak for effect abroad, upbraided Suetsugu, and the home minister promised that Japanese magazine and newspaper censorship would hereafter watch for "inflammatory stuff," as well as "dangerous thoughts." The home minister at the same time also asked that "Japan's friendly nations" coöperate by prohibiting the appearance of such books and articles as this humble author presents herewith!

At the same time the department stores in Japan's largest cities were, with police and government approval and assistance, holding full-floor exhibitions of the "1935-1936 naval war with the United States." Writes the correspondent of the New York Times: "From morning until night hundreds and hundreds of observers and lis-

[2] Magazine Gendai, January, 1934.

teners see these exhibits and listen to the lecturers—and then shuffle away on their sandals visibly impressed." He describes an exhibit in Kobe's largest department store held in the summer of 1934: "The department store in question is a five-storied building of modern foreign style. Over the spacious main entrance was suspended a paper and cardboard replica of an aerial bomber with a wing-spread of about ten feet, and the sign above this, the guide explained, advertised the war exhibition on one of the floors above, and what an exhibition!

"A large portion of the floor was devoted to an elliptical papier-maché relief map of the Japanese coast around Tokyo. The area devoted to the capital city itself was a rough circle about fifteen feet in diameter. The bay and outside ocean were shown, and there was an attacking and a defending fleet of warships, each ship about three inches long. Squadrons of contending airplanes hung from the ceiling by invisible wires. From somewhere a phonograph was giving out sounds like the crash of big naval guns, the drone of airplane motors and the thud of bursting bombs."

Suetsugu's comment on the new foreign policy of "educating the powers to Japan's program" is, "Diplomacy cannot solve our present emergency." Realizing that the navy has always had better care than the army in Japan (due chiefly to the cohesion of the Satsuma clansmen who have filled all the navy's high offices) Suetsugu hands a sop to the sister arm: "As a Japanese sailor I believe implicitly that the Japanese army is the strongest and finest army in the world." Asked what he thought of political circles into which he had plunged like an angry Neptune, Suetsugu replied, "I enjoy the sea's pure air."

A journalist remarks wittily that Suetsugu differs from the army hero, Araki, in that he is a man of few words and no tact. However, he is described as a cool-headed officer with whom the fate of the empire may be trusted in crises.

III

Close to Suetsugu, high councilor of the imperial navy, is the younger Admiral Yamamoto sent to London in October, 1934, to end

Japan's submission to a ratio keeping her inferior to the United States and Great Britain in sea power. He is airminded—a graduate pilot himself. He was in supreme command when Japan's navy destroyed off the seas every rival between the Coral Sea and India.

Suetsugu and his direct-speaking group have pushed completely into the background the navy heads who "came to reason" from the viewpoint of American and British experts. This is the basic situation to be considered in connection with any further dreams of naval limitation by agreement with Japan.

Old papa Admiral Osumi, minister of the navy, liked to talk to newspapermen about the fraternalism of Japanese and American gobs, and to call American naval officers by their first names and gossip over their personal characteristics and domestic affairs, but his ministry's policies were determined by younger men like Suetsugu. One gifted officer among the younger crowd, Admiral Kobayashi (Saizo), is tainted with the odor of Washington and London internationalism. He will have to live that down if he is to reach the fame to which his capacity entitles him.

Suetsugu and Yamamoto were particularly concerned when the American navy surveyed in the Aleutian Islands, which jut out from the coast of Alaska to within six hundred miles of the Japanese Empire, and allocated a cruiser or two from Bremerton base in Puget Sound to patrol them (1933). Up to this time the best we had were the charts we got along with the Alaska purchase from Russia (1867).

The Japanese in Washington in 1922 procured a last-minute victory from Secretary Hughes, after American navy experts had left the table, in the insertion of a clause ambiguously prohibiting military installations on the Aleutian Islands, which are part of Secretary Seward's Alaska purchase from Russia. Japan, through the great "floating canneries" (ships of 10,000 to 30,000 tons) of her fishing fleet, which fleet is an auxiliary of the Japanese navy equipped with naval radio and commanded by naval officers in uniform, continued in strategic possession of the waters around this chain of American islands.

In 1922 both Japan and the United States were building fleets with the immense profits from the World War enjoyed by both nations. America resented Japan's high-handed actions in China during the war and at the peace conference Japan resented America's stopping her when Europe was helplessly amenable.

Woodrow Wilson had sent an American army to Vladivostok to be a "moral" check on Japan's invasion of Siberia. The relations between the two nations were strained. They were drifting into an armament race that logically and historically must have ended in the use of the weapons prepared.

Liberals in both countries and in England, which was also building but had little money and heart for it at the time, arranged for the conference at Washington. Japan suddenly suffered a postwar depression—thousands of her new firms and plants went bankrupt. The ratio in sea power offered her, three to five, was better than she could have maintained through competitive building at the time. The United States obtained the admission of equality with Great Britain in sea power. The bargain struck between the United States and Japan was that in return for Japan's acceptance of the United States Pacific policy, chiefly the protection of China's independence, the United States renounced the advantage greater wealth and construction facilities gave her, and showed her trust in Japan's honor and relieved Japanese apprehensions by letting American bases in the Philippines, Samoa, and elsewhere become completely outdated.

But in 1930 when details of the naval ratio arrangement came up for revision at London, the material premises in the case—upon which Japanese logic is always based—had changed completely. American shipyards had rusted away. The American navy under Harding, Coolidge, and Hoover, those "three American Louis," had fallen actually below the Japanese in fighting strength. More than one-third of it was outdated. The American outposts in the Pacific had come to be entirely at the mercy of Japanese sea power.

Japanese knew that American popular interest in affairs of the far Pacific had evaporated, that they were in the despair of the Great Crash, that their president could not conceivably have sent his fleet sailing in Japan's direction, as did a predecessor, Theodore Roosevelt, and would not begin rebuilding it as his successor was to do. They knew that he was a president who couldn't have effected any European alliance against Japan, who had antagonized his

Congress and lost the confidence of his people and sat in the White
House or on the banks of a fishing stream waiting for his term to
run out. Japan had built the world's second largest ship-producing
facilities; Japan was launching her great world-trade drive. It was
the moment to change the picture—to demand equality with America and Great Britain.

A Japanese may consent that his nation should be humble among
others while there is no other way and destiny's moment has not
yet arrived. But to continue supinely in an inferior status when it
is no longer necessary becomes the unforgivable sin against the
sacred motherland, personified in the Divine Person within the
palace moat of Tokyo. Japanese anger blew the lid-sitters off in 1931
—hence the great naval budgets and the demand for equality which
followed. Hence the mission of Suetsugu's henchman, Admiral
Yamamoto (Isoroku), to London in late 1934 to suggest decreases
in American and British sea strength, relatively increasing Japan's
—or the alternative of "every nation entitled to determine for itself
its needs." Japan preferred not to enter an open building race
with the two western sea powers, but her navy government planned
a 240 per cent increase in navy budget over 1931—just "in case."
And the Washington treaties of 1922, giving other powers any claim
to concern in her conduct in China and Pacific waters, had to go
by the board. The Japanese way of getting out of a contract is first
to ignore it—if that "works," then brazenly to cancel it. Yamamoto
followed through at Pearl Harbor.

IV

Americans naturally saw quite a different picture. From their
viewpoint Japan was most generously treated in 1930. As they saw
it, a nation with only one coast to defend, navally unchallenged from
Singapore to Hawaii, didn't need any more navy, and to give her
equal ratio would merely be to encourage her imperial ambitions.
They apprehended that if Japan became ruler of the waves it
would be difficult and dangerous to keep her cheap goods from flooding the world and putting the finishing touch to western industry.
By her actions since September, 1931, when her armies leaped upon

Manchuria, Japan had in the eyes of the American state department broken the basic bargain of the 1922 contract, sweeping it
aside by brazen force upon the excuse of necessity. Respect for
the independence of China was Japan's "give" in a give-and-take
arrangement. Instead of admitting this, Japan wishes to go into long
arguments regarding the validity of her necessity. Yet there remained, right to December 7, 1941, strong influence in the State
Department sympathetic to Japan's general program in Asia.

United States navy men feel that Japan has played this country
the way a clever woman will sometimes take advantage of a man.
In harmony with the agreement, we gave up fortifying Manila, and
our other Pacific bases became antiquated liabilities. It became
impossible to put the odds back to where they were in 1922. Meanwhile Japan, who also was not to fortify, turned the ocean west of
Midway into a nest of Japanese submarine and air bases—built not
openly but "in the interest of fishing or commerce." The United
States navy neither fished nor traded. Japan quit the League of
Nations but kept the mandated islands which lie between our bases
to the east (Hawaii), north (Guam), south (Pango-Pango), and
west (Manila), and the spokesman of her house of peers' mission to the Philippines, going direct from the American governor-
general's palace to his Japanese warship, said, "If any one bothers us
there, we'll fight!" We blinked at this robbery and illegal naval-
air-base building under our feet. We paid for this neglect by the loss
of dominant sea power at Pearl Harbor. Suetsugu and Yamamoto
had far more than evened the adverse naval ratio of London.

In the 1934 printing of this book, I said:

"The fundamental clash between the two nations is psychological
and ideological. Idealistically (we do not always live up to it) our
way of doing honor to our name and nation lies in adhering to a principle or promise even to our immediate hurt. The Japanese way of
doing honor to his is in alertly taking advantage of every circum-
stance and vicissitude in its favor. We have seen this ethic operating
through Japanese history and lives.

"This difference in mentality was illuminated by President Franklin Roosevelt's withdrawal of the fleet from the Pacific. When our
main battle strength was concentrated in the Pacific Japan inter-

preted its position as a bluff intended to stop her in China. Yet when the president ordered the fleet to the Atlantic she took it not as an act of good will and of manifesting trust but as irresolution on the part of the American government and perhaps doubt of our own fighting strength. And when the fleet started back, although its return had been provided in the beginning, this was taken as another attempt to bluff—coincidental with the beginning of 1934 naval ratio talks.

"Suspicion is strong in Japan. The Osaka *Asahi* says that Britain and America prepare a solid front against Nippon but that the rising empire can no longer tolerate ratios that menace security. It says that Great Britain and the United States will gain nothing by threatening, even though to her bluff of greater building strength America may add the threat of new naval bases in Alaska and the Aleutian Islands.

"Japan proclaims the new ethic, discovered to fit her opportunity, that every sovereign nation is entitled to determine its own defense needs. 'The more Japan is anxious for peace in the Orient,' says *Jiji*, 'the more responsible she is for its maintenance. International arrangements cannot be static and Secretary Swanson is as out of date in insisting upon preserving the five-to-three ratio as the League of Nations and Secretary Stimson were, in a world of changing organisms, in regarding as sacred the borders of China.'"

On October 3, 1934, General Hayashi's information bureau of the war department issued to the nation 160,000 copies of a startling five thousand word pamphlet calling first for more alertness toward the nation's prospective enemies, Soviet Russia and the United States of America, and, secondly, for mental preparation for an economic reorganization of the nation. The pamphlet, an amazing document showing much study on the part of military minds of radical and communal economy, created a sensation among political parties and threw a new scare into the great houses of wealth. It was considered particularly significant as coming just before the London naval talk. When the naval leaders seemed ready to discuss a temporary compromise with the United States and Great Britain the army jumped in thusly and pushed ahead the sentiment of ultra nationalism. Thus did army and navy see-saw the nation

forward in the path of jingoism. The pamphlet pointed out that the
United States and Soviet Russia combined possessed 6,000 airplanes
to Nippon's 1,000 (the Japanese army and navy were generally
credited—1934—with the possession of 3,000). It emphasized the
necessity of the development of civilian aviation in Japan, indicating that the United States possessed something like 10,000
civilian planes—over half the civilian airplanes in the world—
while Japan had only a few hundred. Army leaders in this connection
made much of "America's latest imperialistic drive upon the Orient"
in the shape of the Roosevelt-blessed plans to inaugurate Pan-
American's trans-Pacific air service. War Minister Hayashi demanded a 600,000,000 yen budget for the army for 1934-35,
400,000,000 yen of which was classified as "new projects." The
total asked for army and navy for the new year was 1,100,000,000
yen. The fall army manœuvers were to be participated in by 51,000
troops. Navy plans included the greatest naval manœuvers in the
nation's history to take place east of Japan, simultaneously with
the American naval manœuvers off the Aleutian Islands following the
return of the American fleet in entirety to the Pacific in November.
The final answer of the Japanese navy to the insistence of the
United States and Great Britain upon continuance of the 5:3 naval
ratio was a demand that this ratio must exist in oil and other
supplies to run the boats as well as in ship tonnage in order to be
a true ratio, and that if the United States and Great Britain would
arrange with Holland to give Japan the oil supply of Borneo, Japan
might be content to continue on inferior ratio a while longer.

This chapter closed (1934) with the words:

"Bearing in mind what sort of men control Japan's navy, what the
word 'peace' means to the Japanese mind, and what the 'philosophy
of developing organism' connotes in view of 'Nippon's world mission,' we see that the naval problem on the Pacific is the most difficult and dour international situation ever faced by the American
people."

Chapter XX
Japan's Modern Feudal Lords

W HILE Japan's army, asking no outside authority, was completing the conquest of Manchuria, two great financial figures were shot to death in the streets of Tokyo. One was Baron Dan (Takuma), gentle, slender esthete, entertainer of distinguished foreigners, popularly called the "prime minister of the House of Mitsui" —wealthiest house in Japan and one of the wealthiest in the world. The other was Mr. Inouye (Junnosuke), hard-fisted, rather rotund executive in the House of Iwasaki, second in wealth, known by its trade name Mitsubishi.

The Mitsuis had just made 100,000,000 yen by "selling their country short" in the following manner: They had purchased United States dollars with every available credit. Then, when the entire nation was in a patriotic furore over the exploits of the Japanese army in China, and the restraining Shidehara government was overthrown by assassinations and newspaper denunciations, they slipped their creature, "Old Fox" Inukai, chief of the political party financed by them, into the premiership. He took Japan off the gold basis. When the yen had dropped sixty per cent the Mitsuis sold their dollars to Japanese importers badly in need of exchange. The deal left them in possession of that much greater proportion of Japan's total wealth.

So the patriot organizations sent out their young fanatics to shoot a high Mitsui as well as the politician Inukai. And to play no favorites and throw the fear of God into Japan's other houses of wealth, they shot a Mitsubishi at the same time.

The wise Mitsuis reacted with a thirty-million-yen contribution for the uplift of the peasantry whence spring soldiers and patriots—

the largest benefaction in the annals of Japan. The code of Mitsui which Baron Dan had signed provides for the interests of the firm to be paramount over any member's life. The unique House of Mitsui has eyes for seeing the signs of the times and executive discipline for adapting to them unmatched by other possessors of great wealth in this world.

Japan's western counterpart in trade empire is England; in emotional reactions, Germany; and in internal industrial growth, the United States of America. Japanese speak of their plutocracy as the Five Houses, and sometimes of its heads as the Five Gods of Wealth. Although there are several outstanding families and corporations of enormous wealth aside from the Houses of Mitsui and Iwasaki, and, contrary to the trend in the west, rich men are multiplying in Japan at an astonishing rate—the last census showed twenty-three with an income of one to six million yen each [1]—the Mitsui and Mitsubishi trusts might without great inaccuracy be said to own or control everything that is profit-making in the Japanese Empire. The other two major financial factors are the national treasury itself and the privy fortune of the Imperial Household.

II

There is only one comparison in the world with the House of Mitsui, and that is the House of Rothschild. They are of about equal age. The House of Rothschild was built by an outcast as a revenge on the society that held him and his people down. The House of Mitsui was founded by quartermasters to a feudal lord. The lordly house petered out after the manner of lordly houses, and the quartermasters adopted its heir and along with him its coat of arms. Then came Nobunaga, first of the triumvirate of conquerors who were to unite Japan at the beginning of the seventeenth century, and drove them off their estates.

Japan's most elegant fortune began, as have elegant fortunes elsewhere, with the brewing business. About the middle of the seventeenth century the exiled quartermaster opened a brewery in a small town on the southeastern corner of the main island near the sacred

[1] Survey by magazine *Hinode*.

shrine of Ise. There is a similarity between the instructions Meyer Rothschild gave his four sons, despised and persecuted as Jews, and the dying command of the brewing Mitsui to his four sons, who as merchants and plebeians were subject to the insults of the samurai. "Get money!" and "Work together" were the essence in each case. The four young Mitsuis removed to Yedo (now Tokyo), which by this time was Tokugawa's booming new capital. There, in the opening years of the seventeenth century, the eldest established a silk-goods shop, which, still bearing the family name, is the oldest department store in the world and the largest east of Suez. The seventeenth-century store employed more than one thousand men and women; the giant store on the same site to-day employs fifty thousand, mostly girls.

The genius of the family was the fourth son. He developed business principles that American go-getters may have thought were their own. The first was "cash payments and single price." The old oak signboard, six feet by two and one-half and nine inches thick, carved with this slogan in Chinese characters, now occupies the place of honor in the Mitsui family museum in Tokyo. This youngest son, Hachirobei, began cash-and-carry, large-volume, small-margin business in Japan. He was the first to cut bolts of piece goods. While appealing to the small buyer he maintained a smartness that held the rich, who like a bargain as well as the poor so long as it can be got in a smart place.

He developed advertising to a degree that our clever ad men haven't yet matched. All customers on rainy days were presented with huge paper umbrellas, bearing in bold lines the store's trade-mark, the three bars inside a diamond seen on ships and offices all over the world to-day. It stands for "three wells"—the meaning of Mitsui. Soon the three wells were seen on every important street and veranda in the empire. Mitsui Hachirobei printed wood-block hand-bills and hired boys to paste them over everything. He subsidized playwrights to mention his store in their dialogue and put it in the stage scenery. A struggling novelist could get a book published by having the hero catch his first glance of the heroine in the Mitsukoshi store. One suspects that even the classic wood-block artist Hiroshige got money for one of his gay parties when he made his famous color print of Mt. Fuji with the Mitsukoshi store in the foreground—a prize of to-day's collectors.

This medieval merchandising genius was assisted by his wife Ju-san, who in addition to bearing him fifteen children took a decided part in administering and building the business. Japanese children read to-day in their primers, under Hachirobei's picture: "Deceased gentleman, pure and sincere like the pine tree; his integrity will be admired forever and may his venerable spirit remain long with us." Under Ju-san's picture: "Deceased gentle lady, prospering and radiant, whose virtues will be admired and followed by our people forever."

Like the Rothschilds, but before them, Mitsui Hachirobei went from merchandising into money lending and from that into banking. In 1687 he received appointment as financial expert to the Tokugawa ruler. Money in the form of bullion or currency to settle obligations or pay tribute was being carried around the country in baskets slung from poles. Mitsui Hachirobei developed the exchange system which, with the fall of feudalism, transformed itself into Japan's modern banking system.

Before his death he drew up the constitution of the House of Mitsui, based on the fundamental precepts of the family's twelfth-century ancestors. This remarkable document expressly assigns to each member of the family his part in its enterprises. It creates a sort of early holding company with interlocking directorates. In addition, it is a code of conduct. Divorce in the family it absolutely prohibits—a prime protection to the integrity of the house's estates. Definite maximum allowances are made each member for entertainment and a frugal, simple personal life is stipulated for Mitsuis. Although the income of the head of the house was six million yen in 1933 and five more Mitsuis earn more than two million a year, none lives with the luxury or ostentation of a $20,000 a year man in the United States. They put their increment back into business or into art—and latterly philanthropy. The constitution sets up a family council which is at once the supreme directorate of all its business and a court and police power over all bearing the family name. The council consists of active heads of the branches and is advised by retired heads. By vote of the rest it may depose any of

its members for incompetence, vice, or luxury. It decides when
members must retire, willy-nilly, in favor of the younger generation.
It passes on family marriages, and one of its unique and most valuable functions has been that of adopting into the family the most
gifted and promising executives of its far-flung banks, mines, realty
companies, office buildings, factories, and power plants.

The Mitsui constitution provides for amendment in accordance
with the need of the times "without sacrificing the spirit of the
original." When desirable—every few generations—the house is to
be redivided into families. Upon coming of age every member of the
family must take solemn oath in the "presence of the august spirits
of our ancestors" to place the interest of the house above all personal
interests and swear fidelity to the house and obedience to the constitution. The constitution of the Mitsuis received its latest revision
and adaptation to modern conditions in 1900, when the house was
divided into its present eleven families and the eleven heads given
their order of precedence.

Compared with this the dynasty and house discipline of the
Rockefellers is as kindergarten play. It is doubtful if even the Rothschilds, whose activities are confined to banking, will bear comparison. When our capitalists of the west begin to take inventory of
what the new competition from the east means, they might think
not only of Japanese industry's advantage in cheap and docile labor
and in government support, but they might compare the founded,
consistent, vigilant House of Mitsui with the adventurers that sky-
rocket through western financial skies, governed only by opportunity, greed, and whim.

The great Mitsui Hachirobei is also responsible for a traditional
house attitude towards employees. They are given rest periods, instructions in hygienic living, and commanded to observe details of
dress and cleanliness. Bonuses are distributed to high executives and
exemplary employees. The House of Mitsui has had less trouble with
labor in late years than its rivals, for the Japanese workman is still a
childlike person, who appreciates paternalism. The heir-apparent to
the headship of the House of Mitsui, still in his thirties, spent the
1930's as manager of its New York branch, and makes America his
chief study.

The Mitsuis have for centuries been patrons of art. A few of them have branched out into literature and professional pursuits. The famous portrait of Commodore Perry, with his extremely long nose and fiery red hair, which was the way the Japanese saw the Yankee seadog, was made by a young Mitsui. They are patrons of the great Keio University, founded by Fukuzawa, one of the two great non-government secular universities of the land. Fukuzawa was the founder as well of the Seiyukai, first "western-style" political party. Through Fukuzawa the Mitsui House became its patron, continuing so until the political murder of the Seiyukai chief, "Old Fox" Inukai. Their rivals, the Mitsubishis, naturally took to supporting the opposition political party, known in its last form as Minseito, and the rival university, Waseda, founded by Okuma. It is as if the Rockefellers should finance the Republican party and support Chicago University, and the Mellons, say, finance the Democratic party and support Columbia University. Under such rival patronage Japanese parliamentary elections are known to have cost as much as ten million yen.

III

The great rival House of Iwasaki, known as Mitsubishi ("three diamonds," its trade-mark seen throughout the world), can claim no such ancient origin as the Mitsui House. It is a creation of the last three generations, quite like our oldest American multimillionaire families. As I have pointed out elsewhere, aristocracy tends to become liberal in Japan, and we find that the parvenu Mitsubishis are much more conservative in their control than the older family. They keep high executive offices within the family and they have no such generally suave relations with labor and with the public as the Mitsuis. They lack the elegance and finesse of the older house. The head of the house "made" six million yen in 1933 and two more Iwasakis five million each, but they lack a house council which can sit down impartially to decide when it is time to donate 30,000,000 yen to poor peasants. Some of the bitterest strikes of Japanese labor history have been in Mitsubishi works and some of the worst scandals have involved Mitsubishi slush funds. Whereas the aristocratic

Mitsuis adopted American styles of banking and business, the Mitsubishis preferred the more conservative English styles.

The Iwasaki (Mitsubishi) fortune was founded in a big way at the expense of the Japanese nation when in 1873 the American government ordered the Pacific Mail Steamship Company to stop carrying Japanese troops to Formosa. Washington had just discovered that China was putting forth belated claims to the big island off the China coast, and wished to lean over backwards in neutral rectitude. Iwasaki (Yotaro), business manager for the lord of Tosa until feudalism was abolished, took his ex-lord's eight little steamships and a few more from around the defunct feudal capitals and "held up" the new imperial régime for transporting its troops.

Japan's later independent buccaneer in the shipping game, Asano, says in his memoirs that Iwasaki made ten million yen out of this Formosa campaign. In a civil disturbance which followed this, Asano was appealed to by a Japanese army officer, who felt that Iwasaki's company was holding up the army in asking ten thousand yen for a short haul of two thousand troops. "I'll get a ship and carry the troops for five thousand yen, and I don't mind telling you that I'll still be making money," said Asano. "Oh, just make it seven thousand then," countered the amiable officer. In the founding of Japan's shipping and great industries the most atrocious overcharges against the Japanese taxpayer for supplies and operating expenses of all kinds were winked at, partly because army, navy, and politics were riddled with graft and partly because the men on the top wished even at such costs to encourage the rapid growth of industrialism and shipbuilding.

The Mitsubishi firm got the monopoly of coastwise shipping early and branched out from this into insurance, the financing of bills of lading, storage, etc. Yotaro's favorite proverb was, "You may ladle sake, but you mustn't allow it to leak from a hole." He worked all ends against the middle in a way that might have given pointers to John D. Rockefeller in his predatory days. If you didn't take a Mitsubishi ship, you couldn't get your cargo insured, and if you didn't insure with a Mitsubishi, you couldn't finance your bill of lading. Unless it were "properly" insured and financed you couldn't find a wharf to land it, nor was there any place to store it save in a

Mitsubishi warehouse. While making outrageous charges for government business, Iwasaki procured luscious government subsidies for Mitsubishi ships. At times his companies would be bankrupt, and then again would issue thirty per cent to fifty per cent dividends in a single year.

The Mitsuis got government backing to start a rival shipping firm, but its shares fell. Mitsubishi bought them up. The two companies were merged into the Nippon Yusen Kaisha (N. Y. K. Line), Japan's largest and one of the world's three greatest shipping companies. Iwasaki Yotaro died soon after, at the age of fifty-one, either a suicide or from cancer, but he had founded one of the ruling dynasties of the world's capitalist era.

Iwasaki's heirs do not go in for culture and philanthropy as heartily as the aristocratic Mitsuis, but maintain an economic research body which has become a quasi-official source for business statistics.

Mitsubishi interests have come to be, generally speaking, financial operations, insurance, mining, and shipping. Fourteen great corporations in Japan bear the name Mitsubishi, and these have hundreds of subsidiaries. Mitsui's interests are primarily general manufacturing and trading. They vary from coal mining to tea planting, zinc refining, machine shops, making of synthetic dyes and patent medicines. The two great houses share between them control of Japan's enormous supply of hydro-electric power. Both have their banks. The two touch and overlap at many points.

Just before the resources of both were merged in the supreme imperialist drive of the early nineteen-forties, Mitsubishi preferred a government policy which specially protected the financial capitalist, whereas Mitsui wished such policies as favor the manufacturer and trader. Mitsubishi was especially interested in developing east-coast African and west-coast South American business, and had trained several hundred young salesmen with their wives to invade these fields.

IV

The third house of wealth in Japan is either the Sumitomo or the Yasuda. No two dynasties of wealth could be more different in character. The Sumitomo business claims to be older than Mitsui, dating from the time when Nobunaga and Hideyoshi were unifying Japan. The real fortune began a century later with the development of copper mining and refining in the mountains of Iyo. All through the Tokugawa era the family's interests were chiefly in this metal— the only mineral outside of coal, cement, and lime in which Japan is self-sufficient. With the modernization of Japan the Sumitomos went into banking, and in most smaller Japanese cities to-day the Sumitomo Bank is considered the most conservative and is often the most popular as well. The firm has kept up with developments in copper and to-day turns out a large share of its product with the electrolytic process.

Up until 1921 the business of this old house was conducted as a private family enterprise. In that year it was incorporated and at present has a capital of 200,000,000 to 300,000,000 yen. Of late it branched out into gold mining, steel tubing, electric wire and cable, nitrate from the air, and other fertilizers. Baron Sumitomo (Kichizaemon), whose private income in 1933 was six million yen, made the largest and finest private collection of Chinese bronze ritual vessels and mirrors in the world, and was better known in the world of gentility and culture than that of business.

The house of Yasuda was founded by old Yasuda (Zenjiro) with fifteen ryo which he had saved as apprentice in a dried-fish shop, about the time of our Civil War. He became the individualist of high finance, playing always a lone and unexpected hand. He is the only rich Japanese the author has heard of who declined to buy a peerage. In the crisis of the war with Russia, the war-time minister of finance asked him to save a tottering bank in order that Japan's prospects of obtaining a sorely needed foreign loan might not be impaired. Yasuda replied merely, "Bad business." General Kodama, hero of the land campaign against Russia, asked Yasuda to advance money to continue the war. His reply was, "I don't like to make war-time loans. I would have to charge too much interest." It can be understood why Yasuda died at the hand of a patriotic assassin (1921, at eighty-eight years of age).

Yasuda had the perverse turn of mind often found in Japanese, and loved to stand up before millionaires' clubs and denounce the government's protection of capitalists. This, he said, would precipitate class warfare. Also he advised capitalists to stay out of agriculture. "Landlordism is dangerous." He was not stilled by the slogan attributed to the Mitsui family that "politics are timid in the face of wealth." Perhaps he feared that politicians would strengthen themselves through alliance with wealth until they would make bold to boss wealth. Or maybe he foresaw what has now come—a military and popular revolt against politicians which includes the fortunes that have suckled them. Old Yasuda's death confirmed his saying that it was as dangerous to be a millionaire as a samurai. The comparison is most odious to present patriots, who, being mostly poor, think regretfully of the feudal caste system which prohibited a rich man or usurer from even speaking to a soldier unless addressed first. The hard-boiled Yasuda softened only towards music, to which he contributed handsomely. The Yasuda trust, consisting of thirty companies, chiefly interested in banking, insurance, and the flax industry, gave three million yen to Tokyo earthquake relief and a three-million-yen park to the city.

Yasuda was the lone backer of Asano in the bold moves of that adventurer and pioneer of shipping. Asano, first known as Japan's "concrete millionaire," became to Japan's merchant marine what Katsu was to her navy. Being, however, like most of the merchant princes a plebeian, he showed, like most of them, a deplorable lack of that restraint of egotism which characterized the warrior caste. He was one of the most spectacular figures of Japan's era of rapid fortune building—exactly contemporary, by the way, with our own.

He was a village boy, adopted at fourteen by a physician to whom he became assistant, but he ran away from both this career and his foster-father at an outbreak of cholera. After that he tried and failed in one enterprise after another until his imagination lit on peddling sweetened water at one sen a glass on Tokyo streets. A later fortune was to be founded on sweetened, colored, shaved ice. Asano saved and bought a cement deposit and a little machinery from the government. The age of concrete was beginning. At his height he controlled thirty-five corporations with capital of twenty million yen. He became the greatest entertainer of guests of Japan's history, having dined or teaed in his house between Yokohama and Tokyo more than 150,000 foreign passengers of his steamships. His company goes on, controlled by other houses. When Yasuda and the Mitsubishis got through with him he had little to leave posterity save the fifty-foot concrete statue of himself in frock coat and bowler hat which he felt it appropriate to build on a hilltop.

Asano planned the first long-haul Japanese shipping route, to Bombay, about 1893. He couldn't finance it and the N. Y. K. got it away from him. Then, with the aid of Shibuzawa, he launched Japan's first trans-Pacific line, the Toyo Kisen Kaisha. He was soon in trouble, and only Yasuda would help him out. Asano says that up to this time Japan was paying foreign shipping concerns more than twenty million yen a year for carrying her goods. Asano is responsible for starting Japan's shipyards off in big passenger-ship construction by awarding them the contract for his second trio of ships. The first trio had been Scotch-built, and men along the Clyde Bank in Scotland regretted their shortsightedness in accepting the clause providing for the presence of Japanese engineers during the construction of the first ships.

The *Tenyo Maru* of the second group, which put Japanese shipping ahead of American on the Pacific, is still in service, and is the original of the oft-told story of Japanese imitativeness carried too far. A Scotch firm was asked to submit estimates and detailed plans. Feeling in their bones that the Japanese would build the ships at home once they had gotten the architects' plans, the Scotch bidders falsified some essential measurements. When the *Tenyo* was launched she listed far to one side to the puzzlement first, then the enlightenment, of the Japanese builders, who balanced her with a heavy load of Asano's cement.

E. H. Harriman, who to this time had monopolized regular-run trans-Pacific shipping, was so concerned over this rivalry that he went to Japan, buttonholed Asano and challenged him either to sell or to buy complete monopoly rights over the Pacific Ocean for $20,000,000. This was typical Americanism of the time, and Asano's answer is typical Nipponism: "Knowing that Mr. Harriman's intention was really to bluff us, I told him simply that we were unable to sell, avoiding the other side of his offer—to buy."

Asano had rough sailing with his expensive new ships in the rocky financial seas of the nineties, and on into the first decade of the new century. He patriotically turned his ships over to the Imperial navy during the Russo-Japanese War, and had a hard time getting back lost business after 1905.

The World War saved Asano's neck—and Japan's merchant marine. Asano's company, he says,[2] received 200,000,000 yen from foreign countries during the war years and paid dividends of from thirty to fifty per cent in a year, although it carefully clung to the annual 2,000,000-yen subsidy that Asano had been able to arrange with the national treasury.

And then came the dead years after the World War and the demand for bigger and more luxurious ships, and Asano saw that the only way Japan could save her position in the Pacific was to launch a new fleet to compete with the rising Canadian Pacific and Dollar Lines. This Asano couldn't finance. His old banker, Yasuda, closed in on him, then was slain—and Asano had to give his fleet and his life work over to the Mitsubishi trust, who merged it with their N. Y. K. His son, who retained the presidency of the cement company, got down to the half-million a year income class.

Thus Mitsubishi attained final supremacy in North American and European shipping. In 1931 Kagami, the Mitsubishi smart boy, arranged with the rival Osaka Shosen Kaisha, a Mitsui organization, to trade North American for South American lines, and to coalesce operations. This great Japanese shipping merger led the way to recent mergers such as those of the two old German shipping houses and the two great English companies. Japan, who established her first trans-oceanic line in 1893, had become in forty years the pace setter in world shipping—made so by egotists like Asano, financial pirates like Yasuda, and great trusts like the Mitsubishi—with the support of amenable politicians and tribute from docile taxpayers.

v

Japan produced a Hetty Green in the person of Madame Suzuki (Yone). The Suzuki trust, chiefly interested in banking to-day, is still reckoned by many as the fourth of Nippon's Five Houses of

[2] *Memoirs.*

wealth. The eccentric old dowager, at eighty, passed the headship on to her daughter, wife of the chief manager, Tabataki, who worked up from the firm's London branch. But old Yone crashed in 1927—providing Japan's most sensational bankruptcy, since which time the vast Suzuki interests have been in the control of Mitsui and Mitsubishi, chiefly the latter.

Yone was the daughter of a lacquer-work artisan, who with her husband started a corner cash shop in Kobe—the sort in which sailors and tourists exchange their left-over Chinese, American, or European bills for Japanese currency, and vice versa, at exorbitant discounts. In those days, two years before the promulgation of the Japanese constitution, there was also much money to be made by gambling in depreciated Japanese currency. The cash shop developed into a foreign-exchange business and then branched out into the importation of East Indian sugar.

In 1887 an indigent man sixty-one years old, named Kaneko, signed himself up as apprentice to the couple. At the first new year's bonus time he received from Yone a one-sen (about a half cent) towel, in recognition of his contribution to the firm's prosperity. He walked out and disappeared but Yone found him and fetched him back, gave him his freedom from apprenticeship and eventually made him "prime minister" of the Suzuki kingdom. A pauper at sixty-one, this Kaneko was to die one of the world's richest men. In Japan, it appears, life frequently begins at sixty!

Madame Yone, however, remained distinctly head of the organization. She built the Suzuki palace near Kobe and there bossed her son, his wife, and their five children. She would arise at dawn and study the newspapers, gaining from them hints for many of her buccaneering coups in the financial world. One morning she read that Viscount Goto (Shimpei), governor of Formosa, was stopping in a Kobe hotel. She sent Kaneko hot-foot to make contact with him. Kaneko sat in the lobby three days before Goto gave in and received him, but the result of the interview was a connection between the Formosan administration and the Suzuki interests intimate enough to become one of Japan's standing scandals. The Bank of Taiwan (Formosa) became an annex of the Suzuki interests, and Goto himself showed an effulgence of prosperity.

Madame Yone never admitted a caller. *She* went to see any one she was interested in. Every morning she drove to Kobe, carrying in a lacquered Japanese box the Suzuki seal, which was placed upon transactions by her alone. She was a No singer, a fisherman, an expert in the difficult Japanese military game of Go—a sort of chess game played with five pawns—and an expert in the tea ceremony and the hyper-esthetic art of flower arrangement. She wrote considerable poetry and from time to time cut loose with a devastating criticism of some drama or motion picture.

The Suzuki interests are chiefly bulk raw products: sugar, fertilizer from Chile, tea, raw cotton, and a practical monopoly on the world's camphor supply which comes from Formosa. The profits from these commodities were put into banking. World War years saw a fabulous increase in the fortune, but the dead period after the war saw the old female dictator forced to give over control to an older house which had better tie-ups with politicians and the national treasury. The Suzuki failure was one of those redistributions of losses and winnings in the inner clique, known in New York as a "dry liquidation."

VI

By far the most likable figure in Japan's plutocracy was its "elder statesman," Viscount Shibuzawa (Eichi), usually ranked as the fifth of the Big Five. Shibuzawa was a diplomat of wealth who amassed his great fortune by providing the other buccaneers an essential go-between. It was Shibuzawa who brought about Japan's great shipping consolidation. He became a large stockholder in all the other houses, and the most trusted figure in the Japanese pantheon of wealth. Shibuzawa always had a lucky star over him. He was born in the mulberry and silk-cocoon region back of Tokyo in 1840, of a family that possessed old interests in silk. At nineteen he went to the capital, Yedo, to see what the uproar regarding the foreign barbarians was about. Like Takahashi and all his contemporaries of that generation, he studied swordsmanship under one of the masters who combined that science with Zen philosophy and superpatriotism.

He had the luck to be adopted into one of the Tokugawa families through marriage with its daughter, and then the further luck to be in France as a companion of the shogun's younger brother during the time of the overthrow of the Tokugawa. On his return the deposed Tokugawa house needed a good business man to rearrange its finances on the status of a private family instead of the Empire's lords, and young Shibuzawa did the job—so well that the Tokugawas have not had to worry about where their next rice bowl was coming from. Prince Tokugawa's income became close to a half-million yen per year.

When the statesman Ito put his associate Inouye in charge of Japan's first finance ministry, Shibuzawa was made treasury expert to establish Japan's banking system. He built it on the basis of the new United States banking act of 1870. This, however, was to prove a doubtful success, and to be supplanted, so far as government banks were concerned, by a European-type system. The two exist side by side. The government system consists of the Bank of Japan for note issues, the Yokohama Specie Bank for foreign exchange, and the two colonial banks of Chosen and Taiwan, which in all have a thousand-odd branches. Alongside of them are the private banks of the empire, functioning much as our state banks, with about two thousand branches. The system has held up remarkably well through the postwar banking crisis, although, if western bookkeeping were applied, many more than the several score that have gone bankrupt would be out of existence. The trend now is towards amalgamation. As a matter of fact, both government and private finance have so drifted into the control of the two big houses, Mitsui and Mitsubishi, that there is no longer a true line of demarcation between them.

Shibuzawa's elevation to the peerage—the first ever given a businessman pure and simple—raised businessmen to a position of full social equality in Japan. This, be it noted, did not take place until 1900. Before the military blew the lid off in 1931, wealth had become so influential that any millionaire could get a peerage by donating to political campaigns and charity, as in England. Now caste lines are tightening up again.

Shibuzawa was the introducer into Japan of American service-club ethics in business. He took pride in the fact that he was the founder of the Tokyo Chamber of Commerce and its president through most of his life. Shibuzawa carried Japanese finance beyond shipping and heavy industries into the multifarious manufacturing activities which have made Japan the world's industrial challenger. He was a pioneer in cotton spinning and weaving, electric light, gas, hydro-electric power, hemp, brick work, cement, sugar, harbor construction, reclamation, horse and cattle breeding, hat and shoe making, and a hundred other things. He was president or director of thirty-odd companies, and chief promoter of Japanese railways in Korea. His principal avocation was his asylum for the poor, but he could be counted on to give the prestige of his grandfatherly, paternal appearance at any function of cultural interest or international good will.

Probably no other Japanese ever really liked Anglo-Saxons so well as Shibuzawa. He loved to repeat the slogan for which the London Chamber of Commerce gave him an ovation in 1902: Business knows neither race nor nationality—a catchword hardly borne out to-day. Before his death in 1930, just as the soldier-patriots were making ready to upset that realm of good will over which he presided as happy potentate, he had begun to emphasize that the time had come for Japan to proceed full blast in China. He dreamed this could be done with American dollars used by Japanese capitalists. Maybe it could have if the Shideharas had remained in control of Japan's government.

Perhaps remembering his own start, Shibuzawa made his adopted son-in-law his heir, and under this kindly, frail gentleman, the Shibuzawa fortune continues to be the most conservative, and perhaps the most honest, in the empire. Luck followed Shibuzawa even in his death. Takahashi took his place as "elder statesman" of Japan's plutocracy, to be called upon immediately to face a military bent on making wealth its lackey. For maintaining some of the feudal independence and dignity of wealth, Takahashi was assassinated.

VII

I will give thumbnail sketches of a few more of Japan's money barons. A millionaire sometimes listed among the Big Five, almost as famous as Shidehara for his pro-Anglo-Saxonism, was Baron Okura (Kihachiro). He credited his ambition to the arrogance of the samurai towards plebeians. A friend of his, standing at the side of a muddy road to allow a samurai to pass, dared to keep his high rain clogs on his feet instead of squishing down into the mud in his socks. The samurai had the plebeian's sake shop closed for being "other than expected." In indignation seventeen-year-old Okura borrowed twenty ryo from his sister and came to Yedo, determined to become so rich that he wouldn't have to bow to warriors.

Okura's career was an example of the tremendous energy released in the long-restrained plebeian by the rise of trade and introduction of machinery. He began with a dried-fish shop, but sensing the opportunity of the times, stocked firearms between his slabs of salted swordfish. After the restoration he contrived to become purveyor to the army, making a trip to Europe in 1872 to buy military supplies. The extent of plebeian patriotism and commercial ethics of the time is evidenced by the fact that his fortune was chiefly built at the expense of the Japanese forces—one of the charges against it being that during the earliest Manchurian campaign tins of supposed army beef were found to be full of sand and pebbles. Yet Okura, "the sentimental" who rehearsed his own "wind funeral" on his ninetieth birthday while the Black Dragons condemned his display, attained the rank of baron and died in high repute and is honored by a statue in the gardens of the Imperial Hotel and an inscription crediting him with "opening" Manchuria. His son enjoyed an income of two and one-half million yen a year.

Morinaga is the candy king of Japan. As you went on the electric from your ship at Yokohama to the capital, you passed his acres of sugar and chocolate refineries equipped with an intricate system of overhead cranes. His factories are models of the industrial age. An orphan, at twelve Morinaga began peddling rice bowls from village to village, starting out with 150 pounds each day. He earned his passage to America and worked for sixteen hours a day in a California candy factory, returning in 1899 to open his own kitchen, a tiny room for which he paid two and one-half yen a month. His were the first western-style sweets made on the Asian coast, and he was to make millions out of an oriental sweet tooth which for millenniums had had to be satisfied with cubes of colored bean curd.

Kichigai (Banzai—"Hurrah!") was the incarnation of Japanese egotism. His self-contributed paragraph in Japan's *Who's Who* reads: "Just like the thunder in a clear blue sky did Kichigai bolt over the astonished world. He established the Bushi Bashi Boshi Kabushiki Kaisha; his well-known triple-B trademark authenticates the purity of his hats." In youth this fellow left his humble village to raise pigs in incubators at Yokohama, but switched to straw hats, made millions, and became head of sixteen corporations.

As great an egotist but a much more delightful one is Mikimoto (Kokichi), "king of cultured pearls," who has so successfully advertised himself to the western world that I can save many words on him here. He began as illiterate maker and peddler of bean curd. He got the idea that oysters could be encouraged to speed up their making of pearls, and while all Japan laughed at him he sold his clothing and his wife's family jewels to continue his oyster coddling. He was canny enough, it seems, to have culled his basic idea from a botanist, Dr. Kuri (Minotsu). To-day Mikimoto owns several hundred miles of the coast line of Toba. He employs hundreds of sturdy girl divers upon whom, in deference to the prudery of lady tourists, he imposed a nurse's white costume! When Japan threw off the foreign taint in the late 30's his diving girls went back to gee strings. But they really are nurses to the oysters. Any one who has spent a day in the company of the furrowed-faced, bowler-hatted, kimonoed old gentleman, drinking tea made ceremonially by his granddaughters, and taken snapshots of him standing beside his model of Washington's Mt. Vernon home, will never forget Mikimoto-san. Nor will the pearl industry and the jewelry trade. Mikimoto burned several hundred thousand dollars' worth of pearls into lime to uphold the pearl market. The world price of pearls is in his hands.

Dr. Kikuchi (Kyozo) was known as the "grandpa spinner" of Osaka. He received his degree from a college in engineering and was sent to Manchester in 1887 to study spinning. He returned to advise the mushroom spinning factories springing up along the Inland Sea, and to help amalgamate them under the control of the big houses. He lived to see Japanese efficiency, both mechanical and executive, surpass that of his British teachers.

VIII

Uyehara (Tokuichi), now manufacturer of gas stoves and equipment, began as a laborer on a sugar plantation in Hawaii, where, after saving money, he had a high-school education and started a curio store in Honolulu's Young Hotel.

Hoshi (Hamime), Japan's drug magnate, was the first modern-style newsboy in the streets of Osaka (which to-day has thousands), peddled books for two years to make his passage money to the United States, worked his way through Columbia University with odd jobs, started a one-sheet mimeographed Japanese language weekly for the Japanese community in New York, then returned to Japan and borrowed four hundred yen to begin drug manufacture, from which he has made fifty million yen. He owns the largest tract of cinchona bark in the world, in Peru. A great deal of his success is credited to the use of German formulæ (there have been many complaints from the big American firms on the same score). Probably interest, maybe conscience, is responsible for his two-million-yen postwar gift to Germany for the promotion of scientific study. Like all successful businesses in Japan, his drug concern has become an affiliate of one of the two great houses, Mitsui and Mitsubishi.

Another example of wealth made by the introduction of western products meeting popular demand is that of Ohashi (Shintaro) and his family who began publishing magazines and early procured a textbook monopoly. The Ohashi family, however, have graduated out of the classification of publishers into that of magnates. The splendid Ohashi library is Japan's counterpart for the Morgan library in New York. The publishing business is one of Japan's greatest. The greatest reading public in the world demands magazines of all types from movie gossip through dignified women's magazines to Black Dragon Society publications. In addition to which Japan has a book publication list of thirty thousand titles a year, three times as many as we publish for our twice as large population. Japanese books are mostly issued in paper bindings.

The Hearstlike Noma (Seiji) came along and outdid them in popular periodical publishing, and is to-day known as the magazine king of Japan, turning out eighty-five per cent of her magazine circulation on the criterion that "everything must be of a nature to be read aloud by members of the family, including the servants." His magazine *King* attained nearly two million circulation. He tried to make himself also a great newspaper publisher, but it seems to hold true in Japan as in the United States that the successful man in one field rarely achieves success in the other. He published his autobiography in America. He endowed a society for the study of his life and principles of success which offered membership through full-page ads to Americans and other foreigners as well as Japanese.

Hattori (Kintaro) is popularly called the "watch king." He opened his shop at the age of twenty, and at eighty-six was still coming regularly to work. Hattori's company frightened the European watch trade in 1933 when he began shipping watches, clocks and parts in bulk at less than a dollar per pound, to get around protective import quotas. Hattori is also interested in the bicycle trust, which exported twenty million yen worth of bicycles a year, selling two thousand in England. The Hattori son spends millions upon the encouragement of inventions, his latest contribution to the Hattori foundation being three million yen. His income was more than a million yen a year.

Fukuzawa (Momosuke) is Japan's electrical magnate. He was the poor college athlete who got his start by winning the daughter of and being adopted by the great Fukuzawa, friend of Katsu and founder of universities and newspapers. The old sage had been trying to introduce athletics into Japanese education and here was his chance to show where he stood personally. So the athletic poor boy got the girl and the name Fukuzawa and a considerable fortune amassed by the practical educator, who taught the plebeian generation of his age the slogan he had learned in America, that "money is the basis of independence." Fukuzawa is tied up with the Mitsui interests.

One of Japan's new millionaires constantly watched by the news hawks for his eccentricities is Yamamoto (Tadasaburo), a product of Japan's one great Christian university, Doshisha, at Kyoto. He began with mass cultivation of old Ainu lands in Hokkaido, and then became president of one of the great concerns trading with China. Since 1916 he has been known as the "tiger millionaire." In that year he led a great and luxurious tiger hunt in the mountains of Korea, returned to give a "tiger dinner" to hundreds of noted Japanese and foreigners, and present to each a tiger skin.

A career which will interest all persons who have enjoyed the hospitality of Tokyo's Imperial Hotel—architected in a sort of cave-dwelling style by the American Frank Lloyd Wright, whose style has been copied by Japanese architects for new government buildings—is Inumaru (Tetsuzo), manager of the Imperial for its owners, the Imperial Household, and hence leading hotel man of the empire. He began as a Shanghai hotel flunkey, receiving three yen a month, but met some one there who took him to London, where he was a very popular Japanese bell-hop, and invested his tips in bribing hotel executives to tell him the innermost secrets of the business.

Japan's most spectacular businessman of the 1930's was Matsukata (Kojiro) who, at middle age, was a Harvard classmate of young Franklin Roosevelt. He paid the American president a visit at the White House. Matsukata made a fortune by somewhat dubious means when past fifty, went bankrupt when past sixty, and abandoned his control of Mitsubishi's great dockyards at Kobe, which were closed after a severe clash with the laborers.

In 1933 Matsukata staged a comeback by importing Soviet oil, and gas stations of his company played havoc with the time-established American Standard Oil and the British Shell interests up and down the coast of Pacific Asia. Matsukata, with military support, moved to capture the product of Borneo from the Dutch Shell interests—which caused British haste to complete their Singapore naval base and certain private understandings between the Dutch colonial administrators and the British navy. There was a sudden but after all pathetic doubling of Holland's navy, and the Dutch order prohibiting Japanese ships' officers from coming ashore in the oil ports.

Matsukata met the suspicion of fellow Japanese—aroused when he hooked up with the Soviet Petroleum Monopoly—by putting his enterprise on a philanthropic and patriotic basis. He would take no profit, he said, until he had made gas as cheap for Japanese and Chinese taxi drivers and oil as cheap for the Japanese navy as these products are in the oil fields of California. And he did—a thing which made considerable difference in the lives of old-timers on the

Pacific Asian coast who had to pay fifty cents to a dollar a gallon for the vital fluid. At the same time he proved to the Soviet that the way to expand their business in the Pacific was through Japanese agents.

Kato (Kizaburo) is another Japanese who enjoyed an income of more than a million yen a year. In Kato the Horatio Alger story receives a slight variation. His parents were prosperous but had no use for college education, so at sixteen he went into the chicken business to put himself through college, and invented a steam-heated incubator. He got disgusted with classes, finding that he could learn more by spending all of his time in the library. His first manufacture was western-style hairpins, which netted a small fortune in the home market and soon displaced the British and German products around the world. Not satisfied, Kato took the civil-service examinations and became one of the most active officials in the department of communications, winding up as president of the Hokkaido Colonization Bank.

A "fragrant" fortune in Japan is that of the "esthetic count," Karasumaru, known as "king of flowers." In 1900 he came to America in steerage to study western large-scale operations in the line of green-housing, in the science of which Japan has always been far ahead of us. He is said to name the daily price of flowers for the Japanese capital.

And so we might go on listing the individual characters who saw the chance to make imitations of the Swedish match, German toilet water, French perfume, incandescent globe, and an endless number of products for which the westernization of Japan created a demand, and which the new Japanese industrialists were soon exporting to the west. These built fortunes for their entrepreneurs; then the great houses reached out and absorbed the enterprises. Then they built dynamos and spindles, and, very soon, tanks and guns and airplanes.

A glance at a few of the executives of the great houses will make them more vivid to us. I begin with Masuda, the modernizer of the House of Mitsui, who acquired in his own name one of Japan's great fortunes. He began back in the time of the restoration as clerk to a foreign trading firm in Yokohama, and studied his English from

Townsend Harris, America's first consul to Japan. He was one who early saw the place Japan's water power would play in building Japan's commercial empire. He was a great upholder of the Mitsui motto that "age is for counsel and youth for action." He recalls that at one time the average age of Mitsui House executives was thirty years! He lived out the motto by retiring to a ten-foot-square study on Lake Hakone, which mirrors Mt. Fuji, in imitation of Japan's Thoreau who wrote his famous *Ten-Foot-Square Essays* during the early Tokugawa era. Old Masuda constantly cautioned against antagonizing the United States, maintaining that Japan was still far from through with her need of American help in internal development. He made a point of helping foreigners interested in Japan's arts and did not always discriminate between real students and impostors. Japan's internal development seems to have taken place much more rapidly than even Masuda, one of its chief creators, envisaged.

Another great Mitsui executive is Kobayashi (Masanao), also a graduate of the Christian university, Doshisha. In spite of his diploma, the Mitsuis insisted that he start, in 1893, on fifteen sen a day. He introduced Canton silks into the United States, then became head of the Mitsui's coal department, mining in the southern islands, Hokkaido, and Manchuria, and shipping to China, India, Java, and the other islands of the Pacific. He even shipped coal to San Francisco, raising havoc with the native California coal industry until a tariff barrier was erected. Kobayashi is responsible for the statement that there is no such thing as "pull" in the Mitsui House.

From him we might turn to Ito (Yonejiro), one of the great executives of Mitsubishi, who led an exceedingly varied career until he found his place as a business king. He was first fireman, then apprentice to a physician, later teacher of English to Japanese in the United States (where he attended San Francisco schools), then farm manager in California. After two stays in America, he decided he would like to work for the Nippon Yusen Kaisha (Japan Mail Steamship Company). He applied—was promptly turned down. So he went over to the Bank of Japan and applied. To get rid of him the governor of the bank suggested that he try the N. Y. K. and gave him a letter. Ito went right back armed with the letter and got the job that had been denied him at first. He became president of the Nippon Yusen Kaisha until he was succeeded by the young go-getter, Kagami. Another great Mitsubishi director was Eguchi (Sadai) who left his professorship in the public school system to become a banker and captured for the Mitsubishis the high-grade coal deposits of Hokkaido.

In Takechi (Naonichi) we have a character who reversed the general order, going out of the Mitsui House to found his own. He was born a Hayashi—the family that for generations headed the famous Mitsui dry-goods store—but was adopted into the Takechi family, also Mitsui executives. He turned his back on the house of Mitsui to adventure in Hawaii, where he went to college, won the confidence of the Hawaiian court and was sent back to Japan as interpreter for the Hawaiian legation there. During the illness of the Hawaiian minister he negotiated—at the age of twenty-one—in the name of the king of Hawaii, the treaty admitting Japanese immigrants to the mid-Pacific kingdom and guaranteeing them fishing rights in Pearl Harbor. They fished in this otherwise closed naval base of America until the late 30's—because our government had guaranteed to respect the Hawaiian king's treaties!

IX

This glance into the human side of Japan's new aristocracy of wealth tells us that the story of industrialism in Japan has been much the same as in the United States and covers actually the same period in years.

In the United States great monopolies grew out of the Civil War; in Japan, out of the wars to end feudalism. With the flooding of engineering and machinery into Japan a few buccaneers founded fortunes at the expense of government and people, and then consistently began grabbing up anything profit-making, from dyspepsia pills to coal mines. In both countries the early slogans were: "All the traffic will bear," "To hell with the public!" and "The devil take the hindmost." Gradually the little fellows were tripped up and absorbed into a few great houses, who themselves began to dovetail at many points. An example is Japan's great power fishing industry, owned jointly by the Mitsui and Mitsubishi houses, and operating under supervision of the navy. The sons of the big fellows grew respectable, and in their new Rotary clubs and chambers of commerce began talking "integrity and service." So things went until the expansionists, who believed in taking over rapidly, by violence, closed Rotary and made chambers of commerce offices of the quartermaster's department.

The drawing of the population off the land through the development of industrial communications proceeded at about the same pace in the two lands—in both of which approximately fifty per cent of the people are now city dwellers. Also the creation of a white-collar and skilled-workman middle class has been parallel.

There are some differences to be noted. In both the United States and Japan fortunes were made openly out of government, army and navy, and public-works contracts. But the prestige gained by making the Imperial Household a heavy shareholder is something American promoters had to do without—also the manipulation, through connections with the minister of the Imperial Household, of the imperial block of shares—the trick through which Mitsubishi got control of the great N. Y. K. fleet. The old samurai statesman Katsura had a battle with the Japanese magnates to make railways and communications purely state enterprises. These, with the tobacco, ginseng, opium, and ancient silk monopolies, contribute steady revenue to the national treasury. Another difference is that authority in Japan is centralized, and the plutocrat who bought political Tokyo captured the empire for the time being, whereas American wealth has had both the advantage and disadvantage of dealing with hundreds of little local governments.

The greatest difference between Japanese and American industrial development is in tempo. The swallowing of the little fellows by the big has gone forward much more rapidly in Japan. And the rebellion of the military and peasantry against men to whom profit is god has come up with tornadolike suddenness.

Here are the reasons for this, of tremendous value to students: Modern Japan included a warrior class whose interests are immensely greater than mere national defense, whose influence goes through government and education, and who appropriated the ethics of the feudal samurai and have a definite program maintained by unceasing activity for the building of nation and empire. Here was a ready nucleus for popular rebellion against capitalist industrialism and distribution. The first thing that any student must learn about to-day's Japan is that its army and navy are not policemen for whoever is in power, and protectors of the status quo, but are in a true sense the radical element of the country. They suffer the plutocrats as long as they need them—thus far they have found no way to get along without them—but it would not hurt their conscience in the least to wipe out capitalism root and branch with a stroke as ruthless as Lenin's. On the other hand they are determined that no communism shall get a root which has its sentimental or ideological affiliations with Marx or Stalin or any foreign influence.

Again, the western reader must realize that his conception of the sanctity of property rights is quite foreign to Japan—that as late as 1870 ownership throughout the empire was completely abolished and property redistributed. Then the feudal lords and their vassals were dispossessed by imperial fiat (with a partial, and at the time very doubtful, remuneration in the form of pensions). Farming lands were distributed among the peasantry in one of the hugest resurveying jobs undertaken in history. Nonfarming lands became the privy property of the Imperial House. Under the constitution of 1889 the Emperor owns in fee simple all property in the empire; he permits his subjects to exercise functions of ownership and transference so long as it pleases him.

To the Japanese of to-day the great barons of the industrial age are merely a repetition of the landowners of the feudal age—to be dispossessed quite as simply if the occasion requires. Now do you see why even Japanese communists are often supporters of the Emperor? The simplest way to abolish private holdings in Japan to-day would be with an edict over the imperial seal!

Sometimes the struggle between plutocracy and military becomes open and bitter, as in the three-cornered tussle between Mitsui, Mitsubishi, and the Japanese army for the Manchurian Railway system. The big houses feel more and more harried over the necessity of buying unconvertible treasury bonds to balance Araki's and Suetsugu's military-naval budgets. But the military need the monopolies to carry on Japan's industrial drive against the world, which is half of her empire-building campaign, and to provide the army and navy with the equipment and finance for political expansion, which is the other half. The monopolies need the army and navy to capture and protect their sources of raw materials and hold half the world as a market for Japanese exports.

The Arakis, Suetsugus, and Matsuokas, who are far from free of personal tie-ups with predatory wealth, are beginning to wonder how to explain the divine mission's compromise with capitalism to their backers, the peasantry and proletariat, who, moistened with the typically Japanese "fluid of the gods," are capable of much bolder expression than our underclasses in the west. The way to keep these great undercommunities from asking too many questions is by maintaining an industrial boom at the expense of other industrial nations and raising patriotic fervor to fever pitch by demands for naval or social equality with white nations and by continued annexation of more territory to the empire.

Thus, previously to the American-British embargo of July, 1941, did the Japanese dragon chase his tail. He whirled around in a spiral circle that led him further and further into the west's vegetable garden.

Of Japan it is loosely said either that "government owns business" or "business controls government." The truth is that both are allowed to aggrandize as long as they contribute to national greatness, but both are under the negative, but very terrible control of conceptions within the Japanese soul—and both officials and plutocrats bow to the correction expressed in "popular" assassinations.

Chapter XXI
Spokesmen of Expansion

A MAN named Shiratori (Toshio) made the position of spokesman in Japan's foreign office famous. Shiratori knows America. He has written for "the best" American magazines. He was for years a secretary in the Japanese embassy in Washington. Then for two years he was the Imperial Person's private reporter on foreign news. Although calling himself a liberal and a philosopher he has close connections with the inner army clique. Shiratori substituted sarcasm for the traditional Japanese courtesy in replying to foreign critics. Particularly did he enjoy taking punches at United States Secretary of State Henry Stimson, in return for the latter's criticisms of Japan's behavior in China. When asked how soon Japan would diplomatically recognize its creature, Manchukuo, Shiratori replied: "We are in no hurry. We haven't any canal to build there"—which, being well turned, got him admiration in America, although brazenly false in implication. And Shiratori was copying at the very moment every detail of Theodore Roosevelt's trick for controlling Panama.

In an article for American readers Shiratori said, "The west has always shown a sympathetic, although patronizing, appreciation of the old Japan. Many a foreign observer would remark with a sigh: 'What a pity that things of the past, of beauty and joy forever, should be so mercilessly sacrificed on the altar of modernism!' This criticism fell flat upon the Japanese, feverishly learning from the west; making what it made, trying to think what it thought, even sinning where it sinned. To-day Japan is outwardly as modern a state as any in Europe or America. Her industry is carrying everything before it in the markets of the world.... Having achieved a measure of material progress undreamed of by their forefathers, the

Japanese people begin to pause and ponder."[1] Shiratori then stated
that the opposition of western nations to a Japan doing exactly
what they had done, and what Japanese regarded as unfair restrictions being placed upon Japanese trade everywhere, were driving
Japanese back to an earlier Japanese philosophy. Japan, like ancient
Israel, saw herself the chosen champion of the true god in a heathen
world. The disorderly Philistines on her borders must be made to
bow the knee to Jehovah, and eventually, if the world at large was
to be saved, the law must go out from the Jerusalem of Tokyo.

Shiratori was elevated into ambassadorial rank, leaving a blunter
spokesman successor in the publicity and propaganda bureau of
Japan's foreign office. This swarthy, kinky-haired young man with
long American experience, named Amau (Eichi), had not the sting-
ing jab of Shiratori—he was a heavyweight slugger. But he was
"boned up" on all the inconsistencies between present American
idealism and our record of imperialism.

Amau got western governments all stirred up with an offhand
press release in April, 1934, to the effect that from now on Japan
would assume sole responsibility for the political and economic
regulation of Pacific Asia, and would deal at the proper time with
the fallacious conception held abroad that China was an independent
nation to whom America might sell airplanes or make wheat loans
at will.

This Amau, before the west had heard so much about him, sat in
the dingy barracks which had housed, since the great earthquake of
1921, Japan's world-upsetting diplomacy, and asked me how long
Americans who (he understood) boast of being realists, are going
to talk to Japan on the basis of treaties made by weak-kneed politicians whom the Japanese spirit has overthrown and who are now
either dead or degraded. "If you want to know," he continued, "what
we are doing about Washington Conference commitments to respect
the American conception of Chinese sovereignty, or the surrender of
naval equality made in Washington in 1922 and in London in
1930, look for a parallel in what Germany is doing about the Versailles sanctions. There are two kinds of nations in the world today:
the early comers that treaties are made for, and the late comers

[1] "Reawakening of Japan," *Atlantic Monthly*, May, 1934.

whom they are made against. Germany and Japan belong to the latter category. If you really wish to strangle them you'll have to use more than note paper." Mr. Amau stood up and pounded upon his desk, which means a great deal more than when a westerner pounds on a desk.

The answer to Mr. Amau's proclamation was in a note from the gentlemanly American Secretary of State, Mr. Cordell Hull, to the effect that America expected Japan to keep her commitments. America officially and firmly rejected Japan's assumption of supervision over the affairs of China: "In the opinion of the American people and the American Government, no nation can, without the assent of the other nations concerned, rightfully endeavor to make conclusive its will in situations where there are involved the rights, the obligations and the legitimate interests of other sovereign states." [2]

II

Mr. Amau's chief, the minister of foreign affairs, Mr. Hirota (Koki) was more of a diplomat but possessed of the same heart. In his boyhood in the jingoistic southern island of Kyushu, he became a disciple of the fire-eating superpatriot and expansionist, Toyama (Mitsuru), of the Black Dragon Society. Shortly before taking office as foreign minister in September, 1933, at the age of fifty-five, Hirota wrote to Toyama, then under court condemnation as "the Master."

The Black Dragon Society helped Hirota, a stonecutter's son, through school. To improve his English rather than give his own language—a typical situation—Hirota offered himself to the military attaché of the American embassy, John J. Pershing (the young captain whom the world was yet to know as commander of the A.E.F.) for a position as Japanese teacher and assistant. Pershing turned him down flatly because of his "very poor English knowledge." The now active Foreign Minister Hirota sent a message through Ameri-

---

[2] In the 1934 printing, this statement from Cordell Hull was followed by the words: "Secretary of the Navy Swanson endeavors to have ready, in case of need, more concrete argument." These words were pounced upon by popular pacifistic —now (1942) very belligerent—critics to charge that the book was "jingo" and "yellow" journalism!

can Ambassador Grew some time before he left Tokyo: "Please tell
the General that Hirota is still as poor at English as he was thirty
years ago."

He went out of Tokyo Imperial University Law School (the hatching box of Japanese officialdom) into foreign service; first Peking,
then London, then Washington, then in Europe, culminating with
Moscow where he became Japan's greatest political student of that
neighbor nation.

Hirota believed that the United States would write notes, but
never block Japan with force, and that a high preparedness which
would make the blocking unpleasant and costly, combined with a
polite refusal to discuss matters that to the Japanese mind are settled, would take care of this habit. "America," he said, "is coming
to understand. She has no time for far eastern affairs."

Like Matsuoka, Hirota spent a great portion of his life abroad,
and was made the more Japanese by the experience. Hirota's every
word and action rises out of the mystical Japanese belief in his
nation's makeup and mission. He is the best philosopher of the
younger set in connecting modern situations to ancient motivation.
The superpatriots call him the first foreign-office man whom contact with western diplomats is unable to emasculate.

His definition of diplomacy sounds like a paraphrase of Prince
Machiavelli, but as a matter of fact it is quite as truly Japanese as
the pre-war German paraphrases. As he put it to the congress of
prefectural governors: "Diplomacy is the mirror of national power.
The job of Japanese diplomacy is the study of our relations with
other lands *in conformity with Japan's attitude and mission.* Modern diplomacy is not confined to negotiation but involves the mind
and strength of the whole people of the nation. Adequacy of national defense will lead to diplomatic efficiency. It is thus that war
can be nipped by diplomacy." [3] Hirota has reduced diplomacy to the
simple job of convincing the rival or resister that you are too strong
for him—in other words, the schoolboy showing his muscle.

He lays stress on introducing the world to the feelings and
thoughts of the Japanese people. The cost of this "culture export"
appears in the 26,170,000 yen increase—a five-thirds increase!—

[3] *Nippon-Dempo Dispatch* of May 4, 1934, and *Rengo,* September 23, 1933.

in Hirota's foreign-office budget for 1935. The semiofficial news agency *Nippon Dempo* (*Japan Telegraph*) explains: "The huge increase is to augment and improve the diplomatic forces abroad as one of the means of meeting the crisis due in 1935 and 1936." This is the last year in which budget items were fully published. Of the sum requested 2,500,000 yen would be allotted to an "international cultural bureau," 9,150,000 is for a special diplomatic fund, 3,600,000 is for relations with Japanese abroad, and 7,150,000 is for improving relations with the subject Manchukuoans. In addition to these official government expenditures there has recently been created the Society for International Cultural Relations to which the Mitsui and Mitsubishi, the dominant financial and commercial houses of Japan, have contributed handsomely.

"Culture" is interpreted broadly. "Good will," dressed as Japanese dolls which have so delighted little girls and elderly ladies in the peace movement in the United States, was generously distributed in South America by the Imperial Children's Educational Society. Old diplomat Ishii headed an institute for bringing Japanese young people born abroad to Japan for indoctrinization with the national spirit. A party of American journalists led by publisher Roy Howard toured the Japanese Empire (expenses paid). During the summer of 1934 Japan was host to seventy-nine American college students, who were fêted in Tokyo and toured, at government expense, throughout the Japanese islands, and of course Manchukuo. At the Japan-American student conference in Tokyo, the student-statesmen from American small colleges concluded that Japan had done quite right by Manchuria, and that she should solve her population problem by pushing the Koreans into Manchuria and sending her own surplus into Korea!

The International Young Women and Children's Society began a "hands around the world" movement. The society expected to establish correspondence circles in twenty-one countries. Young women of other countries were invited to Japan to drink tea, view cherry blossoms, and to be indoctrinated with the imperialist viewpoint concerning Manchukuo. Artists, scholars, and jiu-jutsu experts demonstrated their art, knowledge, and prowess abroad. Japanese music and plays were introduced to the foreign public. Chairs of

Japanese culture were established in American, French, English, and Brazilian universities. Foreign students and professors were given scholarships in Japanese universities. Giant radio stations were equipped to drown out any rivals in the eastern hemisphere. Motion pictures depicting the glories of modern Japan—and its benefactions to Manchukuo—were made for the screens of the world. The lovely rock gardens, whose beauty is surpassed in no country, were admired by a party of American women garden lovers. Japan's expansionists seized the ancient pacifist, otherworldly, and non-nationalistic religion of Buddhism as an instrument for mustering east against west. Tibetans, Burmans, Siamese, Mongolians, and Chinese were told that it is to be revived as the great world religion unifying Asia. A great Buddhist congress held in Kyoto drew delegates from the Himalayas to Hawaii. Buddhism, the religion of placid contemplation, was made as much the unwitting instrument of Japanese imperialism as was Christianity the tool of European conquest. The priesthood of Burma and Siam, which is interrelated, was coddled and subsidized and made into a better "Fifth Column" than any that ever operated in Europe, for it was sacrosanct.

Hirota suggested that the powers were overconcerning themselves with Japan's expansion. They ought to know when their day is up, and consider what they *couldn't* do about it, before talking. Great Britain's practical statesmen of the Simon-Chamberlain type, indeed, inclined to see it that way. Hirota said he would have his ambassador, Mr. Saito, see President Roosevelt and explain everything. And if Japan's policy were approved by the President, he would be willing to go even to the extent of negotiating an arbitration treaty with America! In perfect sincerity the Japanese mind, marked by feminine inability to sense reactions that vary from its own, demands that the world acquiesce in its moves. Hitler's Nazis gave us another example of the same mentality, but more German minds sense its inadequacy than Japanese.

Hirota pledged to strive for the establishment of a definite "Monroe Doctrine for Asia." The lack of analogy with the American Monroe Doctrine was lost on the Japanese mind, which assumed that only internal decadence prevented the United States from assuming the same dominance in this hemisphere that Japan proposes to establish in Asia. To Japanese this "Asiatic Monroe Doctrine" is synonymous with "Asia for Asiatics" under divine guidance stemming from heaven itself through the Imperial Family.

The comradeship of Hirota and Minister of War Hayashi made Japan much less of a two-headed monster. The war minister induced the foreign minister to venture more frankness in Japan's diplomacy. At the same time he issued to his underlings this order: "It is imperative that the army be solidified as one mass of steel and that the whole organization abide firmly by the aims for which it exists"—interpreted to mean that foreign policy must not again be the product of spasmodic military hysteria on the part of army cliques. Henceforth the two wings, diplomacy and army, moved forward on an even front.

III

The difficulty in Hirota's negotiations with the president of the United States was that American Pacific Asian policy, if we are to take the words of Stanley Hornbeck, chief of the division of far eastern affairs of the United States state department, "has grown from and is shaped by the belief of Americans that free states should remain free in the orient and elsewhere, and that nations should live and let live with due respect for the interests and rights of one another." [4] No two things could be more contradictory than the theory of Japan's divine mission as Matsuoka and Hirota expressed it, and this American belief that became the greatest obstacle to the consummation of Japan's divine mission.

The United States still regarded China as an independent country! Japan might let that pass as theoretical—eventually to be overcome by the "cultural" process of education. But Japan could not long tolerate the American government's insistence upon the right of American firms to sell airplanes and ammunition to China as freely as to Japan, or the right of American individuals to act as instructors in China. Those things, too, seriously threatened the whole divine-mission program.

On Matsuoka's last crossing to America the reporters got out of him a typically Japanese combination of concealment and frankness.

[4] Speech reported in press of January 18, 1934.

He told Americans: "Japan is no vassal to America!" He remarked that a nation which pledged other powers not to sell naval vessels [5] except by agreement of all the governments ought to be willing to refrain from selling airplanes. And he gibed at America for spending more money on naval defense than any other nation, although being the least vulnerable. A confused reporter, dabbling for the first time in far eastern matters, kept addressing him as Mr. Manchukuo. Matsuoka kept his smile.

"I'm really one of you," he concluded. "Oregon is my second 'native state.'"

A reporter asked, "Does that indicate that Japan will be annexing Oregon?"

Matsuoka laughed heartily. "We haven't gotten to that yet!"

On the radio Matsuoka told us: "It is high time in the affairs of the world for you Americans to know your minds, and clearly decide whether you want a real peace or only the formal pretense of it!" This was in 1934. Still Congress voted against fortifying Guam—and on the other hand we kept our hand in, in Pacific Asia. Almost as much as the British, we relied upon prestige to counter superior force!

Matsuoka didn't want America to think about an arbitrament of arms. "Every Japanese and American," he said, "who says anything that leads America and Japan toward war commits a crime against humanity and against God." [6] But Matsuoka's hope of arguing the United States out of the picture was waning. Lord Palmerston, the czar, or Theodore Roosevelt could have sat down in full heartiness to melon carve with Matsuoka. The only difference might have been over the size of respective slices. But in Franklin Roosevelt's day—practise it or not ourselves—we were upholding a new idealism. The new Russian ambassador to Washington, coming from five years' residence in Japan, succinctly gave the reaction of the western world to Matsuoka's Japan:

"Some nations regard themselves as supernations, destined not to coöperate with others, but to dominate and conquer other nations." [7]

[5] Chicago *Tribune,* April 3, 1934.
[6] *Japan Times and Mail,* January 21, 1934.
[7] Washington newspapers, April 28, 1934.

Then Troyanovsky told the old Russian fable of the cat that ate the meat while the cook lectured and scolded. The question seemed to be: When the lecturing cook pulled the meat away from the cat, would the cat fly at his face?

Japan reiterates that she is actuated by no motive other than her desire to establish enduring peace in eastern Asia. This is the same motive that actuated Cæsar in pacifying Gaul, and Clive and Hastings in pacifying India. Japan believes that people of the future will speak of the thirty thousand cherry trees planted inside the Great Wall as a beautiful memorial to the Japanese troops, who died early martyrs to the eventually successful cause of introducing order in China. One pauses to wonder how "accepted" history has been made in many lands.

According to all the old standards, Japan was right, as was the wolf when it pacified the bleating lamb, and turned it into hard wolf flesh and strong wolf muscle. We hesitated to accept—believing in new ideas of live and let live. And yet we hesitated to prepare force to back our ideas—believing (or did we?) in peace.

Hirota concluded his summary of Japan's problems:

"As long as our people are united and well prepared to face courageously whatever difficulties may arise, and as long as we retain our composure and sobriety and 'stray not from the path of rectitude, and in action always embrace the golden mean,'[8] I am confident that Japan has nothing to fear and her future will be full of hope. We should not forget that Japan, serving as only a cornerstone for the edifice of peace of eastern Asia, bears the entire burden of responsibilities.

"It is in this important position and in these vast responsibilities that Japan's diplomacy and national defense are rooted. Our national defense is organized in its very nature for defensive and self-protective purposes. At the same time our diplomacy has no claims to put forth save what is legitimate and rational and consonant with our national mission.

"That eventually this position in which Japan naturally and actually finds herself will be rightly understood by other powers is, I believe, a foregone conclusion."

[8] Quoted by Hirota from Confucius.

Mr. Hirota's diplomacy was approved by the important, silent Yoshizawa (Kenkichi), a modern incarnation of the dour samurai type who is plagued by children who want to tap dance, run American-style bars, and otherwise express an ultrajazz spirit that is already out of style among the youth of Japan. His short, high career was a tense drama; advocate of Japan tried at the bar of the League of Nations—a defendant who drove his judges, particularly Aristide Briand, mad with his poker-faced silence; elevated to a foreign ministership by his father-in-law, Premier Inukai, "old fox" of the stop-gap cabinet following the military outburst of 1931; plunged into official oblivion upon the assassination of this seventy-odd-year old opportunist who was too much wedded to big business to suit the army junta that had seized power and invaded China, then brought back for the protracted negotiations for oil and rubber with the Dutch Governors of the East Indies.

Yoshizawa did Japan outstanding service in passing off the drastic internal change in Japan on foreign governments without admitting that it was a revolution, and in keeping the conquest of Manchuria and invasion of Shanghai from being called war. He had a profound instinct for the hypocrisies used to cover the rise of nations to empire; Japan needed him. At the same time he represented the group opposed to bandying words with western governments. Let them accept Japan's acts in theory as well as in fact.

Working on Hirota's theory, but not so optimistically, was his wide-awake henchman, Mr. Saito (Hiroshi), who, during his consular experience in New York, studied the United States as carefully as Hirota studied Russia. Upon assuming the ambassadorship to Washington, Saito announced that his business was drinking good whisky with Americans. He was more successful in influencing the American public by means of our radio than any other foreign emissary.

Matsuoka, who grew up among us, threw American inconsistencies, like dead fish, in our face. Saito, better trained in oriental tact, cooked the fish and smilingly suggested a mutual banquet. "The United States of America can readily sympathize with Japan's position in China, because of your difficulties in this part of the world," he said. "Your motives, too, of promoting peace and benefiting small neighbor countries, have been misunderstood." [9]

"The best of customers do not fight," Saito mouthed the epigram of the veteran Japanese hooeyist," Count Ishii. This went over big with chambers of commerce, Rotary clubs, and women's club audiences, although the former two, at least, should know without being told that every great war in history has taken place between the "best of customers."

No American could have safely undertaken Hiroshi Saito's task of predicting this country's actions, but he must have been more accurate than his predecessor, Debuchi of the unerasable smile, who assured War Lord Araki that for three good reasons the United States would never extend the diplomatic hand to the Soviet power. The three were: the American Legion, the Roman Catholic church, and the D.A.R.! He died in the grand new Imperial Japanese Embassy in Washington and was sent home to Tokyo for burial on an American battleship with flags at halfmast, while the men and women of good will among us shed tears of sympathy over the kind little man who worked his life out for peace between our nations and the touching gesture on our part which insured it! But our Navy thought of the mission—wisely—as their last chance to get a ship into and have a good look around in Tokyo Bay.

[9] Newspaper reports of national radio hook-up, May 16, 1934.

Chapter XXII

Light from the East

W E HAVE looked at several score key men of Japan, from founders, through unifiers, revolutionaries, and conservers to the present head-liners. Don't worry about their names. Those with whom we must yet deal will be brought back to you through the radio and newspapers. But the author hopes you have got the taste of their conceptions, their ambitions, a glimpse of their outlook on the world. In their contours you have seen the outline of Nippon's face.

Through the fabric woven out of such human lives, through viewpoints differing from those of the superaristocrat Konoye to the adventurer-fanatic Toyama, through personalities differing from the unexcitable Saionji and Saito to the fervid Araki and the brutally shrewd Tojo, from the argumentative Matsuoka to the coldly cynical Suetsugu and his clever fleet commander Yamamoto, who boasts of what he learned while our guest in Washington, runs one attitude and purpose peculiarly Japanese to-day.

In concluding this survey of contemporary Japanese, we can do no better than to turn back to American-reared Matsuoka for a summary of this attitude and purpose. He draws, in the clearest and boldest strokes, the picture of Nippon against the world.

"As a member of the international community, Japan shares the world's distress. She too has got something restless inside. But Japan can extricate herself with greater promptness than the western countries, for she has a spiritual civilization of her own which is great enough to correct our mistaken imitations of western civilization, to guide occidentals and to save the world itself. Our forefathers' motto was 'The Japanese Spirit with the Chinese Cul-

ture.' In the modern age this became 'The Japanese Spirit with
Western Technic and Science.' There is no gainsaying the fact of
the peculiar excellence of the west's contribution here. But Japan
is hardly in need of copying anything from western life save its
material civilization. As a natural outcome of following the western
peoples' liberal system of education, the sense of national character
among Japanese of higher education became faint, and what is
worse still, their personal conduct became loose. Such degenerates
were fair meat for the Marxist taint. In politics, diplomacy and
education, Japan had gone a little too far in imitating the west. At
least this dangerous tendency was noticeable until right before the
outburst of the Manchurian incident. Through this experience the
traditional Japanese spirit has at last been roused up, and now
pulsates in the hearts of the whole nation.

"It is natural that a Japan that had become too abandoned to
westernism should have begun to suffer when western civilization
itself was collapsing. The task now is not merely to resuscitate the
old spirit which governed and actuated the Japanese fathers but to
interpret it in the tempo of modern life. That spirit is traditional
but is also peculiarly aggressive and creative. We need not fear, for
the Japanese have come of late to realize the strength of their own
civilization, built upon their peculiar philosophy of a family country,
with the Imperial Court as the center.

"Western history is the history of individualism, while Japanese
history is a history of totalism. It is but natural under the circumstances that loyalty and filial piety should be as predominant in the
Japanese character as they are absent in the west. Loyalty and
filial piety are the twin cardinal elements of our morality—the
supreme virtues, divinely implanted in the Japanese and developed
through their long history. They are virtues that demand self-
sacrifice for the sake of the whole. They completely transcend individualism. In fact, they are diametrically opposed to individualism
which takes a point of insisting upon personal liberty and rights
above all else. The idea of loyalty, as the Japanese know it, is
entirely strange to the majority of westerners. In Japan mere school
children understand it without any explanation. Filial piety seems
to be more comprehensible to the occidental than loyalty, but their

sense of this virtue, too, is fast fading away. To them it is hardly anything beyond being kind to parents.

"Not only filial loyalty, but chastity is less marked in the occidental mind than in the Japanese."

II

Matsuoka grew up among the representative institutions of American democracy. Therefore they were not sacred to him. He had for them the contempt born of familiarity. The generation before him thought western institutions had some connection with western material power, even as did some of our material-minded people, and for that reason—not because of moral or humanitarian reasons, introduced them into Japan—in much the same spirit that medieval chieftains used to take their priests and religion on campaign with them, or the Jews carried the ark to war against the Philistines. Japan had early imported from China the belief that certain institutions, purely by intrinsic virtue, have magical material effects. The most modern Japanese diplomat or soldier will ascribe a victory to the virtue of the emperor, which really means the mystical effect of having the Divine Family enshrined in his nation.

So did the creators of modern Japan in the middle of the nineteenth century believe that modern military and economic power were the emanation of the west's god, Representative Government. That Japan might have "his" benefits, in addition to indigenous blessings, they imported the western god and set him up on a shelf just below the Sacred Seat of the Son of Heaven.

Matsuoka and his generation are fully recovered from this puerility. Democracy has actually been worked in Japan about as much as has Christianity over here, which may be a little less than democracy has been worked over here. With the examples of Italy and Russia before them, the Japanese no longer believed that national power was the child of democracy. Those who favor retaining the party system do so for opportunistic reasons. Matsuoka comes out flatly with the statement that "the party system, imported from western countries, does not suit the peculiar conditions of Japan." Some scheme "enabling the nation to act as one man in carrying out both foreign and domestic policies must supersede government by struggle between factions." "The present political unrest in Japan is evidence that the nation realizes before reaching calamity that democracy is a failure," says Matsuoka's newspaper friend Kiyosawa. Matsuoka emphasized his conviction by resignation from the House of Representatives—an act rather beyond the comprehension of the western politician. One might note in passing, that his attendance for one day to submit and help accept his own resignation enabled him to collect the fifteen hundred yen salary for the session. He went out to stump the land, to make a motion picture called *Youth of Japan, Arise!* and to make a war picture called *The Coming Crisis* in which General Araki and Admiral Suetsugu took part!

No opposition is heard to Matsuoka's doctrine. In place of parliamentary forms, Matsuoka suggests an assembly for expressing views—a national edition of the oriental village council. The most liberal great paper in Japan states: "Matsuoka's sentiment is shared by the majority of the nation and the resolution of military people to-day is thoroughly for it."

Modern men like Matsuoka and Hirota identify the ancient theocracy of Japan with the theory evolved in Russia, Italy, and Germany since the World War—that whatever group has unity of purpose and hitting power has the divine right—nay, the divine duty—to rule the nation. Japan applies this fascism internationally, continentally, and, in vision, terrestrially.[1]

III

Let us take time for one messianic message in a vein of assurance and expectancy that reminds of the old Hebrew prophet

---

[1] It was logical that the founder and prophet of fascism, Mussolini, should, more than any other statesman in Europe, have resented Japan's ambitions and been outspoken about the menace in them. Mussolini, too, had a world vision—perhaps a world mission—and the Japanese paper *Nichi-nichi* truly accused him of jealousy. He replaced Kaiser Wilhelm as the warner against the "yellow peril," he restricted the entry of Japanese goods into Italy and her colonies, and his jealousy and fear—perhaps his vision—went so far as to interdict the marriage of a black Abyssinian noble, arranged by the noble through that effective new instrument in Nippon the newspaper ad, to a Japanese young lady of station and wealth.

Isaiah. It comes from the usually hard-boiled army, penned by Lieutenant General Hata (Shinji) in the popular magazine *Gendai*, New Year's number, 1934:

"From ancient times the 'providential wind' has been constantly blowing over the country. This, however, can only be realized through divine communication and none but believers in the imperial way can feel it.

"It is regrettable that among those who know the heavenly aid at the times of the Sino-Japanese and Russo-Japanese Wars, some are unappreciative of the divine help extended in the existing national difficulties.

"Just look back upon the outbreak of the Manchurian incident. If it was not the work of the providence, what prompted the outbreak? Some feared that the unrestrained action of the army might ruin the country. But see how the country emerged victorious and how the dark clouds of apprehension have been wiped away! The nation has begun to put up its head in fresh spirit and vigor. People's understanding of traditional Nippon teachings is now being promoted in great speed."

Japan's seventy million people, so capable of fanatic idealism, are increasingly impregnated with the messianic complex editorially expressed in the newspaper *Kokumin:* "Occidental or material civilization requires to be complemented by oriental or spiritual civilization. Western civilization has been driven to an impasse on account of its utilitarianism and is now in need of aid from oriental civilization. The World War and the Russian revolution prove the bankruptcy of western civilization, and its basis, capitalism. They collapse from want of that moral control which the orient alone can provide. What is aimed at by oriental civilization is the promotion of the welfare of neither the minor nor major portion of the people, but of the whole. Rescue must come from the orient, for the light is always from the east."

When the Japanese say "oriental civilization" they mean Japanese civilization. Confucius and Buddha have been expropriated and set to their tasks by the Arakis and the Black Dragon priest Toyama.

New Year's messages, 1934, from the great Japanese newspapers to their millions of readers read:

Kokumin: "The east is beginning to rule the west. Proof 1: When Japan leaves the League of Nations the League becomes moribund. Germany, the greatest western nation, takes her lead from us. Proof 2: Japan has become the industrial pacemaker of the world. Proof 3: The capitalist powers of the west are compelled to permit this triumph of Japan in order to keep Russia and bolshevism from overwhelming them. Eventually they must call on Japan for protection from communism. The year 1933 leaves this terrestrial globe with the east in triumph over the west. The year 1934 will see greater impetus in this direction."

Osaka *Asahi:* "During 1933 Japan has made economic development at a steady pace. She has learned that in tiding over economic as well as political difficulties, her fighting spirit is a greater asset than the western world's natural resources. This spirit manifests itself in the contentment with a low standard of living so long as that is required. This spirit maintained, Japan can be as sure of triumph in the world's economic struggle as in the execution of the world's divine mission.

"Not only filial loyalty, but chastity is less marked in the occidental mind than in the Japanese. Loyalty is the virtue that maintains the relative position of monarch and subject, filial piety the one that defines the relations of parent and child, while chastity is the value governing husband and wife. The decline of the last-named virtue among western peoples has been particularly conspicuous of late, it having come to the point at which many husbands are no longer able to trust their wives. At that point individualism finds its bankruptcy, which means, in short, the bankruptcy of western civilization, political, economic and moral—thus the heavy atmosphere of anxiety in which the whole world is submerged.

"Individualism has been carried to an excess; it upsets the orderliness of society. Without faith between monarch and subject there will be born republicanism; without faith between parent and child, contumacy; without faith between man and wife, libertinism.

"Party government is an administrative system based on individualism. Individualism seeks protection of self and selfish interests. A government form founded thereon necessarily lacks the spirit of self-sacrifice for the sake of the state; it attaches greater importance to party welfare than to state interest. Certainly it is time now for Japan to cast away this stained cloak borrowed from the west." Translating philosophy into daily life Japanese Minister of Education Masuda issues an edict forbidding children to call their parents: "papa" or "mama"—as derogatory to family discipline. The honorific literary names for paternal and maternal ancestors must be used.

Thus to the depth of her spirit Japan began to find herself in clash with the west. Contempt replaced adulation, inferiority complex became superiority complex. It seems destined to be a struggle to the death. The voice of new Japan is definite enough:

"We have never permitted ourselves to be drawn into political or military affairs of Europe or the Americas," said Matsuoka in 1934, "but the western nations have not similarly refrained from interfering with eastern affairs, and are permitting themselves to be drawn in by false idealism of the clever Chinese. A frank recognition by western countries of Japan's position would have met welcome. However, not only before we became a first-class power, but even now, the western countries continue to act in disregard of us. They respond to Chinese appeals and encourage Chinese violence. The trouble in eastern Asia is fundamentally of western making. It was not Japan that began the aggression upon China. For one hundred years before Japan opened her doors at American request, invasions in China had been going on, and, but for Japan, China would undoubtedly be an arena for western squabbling today. Russia has been the most persistent European nation in making conquests in Asia.

"The methods of western countries in dealing with Japan have been partisan. Germany could take territory in China and establish a naval base at Tsingtao, France could seize the territory of Indo-China and extend her influence into Yunnan, Britain may hold Hongkong and lay claim to a sphere of influence throughout the Yangtze valley, America may acquire the Philippine Islands—an Asiatic territory six thousand miles from her shores—but when Japan drove the Germans out of China during the World War, the

American government objected to Japan's assumption of German rights. When Japan took control of Korea, a country smaller in territory than the Philippines and only one hundred miles from her borders, her action was denounced. To the western mind, what Europe or America does in Asia is always in the nature of duty and in the light of human progress, while what we do is criminal."

When Japan's hero of the battle of Geneva reached Tokyo station, to be greeted by 20,000 compatriots yelling "banzai (viva)!" and to be presented a cask of sake and a case of fish from the Imperial Couple, he told his audience that Lord Lytton, hard-working head of the League of Nations committee of investigation into the Manchurian situation, possessed "an attitude of mental superiority towards Asiatics—looking upon the Japanese in the same manner as the British do upon the Indians." Lord Lytton, as it happens, had concluded that that is the way the Japanese were looking upon the Chinese. To Japanese, one case of superiority complex is the product of innate divinity; the other just plain British.

Matsuoka gives Japan's side of her present controversy with the world: "If the League of Nations, ignoring the United States, were active in Mexico, Americans would object, although Mexico is a comparatively small country compared to the United States, while China is seven times as large in population as Japan. If the action of the League and America had been of a friendly diplomatic character, Japan would have dealt with them in similar courtesy, although she could not have given in. Though the purpose was declared to be peaceful, their action was in the nature of browbeating and saber rattling. Men in the League spoke of the application of sanctions and of bringing economic and financial pressure upon Japan, while the American navy concentrated in Hawaii. The Japanese government and people cannot be dealt with in this manner!" [2]

Matsuoka compared the situation of his country and prewar Germany: "Japan's international position is comparable to Germany's position for many reasons. Japan's astonishing activity in industry

[2] Yosuke Matsuoka, for the North American Newspaper Alliance, as published in the New York *Times,* April 29, 1934. Rearranged by the author, but not contrary to sense.

and shipping is like that of Germany, which overpowered the Union Jack in every harbor of the world. Some persons fear that Japan may be suppressed by force as was Germany, but it is impossible to suppose that Britain and America could wage war against Japan merely for the purpose of checking the latter's activity in business. European and American nations had enough experiences from the World War for even America and Britain to have no courage to make war with Japan. If the Japanese nation goes ahead with grim resolution, it is certain that Japan will always be able to ward off any foreign intervention. As a healthy body cannot fall victim to illness, so a united nation will not suffer from intervention. To substantiate her case, Japan must be backed by sufficient armament. But repletion of armament without consideration of international psychology will defeat its purpose. We must be frank but never rude, resolute but never challenging." [3]

To sum up, the decorous nations of the world treated Japan like a committee of gray-haired vestrymen administering correction to a virile young church member too openly flaunting his conquests of women. Willing to deal with the case in the gentle Christian manner, they suggest that all sit down and sign a mutual pact to leave women alone.

The young blade is put on the defensive. While he argues, he looks pityingly at their sagging lips, and furtively thumbs his book for his next date.

When the time came to fly in their faces, Matsuoka, American reared, Japan's most competent "cusser" of America, stepped down. He didn't want to be in the forefront of war against his "second native land." And the demi-gods around the Son of Heaven, thinking of every eventuality, wished to keep in reserve men who could talk "American." For the same reason, they preserved some of the top communists, paying their way in refuge abroad—men who can talk familiarly with Moscow. *We* shall hear from—be dealing with—the Matsuokas again.

[3] Washington *Star*, 1922.

EMOTIONAL FACES OF JAPAN

Chapter XXIII
Natural and Sentimental Japan

By now the lives and anecdotes recounted in this book will have given the reader the picture of a disciplined yet heady people, regimented yet strongly permeated with a spirit of nonconformism, reserved and yet surprisingly natural.

I think that in some ways they are the most natural people in the world. A Japanese high official or professor is a great man, held in awe as American people hold perhaps no one other than their president, or as humble Roman Catholics might hold their bishop. In no country do great and famous men feel so free to be unconventional in their dress and habits as in Japan, and their people feel this no sacrifice of their dignity. An admiral recently chosen premier allowed newspapermen to take his photograph as he was pulling on his shoes to go to the imperial audience to receive his appointment. Yet, paradoxically, in this same Japan, formalism is carried to the greatest length of any country in the modern world. It is a formalism of ceremony, entirely different in spirit from "putting on dog" as known in the west.

A Japanese wrote me that during his long residence in America he came near to being converted to the American idea that his own people are inscrutable or artificial. Then he strode through Japanese parks and came upon a group indulging in the national sport of picnicking. Spontaneously two elderly women rose, took fans in their hands, and did a graceful amateur dance, and the crowd looked on and applauded in pure childish delight.

On streets, trains, and steamers, in hotels and shops, Japanese unceremoniously accost the stranger. Sometimes a Japanese asks you out of a clear sky the meaning of a word or a phrase in

English. Sometimes he begins with the bald statement that he wishes to converse and improve his English; or he may ask you how much you paid for your hat, whether your teeth are false, or where you purchased your walking stick. Frequently enough he is a government spy trying to make a report on the unwary traveler which will attract the attention of his bureau chief, but in most cases he is a common citizen inspired by amiable curiosity, friendly hospitality, or a real wish to help the visitor see Japan at its best.

A correspondent for the New York *Times* relates one unusual experience of this sort when a smiling, short Japanese, dressed in western clothes and speaking excellent English, bowed and stopped him on the streets of Kobe. "Would you like to see the American-Japanese war of year after next?" he asked pleasantly. The correspondent collected his wits and expressed interest and was led to one of the full-floor exhibitions of the crisis of 1935-1936 being put on by the five large department stores of the city. Here the guide patiently explained to the American the set-up of great naval and air battles in miniature, and interpreted the droning descriptions of the lecturer.

Not so many years ago I stood looking rather aghast at a full-window map exhibit showing the relative situations of Japan and America and the strategy of American defeat by the hosts of the Son of Heaven. Japanese, from white-collared business executives to coolies dressed only in loin cloths and unbuttoned jerkins, stopped beside me, smiled, and asked amiable questions about my reactions. With some effort I told them it was a splendid map and that it impressed me very much, which pleased them like children are pleased when you dodge their toy swords.

An evidence of Japanese naturalness is their unself-consciousness of the human body. Over the most of Japan still, public toilets are co-educational—to Japanese the natural requirements of nature have no gender. Cleanliness is maintained by a woman attendant who presides with the dignity of a maid in a drawing-room. Until the introduction of western salaciousness, the Japanese bathed without thought of sex classification. The author has enjoyed many a charming and thoroughly proper conversation with a nude, wet lady casually met in the limpid waters of the ofuro—the miniature heated pool found in every inn and resort. Lust to the Japanese is a serious thing to go full out about on special and appropriate occasions. There is never the slightest degree of it in casual contacts.

As in many other parts of the world, for instance Russia, the bathing suit was unknown until the importation of western ideas. When people of either sex took off their clothes to bathe, they took them all off. There was to the Japanese mind no reason for compromise in the form of wet clinging garments around particular parts of the anatomy. There still is to them no part of the body more mentally connected with sex than any other part. The Japanese sweetheart, like most oriental women, may be more fastidious about her breasts than the European woman, and she is certain to be the most fastidious about her lips—given only in the supreme embrace, which explains the attitude of Japanese censors about kissing scenes —but there is none of that anatomical classification (constantly varying) which is the core of the behavior concepts of our western ladies.

I think the most natural incident I have ever seen in all my travels took place on the slope of the sacred Mt. Maya ("cloud-scraper"), whose cryptomeria-covered crest, always hung with curtains of mist, towers over Kobe, which contains the largest community of westerners in Japan. On Maya's summit, reached by a thousand or more stone steps lined by several thousand copper fretwork lanterns, now equipped with electric bulbs, stands a Buddhist temple famous for its huge bronze and wood carvings, a monument of culture built as early as Canterbury Cathedral in England. The forest around the Buddhist temple is still dotted with crude carved stones which were shrines to animal and spirit worship before the arrival of the civilizing religion from China thirteen centuries ago. Enterprising Japanese concessionaires have built a cog railroad from the busy city halfway up the steep side of the mountain to a natural amphitheater scooped out through the ages by flowing warm springs, and have placed there a miniature Coney Island amusement resort.

Here on a summer night that was stifling the millions in Kobe and great Osaka, seen as a twenty-mile belt of lights along the Inland Sea at our feet, I stood watching a Japanese reproduction of a Broadway farce. The crowd, some in kimonos, some in western dress, were trying to get the salacious points in a sophisticated conversation between the young top-hatted gigolo and the drunken gay lady on the stage. Suddenly a girl sitting on the aisle looked about her, saw a warm spring flowing from the embankment of the amphitheater into a little pool, slipped from her seat to its side, dropped her clothes, sat in the pool and thoroughly laved herself, stepped out again, donned her kimono, and quietly resumed her seat to knit her brows over the meaning of the play. No one in the banks of packed seats gave her more than a passing glance.

The Japanese is both a good and a poor liar. He lacks the ability to make himself seem as romantic as he really is. He is a combination of conservative and rebel, intensely proud, direct-acting, absolutely faithful to conviction, impossible to drive, but very susceptible to leadership. He has submitted to tyranny through most of his civilization because he has really believed in it. The Japanese is a selfish rather than a social person, taking matters that affect him exceedingly seriously, more frequently than most races brooding upon them to the point of mental unbalance.

No nation acts so cohesively, yet the Japanese person is exceedingly individualistic. A Japanese young lady of New York expressed to me that she believed "the Japanese individually are the most selfish people in the world. They look at everything through their own eyes." Individually and nationally it is difficult for them to see the other man's point of view. Their selfishness contrasts with that of the English—it is much less mature. Englishmen have said to me in Shanghai and India, "If we were in the shoes of the Chinese or Indians, we would do to them exactly what they are doing to us, only do it better and harder." I have never heard a Japanese speak of himself even in sardonic imagination as being in the shoes of the Chinese or Koreans, or of any victim. I think the Japanese mind is too childishly direct to conceive such a thing.

Yet with all of his supersensitiveness the Japanese for the most part tends to view life, when he is not himself concerned, objectively as a fatalistic play, fascinating the understanding—interesting, regardless of how cruel. Once he has given himself over to the supreme ecstasy of his soul, he can view his own life in the same detached manner. It is then that he is dangerous.

II

There is less paradox in Japanese sentimentality than in Japanese naturalness. We are prone to make a mistake in thinking sentimentalism is a trait opposed to austerity and ruthlessness, whereas these traits really go together, and are phenomena of medieval or undeveloped mentality. We find them constantly together in the German people as well as the Japanese. Historically, Japan's nearest parallel in the western world is England, but emotionally it is Germany. Japanese and Germans often show similar lack of sense of humor in its full meaning of sense of mis-proportion.

The two nations have the same attitude to war. Kaiser Wilhelm expressed it in 1908: "We have to fight even for righteousness' sake. The Bible is full of fights—jolly good fights some of them were. It is a mistaken idea that Christianity does not countenance war." The Nazi fanatic to-day is very much of a piece with the Japanese super-patriot—save that he lacks the Japanese patriot's foundation and consistency, being without his integrating center, the Divine House.[1] In the Hitlerian method of handing to traitors or obstructors pistols with which to shoot themselves, in the encouragement of dueling, and in the tendency of trapped political offenders to suicide, we find a working out of the same psychology that lies behind the "honorable discharge" of the samurai. Several times in her brief history Germany has tended to create a warrior caste parallel to that of Japan.

Japanese and Germans have much the same naïveté of self-revelation. Quite the opposite from being inscrutable, for which the world gives them credit, Japanese are perhaps the most self-revealing nation in the world. Even in their efforts to hide matters or evade issues they are amusingly transparent. Their face saving deceives no one, and is childish in comparison with that of the Chinese. They are shockingly frank about data regarding themselves. This trait, combined with their modern passion for statistics, provides the student of their activities with abundant and telling material. Their journalists are the most anecdotal-minded that I have encountered. Their papers love to print items about men and national policies

[1] This as written in 1934.

with bland disregard for any embarrassment they may occasion.

Many an accommodating Japanese official or governor of a corporation, apparently inspired by pride in the sheer fact that you should be interested in his people, will provide you with data which drives you inescapably to conclusions for which he may in turn bitterly condemn you. Just this happened to the earnest and perplexed Lord Lytton of the League of Nations' investigating committee on Manchuria. Eventually the ponderous mills of the official censorship move to prevent seepage of the damaging facts, but they are always too late.

With all this, too, the Japanese are a very gullible people—particularly their officialdom. Japan has been and continues to be a prey to literary fakers, self-advertised world travelers and explorers, small college professors, professional exploiters of "good will," would-be women's club lecturers, and such persons, who, even though they may possess no standing in their own communities, can with a little flattery or promise of propaganda activity procure for themselves free honeymoon trips through the orient, sinecures in some Japanese propaganda organization, or out-and-out gifts.

The most common Japanese charge against one who differs is "lack of sincerity." This is their stock political charge against their own officials and demagogues. I think the Japanese really fail to see how palpably insincere this lack-of-sincerity charge usually appears to the outsider. Nor do I think that they themselves are insincere in making it. It is simply that the Japanese more than any other people are victims of the rather common human failing of being unable to see any side of a controversy save their own at the moment. You will find this as true of shopkeepers as of admirals. The Japanese idea of granting to another the right of free will and opinion is like the Nazi idea of giving a dissenter a fair amount of time in which to convince himself that he is wrong. Japanese simply are unable to understand that one might differ and still be sincere, fair, and even sympathetic. In this particular illogicality and irrationality they are a nation possessing what the male in moments of exasperation thinks of as a "feminine mind."

The Japanese and German races have the same tendency to burst into tears over abstract ideals, hurt pride, or the superficially pathetic aspects of a hopeless love affair. The Japanese newspaper-reading public is always having its eyes dimmed by incidents like these: "The Little Pilgrim. On the morning of January 20, 1931, a little girl with bobbed hair presented herself at the official residence of the war minister. She was Miss Hideko Higashimura, fifth-grade pupil of the Fifth Primary School, Tennoji Ward, Osaka. Although she had no introduction or previous permission, the minister saw her.

"She showed him a book containing the seals of one hundred and twenty-three Imperial tombs which she had visited for the purpose of praying for the success of General Honjo and his army in Manchuria. She desired to have this book sent to the general and her request was granted."

"Two young girls called on the social affairs bureau of Oji ward with the sum of ten yen which they wished to donate to the imperial army. They are telephone girls and saved this amount by doing without the cosmetics which are dear to the heart of the modern girl."

An eighty-one-year-old farmer walks across the empire to collect a loan made ten years previously, to find his debtor sick and unable to pay, and gives his last few sen to a taximan who drops him at a strange place. "If I walk with a well-filled sake bottle in hand, I can negotiate at least twenty miles a day without getting the least bit tired," he tells the sob writer who features his story. The faithful dog Hachiko, who goes daily to meet the train of his one-time commuting but now dead master has a statue built to him by fellow commuters of his lamented master at the suburban station.

The beasts in the great Ueno Park have radio loud-speakers installed in their cages so that they may enjoy music in their captivity. A ten-year-old schoolgirl trudges to the war department to give $6\frac{1}{2}$ yen, which she has made selling bean sauce after school hours, to the army to buy a cannon. Students and merchants collect money to provide the aviation department, Russian fashion, with thirty airplanes. Caps in hand, politely, they solicit us for funds at the doors of temples and shrines. The Japanese community in Peru purchases several airplanes to further the divine mission. Whether or not these are kept in the shadow of the Andes and within striking distance of the Panama Canal is not published. A modern buccaneer, Azure, disciple of Toyama, is sentenced to ten years for attacking Soviet fishing ships. He says his motive was patriotism. But Warden Arima of the model prison says he was influenced by the movies.

Minura (Katsunda) is jailed for graft in Matsushima. His lifetime political enemy, the former communications minister, Motoma, obtains a license as attorney so that he can defend the accused and procure his acquittal.

The republic of El Salvador recognizes the independent government of Manchukuo, and with eyes tear-dimmed by this "beginning of world recognition" of Japan's great constructive work in Pacific Asia, Japanese acclaim the combined Salvadorean consul and minister as a hero, and raise several hundred yen for the victims of a Salvadorean hurricane.

The Japanese army and public are much affected by the voluntary action of the British guard of honor in marching in the rain without oilcoats, the same as Japanese paraders, at Admiral Togo's funeral. We might list a bookful of similar revealing instances of Japanese sentimentality.

Japanese are tremendously affected by the participation of outsiders in their peculiar doings. Nothing moves them so readily as the stranger's sincere reaction to the beauty of their islands. They easily break into tears—not of tenderness, but of sentiment.

Their sentimental side is perfectly mirrored in a well-written Japanese story of the surrender of the Russian commander at Port Arthur: "On New Year's day, 1905, the long-expected messenger from the Russians arrived, and by the fourth Captain Tsunoda and T. Kawakami (interpreter) were ordered by General Nogi to proceed to the Russian stronghold to make arrangements for the meeting of the two generals.

"They found the place in a state of ruin and desolation with wounded men lying about everywhere. Groans could be heard even from the room in which General Stoessel received them. All the horses except General Stoessel's own had been killed and eaten so that the present of fifty chickens and a hundred fresh eggs which the Japanese brought with them was welcome indeed. Arrangements were made for a meeting of the two generals the next day at Suishihying.

"There in a cottage left among the ruins of a fierce battle, the two generals clasped hands. Stoessel expressed his admiration for the courage of the Japanese and said that the guns of the Japanese navy had caused him his worst losses. General Nogi praised the long and brave defense of the Russians. Stoessel expressed his sympathy with Nogi for the loss of his two sons in the campaign.

"Stoessel expressed his thanks for the telegrams which had come to the stronghold through the courtesy of the Japanese, one of which was from the czar. Stoessel told of his indecision as to whether to allow himself to be taken prisoner to Japan or to return to Russia, and he finally asked the czar. The answer was that he might do as he liked. Everybody in the room became silent and all felt a prickling around the eyes.

"Stoessel presented his fine white Arab horse to General Nogi, but Nogi said that much as he would like to receive it as his from the general's hands, it must first be presented to the Emperor. He promised, however, that if it came back to him, as he had every reason to believe it would, he would take care of it as if it had always been his.

"Stoessel himself led the fine animal to where Nogi was and mounted for the last time, showing off its good qualities and the tricks it knew."

General Nogi built a stable for Stoessel's horse better than his own residence and kept the animal there in his front yard till it died. The stable is to-day part of the Nogi shrine, made one of Japan's most sacred altars of patriotism by the hara-kiri of the general and his wife as the gun boomed to announce the burial of the Meiji Emperor.

Chapter XXIV
Individualistic and Nonconformist Japan

SNAP-JUDGMENT oracles have mouthed the statement that no people as repressed, regimented and literal-minded as are the Japanese could excel in world competition or win in the last supreme test. Such persons know too little of Japanese history and lives. The Japanese Wars of the Chrysanthemums were terminated by the glorious individualism of Yoshitsune, brother of Yoritomo, and all Japanese history is sprinkled with examples of a sublime ability to disobey: to break out of routine at the right time.

No religious tenet has taken root so deeply in the Japanese soul as the Zen doctrine that if a man follows his individual impulse with no thought of saving himself in the consequences, heaven will take care of the rest.

Japan always has a man willing to pit his own conviction against the mass mind—even against the accepted interpretation of the Divine Will. Substitution of their own wills for orders by Japanese officers and officials is something with which foreign diplomats or soldiers dealing with Japan must always be ready to cope.

Travelers in the Japanese Empire constantly met the same thing. A few years ago the writer was able to arrange through Baron Shidehara, then foreign minister, for a writer to visit the Bonin Islands, Japan's great "Pearl Harbor" halfway between Tokyo and the American outpost of Guam. This little archipelago was settled a hundred years ago by Americans along with some British subjects and South Sea Islanders; Admiral Perry, between his two visits to Tokyo Bay, annexed it for the United States, surveyed it for a coaling base and trading outpost and bought up the foreshore by way of doing a little land speculation on his own. Washington declined to go through with the annexation, however, and after a dispute with Great Britain, the islands went in the nineties to Japan, who thoroughly Japanized their surviving white population, teaching them to use the Japanese language and revere the Tenno. The object of my writer friend was to take some pictures of surviving Japanese subjects named George Washington, Adams, etc. This was fully endorsed by the national authorities in Tokyo. However, the captain of my friend's ship felt differently, as did the police in the islands. No sooner was he at sea than his cameras disappeared, and when the ship arrived he was escorted directly to an inn and kept inside its charming garden until time to leave a week or so later. His captors wined and dined him and generously regaled him with geisha entertainment, but paid no attention whatever to his documents from their superiors in Tokyo or his protests.

Again, in the summer of 1933, the writer, at the suggestion of the Japanese legation in Peking and with full documents therefrom, took a group of Americans into Manchukuo, only to have the Japanese military there ignore entirely the laissez-passer given by the minister, and, in fact, arrest and practically deport the entire group. When it is convenient the Japanese Empire is an absolute unit; and also when it is convenient it is a loosely connected chain of apparently independent governments.

The complexions of Japan's recent campaigns in Manchuria and Shanghai were several times changed by the independent initiative of commanders on the spot. At Shanghai in 1932 a Japanese aviator made a studied attempt to involve his nation in war with the United States by bombing, entirely on his own, a Chinese cotton factory where American marines were quartered. By the grace of God he hit the wing where women operators had been herded, killing some twenty of them but leaving the marines untouched. Had not the American commander on the spot been able to assure the American forces on the other side of Soochow Creek that such was the case, they would have begun a cross fire on the Japanese flank then and there.

The final terms of the Russo-Japanese treaty being made under

Theodore Roosevelt's ægis at Portsmouth, N. H., to end the Russo-Japanese War in 1905, were changed by the disobedience to orders, or personal initiative if you wish, of young Ishii, then a clerk in the foreign office, with the connivance of Shidehara, then director of the telegraph bureau. They held up the cabinet instructions to the chief Japanese delegate to sign while a movement got under way in Japan to demand the cession of the southern end of Sakhalin Island.

Similar things happened repeatedly during the attempt at Geneva to stop Japan's undeclared war on China. It was quite impossible for our diplomats in the closest touch with the authorities in Tokyo to tell just what the Japanese delegation in Geneva would do. And it was utterly impossible for the Tokyo civil government, or even the war office, to tell what the army in Manchuria was doing. From the Japanese point of view, however, it all came out as a sublime justification of the Zen philosophy, which might be paraphrased, "Heaven helps him who helps the nation"—or does on his own what he thinks ought to be done for it. This independence of action does not go too far. Reverence for authority and individual initiative exist in proportions making a formidable leadership toward world conquest.

II

In spite of his group's decision, the Japanese individual holds himself responsible to his own conscience. This is officially encouraged in high officers. For instance, the minister of war, chief of military education and chief of staff are coördinate but independent officers, each directly responsible to the emperor, and not only this, but each infantry division commander is directly responsible to the emperor or the head of the staff for the efficiency of his command!

A court attaché who had helped convict Kotoku as an anarchist, discovering after twenty years that the accused had been unjustly executed, went insane, and this is not an individual instance. The Japanese conscience is a pervading and terrible thing. Demonstrations constantly occur similar to the following: A woman was condemned to die for killing her husband out of love for an actor. Word was brought to her at the execution that her lover was taking his own life also. This guilty conscience shows in the fortitude with which Japanese meet the natural disasters that visit their islands more frequently than any other populated portion of the earth. The people take these disasters as heaven's punishment for failure in one way or another to live up to the high standards required for the nation of the gods. Once the divine blow has struck, there is a sigh of relief that the sin, whatever it was, has been expiated and that *this* punishment, at least, no longer hangs over their heads.

The Japanese stubbornly refuse to accept a situation with their minds until convinced of it in their hearts. We have seen what manner of martyrs the Japanese make. Other peoples can fulminate and then forget. The Chinese compromises, knowing that nothing lasts forever. The Japanese sullenly but vigilantly bides his time. No Japanese has yet accepted or ever will accept the implication of racial inferiority implied in the American immigration act. He will not accept an inferior naval ratio as compared to Great Britain and America until that appears in an aspect not challenging his pride. The sources of his motivations are within himself and he is unbelievably, often even stupidly, stubborn.

Out of this mentality arose the samurai tradition that a fighter never surrenders. To the present time this is the code for officers in the army and navy. In the Shanghai campaign of 1932 only one Japanese officer was captured alive, and he was wounded. When nursed back to health and released, he thanked his captors, went back to his own lines and shot himself. General Araki commented, "So long as there lives among our soldiers the spirit which Major Koga has shown, the Japanese army can hope to beat any other army."

III

One of the highest forms of individualism is inventiveness. Westerners are prone to assume that the Japanese, because of their success in imitativeness, entirely lack inventiveness, and assume that without it they can never really compete with the western world. It is well to remember that inventiveness in all nations has flourished at specific periods of economic and national growth. The smug westerner to-day might get a historical viewpoint of this by reading the files of the London *Times* of the early nineteenth century. Englishmen were assured over and over again that they need have no fear of rivalry from the Yankees, who "are clever copyists but have no genius for invention." Within the next half century the greatest period of inventions so far in the world's history had its locale in America.

Japan was just beginning her age of invention in 1934. Among the several thousand patents listed for that year by the patent bureau founded by Takahashi were the following:

The 800-horsepower "Hawker's Super-Fury" motors and low-winged monoplanes built for the Japanese army by the Kawasaki Dockyard Company in Kobe, claimed to be the fastest fighting ships in the world and to make 250 miles per hour (autumn, 1934). The "ninety-one model" navy planes made in Japan completely with domestic materials, which on a test flight around Japan proper averaged a hundred miles per hour including stops. The offensive "mosquito planes"—literally, "charges of high explosive on wings"— designed to be flown by their self-immolating pilots directly into their targets, and the "one-man steered" torpedoes to operate on the same principle.

A noiseless, powderless machine gun operated by centrifugal force, said to be capable of firing 10,000 to 50,000 shots, firing 6,700 rounds per minute. The aerial torpedo of Kohara (Tsuneto) of the Patriotic Invention Institute of Tokyo, which, propelled by rockets, is claimed to be capable of reaching any point on the earth's surface within ten hours. New patents on silk-fabricated war goods, such as uniforms, flags, hats, overcoats, and parachutes.

An "air-mine" shot from a gun to suspend from a parachute in the pathway of attacking airplanes. A coding machine that solves the problem that has confronted cryptographers for more than a thousand years, which creates a system of diplomatic and military secret intelligence which the greatest experts cannot decipher. It is praised very highly by Major Yardley of the American "Black Chamber," whose work in deciphering secret messages between the Japanese delegation at the Washington arms conference and their home government in 1922 is said to have enabled Secretary of State Hughes to force the five-five-three naval ratio. American Secretary Hughes learned that the Japanese home government would accept what its Washington delegates in typical independent fashion had refused to accept.

A new method of secret telephoning by Dr. Shiba of the research laboratory of the Tokyo Electric Company—inverting speech with irregular frequency. The Japanese electrical trust announces for sale a pocket radio set.

A new light metal by Mr. Takahashi of the Metallic Research Laboratory of the Imperial University in Formosa, named magnesium number 100. It is an alloy of magnesium, aluminum and cadmium, said to be two-thirds the weight of aluminum, exceedingly strong and ideal for the use of airplanes.[1]

Several patents on new-principle motors have been filed. One on the method of generating power through the permanent rotation of "super-low-temperature liquefied air" has been pronounced successful by professors of engineering at Tokyo Imperial University. Another interesting new thrifty type of power is the charcoal-burning motor, which runs on gas produced from charcoal. In spite of the fact that Matsukata had made gasoline cheaper in Japan than anywhere else in the world (1934), the Japanese government had offered subsidies of one-half the cost of equipping gasoline motor cars—about 300 yen—with this device. The industrialist Masuda led the way by putting the charcoal attachment on his Chevrolet and claims that he gets fifty-four miles an hour at a cost of about one-fourth cent a mile. Another motor scheme is a little town car that Japanese manufacturers have sold in numbers in India, run by steel springs, 250 miles to a winding. Winding stations are provided at various spots in cities.

Other inventions of this same man are the use of dead silk cocoons for chicken feed, a cloth made of rabbit fur and waste silk, and a commercial method of turning out the ancient delicacy of dried persimmons. The annual invention prize offered by the newspaper *Asahi* for the year 1932 was for an electric loom which weaves tapestries in four colors. And, of course, we should include the invention for photographic sculpture.

Every day Japanese papers announce more inventions. Many are

---

[1] Apparently Japan pioneered in the substitution of magnesium for aluminum—not used by us until the midst of the war, 1942.

impractical, no doubt, but there is every evidence that Japan has begun a career of invention which takes up where the older mechanical nations have left off. Great Japanese industrial concerns and universities maintain research laboratories where Japanese scientists excel their brothers of other races in enthusiasm, patience for details, and dexterity of fingers. The wealthy houses of Japan are establishing great endowments for science and research. Certainly Japan is not putting a curb on inventions as Sir Josiah Stamp, a director of the Bank of England, suggested the industrial world must do.

We have already seen the great Japanese penchant for pure science evidenced in the lives of Noguchi, Takamine, and Kitazato. It is evident in astronomy, mathematics, and other pure sciences as well as medicine and biochemistry. Japanese astronomers led the world in observations on the eclipse of the sun observed in the south sea islands in 1934.

Japanese engineering, electrical, mechanical and chemical, is already the equal of that existing in the western world. Some of its recent notable achievements are the installation of radiophones on South Manchurian-railway trains and the fast ocean-going ferries between Manchuria and the Asiatic mainlands.

The new Tokyo subways are the finest in the world, and the quietest and most decent. The world's fastest train built in the Kawasaki engineering plant in Kobe runs 700 kilometers at 120 kilometers per hour from Dairen to Hsinking, the new capital of Manchukuo, with only one stop. A new tunnel connects the principal and the southern islands—a rival of the Hudson and Liverpool tunnels.

IV

Perhaps related to the Japanese penchant for nonconformism is the love of a surprise blow. Togo said to his officers, "If your adversary's sword is longer than yours, close with him," and the present jingo Admiral Suetsugu says, "The secret of success in battle is to remember there is no demarcation between attack and defense." Whether it be in war or in business, the Japanese loves to keep his resources confidential and to himself, and then suddenly to deliver a surprise blow. The Japanese love of the coup, which is such a continuous feature of Japanese history, was shown even by Dr. Noguchi in the realm of science. He always concealed his discoveries until the final proof was in his hand, and he got as much joy in springing a brain child, full-fledged, upon the world as a general does from taking his enemy from ambush. The good commander in Japan has always opened his campaigns with a surprise blow and nations who put reliance in international conventions and law cannot be too often reminded that every war of modern as well as ancient Japan has been opened by a surprise blow, not by formal declaration or a diplomatic nose thumbing.[2]

"Japanese always think and act together" is a common idea in the west. Let us note a few examples to the contrary. When Perry's fleet lay in Tokyo Bay and feeling against the "hairy barbarian" was at its height, a great scholar rowed out to Perry's ship and asked to be taken to the United States to learn. Perry refused him, and he was imprisoned by the shogun for his attempt. Every reform or revolution in Japan's history has been gained through cumulative cases of tough Japanese individualism going against the mass. This individualism has usually come from the upper classes and therefore social progress in Japan has always been created for lower classes by the efforts and sacrifices of those above. The delegate representing Japanese working women in the international labor conference at Washington was a niece of the magnate Baron Shibuzawa, and although radical groups in Japan violently protested her appearing as labor representative, she fought vigorously for improved conditions for the ex-peasant girls in her uncle's factories.

Uprisings among Japanese university students over changes that appear to them unreasonable and arbitrary are frequent. Recently Kyoto Imperial University went through a prolonged student strike over the resignation of a teacher upon demand of the minister of education. The fellow professors of his faculty backed him up and even the president of the university refused to put him out, whereupon the minister of education got a special order from the cabinet of the nation dismissing the professor. Public feeling grew and old Premier Saito himself had to use arbitration to settle the incident. Meanwhile, to the rejoicing of almost every one, the

[2] As published, 1935.

young minister of education was exposed as participant in a shady financial deal and was glad to retreat into private life. Severe measures for collecting tuition fees recently caused a somewhat similar uprising in Meiji University of Tokyo. No one can be arbitrary with Japanese, in spite of the amazing discipline to which they submit. They have to be convinced about it. That is why Japan so much of the time is at white heat. To put over any new or drastic program involves warming up the populace to it and carrying it through on a wave of enthusiasm. No people is so responsive to advertising—in none is propaganda so necessary. In fact, modern advertising began in Japan with Mitsui's prints and umbrellas.

The Japanese spirit of nonconformity under their regimentation is illustrated by the conversation of the individualist statesman, Viscount Goto, when a fellow official highly praised an underling. "If he be so good," said Goto, "let's make him prefectural governor." "Impossible," was the reply, "he lacks the requirements set by law." "Then let's change the law," Goto answered.

But note that he said "change," not "ignore" the law. The Japanese mind is literal about obedience to law and authority. Japanese either openly challenge law or obey it to the letter. And the easygoing westerner or Chinese is as constantly surprised by Japanese punctiliousness in observing meaningless little regulations when no one is about to enforce them, as the Japanese is surprised at American or Chinese petty lawlessness.

It is the paradox of Japanese individualism combined with stern devotion to duty that makes Japanese personalities so much more colorful and interesting than those, say, of China, in spite of the greater human qualities of the latter. One never knows what he will run into in Japan. I had a lady novelist friend who suddenly informed me that she had changed her name, and that I should now call her Kajiko, or Miss Rudder. The explanation was that on a recent sailing trip she had suddenly decided that she was unhappy and that she would change her luck by renaming herself after the first object that met her sight.

V

An outstanding trait of the Japanese to which their history calls attention is their fascination with the new. Dr. Washio says that his people are the most susceptible race on earth. "In my neighborhood," he says, "I see a long-bearded young man who wears a Russian shirt delivering a dozen bottles of goat milk each morning. He is an art student maintaining himself by keeping two goats—which is admirable. But why should he have to look like a Russian?"

"Marxism in Japan," continues this writer, "has been planted in soil fertilized by Tolstoy. The bookstores are flooded with translations and explanations of *Das Kapital*. On the other hand we are invaded by American influences such as the recent café revue showing a bartender dancing on the counter mixing cocktails to the time of the music, and the blacking of the faces of good Japanese jazz-band members to make them look like Negroes. It seems that Japanese youth has become a combination of jazz tastes and Marxian intellect. The term Marx boys has been coined to go with moga and mobo.[3] If intellectual, a youth is a Marx boy. If just a plain 'dumb-bell' then he is mobo. Russian radicalism comes in through the back door, American decadence through the front. Fortunately these infections haven't yet got to the backbone of the nation." Dr. Washio wrote just before the superpatriots rose in 1931 to purge the "empire of the gods," and incidentally to increase its size three times. But what the pungent Japanese essayist complained of is a lively example of Japanese fascination with the new.

Mr. Tokonami, a cabinet member and one of Japan's leading politicians, says that the Japanese are like the Athenians of St. Paul's day: always eager to hear any new thing. "We lie open to Moscow and Milan, London and Chicago." Yet that love of the new is so counterbalanced by the conception of the unique makeup and destiny of the nation, that while it enables Japan to keep abreast of the world, the Japanese people must forever remain as peculiar a people as the children of Israel.

The combination of Japanese love of the new and flair for the

---

[3] Moga—Japanese slang, contraction of "modern girl"; mobo—contraction of "modern boy."

bizarre is shown in the architecture that sprang up in Tokyo after the earthquake and has, in somewhat tempered degree, spread throughout the Empire. Tokyo became the most modernistically architected city in the world. In pursuit of the unusual builders went far beyond accepted principles of modernism. The Japanese are natural-born faddists. Western-style dress or interest in Marx or Margaret Sanger or golf or jazz or bridge or the music of Ravel sweeps the country as a fad. One of the latest fads, according to the newspapers, is the anti-birthday league being joined by ladies of all ages who take the pledge to remain thirty-five years old no matter what the calendar says. Fads with a humanitarian or international tinge have a special appeal. Japanese school children almost fanatically took up the idea of exchanging letters with children of other lands. The fad of exchanging dolls or sending exhibits or presents of dolls to American and European cities has been seized upon by alert geniuses of the foreign office as a very clever means of propaganda.

The tendency in Japan to extremism, whether in ambition, line of duty, patriotism, pleasure, or anything else, has been amply indicated by their history and the sketches I have given of careers. The story of Japan is full of examples of such things as the shogun Tsuneyoshi's deportation of a merchant because he allowed his servants to wear too gorgeous attire, of the official outlawing of dyed, low-laced, embroidered clothes, or of prohibitions against the keeping of unusual birds and beasts.

On the occasion of President Franklin D. Roosevelt's visit to Hawaii (1934), the leading Japanese daily in Honolulu headlined its editorial: "Two things of pride," enumerated as an aged Japanese woman joining hands in prayer as President Roosevelt passed, and the fact that Japanese girls did not stand on books or smoke or wear "wind-window" dresses as did Caucasian girls while they waited to see the President. The Japanese with all their naturalness can have periods of extreme puritanism. Once Yedo had a law compelling women to dress their own hair!

VI

In a land where so many things are regulated and discipline is so thorough, the imagination of the people is easily captured by anything totally whimsical, individualistic, and impulsive—which is the way I would account for Japanese love of eccentricity and extravagance of expression.

This fascination of a people so schooled in restraint with anything which, disregarding all risks, whole-souledly breaks over the bounds, goes far toward explaining the ronin in Japanese history, whether he be of the type of the immortal forty-seven [4] or of the youthful assassins of the last political upset. Such actors on the stage of public affairs would not exist without applauding audiences. Kagawa, the Christian communist, is a ronin of righteousness, and commands universal respect even among his bitterest opponents, because he dares to be different. Even while the nation was mad with militant patriotism, eccentric old Ozaki (Yukis), M. P. and ex-Mayor of Tokyo, could stand aside scathingly condemning and still be spared and admired—because he did it with a flair.

Verve and nerve and flair and a little madness the Japanese nature respects. It is quite possible that respect for what they have considered incurable madness or eccentricity in the author of this book has caused Japanese in various instances to tolerate and spare him.

Most of the heroes of Japanese history have had eccentric traits, or if lacking these, have been provided with them by popularizing historians. I need only refer the reader to the several-score sketches of Japanese lives in this book. The Japanese are unquestionably the most order-loving people on earth. Yet a criminal who commits his crimes with extravagant gestures and fearlessness of pain or death can become a hero. A favorite story is of the greatest thief in Japanese history, who publicly posted notice to the authorities that he was going to steal the golden dolphin off the top of seven-story Nagoya castle. Remove it he did while the governor's guards were posted three feet apart around the castle. Since the prize weighed hundreds of pounds, he could not very well carry it out between

[4] Their story is told in the following chapter.

the guards, but he hid it under one of the high ledges, and nobody knew where it was until he was later caught and told them. He and his twelve-year-old son were condemned to be boiled in oil. He stood in the cauldron holding the child above the warming liquid until he could do so no longer, then plunged the boy under it to strangle to death, after which he stood on the corpse leering at spectators till he was boiled pink.

Again, Japanese adore the "three eccentrics of the Kwansai." As sedate a character as Admiral Togo wrote shortly before his death the inscription for the bronze statue erected by patriotic societies in Kyoto, showing the most famous of the three, Hikokuro, kneeling upon the bridge where he first caught sight of the Emperor's palace. This Hikokuro, one of the swashbucklers who early led opposition to the shogun, proclaimed that his supreme ambition—taught him by his grandmother—was to polish the pebbles in the Emperor's garden. When fifteen he began agitating in a voice which is said to have waked babies, shaken things off shelves, and burst the rice paper stretched tightly on the sliding door panels or shoji. He used to go about the hills yelling, "Katsu!" (victory), scaring even the robbers hiding there. The town once heard him shouting, "Traitor, pariah!" and rushed to find him ripping up a book which mocked one of his heroes. He visited the tomb of the Ashikagas—the same unfortunates who lost their wooden heads to the sword of another samurai—and strafed their sarcophagi with a horsewhip.

Once, traveling the Tokaido, he saw an old woman walking with difficulty and unceremoniously tossed her on his back and carried her to her destination. When his grandmother died he immured himself for three years of mourning in a straw hut. The culminating glory of his life, an interview with the Emperor, came about in this wise, as related by the Japanese who love the sublime and the trifling in juxtaposition: At forty-five years of age, Hikokuro, seeing some children abusing a tortoise, purchased it and set it free. Then he noticed that it had markings on its back resembling a Chinese character—a rare good-luck omen to orientals, in whose cosmogony a tortoise bears up the earth somewhat as Atlas did. Hikokuro took the creature to the palace of an Imperial prince, who was as impressed with the man as with the reptile and reported both to the Emperor, who asked to see them. Soon afterwards Hikokuro made a collection of poems in the short epigrammatic Japanese style, which were really incendiary propaganda against the shogun. Having completed it, he destroyed it and committed hara-kiri. The importance of such a character is not his own whimsical actions, but his hold on the imagination of present-day Japanese.

Another example of Japanese obsession with the eccentric is their interest in the recently published memoirs of the hereditary executioner for the Tokugawa government. He died in 1910. His career began when he was twelve years old and between then and 1881, when the new code substituted strangulation, he severed over three hundred heads. He says that a sort of Yogi breathing exercise was the secret of the profession passed down in the family; also a certain heart-steeling mental exercise. The executioner should never look at the face of his victim until the final moment when he should say under his breath, "Thou, enemy of the state," repeat the Buddhist litany, take the correct breath and strike.

His first head was a square hit, but he confesses that at twelve years it upset him a bit—and his father encouraged him to spend the night in pleasure with friends instead of trying to sleep. On rainy days he killed with the sword in his right hand, holding an umbrella over him with the left.

He relates the tempering thought passed on to his family by a famous magistrate of medieval time, in the form of an acted parable. This magistrate Ooka, walking with the executioner in a bamboo grove after a shower, asked him to show his skill in cutting a cane. The most skilled strokes of the swordsman nevertheless brought down on him a shower of raindrops. "The magistrate," said Ooka, "gives the order from a safe distance. But on the executioner fall the raindrops of hate."

VII

The Japanese love of eccentricity and hyperbole in lighter things adds a great deal of charm to the islands. It accounts for that particular type of humor in which they are supreme: the portrayal of the ridiculous, the assembling of the incongruous, and exaggeration of human and animal foibles—extended even to inanimate things such as landscapes and seascapes. This art of the ridiculous is expressed in their netsuke, the miniature comic carvings, and in their satire of drawn line and phrase. There is a netsuke in ivory not more than an inch tall showing the elegant Chinese emperor, Ming Huang, seated on his throne, teaching his consort Yang Kwei-fei to play the flute. She is playfully dumb, he is adoringly exasperated. It is carved underneath as well, and the bottoms and impressions of the sitters in the cushions arouse gales of laughter.

In that humor which requires a large sympathy with humankind and the universe, the humor close to tears, the Japanese are lacking. But in the humor of misproportion and caricature pointed as a rapier, they are supreme. One who knows how to read the woodblock print, Japan's greatest art, is endlessly fascinated with the delicate lampooning that lurks in what appear to be serious pieces. The Japanese Don Quixote story of the three would-be knights errant who get separated and go looking for one another all over Japan, as done on the great revolving stage of the Japanese Kabuki Theater in Tokyo, one of the world's finest, is certainly the best slap-stick comedy in the world.

A good example of Japanese sarcasm in words I quote from the *Japan Times* of August 30, 1929: "Prime Minister Hamaguchi talked on thrift over the radio, and this will be sent to 13,000,000 homes as a leaflet. His political enemies reply that he is living in the finest villa in Kamakura and travels in a limousine. As for riding in limousines we agree with the critics—a Tokyo tram should be good enough for any prime minister. It would increase his contacts, and he might slip a leaflet on economy in the sleeve of a pretty office girl. What use is there of placing leaflets on economy in homes on the bare sustenance line? It is adding insult to injury for folk aware of the prime minister's fine villa. But Hamaguchi might move to a three-room residence, and he could receive visitors on a floor in a six-mat room. That would require every one to get down on his knees, which would add dignity to the office, while the tannery next door would drive away all but those with real business, increasing the efficiency of the administration."

A sort of netsuke in words is the classic length poem of Mr. Kurusu, head of the commercial section of the foreign office, later to become infamous as the bearer of peace talk to Secretary Hull while Japanese aircraft carriers were sneaking up on Pearl Harbor. "The cherries may bloom and the plum blossoms go, but spring never comes to the chief of a commercial bureau." The Japanese gift for nicknames, almost as general and much more pungent than in Russia, is another example of this type of humor.

There are many popular biographies in Japan, quite valueless other than as collections of whimsical anecdotes. One is of Hojo Fujitsuna, a thirteenth-century regent to the Kamakura shogun, who one night lost ten coppers by the bursting of his money bag on the bridge that spans the dirty little creek flowing to the sea from the fountains around the great Buddha. He hailed up all the neighboring home owners to search the stream bed, and spent fifty coppers alone on torches to light the search. By morning the whole town had turned out to watch this supreme display of miserliness, whereupon Hojo surprised the searchers by paying them for their time and delivering a harangue upon the place of money in social economy which sounds remarkably like postdepression economics. The lost copper currency, said he, represented intrinsic value, which, should it remain lost, would leave society, already short of exchange medium, forever impoverished to the further extent of ten coppers; whereas recovery of the ten coppers would save this amount to society while the money spent in their recovery going into circulation would increase prosperity. Would it not then be the height of selfishness, he asked, for him to save himself the trouble and expense of recovery merely because the amount was trifling?

Many individuals are famous on the streets or in the press for nothing other than their eccentricities, with which the otherwise regimenting police show surprising tolerance. The mentality in this respect is the exact opposite of that in America, where police often overlook the lawless but not the queer. Landing from Japan in rainy Portland, Oregon, I was admonished by a policeman with an Irish brogue for walking down the main street under the only umbrella I had, a huge Japanese paper one, decorated with the bold Chinese characters of the last inn where I had stayed on the other side. Yet we prowl safely about inland oriental cities in our ridiculous-appearing collars, ties, short coats and plus fours that button up the front—or even in shorts that offend every native sense of artistry and decency, and nothing happens to us!

A Tokyo thief captured three times by the same detective asked that he be given a document authorizing him to always be arrested by that officer, to save having to answer the same questions over. "For," said he, "after I have served my term I will have to steal again in order to make a living and we might as well save trouble for both the police and myself." A Tokyo character known as the Time Man goes unobstructed into business offices, hotels and even homes, checking up on clocks. He is an actor of athletic carriage, and usually says, "If you come to my show, I want you to be there on time." Eccentricity in Japan is good publicity. Many Japanese are shameless publicity hunters, which does not fit at all with the race's reputation for reticence. But Japan is a land of paradoxes. It has all kinds of people and some of them have most conflicting traits.

Japanese great men are often better known by their eccentricities than their serious exploits. General Nagaoka (Gaishi), known as the father of Japanese aviation, wore the longest mustaches in the empire, which he trimmed to resemble the propellers of an airship. This maker of sad history for us, although unnoticed by us, is honored by a bust with "propeller whiskers"—four blades—a foot long.

The plutocrat railway builder, Baron Okura, who spent much of his youth following show trains through Arkansas and tenting in Virginia, celebrated his ninetieth birthday by climbing with his family, friends, personal physician, and an escort of news reporters to the top of 10,300-foot-high Mt. Akaishi, which towers among the forests that contributed paper pulp and lumber to the Okura fortune. Here he rehearsed family and friends in the performance of the wind funeral to be conducted upon his death. The industrial "robber baron" covered much of the distance pick-a-back. In addition, his eighty bearers had to handle a portable radio station which sent back flashes on the expedition and carry a barrel of sake and the makings of a feast. He had his friends plant a wooden post on the peak, bury it under a giant bouquet of mountain flowers, and then shoot off skyrockets. Some wood ashes were scattered to show how he wanted his own dispersed. Then, since this was just a rehearsal of his funeral after all, the old man sang and spread the feast. The Japanese people call him "the sentimental baron." His income was a million yen a year!

Chapter XXV
The Hysterical Face

HE Chinese ideograph borrowed to write the word samurai is the two ideographs for ten and for one put together, and is explained as follows: The samurai's mind must be so drilled as to bring ten or more conflicting impulses and motives into a state of *single*-purposed concentration. The actual expression of this concentration in the old days was through sword fighting. The fighter attained a state of ecstasy in which life, death, and all cares alike were forgotten, and the whole being given over to lightning reflexes.

This is the spirit of Japan. The formal flag of Japan, a red spot on a white field, represents not only the rising sun but the quality of supreme and entranced concentration. Recently the "largest flag in the world," eighty by fifty-six feet, was hung over five stories of a Tokyo department store. Done gigantically, the simplicity of the design showed how striking it is. This particular flag was taken to the top of Mt. Fuji to fly "over the whole Empire."

When not concentrated in the face of some crisis, the Japanese people appear to be a collection of paradoxically disorganized, scattered personalities preyed upon by conflicting impulses. In the face of supreme crisis these unite into a soul with as much definition and drive as the polished sword which is its symbol. Yet one who knows Japanese well would say, "What of the pronounced tendency toward hysteria of the Japanese race?" It is true the hysteria comes, but after it comes the integration and concentration. This is the marvelous thing about Japan.

Mr. T. Oikawa, head of the unique consulting bureau of the police department, is authority for saying that hysteria in Japan is due to anxiety over love affairs, economic difficulties, and the state of the nation, in the order named, and expresses itself chiefly in the form of suicide.

The love-suicide is world-wide, but in no society has it ever been so much of an institution with particular code and procedure as in Japan. Undoubtedly this is due to a romantic fascination on the part of overwrought minds with the old samurai ethic of self-immolation. Youngsters who regard their mutual attachment as tragically hopeless—often enough without even finding out whether it is or not —write oaths committing their souls to union in the next incarnation, and then tie themselves together and jump into boiling craters or from an embankment into the path of an express train. Many who cannot arrange the romantic double immolation commit solitary suicide.

A football star of Tokyo Imperial University killed himself by swallowing four tablets of different poisons on the shore of beautiful Lake Yamanaka, which mirrors Mt. Fuji, because the woman who had adopted him opposed the culmination of his romance with his little sweetheart "Charbo"—which throws the spotlight also on the power of even foster-parental authority surviving in Japan.

After the newspapers had played up the romantic death of a youth in the crater of Mt. Mihara on Oshima Island, which you see belching smoke as you enter Tokyo Bay, 149 persons were known by the police to have jumped into the crater within a year. The police succeeded in detaining 571 men and 111 women; five boys and one girl fifteen years of age were detained. The oldest would-be suicide was sixty-five. Family troubles and disease accounted for many, but the majority were between twenty and thirty and were unbalanced by love.

A recently recorded victim of the crater was a wife of a sculptor, who left a note reading: "Good-by to Sangerism. (Her husband had adopted "birth control.") I leave, as without children at thirty-eight I find no future to life." It must be remembered that Margaret Sanger, who personally visited Japan, made quite an impression upon the sensitive Japanese mentality. The police tried to head off the suiciding woman, broadcasting that the husband was willing to give in on the point, if she would stop short of the crater's rim. An enterprising company is now building a railway to the crater, but

the police express the hope that this will take the romanticism out
of death there.

Some years ago the popular place for a love-suicide was beautiful
Kegon Falls, spilling several hundred feet between mist-blanketed
ridges out of the water-filled crater Chuzenji. The "boiling pot" at
the bottom is so furious that nothing but the tiniest scraps of
human bodies that drop into it are ever found, which makes it a
favorite with persons feeling tragic. After several thousand deaths
in the falls the police put up a high barbed-wire fence and a sign:
"Don't suicide here!"

They promptly spot and steer to a police station any young couples wandering through the maples of the neighborhood with a rapt
look on their faces. To-day one descends to the bottom of the falls
in a most modern double elevator shaft instead of down the pre-
cipitous trail, and the volcano has supplanted the falls as Japan's
favorite passing-on place.

Tokyo records seven suicides per day. Yet the suicide rate in
Japan is no higher than in the enlightened United States of America.
The significant thing about suicide in Japan is the difference in
motivation and the ecstasy in which it is usually committed.

Several years ago the respective husband and wife of two of
Japan's most popular writers missed their spouses. When the summer came and the mountain resort of Karuizawa was opened up
their bodies were found in one of the cottages in an embrace of love
and death, with a message: "The climax of love is not marriage but
death." For a time Japan was swept by an epidemic of this sexual
type of love suicide.

The newspaper *Asahi* comments upon the growing number of
mothers who commit suicide with their children, and particularly
condemns this from the standpoint of the mothers' error in regarding their offspring as their private possession. Under Japanese law,
children go to the father in the event of divorce, which like marriage
is merely a matter of a thirty-sen registration in the town book, so
far as the state is concerned. Marriage being a pact between families, the families on each side have to be satisfied about the separa-
tion, of course.

Mr. Oikawa of the Tokyo police recommends an attitude of sym-

pathy for some cases of suicide in spite of their illegality. The
motives of suicide, he says, are often reasonable. This is a modern
expression of the historically fatalistic attitude toward life and
death.

The police official ascribes the present unbalance among Japanese
in part to western ideas, which he says have created a looseness of
morals and a disastrous tendency to experiment with emotions, particularly among women. He blames the men who take advantage of
this new tendency in the women. "The tragic affairs brought before
us are caused without exception by selfishness. Perhaps selfishness
is an inherent and necessary quality in human beings, but its over-
emphasis has destructive consequences." He opines that the moral
standards of the middle and upper classes in Japan are not inferior
to those of western countries (which according to Matsuoka isn't
saying much) and he declares that promiscuity is greatest among
café waitresses. The police attitude is that no woman should
indulge in extramarital sexual relations unless she is a member of
the officially licensed class, which has its own economic and social
status, is cared for medically and upon which eternal vigilance
keeps down emotional outbursts. In Japan to-day—as it was for a
period in ancient Rome, a woman who wishes to lead a free life,
whether she be a café waitress, a bohemian artist, or a "liberated"
aristocrat, is wise to provide herself with a prostitute's license. The
police do not wish to have anything "slipped over" on them, and
sooner or later they know everything.

II

Another aggravated type of emotional unbalance arises from
the intense ambitions of intellectual youth. Students receiving bad
marks in classes frequently kill themselves. Professor friends have
told me that they often fear to give a pupil his proper rating, knowing it would be as good as a death sentence. Suicides have become
frequent among the increasing number of university graduates who
are unable to find white-collar jobs. This is in part due to the
antipathy of the now dominant military classes to intellectuals and
the fear of the superpatriots that college men are impregnated with

radical and non-Japanese ideas. On the other hand, successful students overbalanced by the emotional strain frequently commit suicide upon learning that they have graduated. Many years ago one of the greatest of that admirable group of American educators who gave their best to Japan, working themselves at the same time out of their jobs, wrote: "The expression on the faces of many students upon coming forward to receive their diplomas is impossible to describe. A student takes his sheepskin, rushes to his lodgings, and will not be comforted. A melancholy of unsatisfiable ambition lies at his heart."

The Japanese intellectual is hard and stern while his task is on, poignantly self-conscious in relaxation. His sternness borders very closely upon sadism and can easily turn into cruelty. His self-consciousness frequently becomes an unbalanced sentimentality that may break out in tears—not of sympathy or self-pity, but purely of hysteria. A Japanese scholar lays this trait of Japanese men to the intimate association of mothers with their sons, and the large part women play in molding the male character. The Japanese, he says, is trained in the school of his father, but remains dominantly the child of his mother, and what might be regarded as the particularly feminine traits of supersensitiveness, touchiness, and moodiness are strong within him.

These traits are not confined to the intellectuals. A cook on a Japanese ship chartered by the writer jumped overboard in mid-Pacific because he had been tongue-lashed by the purser, after warning, for continuing to put onions in the morning eggs.

The exaggerated teachings of pride and personal dignity tend to send Japanese boys into the world furtively expecting offense, and the fearlessness taught them by their fathers tends to develop this into belligerence. "If you will watch the eyes of Japanese hearers when incidents of deep significance are mentioned," says an old American educator, "you will understand what is going on." I have seen a mist come over the eyes of Japanese when American immigration discrimination was mentioned, or some historical flouting of the augustness of the Emperor was referred to. The revelations published in the *Saturday Evening Post* and then a book, by U. S. Captain Yardley (of the "American Black Chamber") that he had decoded official Japanese instructions to the delegates at the disarmament conference, 1922, drove friendly Japanese into trances of cold fury. Japanese are often so overcome in academic discussions of such matters that they find it impossible to take active part.

It is the outward manifestations of this emotional unbalance that make the Japanese appear beyond understanding or sometimes ridiculous to us of the west. For instance, the tendency of a Japanese suffering sudden great embarrassment or even fright, is to giggle or laugh. Many a foreign housewife in Japan has been outraged by a dainty housemaid appearing, bowing low, and announcing with un controllable laughter that she has just broken the household's greatest treasure. As a matter of fact, the little maid is scared to death. Again, a group of modest maidens caught bathing or otherwise unexpectedly by an intruding camera man will nearly always laugh— which accounts for a great number of the laughing groups available in picture postcards. They may be anything but pleased, even though they are the friendliest creatures on earth.

The Japanese guide or railway clerk or official who brings you bad-temper-arousing news is likely to put on a most irritating semblance of being highly pleased about it. He tries to make the news more agreeable to you by appearing as if he were bearing a pleasant surprise. When a Japanese, whether he be a hotel room boy you have asked for a fly swatter or the secretary to the premier whom you have asked to arrange an interview, comes to you in this manner, you should recognize that bad news is coming and get hold of yourself.

III

An incident which set all the world laughing at Japan, and yet came very near to lighting the flares of war on the China coast in 1934, is a perfect example of these various phases of Japanese emotional unbalance. The young Japanese vice consul, Kuramoto, left the Chinese foreign office at Nanking after delivering one of the unpleasant messages that Japan hands China daily. He failed to arrive back at the Japanese consulate. After a few hours the local Japanese authorities began to get excited. In a few days there was a demonstration of the Japanese populace in Shanghai. The patriotic

societies and newspapers in Japan took up the matter and pressed
the fairly susceptible Foreign Minister Hirota and the army and
navy ministries into action. Additional warships were dispatched
in the direction of Shanghai, Japanese gunboats went two hundred
miles up the Yangtze River and anchored off the Chinese capital,
and an ardent Japanese admiral landed a force of their new tank
marines, who clattered in their steel monsters through the crowded
streets of Shanghai.

The incident was exactly parallel to one of those used by the
patriots to bring about the seizure of Manchuria four years previously. Then it was claimed that an adventurer named Nakamura,
traveling with much money in the guise of a geology professor on the
Mongolian-Manchurian border, had disappeared and that Chinese
soldiers had murdered him and stolen his funds.

Japanese touchiness about Chinese retaliation on Japanese subjects and officials, who moved freely about China and claimed extra-
territorial protection as well as the protection of the Chinese authorities (while their country's armed forces were bombing the cities
and seizing the territory of the land where they were guests), is
rather amusing to the outside observer who happens to know how
Japan, in the last century, attacked and murdered foreigners who
merely claimed the privileges of ordinary international intercourse.
Japanese commanders attempted to drive the Chinese populace into
hysterical reaction by conducting unannounced machine-gun practice in the middle of the night in crowded cities. Japanese soldiers,
tourists, merchants, and priests acted most arrogantly toward
Chinese officials and citizens.

The patience and restraint of the Chinese populace have been
amazing, and the diligence of Chinese authorities in protecting these
Japanese, all of whom were acting as spies or who composed forces
for attack from within on the land where they were guests, was
far more than might be expected. Yet Japanese touchiness is always
ready to spring in retaliation against any wrong done to a Japanese
in China.

One of the most illuminating conversations I've ever heard on the
mentalities of these two very different neighbors took place in my
room in the Imperial Hotel in Tokyo over the Nakamura disappear-

ance in Manchuria. We had spent a most pleasant summer evening visiting the cabarets and driving around the shrines of Tokyo. Said Kato, a fine young Japanese who had worked with me for years, to his good friend Ning, an upstanding, soft-spoken, elegant, and brilliant young Chinese who before he was thirty became chief of police of one of China's largest cities: "But why did you kill our Nakamura?"

"In the first place," said Ning, "we did not kill your Nakamura— not until you have proved it. In the second place, we *should* have killed him, just as you would have killed a Chinese snooping around the hinterland of your kingdom under false pretenses with a lot of money."

Such was the background for the disappearance of the consul in Nanking. Just as Japan's army and navy were set to avenge him by taking over all of central China, he wandered into a Chinese sheepherder's hut on the scrub-bamboo-covered slope of Purple Mountain back of the Chinese capital, and asked for food. Many years ago, when it was much wilder, the writer happens himself to have been lost all night on that slope. But he encountered no wolves. The disheveled consul said he had been smarting under a rebuke given him by his superior and had gone out to have the wolves eat him. Finding no wild animals on Purple Mountain he tried to starve himself to death. That seemed to be an interminable process so he thought of committing hara-kiri but found himself already too weak. So he stumbled to the sheepherder's hut for food, and allowed himself to be escorted back into civilization, which was on the verge of being plunged into war over his disappearance.

IV

The type of Japanese hysteria which most concerns us of the outside world is that tied up with the national pride and alert devotion to the embodiment of that pride, the Emperor. As a protest against Japan's surrender to America and Great Britain at the London naval conference in 1930, Lieutenant Kusukara committed hara-kiri with his officer's sword, kneeling in his night clothes in a narrow-gauged train berth. That was really the beginning of the agitation which brought about the downfall of the Shidehara government, the seizure of Manchuria, the withdrawal of Japan from the League of Nations, and her preparations against Russia and the United States. When Admiral Takarabe, chief naval delegate to the London conference, arrived home, he was met, of course, by a patriot who elaborately presented to him a dagger with which to commit suicide. Later a twenty-six-year-old student of political science appeared at the admiral's office, read a high-powered protest, and slit open his own belly in the presence of the admiral's secretary.

In due course the assassinations of premiers, plutocrats, and liberals took place. This emotional frenzy reached its climax at the civil, military and naval trials of the young patriot-assassins in the fall of 1933. It was no flash in the pan. It was guided by a junior officer named Tojo (Hideki)—he who in 1942 was to be warlord of the west Pacific and Premier of Japan. It was rooted deep in the emotional life of the Japanese people, bolstered by historical incidents, and drew the support of most of the Japanese newspapers and millions of soldiers, sailors, officers, and populace. The accused boys were permitted to engage legal counsel to use at the trial, to give unlimited statements to the press, to denounce publicly the white powers and all those Japanese who had "truckled" to foreign governments, and to expose political corruption and the oppressed state of the peasantry.

The old lid-sitter Prince Saionji knew his Japanese people too well to compel the usual custom of having the proceedings in camera. Cadet Kuroiwa confessed that he shot Premier Inukai as the "Old Fox" was saying to the invading assassins, "Shouldn't you take your shoes off on my mats? Have cigarettes, and let's talk matters over calmly." "Shooting might be dispensed with," murmured the aged man as he fell back mortally wounded. Young Cadet Goto, who led the group, proudly testified: "Regions in northeastern Japan were stricken by terrible famine, and men from the distressed agrarian districts were enlisted in the eighth division in large numbers. It takes no stretch of imagination to feel how their hearts were torn with anguish, as they were sent to Manchukuo to fight for the sake of their country, not that they were devoid of patriotism, but because they had to leave behind them their parents and dear ones without food, without any one to take care of them.

"And while these poor fellows were fighting in bleak Manchuria, where the mercury fell to forty below zero, what were the politicians in the grip of financial vampires doing? Busily occupied in feathering their own nests, they had done absolutely nothing to give relief to those suffering farmers. Not only that, but no attempt was made by them to rectify our relations with other countries."

The young assassin Shinohara stated that the hara-kiri of Lieutenant Kusukara had first opened his eyes to the necessity for drastically purging the country of those who weakly submitted to Anglo-Saxon domination and those who considered political and personal interests before the interest of the nation. The clever defense attorney quoted the examples of the heroized forty-seven ronin and of the patriotic murders precipitating the downfall of the Tokugawa régime, then shifted from that to Shakespeare's speeches of Brutus and Cassius after the killing of Cæsar, and wound up with the declamation that "the accused had as their purpose the establishment of a better, purer state. Their aims were unselfish; their heroic decisions should make even devils weep." The lads confessed that they had intended to kill among others the American ambassador, and the Japanese populace heard this with as little shudder as Germans heard of the murder of Dollfuss.

V

In such tremendous waves of emotion, as well as the cautious, cold, steady scheming of the Lords Hottas, Okumas, and Arakis, lies our danger from Japan. The trial court, as well as all Japanese cabinet offices, were flooded with petitions said to total more than a million signatures, demanding the release of the young assassins. Even the family of the murdered premier spoke up in their favor. Many of these petitions were signed by women, many were in blood, and many were accompanied by boxes of fingers packed in silk floss, chopped by petitioners off their own hands to show their sincerity and how far they would go if the court did not show mercy. The powerful new reactionary association of retired army and navy officers, the Meirinkai, issued portentous warning to poor judges trying to do their duty. The lads eventually got off with short terms and the court was relieved by the proud acceptance of the terms by the assassins, who desired to cap their heroism with some degree of martyrdom. They will soon all be promoted officers somewhere in Japan's empire-building forces.[1]

The less spectacular outbursts of this patriotic emotion are also significant. A man named Nojima, sending the minister of interior a five-foot long petition for unemployment relief (this was just before the 1932 boom), accompanied it with his finger. Three non-commissioned officers at Shanghai tied dynamite on their backs, went into the Chinese barbed-wire defenses, and set themselves off, and are now enshrined in the great military museum in Tokyo. Their mothers were taken about the islands on a special train and tens of thousands pressed forward to kiss the hems of their kimonos. Japanese in Peru sent money for the erection of a monument to the san yushi (three heroes). Mrs. Chiyo (Willow) Inouye, learning that her doctor husband was to go with the medical corps to Manchuria, put on her wedding kimono and cut her throat, leaving the following letter:

"To my dear husband: My heart is filled to the brim with gladness. I cannot find words to congratulate you. Before you depart for the front to-morrow, I leave this world to-day.

"Please do not worry about your home, for there is no longer anything to make you worry. Powerless as I am, I am doing what little I can so that you and your men may fight with heart and soul for the country. That is all I wish and no more.

"Thanks to your kindness, my life has been happy. Though this world is ephemeral, the next world, it is said, is eternal. Some day you will come to join me there. I shall be waiting for you.

"They say it is very cold in Manchuria. Please take care to keep warm.

"I enclose herewith forty yen. When you reach the front, please distribute it among the soldiers.

"I pray for your success.   "Your wife."

---

[1] This paragraph stands as printed in 1935. Tojo and his boys in 1942 have crashed the Dutch and British empires and driven us from the west Pacific.

With a halo of heroism placed over him by his wife, the doctor went to Manchuria and acquitted himself gallantly.

The fifth-year (primary school not counted) pupils of Tsuyama middle school, not permitted to cut classes to see Major Yamamoto off to the Manchurian front, drew an inkpot full of their own blood and wrote him the following message: "It is our sincere wish that you will fight bravely and distinguish yourself at the front. We look forward to the day when you will come home in triumph."

Overcome by a feeling against America for its refusal to recognize Manchukuo, a nineteen-year-old Japanese lad in the uniform of the youth-training organization tore the nameplate off the Mukden United States consulate with his bayonet, invaded the consulate, and was stopped only when an American vice consul parried with a chair. The lad escaped over a wall and the Japanese authorities rendered the usual apology, declaring that he was insane—a delicate point, it would seem to outsiders, in many of these cases. Significantly, Japanese news agencies failed to mention the incident and a Japanese-censored British news service consistently failed to state the nationality of the youth.

And so we might pile up incidents of exacerbated emotionalism until they made a book—even as the Black Dragon Society has done, naming it *The Fragrance of the Cherry*. Such emotionalism, as well as the concept of innate divinity and the worship of the Emperor which chiefly aroused it, is essentially medieval. It is manifested in multifarious ways, such as the common one of daughters selling themselves for periods of prostitution to procure money for their parents; strikers sitting on chimney tops, or miners refusing to come out of mines; strikers' wives making daily pilgrimages barefoot to shrines; entire governments resigning when some fanatic shoots in the direction of, or even tries to hand a petition to, the Sacred Person. It is manifested even in the telegram signed by thousands of Japanese to General Araki when he was ill of influenza: "The people of Nippon are fasting and praying for him who has Japan in crisis on his shoulders," and in the reaction of the little patriotic leader—registered by the ever alert Japanese press—who said, "Even such a hard-boiled man as he wept."

VI

The Japanese tendency to hysteria is very manifest in their festivals and folk dances. At these times primitive release of emotions and inhibitions takes place, usually facilitated by the national drink, sake, or the now excellent and cheap beer made by the national brewing combine, or by the more recent imitated liquor which they spell ouisiki—pronounced whisky! The Japanese are, on the whole, given to sobriety, but on occasions set apart for gaiety they indulge, and with few exceptions it takes but a wee drop indeed to flush their faces. An exception who is proud of it is Premier Admiral Okada, admired as well as lampooned for his drinking capacity.

Many Japanese, it must be said, do not drink, being members of Zen temperance societies. Few Japanese ships' officers drink on duty. Christianity in Japan is "totally abstaining" from both alcohol and tobacco, so that a Japanese will frequently say, "I do not smoke—" or "I do not drink; I am a Christian." The anniversary of the terrible Tokyo earthquake of September 1, 1923, has come to be observed, no one quite knows why, as a "sakéless day."

Once in the mountains about Nikko I came upon the celebration of the rectification of some centuries-old grievance in the copper mines. It was a dance for the miners' guild, now a labor union. Up on a scaffold in the center of a causeway that crossed an oblong lake musicians played, over and over, a clipped melody on high woodwind instruments until listeners were bewitched; while the dancers, men and women, the latter often with babies strapped upon their backs, sidled around the lake and over the causeway in two lines facing one another and moving in opposite directions in a figure eight. As they stepped, they sang and made postures with great straw hats, which they placed upon one another's heads and passed from one to another. By the time they continued this for an hour a frenzy like that of the whirling dervishes had possession of them. I was told that the dance continued incessantly for two days and nights. These folk and religious dances of Japan are said to be of Chinese origin, but one never sees anything of the sort even in most remote China to-day. Tibetan and Mongolian lamas (priests) have their devil dances, but these are not participated in by the public. The Chinese, it seems, have become too old a race to dance, and mass emotionalism in China is scarcely seen apart from the impulse of anger.

There is a great midsummer festival in Kyoto in which juggernauts several stories high, carrying immense floats and weighing tons, are pulled through the streets by thousands of yelling, sweating people. The city light and telephone administration wisely sends mechanics to cut all wires in their way and put them up again once the moving towers have passed. Devotees go around the great sacred park in dead silence and if any one causes them to forget their vow and speak a word they begin the circumambulation all over again.

The followers of Nichiren indulge in violent hysteria on the festivals to the egotistical old saint. But the most dangerous demonstrations for the innocent bystander take place on the nationally celebrated O-bon, the Japanese Halloween, when the spirits of the departed return. Young men collect contributions from householders and shopkeepers to build ornate portable wooden shrines or arks (and, quite obviously, buy great quantities of sake).

Groups of young fellows any time of the day or night during the week of festivities get hold of the carrying rods on all four sides and give themselves over to the spirit in the shrine to direct them whither he will—this direction being the resultant of the four pushing forces. The spirit has a very common way of taking both ark and trampling feet right through the shop fronts of merchants who have been a little stingy in contributing, or of suddenly lunging toward an observer trying to focus a camera. The O-bon dance is presided over by a hired geisha who leads off with the intricate correct steps. Drummers beat the interweaving rhythms. Conducted in private homes and inns, in which every member of the family and guests are constrained to participate, it is an altogether delightful thing. On the streets it can become a terror.

Japanese emotionalism of the present day is sanctified by the story, now sacred scripture, of the vendetta of Ako. Ako's forty-seven ronin have become the saints of the patriotic societies, and Toyama claims that the Black Dragon Society originated with them. The story has become a classic inspiration of patriotism, the lesson of loyalty, self-sacrifice, perseverance, and avengement drilled into all school children, hundreds of thousands of whom visit the tomb of the forty-seven ronin in Sengaku temple grounds, Tokyo. Millions throughout the empire hope to visit there. The story is produced in a score of versions on the Japanese stage, and in movies and talkies. I give the historical incident. To get all the embroidery of imagination that has been woven about it, and the nuances of emotion put into it, you would have to live much of your life in Japan.

This bloody affair is held to have started Japan upward from the low ebb to which her spirit had sunk due to the long peace of the Tokugawa and the infiltration of pacifist Chinese philosophy.

In 1701 the Lord Asano, daimyo of Ako, a tiny mountain fief four hundred and twenty miles south of Yedo, was assigned his turn to act as Yedo host to the imperial envoy annually sent to the shogun's palace. The shogun handed around this job of acting as host as a means of impoverishing vassals who were becoming too prosperous. Nevertheless, it was a great honor. Hosts-designate studied intricacies of court etiquette in order that no dishonor might be done the Emperor through faux pas committed in the presence of his envoy. There were two hereditary official Emily Posts of the time qualified to teach the etiquette and held responsible for seeing that no mistake was made. Called in this case was a certain Lord Kira who made his specialized knowledge a means of mulcting rustic lords unlucky enough to require his instruction. The polished but grafting Kira was openly contemptuous of lords from the backwoods who didn't know the tea ceremony, and they in turn heartily reciprocated contempt for a samurai who knew more about pouring tea than fighting.

While the rustic Asano was carrying out his duties in the presence of the imperial envoy, Kira subjected him to some slur beyond bearing. Asano lunged with his short sword and struck the master of etiquette in the shoulder. He thought he had killed him. He then gave himself up. The men about the imperial envoy, who were fellow tea pourers of Kira, connived to have Asano commit hara-kiri under official order. By evening of the same day he was set upon a dais of three mats, and lighted lanterns were hung. He was not allowed to know that Kira had not been fatally wounded, and he returned thanks for being permitted to die as befits a samurai.

But before he could plunge the short sword into his abdomen an assistant censor lopped off his head, which from the standpoint of the samurai was adding the ultimate insult to injury. The excuse given was that the short sword lent to Asano by the Tamura family (he had lost his own short sword in the scrimmage in the palace), ordered to provide the setting for the hara-kiri, was an heirloom, and the Tamura gentlemen didn't want blood on it.

The whole incident was one to bring down the hate of the warriors of the back country on the dilettantes of Yedo. Two of Asano's vassals ran one hundred miles a day to carry news of the tragedy to their clan. A demand arose for the punishment of Kira. After all, a man had been put to death for killing him. Then what right had he to be still alive? they asked, in good Japanese logic. Asano's old steward prevailed with calmer councils. It was hoped that Asano would receive posthumous pardon and his son be allowed to succeed to the fief.

But at the end of a year the fief had been divided by the shogun's order among covetous neighboring lords, and even the noble widow put out of the ancestral castle. Also Kira, fully recovered and back at his tea pouring, was hounding to death the scattered retainers of the dead lord, fearing the vengeance that they now began to plot in earnest. A year and a half after the death of Asano, forty-seven of his retainers met secretly in Yedo and swore a bond in blood. The old steward had died of a broken heart and his son took the headship of the vendetta.

The stage plays of the affair dwell on the terrific hardships of these forty-seven in escaping the hand of Kira while preparing their vengeance. One is pictured as having abandoned wife and family and devoted himself to the prostitute quarter and a life of continued drunkenness in order to escape the watchful eye of the shogun's police, who finally decided that he had gone to the dogs and relaxed their vigilance over him, making it possible for him to join his fellows.

On the night of December 14, 1702, word came to the waiting forty-seven that Kira was having a tea ceremony in his house. Wearing white sleeves to distinguish one another in the darkness, the band stole through the snow-covered streets and with howls of vengeance broke into the front and rear gates, killing Kira's guards and his friends who resisted. The cowardly Kira hid in the charcoal shed, but one of the ronin found him, lopped off his head, and led the band ecstatically to the temple grounds where their ashes now repose. In the spring from which thousands of their present-day worshipers dip water for ceremonial mouth rinsing, they washed Kira's head, then presented it at Lord Asano's tomb, informing his spirit that he was at last vindicated. The youngest of the forty-seven was immediately dispatched to the other end of the country to inform Lady Asano and the young son and heir.

The head of the group then drew up a statement of the crime. All appended their names, handing one copy to the abbot of the temple and sending another by two of their members to the office of the shogun's censor—the principal justice official of the time. After many hours the ronin received word that they were to be divided into four parties as wards of four great lords to whom they would be responsible until their sentences should be passed. One of the lords came personally with seven hundred and fifty men to get his contingent of seventeen, which was regarded by the captives and public as a mark of great honor and silent commendation.

Yedo was in a ferment over the deed. Every member of the high court, the temple magistrates, the four finance magistrates, and the two city magistrates signed a petition which, although it did not dare to demand the pardon of the ronin, adopted the oblique Japanese method of demanding the extirpation of the family of Kira. The shogun, fearful of creating a wide-open schism between his metropolitan courtiers and his country vassals, passed the question on to the Imperial Court, suggesting to the abbot of Uyeno temple, who was a prince of the blood, that he might ask amnesty for the avengers. The prince-abbot failed to take advantage of this opportunity which would have been so in harmony with his religion, and several months later the men were sentenced to "the happy release" (ceremonial hara-kiri) to be carried out in groups on the precincts of the various lords to whom they had been committed.

Their sympathizers consoled themselves that the punishment was that ordinarily accorded only the highest samurai of the realm, whereas being merely disbanded retainers of a lord already put to death as a criminal, they were no longer entitled legally to treatment as samurai at all and would normally have been beheaded by the common executioner. Also the condemned had the pleasure of learning direct from the censor as they sat on their death daises that an excuse had been found for confiscating Kira's estate and turning his heir into the streets.

A year after the death of the forty-six, the forty-seventh ronin returned to Yedo and demanded that he also be commanded to die in the same manner as his fellows. He was reprimanded for the imputation of slackness on the part of the shogunal government, handed traveling expenses secretly by the chief censor and told to get out. Eventually he returned to Yedo, where he died a hero at the age of eighty-two. His ashes were put in a hole in a stone tablet erected beside the other forty-six.

Thus runs the official record of the vendetta of Ako. The reader can imagine some of the changes that have been rung upon it by dramatists fascinated with forty-seven lives devoted to the single purpose of revenge for a wrong done their lord. When you go to Japan, ask for that professional host who is chief clerk of the Imperial Hotel, and whose proudest legacy, known only to his intimates, is that he is a descendant of the ronin who cast away family and reputation to avenge his lord.

You have to build up for yourself an idea of the mentality of a nation which regards this as the greatest story of their history, and which weeps over the weather-worn granite tablets in the Sengaku-ji as devout Christians weep over the Passion, or Shiite Moslems over the death of Hossain.

This medieval Japanese emotionalism is T.N.T. in the modern world of population pressures, trade wars, international rivalries, and naval competition.

Chapter XXVI

Humanitarian Japan

CTS of God" have played a large part in making Japanese history and shaping the Japanese mind. It has been said with much truth that the Tokyo earthquake and fire of September 1, 1923, postponed for ten years the brewing of a Japanese-American war.[1] The great typhoon and cloud-burst of September 21, 1934, recording the lowest barometer reading in history and destroying 5,000 lives and 20,000 buildings, may have come at a crucial time to dampen war ardor over the naval ratio. It cut Japanese electrical and novelty goods exports 20 per cent for the fall of 1934 and caused an attempt to cut the military budget. On the other hand it characteristically tightened up Japanese national morale, causing the postponement of a seamen's strike. The Emperor expressed his concern over the great loss of life of school children, which inspired a rebuilding of Japan's public schools with wind-, fire- and, as far as possible, bomb-proof construction. A Japanese editor in Hawaii comments on the Japanese spirit in American slang: "Constant disasters are making the Japanese hardened and stoic, with guts enough to face whatever dangers may come. Courage created by disaster accounts for the progress they are making."

Japan has thoroughly institutionalized the care of human suffering. The methodical and undaunted Japanese mind has reacted in this way to Japan's recurring natural disasters and wars. The Japanese Red Cross Society has the largest membership and best support per capita of population of any—and needs them! The International Red Cross convention was with propriety held in Tokyo in 1934— where it was treated to an experience of the precision of Japanese

[1] As published in 1935.

formal relief following the great typhoon. Japan's imperial army is a prime relief agency—the Japanese civilian Red Cross is in effect part of the nation's military machine. Then there is the Buddhist-inspired Red Swastika [2] Society which took part in the international Red Cross meeting, and has a large organization throughout China, India, Siam, Burma, and the rest of the Buddhist world. It is a modern expression of old Buddhist humanitarianism, inspired by Christian competition. It is quite non-sectarian in spirit—many of its members belong to the Red Cross and vice versa.

The sentiment behind Japanese humanitarianism, a dominant feature in the closely knit nation, is more paternal than compassionate. Hospitalization, education, relief, and policing are based upon the conception that the Tenno is father and the people children of a sternly ruled family. The Japanese is taken care of by his government in order to make him an orderly asset, a well-behaved and helping child in the family, rather than out of the spirit that "all men are brothers" as the Chinese expressed it, or all are "sons of God" as Christ put it, or that every man and woman is entitled to an equal chance, as radical western thought has it. To this the Buddhist religion added a negative tenderness towards suffering. Upon this compassion, again, an active social conscience has been built from the practical-minded oriental's interpretation of Christianity.

The Japanese sensitiveness for propriety in their own house is likewise not what we would call conscience. Japanese, for instance, are the biggest sellers of body- and soul-destroying narcotic in the world. There are very few individuals in the nation who feel a sense of wrongdoing over the government-protected poisoning of neighboring populations wherever Japanese influence prevails. At the same time, Japanese themselves are strictly interdicted from using the drug. Few Japanese see anything incongruous about this. Of the same psychology would be Japanese use of plague as a war measure against others, while preserving strict health measures at home.

To have a conception of the tight and tough fabric of Japan, you must know something about her great historical religious characters.

[2] The Swastika is an ancient Buddhist emblem and design symbolizing long or eternal life. It is used as a short writing of the Chinese numeral for 10,000.

They have many counterparts in our west, but none in China, whose people never were in historical times religious-minded in the sense of responsibility towards mankind which comes from the feeling of being God's special spokesmen or people. If the reader is not interested in the influence of a nation's religious personalities in flavoring its mentality, let him skip the following sections, as far as "The Divine House"—which is *not* about religion!

II

The great Kobo Daishi, the first personality who attracts us in Japanese history, brought into Japan something of a religion of charitable works, although his mission was dominantly cultural and intellectual. The two great humanizers of religion in Japan were Shinran and Nichiren, whose lives overlapped four hundred years later, and who mean as much to Japanese civilization as Francis of Assisi and St. Paul to our civilization of the west. In addition to Kobo Daishi's Shingon sect, which still has twelve thousand temples, the great churches of Japan to-day are Shinran's sect, Shin, with twenty thousand temples; Zen, with twenty thousand temples in two principal communions—the "high church" warriors' faith which became the spiritual basis for impulsive action during the Tokugawa period, but since has developed into an evangelical movement with missionaries and churches throughout the Japanese Empire, in Hawaii, Singapore, and California—and, latest, smallest, but noisiest, the fanatic Nichiren, with five thousand temples. Some of these are exceedingly prosperous—as well as their abbots. The noble abbots of the great East and West Hungwanji temples in Kyoto, the brothers Otani—most sought after by western visitors of Japanese prelates—are listed as having private annual incomes of 400,000 and 200,000 yen, respectively.

III

Shinran, long-suffering, tolerant, immensely human in his mistakes, the incarnation of kindliness, is perhaps the most attractive figure in Japanese history. One of the most popular of modern Japanese plays, called *The Priest and His Disciples*, is a story of religion and love woven about the lives of Shinran and his disciples. Since its publication in 1918, it has gone through more than a hundred editions and been played before crowded and almost worshipfully attentive houses at the Imperial Theater and other theaters.

Shinran's romance with the beautiful Princess Tamaki, his simple, spiritual, ethical, and economic preachings to the common people, his nursing of the sick and injured, his sorrows over his son's entanglements, and his placid death in poverty endear him to all generations. Nichiren, on the other hand, was the very epitome of a hateful man, a fanatic like Savonarola, who believed he had a private wire to God. He went about telling people who differed from him in the slightest degree that they would suffer forever in the fifty different Buddhist hells, and was constantly making them uncomfortable by spying on their weaknesses, inveighing publicly against their pleasures, and predicting calamities—regarding which he did have a most unpleasant premonitory sense. Yet this Nichiren is called the Bramwell Booth of Japan, and his church going by his adopted name, "Sun-Lotus," its original Salvation Army.

Time and again Nichiren was banished, but he always came back, and in supreme exasperation the authorities of the great shogunal capital at Kamakura, with the apparent approbation of the majority of the populace, condemned him to be beheaded. After exacerbating them with a final piece of sublime insolence, he stretched out his neck to receive the executioner's blow—only to have a sudden stroke of lightning knock down the executioner and some of the guards. The miracle was as much a surprise to Nichiren as anybody. But he had no hesitation in making full use of it. He was the sort of vitriolic-tongued Jeremiah or John Calvin who raises up a host of devoted worshipers, self-perpetuating down through the centuries. To the present day, one of the worst places in which a scoffer can find himself is among the crowds which mass about the shrine of Nichiren between Yokohama and Tokyo on the annual ceremony for the founder of the sect. Young men eccentrically undressed and well liquored go through the streets carrying tree branches and looking for a shrugging shoulder or a disdainful eye as Nichiren spotted sin and luxury.

Shinran, like Kobo Daishi, came from an aristocratic Fujiwara family. He studied with a great monk of the time, Honen, also founder of a great Buddhist sect. His spiritual enlightenment at the close of his novitiate on Mt. Hiei, where the self-indulgence and belligerency of the monks disgusted and puzzled him, took the form of one hundred nights of prayer before the goddess of mercy in Kyoto. The vision vouchsafed him on the final night had a delightful feature for a young man. The goddess promised to incorporate herself as a beautiful woman to be his helpmeet. Thereafter he waited for his lady in some girl child born after this vision, and when he found his princess, availed himself of this divine sanction, becoming the Martin Luther of the Buddhistic priesthood in the sense of taking a wife. In other ways, too, he humanized the priesthood and brought religion nearer the people, but his spirit of tolerance and sense of oneness with commoners, although they sprang from the aristocracy, were centuries in advance of Luther's.

Nor did he preach salvation by deed. That was left for Nichiren. Shinran preached that all beings, high and low, wise and good, stupid and simple, may be saved by the grace of Amida Buddha. Thus through religion he became the great commoner. His doctrine "tariki," or "strength of another," was opposed to "jiriki," or "one's own strength," adopted by the aristocratic Zen.

Shinran agreed with Nichiren that the times had become degenerate and that it had become most difficult for men to live a high life, accepting the Buddhist eschatology that the age of the decadence of the law had begun in A.D. 1052. But Nichiren on this very account demanded additional chastening of the flesh, whereas the human Shinran preached that where evil abounded, grace did the much more abound. Said Shinran's old master, Honen, "Even a bad man will be received in Buddha's land, and much more a good man." This Shinran turned around, "Even a good man will be received in Buddha's land, and how much more a bad man!" which is very near to Christ's saying about the angels of Heaven rejoicing more over one sinner who is saved than a thousand righteous men. The doctrine of salvation by grace usually involves mysticism such as that of "the blood of the Lamb" in Christianity, but not so in the humanistic Shinran's religion. In spite of his own very interesting illumination he preached that grace could be relied upon in the absence of all inner ecstasy and spiritual manifestations such as visions. This was indeed a comfort to the average non-mystic-minded devotee, and greatly tended to purge Japanese Buddhism of superstition and end emphasis on miracles.

Shortly after the opening of the thirteenth century bitter charges brought by the priests of the older sects against Shinran, particularly based upon his marriage to the princess and his tolerance of common human amatory propensities, brought Shinran's banishment to the northernmost province, Echigo, His old master Honen, at seventy-five years of age, was sent to the other end of the Empire so that they could have no connection, and Shinran was separated from his beautiful child-wife and children.

He took all this in the same spirit of calm unresentful long-suffering with which he took everything—oppositely to Nichiren, who found in his difficulties the very proof of the depravity of his attackers and the justification of his polemics against them. "Echigo, so far removed," said Shinran, on his part, "might never have had a chance to listen to the good law of Buddha if I had not been sent there, and it was my conducting myself as I did that caused me to be sent here." And so, without regrets or condemnations, he set to work to civilize this neglected end of the empire. Eventually his delicate wife joined him. When in after years his pardon came, he signed the receipt merely "Gotoku," "simple-hearted bald man." His great grief was that he was unable to get back soon enough to see his old master Honen in the flesh. At the age of ninety in 1262, after devoting the last thirty years of his life to guidance and instruction of all who came to him in the capital, and conducting a huge correspondence throughout the empire, he died repeating the formula "hamu Amida Butsu" ("by the grace of Amida Buddha").

IV

Nichiren survived Shinran by twenty years. He had been ordained at the age of fifteen and at seventeen passed through such a violent psychological struggle that he spit blood and fell into a swoon. In more than one way he reminds us of St. Paul. Nichiren had the resistance, confidence, faith, and narrowness of the apostle to the gentiles, but lacked St. Paul's profound side. He believed that evangelism began at home, and made his parents his first converts. His teacher, the old abbot of Kiyozumi, remained unmoved, however, and consigned his young pupil to the flames of hell. Yet he smuggled the lad away from the anger of an offended feudal lord.

This was the time of greatest internal strife and breakdown of governmental dignity Japan has known, and storms, earthquake, and fire ravished the land—all of which Nichiren said was predicted, and which he blamed on the sins of the people. In public parks and on streets he denounced the corruption and sybaritism of the lords, and published little tracts reeking with libel which he distributed where they were least appreciated. A mob burned down his house and he had to take shelter with fishermen. All these hardships were to him proof of his divine mission.

In 1263 the shogun relented and invited him back, but Nichiren denounced sin more openly than before. His mother became sick unto death. Nichirenites believe that he prayed her alive. Shortly afterwards he and his proselytes were attacked and his disciples killed or scattered. Nichiren was wounded on the forehead, but survived to conduct a fiery "I-told-you-so" revival when Kublai Khan began preparing his great campaign against Japan. Eleven of his letters still survive, in which he told high officials that heaven was going to exterminate them in fulfilment of his prediction. When the majordomo of the palace called him to account, he wrote that dignitary a threatening letter accompanied by one of his most unpleasant tracts. Unable to bear it longer, the official surrounded his house with troops. Nichiren stood on the veranda, a roll of scriptures in his hand, saying, "Behold the pillar of Japan is now falling!"

On the way to the execution ground, called the Dragon's Mouth, Nichiren was led past the great temple of Hachiman, Emperor deified to god of war, in the outskirts of Kamakura, which to-day is a museum of priceless treasures of medieval accouterments and swords. Nichiren stopped, turned towards the temple, and addressed the deified Emperor in words so brazen that his executioners heard him out: "When to-night, I, Nichiren, shall be beheaded and go to the paradise of the vulture peak, I shall declare that thou, Hachiman, and thy progenitress the Sun Goddess, have failed to fulfil

your oaths, which, when you entered the sacred fields, were taken
to guard those who perpetuate the truth of Buddhism in this world.
Are you not afraid of that?"

It is perhaps the only time that the Sun Goddess and an emperor
have been publicly scolded in Japan, or that a Japanese has summoned these godheads before the seat of the alien lord Buddha for
punishment. Catching their breaths, the soldiers and following mul-
titude hurried Nichiren to the Dragon's Mouth for execution—then
the stroke of lightning fell.

Nichiren afterwards claimed that in that instant he had died and
been resurrected again. It seemed impossible to try to kill him now,
and officialdom contented itself with keeping him at the greatest
possible distance. He nearly starved in a hut in a cemetery but
claimed that he had been fed with spiritual ambrosia. A samurai
who went there to kill him became his greatest friend and disciple.
Nichiren now wrote his famous essay called "Opening the Eyes," in
which he used his life story as symbolic of the whole way of man
towards heaven. It became the scriptures of his devoted sect.

When the Mongol invasion took place as Nichiren had prophesied,
people began to regard him as a supergod or superdevil. He returned in triumph to Kamakura, but right away queered himself
again by damning the officials because they had asked Shingon monks
to pray for rain. He withdrew, accompanied by a few followers, to
the slope of Mt. Fuji, where he spent the last eight years of his life,
founding there the holy see of his religion of which he would be the
dictator, and which would conquer Japan. Japan would then conquer
India and China, uniting the Buddhist world. Eventually the entire
world would bow to the holy see and its dictator on the crest of
Mt. Fuji. Just before his death he organized his church under six
elders, and gave a fourteen-year-old disciple the none too simple task
of converting the Imperial Family.

Nichiren is one of the greatest personalities, as well as one of the
greatest egotists who ever lived. So great was his force that its impetus continues undiminished in his followers of seven hundred years
later. Nichirenism has had a renaissance through the efforts of two
scholars and two admirals. Inouye, the jingo head of the blood-
brotherhood who, along with Hideki Tojo, planned the assassina-

tions of Baron Dan and Premier Inukai, and many others less successful, and who is an associate of the old chief Black Dragon, Toyama, is a Nichiren priest. In Nichiren we may see magnified the traits which account for both the greatness and the dangerousness of Japan.

V

No nation that has produced and been affected by such characters as Kobo Daishi, Shinran, and Nichiren can ever become entirely materialistic, and we see the reincarnation of their spirit in a man like Kagawa. They implanted deep in the nation a consciousness of brotherhood and social responsibility which Japan's unending succession of disasters converts into a businesslike humanitarianism.

The emperor is always the first to give on occasions of earthquake, tidal wave, flood, hurricane, and fire, although his gifts are relatively not large; and the army is always the first to act. A tremendous appreciation of nature and beauty and racial love of play and leisure have made Japan's rulers at all times sensitive to their responsibility to provide the city population with parks and recreation grounds. Also it is the accepted duty of the authorities to see that their people have facilities for keeping clean. A municipality maintains public bathhouses whose wooden tanks of hot water are within reach of every laborer for communal stewing and soaking after the body has first been cleansed by lathering it with soap and pouring water over it.

We have mentioned the consulting bureau of Tokyo's police department, which handles such cases as that of the old man who could keep going as long as he had sake. It has six sections with more than sixty subdivisions, and annually cares for fifty thousand cases of destitution, petty money complaints, psychological aberrations, and legal advice. City swimming pools dedicated to a Shinto water god are new summer features for a people whose ability in the water enabled them to take the world's aquatic sports record.

A unique example of the paternal-humanitarian element in Japanese government is the Tokyo municipal marriage bureau, closed, alas, on April 1, 1934, because each marriage arranged within the year had cost the city 240 yen! "Yedo kids," bachelors and spinsters, have to go back to the professional go-between couples—or rely on their own devices.

Highstrung Japan has a high insanity rate. Harmless cases are left in the care of their families and are tolerated about the streets, although a number of modern insane asylums have been built. Workhouses for the poor and lodging houses for the unemployed have eliminated begging, which under the example of saintly Buddhist indigence has flourished between suppressions in Japan's history.

There is a tremendous interest in prison reform from intellectual rather than emotional motives. Any number of model prisons exist, whose chief fault is the literal mindedness and rule of bookishness of the Japanese. The great Tokyo earthquake of 1923 gave the Christian prison reformer Arima his chance. While the ground was still quaking he walked through burning Tokyo to the military headquarters and requested permission to handle without guards the inmates of the great Tokyo penitentiary, whose walls had fallen. Only one of the thirteen hundred prisoners left. This convict, concerned over his poor mother, had tried to get the warden to attend to forwarding her a certain sum of money. The warden would not act; the life-termer crawled out through a quake crevice, delivered the money, and gave himself up for arrest. The prison reformer reprimanded the warden. Soon after Arima was made governor of all Japan's new model prisons. He pays his convicts five to ten yen a month for their work and turns them out after ten to twelve years, instilled with the old samurai discipline and equipped with capital for starting business or farming.

Japan's crime rate is, after all, exceedingly low in comparison with our western communities. There are not as many armed robberies in the empire during a year as there are murders in one of our large cities. Even thieving is low, and this in a land where most of the houses are walled with wood an eighth of an inch thick, or with panels of rice paper. It is almost impossible to lose anything in Tokyo. Leave what you will on a tram car and, whether you want it or not, some honest fellow passenger turns it over to the police, whose lost and found bureau is one of the most efficient in the world.

A traveler must be registered with the police wherever he spends the night. Train boys turn in complete lists of passengers to the railway police. In a small, compact country, whose police are under national and not municipal control, and who have a record of every individual within their jurisdiction at any given moment, there is very little hope of getting away with a crime.

Not ordinary criminal tendencies, but the patriotic assassinations of the blood-and-iron societies, have recently compelled the police for the first time to carry guns and wear bullet-proof vests. Ordinarily a police officer's uniform, in summer spotless white with white gloves, and sword, the badge of authority, are sufficient to overawe a criminal. Crimes of passion are frequent, violent crimes for profit almost non-existent, gangsterism is obviously impossible, and the records of arrests and convictions is almost one hundred per cent. England alone among the white nations has a record that approaches comparison. Japan's police, even more than the army, inherited the samurai tradition and are popularly regarded as incorruptible. Recurrent scandals make it sometimes seem that almost any big man can be bought in Japan, including the chief of the nation's police himself, the Minister of the Interior. But you can't buy the cop on the corner, and it would be dangerous to try! He is usually a college graduate, proud to work for sixty yen a month—for it is still an honor to be a policeman in Japan.

Twice a month or oftener a local police station checks up on every household within its precinct, and some one in the house must answer a full list of questions about each occupant and guest, his means of livelihood and interests in life. Twice a year the courteous but firm policeman inspects the entire house, even to the contents of every cupboard. The little Japanese housewife is proud to get his okay of her semiannual official housecleaning. This irks the non-Japanese resident and also the Korean and Chinese under Japanese rule, who feels that he has an individualistic right to his dirt and privacy. It is one point which makes complete submission to Japanese rule by other oriental races difficult.

Japan is an ideal-worshiping nation. The reformer complex is always present. Many individuals, often of eccentric type, start out in humanitarian or religious enterprises. Little sects of the "holy roller" type are constantly having their day—some sentimentalist (usually egotist as well) is always starting some new movement for humanity.

In connection with the life of Kobo Daishi we have shown how Japan's religious sects stem from such personalities. Ever since Buddhism entered, religious and humanitarian activities have been found together, as in Kagawa who established with sweat, blood, and starvation the slum rescue missions of Japan which have flowered into a great government program of housing and slum elimination. There are many other contemporary humanitarians worth noting, such as the socialist, Iwasaki, who conducts a home for the destitute under the arches of the elevated railroad tracks in Tokyo. He personally dresses like a fishmonger, wearing a white shirt with inscriptions on the front: "Those who won't work should not eat—those who can't work must be fed."

Women's organizations, in emulation of American women's movements, have begun reform campaigns, and are earnest enough about them to be quite annoying to politicians and police. Thus far their campaigns against cruelty to children and animals, against dust and noise and for admission of women to the bar and medicine have been notably successful. They have made some progress toward coeducation and equal educational facilities for girls above grammar school. Women in business have become as common as they are in America; they are conductorettes on the buses, and a few have gone into such spectacular professions as flying. Efforts for woman suffrage, prohibition, and abolition of licensed quarters, however, have failed.

Great improvement has been made in dormitory conditions of women in industry—largely under pressure of reformers. However, women's labor movements have, on the whole, gotten nowhere—save the union of dancing revue girls who forced theater magnates to terms in the summer of 1934.

Christianity is responsible for many of Japan's modern humanitarian enterprises. In 1925 a Japanese Christian named Shimizu opened an orphanage for Chinese girls outside of the North Wall of Peking, financing it entirely by his own efforts. He has sent several Chinese girls and one boy to Doshisha University and returned them to Peking to carry on the work for which he now raises money at the same time that he teaches in Kyoto. He refused an endowment from the South Manchurian Railway Company, which brought him under suspicion and shadowing by Japanese military spies.

The great and wealthy Buddhist sects of Japan operate many philanthropic enterprises in connection with their beautifully kept lacquered temples. The Young Men's Buddhist Association and Young Women's Buddhist Association provide all the humanitarian facilities of our Y. M. C. A. and Y. W. C. A. after which they are modeled, with the addition of a strong flavor of super-patriotism. The Salvation Army was a very prominent institution in Japan under the command of one of her strongest characters, General Yamamoto, and its foremost annual contributor was the empress-dowager. Antiforeignism closed it and Rotary in Japan about the same time, in 1940.

Japan's humanitarian plant recently received substantial foreign aid in a gift by the Rockefeller Foundation of four million yen for the improvement of public sanitation, accepted after careful consideration by the home ministry. Many foreign contributions have been made, such as St. Luke's hospital, Tokyo, built by the enthusiasm of Dr. Teusler, cousin to the first Mrs. Woodrow Wilson. And, commendably, a dozen or so model prisons for juveniles have been built. Yet the reformer-saint Kagawa complains bitterly of lack of social conscience and paucity of its expression among the individualistic Japanese.

The Japanese urge to save humanity—another expression of the divine-mission complex—remains unappeased.

Chapter XXVII

The Divine House

Two days before Christmas, 1933, Tokyo was awakened by a siren. The five million people within earshot sat up on their mats. When a second long blast rent the air they leaped out of their padded kimonos, laughed and danced hysterically for joy, and crawled to their bedroom shrines to kowtow in thanks to the gods. After four previous august accouchements resulting in daughters, the Empress had borne a son! That second blast was the stuff of which history, quite independent of the economic theory, is made.

Nowhere, at no time, could the birth of a male imperial heir have promised more definite effect on history. The "auspicious event" may be chosen by Japan's future official historians for the beginning of the era of *greater* Japan, as the birth of the Emperor Meiji was made the beginning date of the era of modern Japan.

A month before the birth, seventy million Japanese subjects had prayed that the child should be a boy—that the throne of the "one line unbroken from ages eternal" might have a direct heir. Seven prefectual governors had been ordered to send up young women of unimpeachable moral character and proper physical condition to be candidates for the position of wet nurse to the divine child. Thousands of young women presented themselves in each prefecture. Of the seven who reached Tokyo two were chosen who had to learn the special court language called the Yamato tongue, supposed to be preserved from the time of Jimmu Tenno and his Yamato tribesmen. Wet nurses have become strong figures of the court in past Japanese history.

There was national rejoicing over the special ceremony of the court when the Empress donned the sacred maternity obi,[1] of white silk. Bulletins were given the press regarding her condition up to the one announcing that her majesty had entered the specially constructed delivery room and taken her place on the birth-giving couch, surrounded on three sides by a three-leaved Japanese screen. Shinto priests and old women had read the signs and portents strongly predicting a son.

After the two whistles blew and the cannon boomed, the government radio station JOAK briefly announced the "honor of the auspicious event," giving in the metric system recently legally adopted, the Divine Infant's exact weight and length, following this information with the Kimigayo: the national anthem which expresses the sentiment that the Divine House shall reign until every pebble on Japan's shores grows into a great rock covered with hoary moss. Every town and village broke out with rising-sun flags and the inhabitants gave themselves up to felicitations and gaiety. Residents of each block assembled voluntarily before the local police box and shouted banzais [2] before the policeman as local representative of sovereign authority. The Women's Patriotic Society of Tokyo got into the streets with the first lantern procession and by midnight a million cheering people had assembled in the great plaza before the Imperial Palace. Police lifted restrictions on cafés and dance halls. One of the great newspapers offered a silver medal to every boy born in Japan on this auspicious day.

As soon as the imperial gynecologist had completed the parturition, the imperial chamberlain, a retired admiral, bore on a pillow to the infant a sword, symbol of life force and potent to ward off all evil. This sword had been newly beaten for the Crown Prince by Japan's master swordsmith, Gassan—hammered only after ceremonial ablutions and dressing in ceremonial costume, including a wooden topknot held on his shaved head by a cord to imitate the old samurai hairdress. The sword must remain the close possession of its owner all his life.

Within the week, representatives of President Roosevelt and of all

[1] The wide band of heavy cloth, usually silk brocade, worn about the waist over the kimono and ending in a roll behind, which is the most important article of woman's dress and formerly designated her station or class.

[2] "Ten thousand years!" Also, with different characters, "Welcome."

other foreign governments called to offer congratulations. At the end of seven days the baby received his ceremonial bath in a special cypress-wood tub, a rite so ancient that the meaning of its special motions is forgotten. During the bath, standing behind a screen, one of the most venerable scholars of the empire, an assistant reader, two twangers of the great decorated samurai bows (one of whom is a retired general and the second a viscount), and two assistant twangers, both viscounts, costumed in robes and headdresses copied from some ancient Chinese court, chanted and twanged to keep evil spirits away.

Then the name selected for the prince by the wise men of the court, and written on a silk-faced scroll by his Imperial Father, was passed to the minister of the Imperial Household, placed by him in a lacquered box and handed to the lord steward of the Empress, who in turn gave the box to the chief lady-in-waiting, who placed it before the infant Prince. The grand chamberlain then reported back to the Emperor that the little being scheduled to be the one hundred and twenty-fifth Divine Sovereign of the empire in unchanged line from Jimmu Tenno had received his name: Tsuguno-miya Akihito, meaning "Succeeder, Enlightened Benevolent Divine Person." The new Crown Prince then received his first presents from his dowager grandmother in the form of rice and fish.

Meanwhile the guns of military batteries and warships roared and Japan's citizenry assembled in parks throughout the empire. Led by Premier Saito standing under a huge red panoply erected in Hibya Park, Tokyo, they shouted "Banzai!" three times. The mayor of Tokyo then read a speech of fealty and felicitation carried by the radio to every part of the empire.

Imperial messengers were dispatched to the shrine of the Sun Goddess, progenitress of the line, at Ise, two hundred and fifty miles southwest of Tokyo, and to the sanctuaries where are enshrined the spirits of the one hundred and twenty-three dead Tennos and the eighty deities of the Shinto pantheon, to apprise these spirits of the name of the Heir to the Divine Seat.

Japan went into a period of rejoicing for a week which tallied with the New Year festivities. Large cities provided free entertainments of music, drama, and dances in the public parks, and free meals to all who applied. A month and a half after the birth, official celebrations thereof were held with solemn worship at all ancestral shrines, concluded by the proclamation of imperial clemency which commuted all death sentences, freed or reduced the terms of thirty-five thousand prisoners, and restored civil rights to one hundred thousand ex-convicts.

II

The ceremonies attendant upon the birth of a Japanese crown prince sound fantastically medieval to us, but to the Japanese, whether they be scientists, bankers, or commanders of air squadrons, they are as serious as a political caucus or an election to our leaders. In addition to its political significance, every Japanese feels that an imperial birth concerns the nation as a family and himself as a member of that family. To praying and waiting millions, to stern-mouthed leaders convinced of Japan's destiny and their position in it, and to the Imperial Couple themselves, after the royal pilgrimage of supplication from shrine to shrine, the birth of a prince at the moment it took place was heaven's utmost stamp of approval upon Japan's progress and plans. In the terse words of General Araki, evangelist of Japan's destiny, "The foundations of our Empire are now based more firmly than ever." And Admiral Suetsugu says in effect, "The basis for greater Nippon is now firmly laid."

The combination of ancient Chinese costume and Prussian court dress, of bow twanging to drive off evil spirits and announcements by radio, epitomize the position of the Imperial Household in modern Japan. The mother of the Divine Infant, Empress Nagako, thirty-one years old at the time of the birth, is a gracious, charitably inclined, modern-minded sovereign. As consort-designate she was trained in tennis and other sports and gymnastics that the imperial progeny might have added vigor. She is an accomplished musician with a taste for Beethoven and Chopin. The Crown Prince, when he is fifteen years old, will take up residence in a replica of the palace of Versailles that stands at a distance from the Forbidden Precincts, in the city of Tokyo. Yet he is an oriental potentate and a god.

What is the Imperial House of Japan? If it were a medieval

institution surviving in a truly modernized Japan, it would be unreal
or very soon become as modern as the nation. Instead, the Imperial
House is the visible front of the still profound medievalism of a
Japan that boasts machines and transportation, a literacy rate
higher than ours, stunt newspaper reporting and huge circulations,
and a superficial appearance of modern sophistication. It remains
the one thing for which every Japanese of the most variant political
beliefs would forthwith lay down his life.

The old Jesuits, who were the first white students of Japan, tried
to explain the position of the Tenno by comparing him to the Pope
at Rome. But this comparison is most insufficient. The Pope is anything but a racial and national symbol, nor has he ever inspired
among the most faithful the fanatic personal devotion accorded the
Tenno by present-day Japanese. The attitude toward the Imperial
Household in Japan is the nation's sublime expression of self-wor-
ship. The Divine Family is visual evidence that heaven is with it
and in it. As Nippon's ship of state is launched into more and more
perilous waters, and as world pressures increase, this concrete expression of unity is more and more needed. Any Japanese would die
to preserve it now.

The emperor has nothing to do with politics directly. Mutsuhito,
by nature a strong character, did control the elder statesmen or
political machinators or warlike generals who presumed to speak in
his name, but it hasn't been done since. The Son of Heaven's prestige
is never endangered by open declarations against movements that
have not yet run themselves out. As long as it is not tested, imperial restraint is a tremendous factor. If a mistake is made, some
official's or councilor's head goes off. The emperor is never wrong.

Vast sums are spent on ceremonies, and that the people want.
The last coronation cost three hundred million yen, but the Household itself lives frugally, almost austerely. The imperial princes are
trained to be expert horsemen and kept in riding and fencing form.
I have heard stories of their climbing over the wall of the palace into
the contiguous British embassy grounds to play tennis with the
clerks and young women of the embassy. The princes are encouraged to follow scientific interests in their private laboratories.

The Divine House has had its human vicissitudes and has "maintained one unbroken line" only through concubinage and adoption. The blood of many noble Japanese families is stronger in it than that of the descendants of its founder. Wisely, collateral branches have been regularly lopped off. In 1889, influenced by contact with Germany, Japan's elder statesmen adjusted the Imperial House to modern conventions and strengthened it against sophistication without any dissension within, by limiting the inheritance to a son by the imperial consort, although the heir at the moment was the son of a concubine, and although several outstanding figures in the line have been women.

Hence, the extra care with which the imperial consort is nowadays selected. For years the mother of the present Emperor was required to act as regent for her mentally-failing Imperial Husband. "Grave incidents"—this phrase in the press always means something concerning the unmentionable Household—have several times in recent years been connected with free expressions or political machinations concerning the Imperial House. The supreme instance of the modern determination to protect the sublimity of the Imperial House is the police prevention of the dramatization of the classical novel *Genji Monogatari* after the theater had been sold out for the entire season. The *Genji*, written by a court lady herself in the eleventh century, has always been accepted and popular despite its picture of the humanness and emotional foibles of godly personages. Its hero Genji was historically the son of one emperor, illicitly father of another by his imperial father's favorite concubine (as revealed a generation later), and additionally father through other *affaires d'amour* of an emperor and an empress.

III

Obviously the westerner going to Japan must relate himself to a whole new set of ideas. The charge of lese majesty is the nastiest that can be made. A great deal of immunity was granted to the "foreign barbarian"—not merely out of Japanese courtesy, but because of the feeling that the barbarian perhaps should be excused in the same way as are dumb creatures incapable of really knowing reverence. But that kindness, if it were such, is no longer extended.

An English editor was fined for omitting capital initials on the words Imperial Household and the names and titles of its members. One of Japan's veteran English papers got into police difficulties for slightly lampooning a school principal who in a fire neglected the lives of his pupils and suffered injury himself to rescue the emperor's photograph. This brought a gracious expression from the Tenno relieving teachers and pupils of the duty of risking their lives to save the presentation picture before which every class bows daily. The upshot is that teachers and pupils are all the more ardent about doing it. Another English journalist was sentenced in Korea for mentioning the malady of the late Emperor, but after his apology and several months' incarceration he and the authorities contrived some sort of a compromise whereby he became a propagandist for Nippon.

How seriously the Japanese take this sort of thing is shown by their threat, in violation of all international law, to bomb a Chinese paper in Peking if it did not go out of existence after printing a happening which was the convincing symptom of the sick Emperor. Japanese indignantly looked forward to the time when it might be possible to do the same to a New York news weekly that was flippant about the Sacred House.

One of the leading Honolulu dailies, published half in English, half in Japanese, but calling itself an American newspaper (edited by an alien Japanese gentleman with ownership vested in his American-born son) editorialized upon the birth of the Imperial Heir: "Coming at a time when the nation is facing a crisis it has added significance. The people of Japan virtually went wild. This is a psychology that isn't understandable to any one outside of the Japanese. . . . We extend our blessing to the Royal Child." Some one signing himself "A Visiting Tourist" wrote a letter to the editor of a rival American paper expressing surprise "that a leading Honolulu paper should get excited about the birth of a son to the Royal Family of Japan, much in the tone of subjects of that family," and ridiculing the conception of the Japanese ruler as a direct descendant of the Sun Goddess. Whereupon Japanese of Honolulu, its largest community, held an indignation meeting and the board of the United Japanese Society considered a resolution to boycott the American paper. Calm counsel prevailed. But thus does the Japanese "hangover" of medieval reverence, charming enough in itself, become of concern to the world. A Japanese might say, of course, that westerners should not complain of this so long as a Mussolini can order his name always to appear in capitals.

The westerner's Japanese associates convey to him quietly, by looks only, that their emperor worship is something on a different plane from anything known in his world, and so genuinely a part of their souls that he has no more impulse to be frivolous or impudent about it than about a child's worship of its mother. One comes to accept the kneeling adoration of thousands who, after all-night vigil, never raise an eye to the bespectacled, "divine" figure riding past them in an enclosed carriage. The foreigner willingly puts down his umbrella in the usual rain and as often as not surprises himself by literally not standing out against the mass, but kneeling also at the last minute, although (until 1938) uncompelled.

The Imperial Household of Japan is the twentieth century's greatest anachronism. Yet even in it exists the paradox of new and old which we find throughout Japan. It is the world's oldest ruling house, yet in a sense its newest. For its present position dates only from the Tokugawa overthrow, 1867. When Daniel Webster composed President Fillmore's message to the Emperor of Japan, no western government knew that Japan had a ruler outside of the shogun at Tokyo, and Perry delivered the message to the shogun's officials. The dynasty's present court dress comes from the Hohenzollern court of Bismarck and when one is invited to a lawn fête in the imperial grounds, he must wear long tails, and a stovepipe hat even if it be made of paper, while a lady must dress in Victorian style. Just as an isolated chain of feudal islands has become in a half-century one of the world's first-class powers, so an impoverished, ignored royal house, preserved for nine centuries by the fidelity of an oriental population, has taken its position as the world's grandest and richest ruling dynasty during those same fifty years.

IV

In Japan as many things in the life of the ordinary Japanese are hooked up with the Imperial Household as with sectarian

churches in the life of a small-town western community. Imperial
rulers may become the popular gods of later generations. The Emperor Ojin, A.D. 283, became the god of war Hachiman, much worshiped at present. Japanese Buddhism maintains a close connection
with the Imperial Household in spite of the fact that the Shinto
cult exists chiefly to bolster it. An image of the female Buddha of
mercy, Kwannon, made by the great idol carver Takamura, has
already been dedicated in honor of the new Crown Prince.

Every private home and inn in the empire is Tenno-conscious,
containing its never-occupied "emperor's seat," a niche with a
miniature raised dais. Agriculture, education, and even modern
world-market-capturing industry are ceremonially connected with
the Sacred Person. Any one entering one of Tokyo's large department stores during the summer following the imperial birth, would
have seen wide counters covered with nude babies—and nothing is
much more attractive than a Japanese baby—shown to celebrate the
event. Every grammar-school boy and girl in Japan carries his books
in a knapsack because years ago an imperial child saw soldiers wearing knapsacks and insisted on having one to carry his books in.
Crates of fireflies for the emperor are caught by students in Fukuoka
where they first appear, and sent by airplane to the palace. To keep
his paternal relationship to the peasantry always fresh the emperor
once a year transplants rice shoots in a special paddy in his grounds
—a rite taken from imperial China. Japan planned a great imperial
exposition in 1940, to honor the twenty-six hundredth anniversary
of the founding of the nation, to open on April 3rd, the day of the
death of Jimmu, the founder, and to close on November 3rd, the day
of the birth of Meiji, the refounder.

A very human description of what a Japanese feels upon entering
the presence of the Sacred Person is given by Mori, the patron of
Takahashi, who was assassinated on the charge of carrying a walking stick into the sacred shrine of Ise. He tells that he and other
officials went forward, one by one, on their knees, and the waiting
ones were overcome by emotion. When at last Mori's turn came and
the sacred curtain slid up, revealing the Divine Person, try as he
would he could not lift his face. Finally, he says, he got his eyes
as high as the Tenno's chest, but he never saw the Countenance.

The reverence given the Imperial Family, and also a significant example of how it may go wrong, is illustrated by the good-will mission of the Emperor's younger brother, Prince Chichibu, to Manchukuo. When the Prince, who is himself a gracious and democratic-mannered person, reached Mukden, regulations were imposed that violated treaty rights of foreign residents and caused diplomatic protests. To insure that no one might look down on the Prince from an elevation, the Japanese police forced their way into private homes, and bottled up the families in lower rooms for several hours. In Chinese homes and shops, they helped themselves to tobacco, candy and foodstuffs, and made sport of ladies, and in an American home the young bucks presented a demand that the wife teach them to play bridge and dance with them.

No publication in Japan has ever criticized the Emperor. A large daily did begin a series of criticisms of officials of the Household ministry, but the public considered this bordering on indelicacy and blasphemy, and the articles stopped.

v

The Japanese Imperial House is richer than Morgan—is unquestionably the richest ruling house, in privy treasure as distinguished from its realm, that to-day's world knows, and perhaps that the world has ever known. It privately owns and operates the millions of acres of forestry land in Japan, and does all the reforestation. It owns enormous blocks of shares in every great Japanese corporation. At the time, about 1925, when under Baron Shidehara's influence freedom of criticism and investigation was greatest, I interviewed the (then) Baron Makino who, as minister of the Imperial Household, was one of the world's greatest business executives. The minister of the Imperial Household must be one of Japan's most experienced men in statecraft as well as in business. Count Makino has held every important cabinet office but that of premier.

Some Tokyo taxpayers, already burdened with rebuilding the city after the earthquake of 1923, were daring enough to complain of the unfairness of having to support the police, streets, and sanitation of the whole central business district of Tokyo, which as well as the vast areas of the palace grounds, is owned by the Imperial Household and pays no taxes. One hears no such whimpering to-day —the superpatriots would soon quiet such irreverence.

I dared to ask the minister to give me an estimate of the wealth of the Son of Heaven.

"That," he replied, "has never been reckoned and never will be. Never before has it been requested, and I trust never again will be."

He was gracious, while carefully keeping me within bounds, and presented to me the theory, in which there is great truth, that the imperial fortune represents the finest reserve untouchable by politics or public prodigality possessed by any nation in the world. It is always available in time of great catastrophe or supreme national crisis. The first donor to earthquake, fire, flood, or famine sufferers is the Imperial Family, which contributes also regularly to the Japanese Salvation Army, Red Cross, Buddhist charities, and like institutions. It has contributed to help prosecute each of Japan's great wars.

Recently a patriot, a stevedore named Kuroda, called upon a socialist member of parliament named Yamamoto and left him dead. Arrested, Kuroda defended himself with the statement that he called to scold the member of parliament for appearing in ordinary clothes at the opening of the Diet session attended for a few minutes by the Divine Person. "I told Yamamoto I held to the Emperor-centric principle. His sneer at this infuriated me. We fought, and he died." Such is the way the emperor is regarded in Japan.

Recently the newspapers have publicized a retired army officer, who, it was discovered, had gone daily, rain or shine, for five years, to the north entrance of Meiji shrine at daybreak to show his devotion to the Imperial House. Another newspaper tells on the same page with the comic strip of "Bringing Up Father" the story of Squad Leader Higashijima, called to pass the bier of his dead comrades in Manchuria. "He stood a long minute of prayer, pressing his palms together before him. He was to say something for the service. Tears rolled down his cheeks. His lips quivered and at last he managed with difficulty 'Tenno Heika (His Majesty the Emperor)!' He could not add 'banzai,' though he made several attempts, and retreated to his place, drying his tears with his fists. The entire company of soldiers dropped their heads and silently shed tears. Many words are not needed for the soldier who lives in the world of nonself. 'His Majesty the Emperor' is enough. In this one phrase, everything is found, and from this one phrase everything comes. Courage and strength of our soldiers, the power of our army and navy, and the glory of our nation all spring from this one phrase: 'His Majesty the Emperor!'"

The medievalness, as well as the majesty of the Japanese throne, were never better exhibited than when the Tenno on March 26, 1930, repaired to the Kashikodokoro, the Place of Awe, and holding aloft a scroll read in stentorian tones this message to the Sun Goddess, progenitress of his race: "We herewith report the completion of the reconstruction of our capital. We accord the thanks to the august virtues of our Imperial Ancestors." Thus was announced the recovery of Tokyo and its five million tough inhabitants from the greatest disaster to befall a city in the recorded history of mankind.

Chapter XXVIII
Radicalism in Japan

COMMUNISM in Japan, like superpatriotism, is an emotional rather than a political or economic outburst. Malnutrition among those who grow Japan's food, and long hours and bare existence among those who make ammunition for the nation's drive into the world's markets, look like orthodox soil for communist growth, but results thus far have been utterly discouraging to Marxists taught that so much pressure of misery must inevitably produce such and such an explosion.

Rather, the impulses which make communists in Japan are exactly the same as those which make Black Dragons or any other of the superpatriots at the opposite end of the political spectrum. Marxists will not get anywhere in Japan until they learn to take full advantage of the psychology of frenzy, of martyrdom, of craving for a cause for which one may run the risk of physical torture and death—in short, the devotee psychology which is so large a part of the Japanese mind. Such radicalism as has already existed in Japan is a manifestation of this, rather than of economic creeds.

After the Japanese army broke out of bounds in Manchuria and the patriotic societies got control of the government in Japan by a few well-timed assassinations, police records showed between thirty thousand and fifty thousand arrests in Japan for radicalism. Yet with fifty million subjects fervently devoted to a divine mission, and regarding communism as an unendurable heresy, it was foolish to picture Japan as containing anything like a communistic menace. Such predictions were like those that Germany was heading into communism at the time Hitler was receiving a "yes" vote from ninety-odd per cent of the German people.

Yet let great disillusionment come to the masses who are fanatically convinced at this moment of Tojo's, Araki's, Suetsugu's, and Matsuoka's way for the nation—let these men lead their people into great slaughter and humiliating defeat, and the same millions could turn with an equal fanaticism and spirit of martyrdom to the light held out by Marx and the activities promoted by the Comintern.

Communism is no such new idea to the Japanese as to us. According to Okuma the essence of national socialism was the political ideal in Japan all through feudalism. The historian Fukuchi says: "A person living from another's labor is a criminal, according to the fundamental national ideals." Ieyasu forbade the transferring of title to land, thereby decapitalizing it, and in 1869, arable land in Japan was distributed among the food-producing population rather than sold to the highest bidder. During the long Tokugawa period, all wages were fixed by law—a high development of socialism or communalism. On several occasions in Japanese history the supreme authority declared the cancellation of all private debts.

Communal enterprises have always been, and still remain, a strong feature of life in Japan as in all oriental communities. Scores of brotherhoods and many of the artisans' guilds shared on a communal basis. Villages communally educated their brightest boys. Societies of peasants and small townsmen save capital on a dime-a-week savings-society scheme, lend the capital and interest within their own membership, and when enough has been accumulated liquidate the whole business and take all living members on pilgrimage to famous shrines and historical points. They may be seen in their broad-brimmed hats, unbleached cotton costumes, and taped legs, climbing Mt. Fuji, crossing the Inland Sea or reverently kneeling at the Imperial Shrine of Ise. Similar societies exist for burying members or insuring against drought.

The miners of Japan have a communal organization that long antedates labor unionism in the west. The fact that in feudal times miners were considered the roughest class of society, virtual outcasts, caused the formation of the national guild. Travel money from one mine to another was provided by the brother miners, who also collected retirement pensions among themselves, and supported arrivals until there was work for them. The unmarried miners lived in communal houses.

There still exists in Yaijiri peninsula of Aoyama prefecture a communal village of several hundred fisher and farmer folk who since time immemorial have married among themselves and excluded outsiders. Individually, they live in Spartan poverty, all their excess earnings going into the village chest to make the village itself rich. The present age in Japan is so near the feudal period that basic principles of communism known in the guild life that flourished under feudalism are still live memories to the Japanese public.

The history of modern radicalism in Japan can be very quickly summarized. Japanese intellectuals followed Kropotkin, Tolstoy, Marx, and Lenin with great interest before the supremacy of bolshevism in Russia. Sen Katayama, a typical Japanese idealist of the intellectual class, became acquainted with European radicalism during his long American experience, took it in literal fashion and went back to preach it in Japan. Kagawa's Christian reform group helped organize labor unions. The mushroom war industries of 1914-1919 experienced many strikes. The first great violence was in Asano's shipyards in 1917, when the damage ran into six figures.

Katayama was more of a Kropotkin anarchist than a Marxist, but he made the mistake of being perfectly outspoken. Also he antagonized the patriots by opposing war with Russia and fraternizing with Lenin's budding bolshevik party. For a time other leaders, inspired by Katayama, sprang up, such as Fujita, who started as a newsboy; when he wished to propagandize Tokyo with his socialist leaflets he would call on the five hundred or six hundred newsboys of whom he was the dean to cover the city in an hour. Comrade Nagaoka, an ex-miner, became a street vendor to enable him to speak to the workmen without suspicion, and supported his propaganda by selling songs of his own composition. Fujita's successor as principal socialist of the islands, Abe (Iso), was much caricatured because one of his eyelids is almost constantly closed. Abe was also one of the first champions of birth control, although—or maybe, because—he himself fathered eight sons. Abe's socialist party has been squeezed between communists and "anti-dangerous-thought" squads of the police.

There is nothing fit to bear the name of organized socialism left in Japan at the present moment. Old Abe sponsored the first inter-collegiate and international baseball games and is honored to-day much more as the father of baseball than of socialism. Other splendid intelligentsia who favored socialism and many of whom, like Abe, were Christians, particularly Dr. Yoshino of Imperial University of Tokyo, died under a cloud. With this digression among the "pinks" we go back to the progress of extreme radicalism.

Katayama was forced to flee the country on the charge that he had spoken against the Emperor rather than because of his economic theories. Socialism became so distasteful that a convict committed suicide in prison because a fellow jail-bird called him a socialist. Moscow gave Katayama refuge but not very much in the way of physical comfort, and he eked out long years of ill health there until Stalin helped bury him in the wall of the Kremlin alongside the Americans, John Reed and Bill Haywood. Shortly before Katayama's death, at the Emperor's own request, the Japanese government finally permitted Katayama's daughter to go to Moscow and nurse him. She had to give a pledge that she would try to convert him from his doctrinal error.

Katayama encouraged the apostles of the Comintern as to the hopes of communism in Japan. The opening of diplomatic relations between Russia and Japan in 1921 was seized by the Comintern for the beginning of an intensive propaganda throughout the oriental empire. A communist party was openly formed, and was not outlawed until 1927. There was just enough of the risqué about the idea of being a communist to attract many of Japan's intellectuals and students looking for a cause to which they might devote themselves.

Right away, on orders from godless Moscow, the party came into clash with Kagawa's school of Christian socialists whose economic theories were quite as drastic as those of Marx or Lenin, but were based upon Kagawa's studies of the communalism of the early Christian church. In order to combat the agnostic influence these older and Christian leaders in social reform began calling themselves Christian communists. It was Kagawa and his comrades who had first organized labor into unions, first demanded and put through factory laws, first protected the peasant girls who were being drawn by tens of thousands into cotton and silk factories, and first organized the peasants into group resistance against the exactions of landlords. These pioneer reformers of Japan's industrial age founded and built farmers' and laborers' coöperatives and, in spite of the government's connection with big business, forced it to be friendly toward coöperative manufacturing and distributing of food and clothing at cost. They had gone to jail in the first workmen's strikes. These Christian social reformers were too deeply entrenched in the affec tions of farmers and laborers to be readily swept aside by the tide of venom from Moscow. The result of the struggle was merely to weaken both sides, break up proletarianism into a half-dozen warring factions, and leave the most radical communists exposed where they were readily pounced upon by the police.

A significant bit of Japanese psychology profoundly affected the radical movement following the great earthquake and fire disaster which destroyed Tokyo and cost one hundred and fifty thousand lives in September, 1923. The most brilliant and perhaps most sincere radical in the country, the socialist Ogawa, was in jail awaiting trial at the moment of the holocaust. His common-law wife and little son were in cells nearby. The sympathy of the public in the trial had been notably with the radical. During the excitement of the disaster, a major in the Japanese army went to the prison, demanded access to the prisoners, pounced upon Ogawa and broke his back with a jiu-jutsu hold, then went into the other cells and strangled to death his wife and son. There was some indignation afterwards, but the Black Dragons and other patriotic societies saw to it that the major ended up with a promotion in Manchuria, where such a man could really give all that was in him. While he was doing his little job in the prison, patriots started rumors among the frenzied populace that Koreans and radicals were spreading the fire and plotting the overthrow of the Emperor—in duplication of the great fire and gunpowder plot of the Tokugawa period.

Thousands of Korean laborers had filtered into Japan, brought in many instances by employers who paid them less than Japanese workmen. A few of the more intelligent of them had been attracted to the radical cause. While American sailors were feeding Japanese refugees from American warships in the harbor, these same refugees were slaughtering scores of "radicals" and Koreans. The massacre was eventually stopped under martial law and the matter hushed up. It might be of interest to interpolate that some of the superpatriots even agitated for an attack against the American ships in the harbor which were saving thousands of Japanese driven into the sea by the fire.

Japanese history shows that every great crisis has rallied the people about the Divine Head and produced a reactionary period. So strong was this trend after the earthquake that the communist leaders felt it wise to disband their party. It was not reorganized till 1925. It became important enough to cause police round-ups in 1928, continuing ever since. But these had no great purpose behind them until the superpatriots replaced the mild Shidehara government in the winter of 1931. Since then methods used against communists have been very reminiscent of those used in the early seventeenth century in exterminating Christianity, although police tortures have improved from those of the inquisition to those of the American third degree—if this be regarded as improvement.

The communists had begun to win laborers in considerable numbers in the late nineteen-twenties, but they proved to be a helpless herd when the police picked off the intellectuals who were their organizers and brains. Police state that it is not usually necessary to treat proletarians to more than a stay in jail awaiting trial in order to procure their recantation. A writer in the *Japan Times* of Tokyo is authority for the statement that of twenty-seven thousand five hundred communists taken up between March, 1928, and March, 1933, it was possible to release twenty-five thousand without indictment. Of the twenty-five hundred committed to terms of prison, two-thirds had already announced conversion to orthodox Nipponism. This writer expected that perhaps three hundred out of the lot would remain incorrigible.

Such conversions and betrayals among party members drove party leaders to attempt a discipline of terror including murders and tortures such as the pouring of molten metal into the navels of suspected squealers. Also an attempt was made to carry out the sort of "party sequestrations" perpetrated by Stalin in the Caucasus in his young days—robbing banks to provide funds. This lawlessness turned the Japanese public at large against communist leadership. Some went toward the Christian Kagawa but most were won by the national fascism of Araki and Matsuoka, with its pledges to provide plenty by making Japan the dominant nation of the world.

Superpatriotism swept the nation in the wake of the Manchurian campaign and Japan's defiance of the League of Nations. There was more kick to defying America than the local police, mill owners, or landlord. An enlightening incident was the deferring of the mill workers' strike in Osaka upon declaration of popular air-defense manœuvers. Also a war boom got under way. With factories turning out army and navy supplies twenty-four hours a day, and the great Mitsui and Mitsubishi foreign trading companies capturing the world's cotton goods market and making hundreds of new quantity products to shoot into new foreign markets, large-scale unemployment vanished. Radicalism hasn't much chance in a country almost doubling its foreign trade in a year. The Takahashis were wise enough not to increase taxes, but instead to issue bonds, allowed to lie in the Bank of Japan, or taken up under pressure by the wealthy houses. Meanwhile Japan was blessed with good rice crops and although the currency was depreciated some sixty per cent, the cost of food did not materially rise.

In August, 1934, the Japanese ministry of commerce and industry announced that the great world depression had ended in Japan. Certainly from the standpoint of the capitalists Japan went into her most promising boom. Unemployment was not serious and workers' conditions improved. The farmer's lot continued to grow worse until war brought a rise in foodstuffs. Then the peasants had paper money, too. There was little to buy with it, but they felt richer than ever before. Paradoxically enough, with her population growing at the rate of a million a year, Japan proper, dangerously short on her rice staple during the nineteen-twenties, now produces a surplus, and the government, following the old Tokugawa example, has filled its granaries to keep up the price for the peasants. The rice surplusage was caused by the turn of the Japanese eating public from this ancient staple of diet to millet, rye, wheat, meat, butter,

cheese, and eggs imported from abroad in exchange for manufactured products. Also, potatoes and fruits and milk are now being
widely produced at home. A further factor is the necessity of absorbing the product of Japanese large-scale capitalistic farming enterprises in Korea and Manchuria. As embargo and war preparations
put the Japanese back on their old diet, trade conquests in Siam and
military conquests in China, Burma, and Java brought a great surplusage of rice. Japan could now supply Hitler his full needs of food
(if Germans would eat rice—and they would) as well as of rubber
and oil. The same goes for fence-straddling France.

The condition of the silk raisers is the second largest element
of the agricultural situation. It is yet more serious. America, Japan's
one silk outlet, has been turning more and more to rayon, and so
has even the Japanese public. Then the Roosevelt-Hull embargo of
1939 spelled the death sentence of silk. But before that Japan's
agricultural experts had definitely foreseen the end of the glorious
ancient silk industry of Japan, and have been promoting rayon in
its place so effectively that Japan in 1933 became the world's second
greatest rayon-exporting and third greatest rayon-producing nation.
This was fine for the industrialists and for the militarists, who, with
an eye towards possibilities in the Pacific, wanted Japan economically independent of the United States; but bleak for the farmers,
for cotton from which rayon is made is not a crop for Japan. The
ministry of agriculture advised the farmers to cut down mulberry
trees which had taken years to grow.

The government adopted a new scheme of industrializing agricultural villages, setting aside a million yen as a start to carry the
hydro-electric power into the peasants' homes and equip them with
machinery for turning out parts for Japan's watch and clock, boot
and shoe, and new airplane and motor manufacturing industries.
When Japan showed herself as an air power second only to Germany, the rest of the world asked in amazement: "Where did they
make 'em?" Millions of parts were tooled in these peasant home
factories—faithful copies of the imported parts from starved American aviation factories which ranked below iron and oil as the third
item of U. S. sales between 1934 and 1938. The parts were partially
assembled in small plants and finally given wings in a few plane

factories hidden in valleys where no foreigner went, and labeled "fabric mills."

In many cases peasants were helped by the earnings of their daughters in the cotton and new rayon mills. Where they became desperate and refused to pay rent, they were backed by the military against their helpless landlords. They came to look upon the army officers who sprang from their villages as their saviors, and naturally followed them into imperialistic wars. The Mitsuis donated thirty million yen for peasant relief and government budgets provided a million more for relief and five hundred million up to March, 1935, for public works in rural districts—still not a tithe of enough to satisfy the demand.

By 1940, War Lord Araki (Sadao) had left his peasants worse off than he found them, but he dreamed of a coming crisis so great that he could requisition all wealth and all production in the name of the Emperor; a time when Japanese would no longer talk in terms of money, whether in regard to external debt or internal bonds, but would simply work or fight where they were told in return for sustenance and a share in imperial glory. Some remarks of his should have caused uncomfortable thoughts to Americans in regard to our own country: "The illness is not yet diagnosed. We don't know yet where to put the plaster. It is no use to paste a plaster on the head when one has the stomach ache. When the right place is found, the plaster must be applied immediately, but I can't understand why people fiddle around so much. Now take all this talk of surplus rice causing trouble. People complain about that in one breath, and then in the next wonder what to do about undernourished school children. With surplus rice, there should be no undernourished school children, yet what are the officials doing about it? Such matters should not be left to charity. If it is money that is wanted, I will find it somehow!" How long Japan's new urban middle class, tied to the great houses of wealth, can stand between the reactionism of the superpatriots and the peasantry from which the military have sprung, is a question.

The patriot Tachibana, serving a life sentence for assassination of Premier Inukai, says in his book, *Principles of Patriotic Reconstruction of Japan,* that there must be a return to oriental civilization, that farmers and army must be made the basis of the nation, and cities with their banks and industries no longer allowed to drain its wealth.

Although the program of the fascists and the military reactionaries is so similar to that of communism, its foundation in popular sympathies is historically established and beyond comparison greater. If Japan's rumbling pot boils over it will carry a Matsuoka and not a Katayama to power.[1] Japan will launch upon intense nationalistic communalism, not Marxian idealism. The similarity, for instance, in the programs of General Araki and the Marxists accounts, however, for the relentlessness of the patriots against the communists. The fight bears all the bitterness of the usual factional fight among fanatics. Militarism in Japan doesn't mean an army acting as policeman for rich manufacturers and financiers, as has usually been the case in the west. As a matter of fact, the only really dangerous radicals in Japan, or that can exist there short of her defeat in a foreign war, are the military and patriots.

A glance at some of the communistic fish taken in the police net will give us the human flavor of this struggle. Japan's most successful young authors and most modern young women have been notable victims. The radical hereditary noble, Count Hijikata (Hisatake), patron of the little theater and proletarian theater movements in Japan, was deprived of his peerage by the ministry of Imperial Household's bureau of heraldry—an unprecedented action. Authorities find themselves glad that all heirs of created nobles in Japan, under the constitution of 1889, must reduce one degree in rank with each generation until they are commoners again. This, too, they owe to Bismarck. The authoress Miss Hayashi and a group of women artists and writers about her were seized for distributing the *Red Flag* magazine. A famous scenario writer was jailed and "moving-picture clubs" in many of the higher schools were disbanded. Nine judges of higher courts were sentenced for "dangerous thoughts." Many leading university professors had to languish in jail. Two girl typists of the army general staff were seized while this book was under preparation; also six clerks out of the very stronghold of capitalism, the Mitsubishi Bank of Tokyo. Their "cell" was accused of

[1] As written in 1934. Matsuoka became Foreign Minister in 1939.

diverting large amounts of money to the communist treasury. An entire picnic party of intellectuals was taken up on the beach at Kamakura by dangerous-thoughts-police skulking in the bushes, and the picnic sandwiches were the last nonprison food they had for a long time. Prison fare for communists doesn't seem to be too good— journalists have noted that many of them have been scarcely able to walk into court for their trials after the waits of from several weeks to two years.

The great women's societies, the Japanese W.C.T.U. and the Japanese Federation of Women's Clubs, were organized under the influence of the Christian Kagawa, and have therefore been out of the orbit of the Marxian communists; nevertheless when they conducted mass demonstrations and published pamphlets against the war spirit and sent the longest petition in the history of the world, containing over a million names, in the shape of a sixty-pound Japanese scroll to Geneva, they were severely warned by the police, and their outstanding leader, Miss Kawai, was told that she stood in the shadow of prison. Japan's psychological and material war boom has effectually dampened the ardor of the women's clubs, although individually many of the members carry on with true Japanese recklessness of punishment.

Contemporary literature for a time "went radical" and the more bolshevik a young novelist's heroes the better his sales. The reaction since 1931 has brought back to favor the older writers who tried to entertain rather than preach. A new school dramatizes Japan's divine mission and writes of wars with Russia and the United States of America, or conquest in China. One radical writer worth mentioning, Fusao Hayashi, in jail like the rest, turned out there his novel, *Youth,* using the scene of the last Tokugawa days to undercut present exponents of "Japan against the world." Matsuoka countered with a fervid nationalistic movie called *Youth.*

The police have had considerable difficulty with youngsters of the nobility and children of officials. They felt forced to arrest the son of Viscount Mori on the very day his father became chairman of the Tokyo municipal council. Five members of peer families were under detention at one time. The daughter of Professor Mitsu Inoue, former mayor of Kyoto, provided a sensation. She and the daughter of Dr. Kawakami, an intellectual of Marxist leanings, had fled their homes when they knew they were being sought by the police. In spite of the registration system of the Japanese police they contrived to evade these all-knowing ones for a year, during which time they had gone through every sort of experience from seeking refuge in houses of joy to working their way up to the managership of a service station for an automobile company. The police were later able to announce that "owing to mother love and ten weeks in prison"— indicating that the young woman was with child—Miss Inoue had seen the error of her ways and abandoned communism. The other girl was sentenced for two years, but given a stay of three years in which to reform.

One of the most unusual seizures was that of a priest in one of the great Buddhist temples, where more than one hundred communists were taken in a raid. Another round-up of 736 people included a young Englishman who was translating and giving one hundred yen a month to the cause.

On May Day, 1934, the proletarians were permitted to march— after being relieved of everything that looked like a weapon, including canes, and provided that they wore distinctive costumes and moved in ranks several paces apart with police between! About ten thousand paraded, including two hundred of the miniature conductorettes singing out their station in interminably long phrases of formal courtesy such as, "If the honorable passenger will deign to take notice, would he kindly permit this unworthy one to intimate that he is approaching the honorable suburb of Wakahatsu." These have been a notable feature of the last few years in Japan. No girl over four feet three inches tall is employed. They receive about two yen a day. As gas shortage increased in Japan, even the "bus dolls" were dispensed with.

Paralleling the leftists were three thousand reactionaries sent out by the patriotic brotherhoods. The paraders were allowed to listen to harangues in Shiba Park, but as soon as a soap-box orator spoke a forbidden phrase he was forthwith removed from the stand and arrested. Out of forty-five speakers, twenty-four contrived to get through their short addresses; many of the others got out only one word. Many of the leftists were quickly picked up by the police when the parade was over. In Osaka some twelve thousand paraded on May Day, many of them girl mill hands. In this industrial center, fifteen hundred and thirty radicals holding a demonstration in opposition to the annual ceremony of the foundation of the nation by Jimmu Tenno were arrested. Police announced that they found red groups from the prefectual office, from the staffs of several banks and hospitals and from the community of lawyers.

The Japanese police became very suspicious of foreigners, and searched tourists' trunks carefully for books that might have the slightest taint of radicalism. A book bound in a red cover was apt to delay the visitor for hours. He was well advised to leave his reading matter on the ship. Yet, at the same time, almost anything in the way of radical literature could be purchased at the thousands of bookshops clustered like beehives in all the cities of Japan. Again, at the same time, the august head of the law department of Tokyo Imperial University could be indicted for a book on legal dissertations!

Among foreigners deported were Lord Marley, left-wing leader of the British Labor party in the House of Lords, and, though a military officer, a noted antiwar advocate; Langston Hughes, the American Negro author; a deputy mayor of Brussels, and several American students and intelligentsia. Great perturbation possessed the Japanese police when they heard Theodore Dreiser was en route to Japan, but he did not land, to their great relief. Twenty-two Chinese students in Japan, including one girl, were deported for having contact with the Japanese Communist party.

The ministry of education in 1932 established an "Institute for Study of National Spirit and Culture" which was to discover the formula for attracting active brains to support of nationalism rather than radicalism or violent reactionism. It banned what it called social studies from high schools and lower colleges, but instead of trying to ban Marx from the universities, installed specially trained teachers to conduct courses in radical economics which aimed to convince the unlearned that Marx was not worth studying in the beginning. It examined all college teachers, students, and grade teachers biennially. Also students were organized in groups with mentors over them, and the members of groups were set as informers upon one another—an application of the old Tokugawa method of keeping track of the populace. However, in modern days mentors and informers have to be well paid and one of the increased budget items with which old Takahashi had to struggle was for millions of yen for "thought control" in schools. "Thought control" in Japan is strictly constitutional. It is to be remembered that the charter oath of Meiji says: "High and low shall be of one mind and social order shall thereby be perfectly maintained."

A business man remarked that the police of Japan seemed to think their duties more to incriminate, than to protect, the citizenry—a fault common where opinion is suppressed. One understands the cleverness of young Hawaiian-born Japanese who hide their American passports and travel in the Japanese Empire as native Japanese —then in north China as Cantonese,[2] and south China as northern Chinese—speaking English exclusively the while!

Leaders in Japan have begun to realize that near-persecution of radicalism was simply making the youth of the nation sullen. They are now conducting positive patriotic propaganda, which includes giving amusements and support to students of dominant personality. The "dangerous-thought" authorities have become interested in special measures to protect Japanese fishermen in Russian waters from contamination. In view of the constant clash between Japanese and Russian fishermen over spoils of the sea, one wouldn't suppose that the Japanese fishermen were in any great danger.

In spite of this vigilance a desperate attempt was made to revive communist activities. The San Francisco general strike of July, 1934, was said to have been renewed inspiration, and Japanese authorities were disturbed when Japan's seamen's union ordered its members aboard Japanese steamers in American waters to do nothing to harm the strikers' cause. The revival of the movement was accidentally discovered by police who were examining a burglar suspect. He swallowed a ball of paper, but it was recovered and gave the key for seizure of 825 persons within a few days. In all, two thousand persons were arrested, including operators of grapevine radio sta-

---

[2] The Cantonese resemble Japanese more nearly than north Chinese, and it is impossible to distinguish between foreign-reared Japanese (who do not have "bandy-legs" from sitting on their feet) and westernized Cantonese.

tions and many laborers on public works projects, particularly Koreans. The leaders of this reformed communism were given sentences of seven to fifteen years, but the tendency is in general to lighten the punishment, on the ground that any one who could so far lose the true spirit of Japan as to become an adherent of international communism is suffering from madness rather than criminality, and as long as such madness is no longer sufficiently prevalent to be a menace it can be dealt with leniently. Exactly the same attitude was held toward Christian converts in the early days of the sixteenth-century persecution.

The emergency peace-preservation law passed by imperial ordinance has given Japan's anticommunist corps so much confidence in their ability to handle the situation that they have become boastful of their leniency. They have been giving much publicity to the recantations of noted professors, scholars, young women and laborers. Some suspicion is cast upon these recantations by the fact that the recanters frequently state they are moved by considerations for their dear ones still out of jail, and by a note left by a converted communist who hanged himself saying, "In spite of my conversion I see no other solution."

Of most value to us who are studying the psychology of Japan is the mentality of the dominant element which demand these recantations. "We speak," says their authority, "of a communist as having been converted when, having recognized the special nature of the Japanese nation, he recognizes the extraordinarily strong power of internal development attested to by the fact that the Japanese nation from ancient times to the present has followed a course of social progress stage by stage, coupled with an extraordinary racial solidarity cultivated through continued maintenance of the independent and unmolested national life of the people." In sum: a radical is converted when he recognizes the special nature of the Japanese nation.

Converted communists are expected to repudiate the internationalism of the Comintern and affirm their belief in a nationalism based on the divine character of the Japanese nation. They must repudiate the materialistic dialectic of Marx, and recognize that the dialectic of Japan must be a synthesis of idealism and materialism. They must recognize that all radicalism in Japan is fundamentally mistaken which conflicts with the divine position of the Sacred Person, and must regard the uninterrupted lineage of the Imperial Royal Family as the symbol of the national development, future as well as past, and the center of national solidarity. Says my informant, "They must remove indiscriminate opposition to war, rather insisting that Japan must take the initiative in war for the benefit of the backward nations of Asia. They must recognize that the campaign now going on against Chinese militarists, as well as the future war to be waged with the Pacific Ocean as its center, will prove to be a contribution to world progress by liberating the working masses of backward Asians from the yoke of European and American capitalists.[3]

"They must repudiate the Soviet principle of racial self-determination, applied in Russia to the various Moslem, Jewish, and Asiatic republics of the Soviet Union. They must even go so far as to insist that in future the peoples of Manchukuo and China proper, as well as those of Chosen and Formosa, combine to form one great nation."

My informant opines that there is little doubt that the arrest of communists is an important factor in their conversion. Police stations and prisons make excellent sanitoria, he says, giving time for sober reflection in an atmosphere in which the dazzling attraction of the new school of thought rapidly pales. Also a man in a cell comes to realize the strength of family ties and the extent to which parents and relatives can suffer by one's own mental aberrations. This causes a new recognition, he says, of the strength of the family system in Japan which has turned the entire nation into one great family with the Emperor at its head.

These considerations, with the natural Japanese reaction to the development of narrow nationalism in western nations, put an end to communism with its jargon of class war, and internationalism became to all intents and purposes dead. For a new economic interpretation of the Japanese principles, people are turned rather to ideas such as the corporate state. Instead of communism Japan became a divine right fascism appointed to conquer and rule the world.

But this was before defeat.

[3] As published, 1934.

Chapter XXIX

Esthetic and Pleasure-loving Japan

THE pleasantest face of Japan is that illuminated in the adoration of beauty.

I am convinced that the Japanese nation is the most esthetic nation in the present world, and, more than that, the most esthetic this world has ever produced. I do not forget ancient Greece. Only the top crust there had commerce with beauty. In no society other than Japanese has the cult of beauty seeped so far down into the mass. Nowhere else does the ditch digger so unabashedly drop his pick to preserve a flower or a shard of porcelain, or the factory operative go out after long hours to view the moon; nowhere else are the very poor so cleanly, so sensitive to order, simplicity, and arrangement; nowhere else do people close to the sustenance line devote so much time and interest—at peril of starvation—to things of beauty. No other common folk are so well equipped from childhood with criteria for judging beauty and art.

I have seen a rickshaw coolie coddle a single blade of grass with its tiny ball of mud around the roots until he could plant it in his foot-wide lawn around his three-mat cottage on the hill at Shimonoseki. I have been nearly trampled to death in the clattering rush of clog-shod mill hands, carrying infants pick-a-back, with heads wobbling in weird positions like the heads of sunflowers, boarding an excursion train to see maples in autumn. A special leniency is allowed to flower stealers and a special name—hana-dorobo—given them, provided they are gentle with the flowers and steal them for love. In Japan a chrysanthemum show or showing of wood-block prints or the amazing art of miniature landscape sculpturing (in plastic mud, with carved figures and really pygmy trees) has as popular an appeal as a baseball game, prize fight, or cinema show.

The Japanese love of beauty is, like everything else Japanese, a compound of ancient Chinese culture with the native pride motif. The most delicate sensibility to beauty this world has known developed in esthetic China. Its spirit and criteria passed over to Japan, and spread through the mass of the people as they never had in China. In islands so beautiful that (by popular belief) the progeny of the Sun Goddess left Heaven to dwell therein, the love of beauty became an essential part of patriotism. To dote upon mountain and mist and sea, tree and frond and blossom, to identify the moods of the Japanese soul with their phenomena and not to mar them with filth or incompatible constructions were synonymous with worship of the kami—the spirits of hill and tree and streams and of ancestors who watch over the incomparable islands. Japan lived out the beautiful old Chinese philosophy which refused to consider the tree primarily in the light of lumber or the stream in the light of power, or both as made for man any more than made for themselves or man for them. All are equal units in a universe that loves a frog as much as a saint.

And so the Japanese village was built to nestle into the mountains and mist as naturally as a group of mushrooms, and all the Japanese scene remained harmonious until cacophony came from the mechanized west—creating the landscapes of belching smokestacks and crazy shop fronts which Baron Shibuzawa approved. After extremism and experimentation the Japanese sense of beauty will conquer these too. Japan is now developing a hydro-electric-powered industry whose mighty sinews will hide under the trees and mountains and whose workers will have hours off to watch the lotus open, the cherry fall, and the maple leaf turn. Even her new stone and concrete cities will achieve what now seems the impossible and become, in a new way, beautiful and fitting.

II

Art to Japanese is not confined to the fine arts, but manifests itself in dress and in all the appurtenances of daily life. The national dress for both men and women transforms their often squat figures into a delight to the eye, and the fabrics worn are unsurpassed in the whole world for conservative beauty of texture and design. Every Japanese "modern" who attends office in uniform or western business suit gets into kimono in the evening for meditation or social pleasure, and enjoys this simplest yet profoundest civilizing influence, beautiful clothes. Japanese responsiveness to dress and color is utilized even in prison uniforms. In Dr. Arima's modern prisons, convicts begin in brick red and graduate into blue.

The tiny Japanese farmhouse among the omnipresent hills seems a living thing, its brown thatched roof contrasting with the ecstatic green of feminine bamboo fronds, or the dour blue-green of masculine-appearing pines. Rows of shops on a village street are a kaleidoscope of design and arrangement.

Temples and shrines are especially designed for their surroundings. The shrine of the Sun Goddess at Ise is the epitome of simplicity; its wooden buildings with their slanting crossed beams embody the spirits of the pines and cryptomerias which have gone into them. The buildings of Danzan Jinsha, another Shinto shrine near Sakurai, exhibit their thick, rich, red-brown thatches against the green of the tall cryptomeria trees in a vision of unearthly loveliness. Buddhist temples, with their bell towers and pagodas, demonstrate how Chinese architecture, originally of the plains, can be fitted to hills and forests. The pagoda of Yakushiji at Nara is a ringleted finger against the sky at dusk, shadowed in the mirror of the pools about its base.

Japan's most noteworthy esthetic contrast with the west, however, is the Japanese interior. The long hall of a recently built temple stretches to an almost unbelievable length, entirely undecorated, save for the beautiful black-edged mats and the fusuma, or sliding doors, along the side, on which Matsubayashi Keigetsu has painted gnarled old pine trees. Beauty of this kind is not confined to the temples and the homes of the rich. Even the cheapest inn welcomes the guest into a haven of clean, simple beauty. Immaculate tatami (thick matting, replaced yearly) covers the floor. The only furniture is a low table, for the mattress is kept in a cupboard and only brought out at night, when it is laid on the floor for use. In the alcove is a single painting and a vase of flowers.

Factory dormitories (in which eighty per cent of women workers live) may provide only one mat (six by three feet) per girl, but every great room contains the little altar niche, hung with pictures of the Emperor and Empress, or a kakemono (painted or written scroll—literally, "hanging thing") with daily replaced flowers. The ofuro bath provides a "pour and stew" a day for every occupant.

The neatness of the Japanese house is a combination of the natural cleanliness of the South Sea Island home raised on sticks with neatness developed in North China and Korea by the custom of sitting and sleeping on brick floors heated by flues in winter. Since Japan found Chinese culture this manner of life has been supplanted for the most part in China by use of heavy furniture on exceedingly dirty floors. The Japanese no more thinks of stepping on his floor mats with his shoes than you would on your bed. Only one or two objects of art are exhibited simultaneously, that they may have the full concentration of the family and guests. When their fine points have been thoroughly enjoyed, they are put back into the storehouse, and one or two other objects brought out.

Always something living is kept in the room—a conventional flower arrangement or a branch of willow or frond of bamboo or a potted plant. Historic pieces of polished but untrimmed wood often worth more than the entire house are placed to support the sacred niche in each room, known as the Emperor's Seat, which, barring the dreamed-of visit of the Sacred Personage himself, can be occupied only by an object of beauty. The outside of the house is not painted, it being desired that the wood shall fade into subjection to its surroundings. The veranda, floor, and stairs are rubbed with nothing more than a rag until they have a patina like black glass. The kitchen with its charcoal stoves is a delight, and every upper-class house has its tiny private ofuro—a high wooden tub just big enough to squat in with charcoal fire pan under its earth-protected bottom. Public ofuros, of course, increase to the size of small shallow swimming tanks.

Every house higher than the very poorest slum dwelling has its little private patio garden of miniature trees and cascades though it be not more than two feet square. Among scholars, and often merchants as well, the little garden is faced by a meditation room decorated only with the fresh matting floor of golden straw and the unpolished grained wood, the wall supports, and the translucent paper panels of the shoji. This is the withdrawal room of the master of the house, sacred to him alone. Likewise no servant or child would think of disturbing the mistress within her private inner sanctum. A guest to dinner may be invited to the meditation room to compose himself before the host receives him.

III

Wherever the Japanese expand they plant cherry trees, as in Shanhaikwan and Tsingtao. In the latter place, besides the park, which is full of them, a double row leads up to the beautiful Shinto shrine which commands a striking view of the harbor. Prison grounds, instead of being the bare tramped courts of our prisons, are planted with cherry trees tended by the convicts themselves, and this national flower is expected to exert a spiritual influence toward docility and reform. The grounds of barracks, arsenals, and factories are likewise planted with this flower—the emblem of the soldier.

To the Japanese each season has its own personality to be met in an individual manner. A contemporary writer delightfully describes a man's manner of meeting summer:

"On the tokonoma (Emperor's seat) he hangs a kakemono (hanging scroll) of cool waves breaking over rocks, and above the balcony of the house, a gifu lantern of soft blue light. Wind bells made of bits of glass, and bought for a song, catch the whispers of the evening breeze and tinkle like tiny rivulets. The garden, though it may measure but six feet square, and the entrance to the home are carefully watered as if by a summer shower, refreshing the sultry air. A tiny cage of insects who dutifully chirp and sing, add their song to the illusion, while goldfish in a porcelain bowl give a touch of color and of movement. The paper shoji are replaced by screens of split bamboo permitting the free play of air, while the silk cushions are changed to those of linen, dyed in light summer colors. A cheap cotton kimono, of blue and white summer design, clothes his outer being and completes the harmony of his inner contentment."

In gentle satire this writer calls attention to the effect that advertising and mass salesmanship is having on the methods of practice of the national cult of nature worship:

"Lafcadio Hearn marveled at the sight of the Japanese townsman enjoying a holiday in the mountains. On his feet were straw sandals bought for a few sen, to be discarded when worn through. For rain coat, a single piece of matting sufficed, while for sun helmet and umbrella he used a large straw hat. A cheap cotton kimono bought for a yen, tucked up at the belt and readily washed, was all the outer clothing he required, while a square piece of cloth, carrying a few rice balls and pickled plums wrapped in the husk of a bamboo sprout and tied around his waist, constituted all the baggage he required:

"That was the way of the old Japanese. How his grandchildren can now start off on a trip to the Japanese Alps or to the Hakone region bent double under enormous rucksacks loaded heavier than a coolie's burden, how they must carry an imported ash stick instead of a stout pilgrim's staff of Japanese wood, how they must imprison their feet and incidentally their souls in thick leather boots armorplated with climbing nails, how they must carry all manner of metal contraptions for cooking and a first-aid kit for snake bites and germs which happen only in medical journals, is one of the mysteries of modern Japan. The answer may be found perhaps in that aspect of modern capitalism where vendibility and not necessity of an article is the basis of creating sales, a process by which profits may be made —and a soul of a people destroyed."

Japan's big business is taking full advantage of the Japanese love of beauty, but that may prove a good thing, overcoming the hideousness of the first mass products, stores, and factories badly copied from the west. To-day every great department store in the realm has one floor constantly devoted to art exhibitions, musical recitals, contests in pan sai—the making of miniature landscapes—etc. Like everything else in Japan, art is going nationalistic. In music Japan is turning back from Beethoven and Ravel and Tin Pan Alley to native melodies orchestrated for ancient instruments. The twenty-seven government broadcasting stations (owners of receiving sets must have licenses and pay rent) broadcast twice as many hours of Japanese as of western music last year, and the Tokyo Symphony Orchestra headed by Prince Konoye's brother is having a desperate struggle, although visiting mæstros like Kreisler, Elman, Zimbalist and Henry Hadley do well.

But in a Japan rapidly becoming the world's greatest factory and mart, still not one passerby on the Tokaido fails to look up for a glimpse of snow-clad Mt. Fuji, not one person goes out at night but greets the moon.

IV

Japanese fine arts, long and deeply appreciated in their own country—barring the few years of inordinate desire for the things of the west—are gradually receiving from the world the appreciation they deserve. Besides the Buddhist sculptures and paintings, there are the long makimono, which present moving scenes as we unroll them of battles and burning palaces (the scroll of the famous saga Heiji mongatari, now in Boston, for example), the lives of exiled priests, the peregrinations of a flying storehouse and the journeys of a nun (the Shigisan Engi). Even the famous "Scroll of Diseases" is a thing of beauty. And it is to the Japanese esthetic sense that we owe the preservation of most of the best works of Chinese art extant to-day. Not only the collections in Japan are to be included in this category. Much of the best Chinese stuff in the west came there by way of Japan.

From cartoons comparable to our comic strips Japanese artists developed the popular art of the Tokugawa period, known as the Ukyioe school. Its wood-block prints by Hiroshige, Toyokuni, Eishi, and a score of others are collected all the world over to-day. They vary from the most ribald subjects to patriotic and classical themes, caricatures of the foibles of lords, warriors, merchants, and professors; and from peasants gathering their crops to Harunobu's ethereal maidens of exquisite oriental hands and feet and bamboo-slender bodies clad in kimono of delicate yellow, lavender and mauve, or very earthly ladies of the demi-monde carrying their red lanterns. Misty landscapes, snow scenes, rain portrayed (first in art) by slanting lines, are part of this popular art that began with cartooning.

In Japan the composing of the short epigrammatic poems which convey subtly anything from criticisms, political schemes, and business decisions to nuances of emotion is a matter of hourly occurrence.

"Whatever your misfortune, write verses for moral exercise," Lafcadio Hearn quotes an old Japanese precept. These hokku are the outlet of a man or woman overjoyed, bereaved, or ruined. When the Lion Premier Hamaguchi was shot by an assassin in 1929 his bitter political rival Suzuki condoled him with a hokku, and Hamaguchi from the operating table replied with one. The poems are built of nature descriptions and allusions to legends, history, classic Chinese literature, and the whole body of poetry which has gone before. Japanese find it very necessary to know all these things. It is still the custom to write a death poem, summarizing one's life for posterity.

Yearly a nation-wide poetry contest is held by a board especially appointed by the government, and the hundreds of thousands of entries increase each year as the population increases. The Emperor himself announces the subject of the contest. He always writes a poem for it and is always, of course, awarded the Emperor's honor; next the offerings of the court nobility, and thirdly the tens of thousands from the commoners and created nobility are judged by the committee of scholars appointed by the ministry of education. Anonymously, winners are chosen and ranked. Fame (there is no other award) attaches to the winners of first, second, third, or fourth places in the "people's" contest. Great was the amazement—and generous the acclaim of the nation—when a few years back a prize was won in this most difficult alien form by a young American woman, wife of the United States military attaché. Not more than a half-dozen aliens in all have mastered this Japanese poetic form. The writer learned of a poetry contest being held in America through the attention being given it in Japanese papers. Few American papers mentioned it.

The sages of Japan have done much of their teaching through the short epigrammatic poems, and one delightful figure, Basho, of early Tokugawa times, who gave up a lucrative position to become a peripatetic teacher of humanitarianism and applied economics, is known as Japan's greatest master of the form.

On one of his travels he passed through a rural district on a moonlight night and came upon a party of men drinking sake in

the open and enjoying the moonlight. They fell to composing haiku
—very short poems—and asked the wandering priest to join them,
not knowing who he was. He took the lowest seat. The theme was
the full moon. When Basho's turn came he started out, " 'Twas the
new moon,"—Here he was interrupted by a drunken voice: "Oh!
the stupid priest! The subject was the *full* moon." Basho continued,

> " *'Twas the new moon;*
> *Since then I waited—*
> *And lo! to night!"*

amazing them all. This verse illustrates the brevity and suggestive-
ness of Japanese poetry; and the whole story shows the genuine
esthetic interest of ordinary Japanese. What drinking party, even of
the upper classes here, would enter into a poetry contest or recognize
a masterpiece recited to them for the first time?

The poem of Motoori, critic and historian who was forerunner
of Japan's emergence into world affairs:

> *"Isles of blest Japan!*
> *Should your Yamato spirit*
> *Strangers seek to scan,*
> *Say, scenting morn's sunlit air:*
> *'—Blows the cherry wild and fair!'"* [1]

may be taken as the key to both doors of Japan's inner heart. The
cherry blossoms, falling in their prime, symbolize the voluntary
death of the warrior for his country, but they also stand for that
beauty which never yet fell upon those "who have eyes and see
not." And speaking of cherry trees, it is appropriate to add in this
1942 edition the saying of Baron Shibusawa, when he paid for the
trees planted around The Basin at Washington, D. C.: "America
and Japan will remain friends so long as these trees blossom pink."
In 1941 a Japanese correspondent wrote home that they were more
and more blossoming white—due to some strain losing its effect
with age!

Laurence Binyon, in his *Painting in the Far East,* tells the story

[1] Translated by Chamberlain.

of a Japanese in Paris. In the night, snow had fallen and early in the morning this son of Nippon went to the Bois de Boulogne to see the trees in their feathery mantles of white. He was surprised to find himself entirely alone, until in the distance he descried two figures. When they came nearer, he saw that they, too, were Japanese.

From the Emperor down to the lowest laborer, all the sons and daughters of the island empire watch for the blossoming of the first plum, all go picnicking under the cherry trees in spring, the maples in fall. It is not for nothing that nature has placed her loveliest effects of misty mountains, crystal streams and silvery cascades in Nippon; there dwell her most ardent and sincere admirers.

Nor is it for nothing that Japanese know to-day their world paramountcy in esthetic appreciation, in sensitiveness to beauty, in drawing as much sustenance from white lilies as from a loaf of bread. To them it is another proof that they are heaven-descended, that theirs is the empire of the gods, that they have a divine mission in the world.

v

Closely interwoven with their love of beauty is the love of pleasure in the Japanese, which survives and is a reaction from their stern devotion to duty, idealization of Spartan simplicity, and puritanical streaks. This reaction is encouraged and developed by the hedonistic importation from classical China, which has always battled with Japanese puritanism as has French abandon battled with Anglo-Saxon puritanism in many an American soul. Lives shamelessly devoted to pleasure are more generously tolerated in Japan than here, and in spite of the antiprostitution movements of Kagawa and the women's clubs it is still generally considered permissible to devote a whole class of society to pander to the sex-pleasure-seeking instinct. Nowhere else has prostitution reached such a point of refinement or been so socially accepted.

The puritan superpatriots believe that there are places and times and ways to indulge the lusts—they insist, however, that this be done in good old Japanese ways, and in no manner that smacks of western degeneracy.

In striking contrast to the houses of prostitution of the west, the Yoshiwara, or licensed prostitute quarter of Yedo in the Tokugawa period, appealed to the esthetic sense. The whole enclosure was planned after the imperial court itself, and the best of the houses vied in beauty of construction and decoration with the palaces and mansions of the nobility. We can see by a number of paintings and prints that here was no tawdry elegance, but an architecture, exterior and interior, appealing to good taste. Moreover, not only were the inmates exquisitely dressed, but they were trained in all the accomplishments of a great lady: they could play the koto (the Chinese harp, more classical and musical than the still common samisen or guitar), sing classical songs, write impromptu poems in calligraphy of the finest, and quote classical authors both Chinese and Japanese. The question of morality aside, the Yoshiwara was planned to give the esthetic sense satisfaction in various forms of beauty, a tradition that continues to-day even when the flapper "beppin-san" (extra guest) has supplanted the courtesan geisha. Japanese feeling may be as inconsistent, but as accountable, as that of the old-fashioned deacon of a church in Iowa who once verbally chastised me for smoking in the churchyard, but took the sting off by offering me a "chaw" from his quid of tobacco. Patriots in Japan are scandalized by such things as the decorating of Yoshiwara house fronts with Greek nymphs romping under verdant groves. These fronts should be occupied by sedate, kimonoed, soft-spoken girls winning their way to the heart by no more than a lifted eyebrow and the gesture of a perfect little finger.

VI

The answer to the paradox of stoical and hedonistic Japan is that the Japanese regard duty and pleasure as irreconcilable—this in spite of the still common custom of having official or business gatherings in eating houses, and presided over by courtesans. The Japanese takes his pleasure in distinct, defined doses and appears to work very hard at it. He will smile about his work but be deadly earnest at golf or tennis. He will go about his business with an air of leisure and conscientious calm, but in his pleasure he always seems to be overhung with the impelling sense that it is up to him to get himself thoroughly amused. A group of university boys had gathered in a dormitory room and discussed to the end their lessons. "——Now, let us talk about sex!" remarked one, blushing but brave.

Japanese sports since Fukuzawa's day have developed enormously. Professional baseball in Japan is as great an institution as it is in the United States, and amateur baseball greater, and the American university teams that go to Japan to play each year suffer a large proportion of defeats. The Young Men's Buddhist Association in Tokyo is one of the greatest centers for organized sports in the world. Rugby football is played by the colleges and tennis and golf have swept the land. Sports in Japan have had somewhat the same effect as in England: building up the code of the gentleman, giving a conception of sportsmanship to the classes that did not benefit by the samurai code. Yet an upholder of the theory of the feminine-mindedness of Japan might say that Japanese take sports in a determined feminine manner in contradistinction to the British way of taking them.

The sportsmanship as well as the deadly earnestness of the Japanese participants in recent world Olympics has been commented upon by all observers. The Japanese women's teams of runners, jumpers, and swimmers have been remarkable for their morale, and in the 1932 Olympic Games at Los Angeles the Japanese carried off the main honors in aquatic events, and a remarkable little nobleman and his beautiful horse carried off first prize in horsemanship. Before the world went to war, the 1940 Olympics were to be held in Tokyo.

This code of the gentleman, like Japanese stock courtesy, is not allowed to curb ruthlessness if some vital interest is at stake, any more than in England. A flagrant example of this type of sportsmanship upset Pacific Asia when, in 1934, Japanese bluffed the Filipino delegates of the Far Eastern Amateur Athletic Association into agreeing to scrap the far eastern Olympic Games held by the Philippines and China since 1912 and joined by Japan in 1917, because China was unwilling to admit participants from her severed province of Manchuria as the representatives of a separate country. Remarked a Filipino editor: "This is a piece of unmatchable stupidity on the part of the representatives, not of the Philippines but of the Amateur Athletic Federation. Their addle-headed and cowardly action has not found a single defender outside of those concerned."

Thus does Imperial Japan even use sports for her world conquest.

Through all this variegated Japan, as wherever love of beauty and pleasure grow tired, there runs a strain of dilettante sophistication. You see it in Japanese art, and you read it in their poetry and essays. Japan's greatest novel *The Tale of Genji* is as full of sophistication as Cabell or Chesterton. Japan's master of sophistication was a little court lady who, nearly a thousand years ago, wrote comments on her world and hid them beneath her pillow, which, known as the *Pillow Sketches,* remain as modern as anything the twentieth century can boast. "A hateful thing," she says, "is a commonplace person who talks a great deal with the air of being an authority on everything. A thing which makes the heart beat faster is a handsome man who stops his carriage to say he is coming to see you. An object of disdain is a man with too good a reputation."

There are indeed many sides to this nation called Japan.

Chapter XXX
Nippon's Economic Challenge

WHILE the production and trade of the industrial west were drying up as if chopped off at the roots, Japan's production expanded to embrace all articles of modern industry and Japan's trade invaded every market of the world.

While the imperial white nations were making concessions, as in British India and the Dutch East Indies, or squabbling about tiny areas like the Saar or Austria or about barren regions of Africa, Japan increased the size of her empire three times without so much as a formal war, annexed three archipelagoes of Pacific islands entrusted to her by the League of Nations and went to war for trusteeship of all China. Sheer economic necessity and political logic tend to bring the rest of Pacific Asia, particularly the Philippines, under her spreading wings.

While larger proportions of western citizenries were fed with government bread, as in declining Rome, Japan enjoyed a boom and operated her factories overtime.

Youths from the "backward races" who once came to America, England, Germany and France for higher education and technical schooling now went to Japan. In spite of her aggression upon China, the number of Chinese students in Japan increased to more than one thousand while it fell to nearly nothing in the United States and Europe. Siam replaced her European financial adviser with one of Takahashi's pupils. India, Afghanistan, Abyssinia, and Mongolia made industrial tie-ups with Japan and sent students there. The hardy sons of the central Asian desert may have been drawn as much by the reputation of the dainty Japanese women as by serious motives—but to Japan they went!

Any one not suffering racial astigmatism could see who was going up and who going down in the fourth decade of the twentieth century. The west could not compete in its own game. The Pearse report in parliament said: "With fewer than 9,000,000 spindles Japan has more export trade than Lancashire with 50,000,000. . . . Cheap labor alone does not in itself spell the doom of Lancashire. . . . The prosperity of Japan's export trade is due to efficiency and organization and monocratic control."

Major Dunlop of "tyre" fame and of Britain's Chamber of Shipping said Japanese competition was killing British shipping. "If oxygen isn't applied we may have to ask for chloroform." American shipping companies were unable to compete with Japanese—even though they actually received post-office department favors (which Postmaster-general Jim Farley found it unwise to cancel) amounting to twice as much as the open subsidies received by Japanese lines from their government.[1]

Japan was doing the world's business. Because she was selling, Japan could buy. So her ships went loaded both ways: rayon, piece goods, and toys to Australia, wool and meat back; piece goods and machinery to Latin America, hides, saltpeter, and cotton staple back; piece goods, soap and watches to India, raw cotton back; raw silk to the United States and raw cotton back. Then, when Toyama and Araki had determined upon war—scrapiron and oil and airplane parts.

It is now clear that the indomitable people of Japan marching towards their "place in the sun," are jostling the earliest squatters in a manner neither imperial nor Nazi Germany succeeded in doing. It is now evident that the supreme thrust against western capitalism and industry is not the Soviet collective system—now seeking profitable dealings with it—but western capitalism's too-apt pupil in competitive credo: the industrialized Asiatic who outproduces, outsells and outsails it.

Japan's development was seen most significantly for Americans in

[1] Japan's launchings of tonnage in 1933 (the last year of authentic reports) were 40% over the previous year while American tonnage fell 10%. Japan constructed six new fast Diesel freighters for the Yokahama–New York run via Panama. Japan renewed her ship-improvement subsidy for five years—24,000,000 yen to retire old bottoms.

Latin America. There Japanese trade increased 200% in a year. There a Japanese syndicate negotiated with Uruguay for a vast free port on the River Platte to contain manufacturing plants using Japanese labor, and the Japanese foreign office presented many-statued Montevideo with a bust of Admiral Togo. Japanese Imperial Princes visited Chile to establish good will. Japan built an overseas community, her largest, numbering already more than two hundred thousand and increasing at the rate of two thousand a month in spite of the immigration-restriction clause in the new Brazilian constitution, far up the Amazon in Brazil—that coming United States of the southern hemisphere with a population of forty-five million and an area larger than continental United States of America.

In Peru the Nipponese community bought airplanes and erected statues to the Shanghai heroes. El Salvador, baited by a Japanese commission promising to buy coffee, recognized Manchukuo.

From South America Japan imported some of her most important war materials: nickel, molybdenum, cotton, beef, wheat and nitrates. The United States could not cut off this trade without causing South American nations to feel towards her as the United States had felt towards European powers who interfered with her freedom of the seas. And the South Pacific is a big ocean to police!

Peru, Brazil and other Latin American nations put restrictions upon Japanese immigration and trade which threatened local interests—usually none too efficient or even honest. Great Britain countered Japan's advance by flirting with Argentina for the reflotation of her entire national debt.

In the face of challenge from the, to us, heretical totalitarian systems of Russia, and then Germany, we industrialist westerners roused ourselves. But in the face of rivalry from the pupil who got her finishing-school education in our own churches, factories and war colleges, a rivalry proving itself so easily successful over our handicap of a century's head start, we were haunted with the hopeless feeling of a graying matron who watches the flappers making up to her husband.

In this struggle between the western man and his pupil, exemplified in the trade war already ruthlessly under way, the white man found himself hindered not only by an ennui along his muscles and a general let-down of the nerves, but by the conscience which has gradually developed in him during his period of liberalism from Rousseau to Woodrow Wilson. Not that he has followed this conscience spectacularly, but it is there, interfering with his philosophy of survival of the fittest, making him a man divided, fighting against himself, handicapped in struggle with more primitive minds. This conscience was reinforced since 1914 by an emotional disgust with war, and an increasing intellectual conviction that it does not pay.

The man of Nippon was left the world's true believer in the philosophy of the survival of the fittest. He will continue to believe in it, just as other humans have done, until it no longer seems to operate in his favor. Japan, now, became demander of the "open door" into the west's hallway.

Remarks the pithy "flash" writer on the Osaka *Mainichi* English edition, which is the mouthpiece of the Japanese exporting community: "Seventy years ago the powers forced Japan to open her doors. Now they are forcing Japan to open *their* doors." "Freedom of trade," says Dr. Saito (Yoshiye), former head of the commercial bureau of Japan's foreign office, "is a fundamental principle underlying Japan's economic policy and also an established axiom governing her economic diplomacy."

In 1933 Japan's foreign trade increased 40% over the previous year the outward evidence of the most rapid rise of a nation in industrial history. Japan's production index with 1928 as a norm rose in 1934 to 140, while Britain's was 103 and America's 77. In Latin America the gain was something like 200%, in Africa 60%, in Haiti 1000%, in the Philippines 30%. All the tricks of trade were used, of course: depreciated currency, false labels, and imitated trade-marks. Labor costs were approximately one-third of labor costs in America, and one-half of labor-costs in England and Europe, taking into account that most industries in Japan, with all their modern technique, still use three times as many operatives for the equivalent output. The cotton-spinning industry is a notable exception, using fewer workers per machine.

But the real reasons for Japan's competitive success were rationalization of production, modernization of machinery, cheapness of power, absence of false and prodigal capitalizations and huge executive salaries, artistic and lively advertising, government-subsidized sales efforts, government-supervised production and delivery, coöperation instead of throatcutting within each industry, and above all the morale of workers and bosses—their belief that they were winning and *must* win over the western world.

The greatest of the reasons for Japan's trade success—the one which makes possible all the others—is this morale. Mussolini could not match it even though his oratory might persuade his workers to accept lower wages and his bayonets might prohibit strikes. Stalin could not equal it in his Russians, whose spirit is willing but whose minds and bodies must be, for a generation or two yet, slow and clumsy. The Rockefellers could not resort to the paternalism of the Mitsuis and the N.R.A. could not make capital and labor mingle their sweat in a common pride.

It was the Tokugawas who, although setting Japan behind the western world in commerce and invention, put her ahead of the west in the discipline and regimentation which feature to-day's climactic period of the competitive world. The Tokugawas stand out as history's greatest morale builders. The morale they implanted dictated that Japanese should not sell or give any improvement of technique or any services to the competitors from whom, on the other hand, they learned so much. In reverse, Japanese were able to purchase any western services and technique they require, as they recently purchased Du Pont formulæ. By distribution of favors such as free trips to cherry-blossom land given American school teachers, or orders distributed through an American chamber of commerce, they created almost any local attitude they wished among us. Lacking their morale and solidity, individually more greedy and at the same time more sportsmanlike than Japanese, we westerners are put under a great handicap in our rivalry with them.

"The fundamental factor which enabled Japan to make industrial advance is spiritual," writes the piece-goods manufacturer, Yamamoto (Koyota).[2] "It is the Nippon spirit. This spirit is peculiar to Japan." The new Osaka spindles that use one girl to twenty-five machines while Lancashire spindles use one man to six could not

[2] Osaka *Mainichi,* May 31, 1934.

have been invented, installed and operated without the sacrificial loyalty of all concerned known as the Nippon spirit. In Japan no invention is held in cold storage to protect either capital or labor interests—discovery of such a situation would be red meat for the Black Dragons!

The Nippon spirit enabled "rationalizing" textile industry bosses to dismiss at one time 23% of their workers and cut the wages of the remainder 50%, appeasing them with bi-weekly lessons in music, religion, etiquette and ethics. The ancient principle of family solidarity is applied to cut labor costs by making operatives one big family, living and sharing under the same roof. Again, it is used in the "cottage industries," powered from Japan's handy hydroelectric plants, which make motor parts and electric bulbs. Their piecework pay does not reckon as of value the labor of the women and children of the family who help.

The Japanese laborer is not unhappy. His wages in relation to commodity and amusement values have risen much faster than wages in Europe. Japan's veteran American correspondent, Kawakami (T.), said:

"The truth is that there is no higher or lower, no superior or inferior standard of living as between Japan and the west. The question is simply one of difference. Transplant a Japanese mill hand to Lancashire, give him an iron bed with a soft mattress, put him on a ration of bread and butter, beefsteak, coffee and cream, and he will go on strike, demanding Japanese bedding spread on a matted floor, and a ration of fish, rice, and vegetables which to him, are more palatable and wholesome. It is the misfortune of the British or American that his standard calls for higher-priced materials than the Japanese, that is all." [3] "—The difference between cheese and pickled radish," Mr. Tsuda, head of Japan's greatest cotton-milling company calls it, maintaining that "the living conditions of Japanese spinning workers are much better than in England."

League of Nations Labor Commissioner Maurette decided after investigation that Japanese labor was not excessively underpaid. It is much better paid than in central Europe. He found that the best conditions were in export-trade factories.

[3] *Foreign Affairs*, April, 1934.

Japan's spectacular rate of market invasion (continuing throughout 1934) inspired open attempts at protection of their home or subjects' markets by thirty governments. India's government abrogated an old commercial treaty with Japan to put prohibitive duty on Japanese cotton goods. Japanese cotton manufacturers retaliated by boycotting Indian raw cotton. After months of dispute Japan accepted a quota giving her a large but to her still unsatisfactory share of the Indian market. Her latest move before war was to combine with Indian mill owners to produce within India.

Governments as far apart as Egypt and Peru acted to protect budding home industries. The Dutch East Indies timorously followed the British example, then began interminable discussion with the angry Japanese. England clamped down in the British West Indies and the docks of Cristobal were glutted with textiles and shoes. But Japan continued to turn out new products and find new markets for old ones.

The measures taken by western countries threatened to react disastrously upon their heads. It appeared a question how far they could controvert the essential philosophy of the competitive system and still continue to be capitalist nations. Those barring cheap goods out of their own national boundaries thereby set themselves up on an economic pinnacle and found themselves unable to buy from or sell to others. Their action tended to force them into an isolation economy of self-sufficiency reminiscent of that of Tokugawa Japan, and their growing isolation from world trade left Japan the more unique and supreme therein.

The imperial nations which endeavored to bar Japanese goods from their dominions and subject peoples endangered themselves yet more. The president of the Japanese Kanegefuchi Spinning Company, Mr. Tsuda (Singo), published and Japanese consulates distributed a pamphlet which flung down the gauntlet to England in no uncertain words: "One-quarter of the world is in Britain's possession and she intends to sacrifice the happiness of those countries only for her own sake.... To force expensive clothing upon a nation of low purchasing power means an utter disregard of the interest and well-being of the consumer.... If England goes on raising her tariffs, that may usher in a state of things which England would least wish to see. Was not the independence of America the result of interference with the colonies' free trade by the mother country? Should England continue to impose upon her possessions, the solidarity of the British Empire will not be maintained. . . . An industry that cannot exist without a 70% to 80% handicap against its rivals should die anyhow! England will do well to emancipate all her possessions economically and return to her tradition of free flow of trade."

Mr. Tsuda then went on with a hint to Australia: "Does not Australia depend upon her sheep-farming industry for her national subsistence, and doesn't this largely depend upon our patronage? Let it be remembered that Indian cotton and Australian wool are Japan's greatest purchases from the British Empire."

It seems that Great Britain had caught a tiger by the tail. As Japanese predicted, the 214 native principalities of India were not pleased with the embargo on Japanese goods. They are not subject to British-Indian-imposed tariffs save as they have to use British Indian ports of entry, having none of their own (a far-sighted arrangement made by Britain's empire builders). Inspired by Japanese influence, and lent Japanese money for the purpose, the rajah of Kutch, north of Bombay, set out to construct a port of his own. The council of Ceylon refused to enforce the new tariffs against Japanese textiles and beer and challenged the British governor to declare them arbitrarily. The Ceylon Labor party held a mass meeting which protested against "penalizing Ceylon workers for the benefit of Lancashire," and a Senegalese member of Parliament threatened a boycott on British goods in retaliation.

Even more startling things happened in Australia and New Zealand. Australia withdrew the embargo on Japanese toys, writing a death sentence upon the native Australian toy industry because of a hint from the Japanese consul in Melbourne that Japan could buy her wool from Argentina. On the heels of the visit of Australian Trade Commissioner Latham to Japan, during which he presented sacred cocks and hens to the Shrine of Ise, a trade war broke out within the British Empire—Lancashire boycotting Australian wool in retaliation for Australian tariffs on Lancashire piece goods, and Australia boycotting Lancashire piece goods in favor of Japanese yardage!

T. L. Tourrier, Brisbane wool man visiting in Tokyo, told his
Japanese customers: "As the Japanese girl discards her kimono for
western style clothes she is deepening international relations between
Australia and Japan. Because we are part of the British Empire we
must buy certain articles from England, but this condition is not
as important as it used to be. We know that it is more economical
for us to trade with Pacific countries. We know that Japanese goods
conform to a high quality and that they are cheaper—hence we are
anxious to buy from Japan and we want to see tariff barriers removed. Our purchasing capacity per capita from Japan is three
times that of Japan from Australia. Yet last year we bought only
52,000,000 yen worth from Japan, while she bought 250,000,000 yen
worth from us. Japan's consuming power is five times greater."

If a generation ago Australians had shown as much ambition,
vigor, and national spirit as South African pioneers, they might have
built the empire of the southern hemisphere, including the great
rich areas of the Dutch East Indies, but, weakened by impractical
labor domination and the popular desire to live well, Australia fell, a
rich plum, into Japan's economic lap.

The New Zealand minister of customs announced that Japanese
imports would not be specially selected for tariff treatment (at the
same time that New Zealand started building a navy!) and British
East Africa almost took the Japanese side in the trade war between
the mother country and her rival.

Another factor in the Indian tariff against Japanese cotton goods
was that two-thirds of Lancashire's market is outside the British
Empire. In these markets Japan's cotton-goods salesmen now made
a special drive against British products. Tsuda's boast seemed in
process of fulfilment: "No tariff, however prohibitive, will be able
to check the inflow of merchandise which is better in quality and
cheaper in price."

If Tsuda's prediction were to prove true, then Japan would have
commercially conquered the world. All goods sold between nations
would be Japanese goods, all ships plying between nations Japanese
ships, all foreign trade Japanese trade. For men and women will
always buy where they can buy cheapest. Even the United States
army in Hawaii, Guam, and the Philippines, hard-pressed for funds,

bought its sugar and cement from the Mitsuis, who made the prices especially low. Some years ago, on a trans-Pacific crossing the author listened for days to his British captain inveighing against Japanese industrial piracy. The last day out the captain confidentially exhibited a pair of seaman's boots he had bought in Yokohama for seventy-five cents. "They would have cost me $3.50, regulation," he said. "And you know my salary has been cut!"

Patriotism will always, I fear, bow to the pocketbook—save among the Japanese themselves. Can flotillas of war vessels keep thirty-cent shoes away from barefoot people who feel they have a right to be shod, but cannot pay for Manchester's or Boston's leather goods?

England knew only one answer to Japan's trade drive: tariff barriers, which predicated gunboats and air navies.—Just as the United States had only one real answer to Japan's imperial drive in the Pacific. Honolulu customs inspectors refused to admit goods marked "Made in Nippon" on the ground that they were officially unaware of such a country of origin. (Officially, they listed "Japan," no "Nippon.") But that was not the answer. Rather, consciously or otherwise, it was the visits of Secretaries of Navy Swanson and War Dern to Hawaii and the building up of America's naval establishment in the Pacific.[4]

Japan, with naval control of the west Pacific, played a world-scale game against the European industrial powers, pitting their fear of being driven entirely out of the orient against their impulse to bar Japanese trade out of other parts of the world. Japan has a coördinated economic and political life which enables her to play the game more consistently than her opponents.

In China proper Japan turned the tables by procuring, through purchase and pressure, the establishment of new customs tariffs which discriminated in favor of her goods and against those of the United States, Great Britain and Italy. The head of China's legislative department, Dr. Sun Fo, son of the founder of Chinese nationalism, had to take a sudden vacation to Hawaii—but the new tariffs

---

[4] For thus suggesting, in 1934, that the commercial rivalry was heading for a military climax, the author was roundly condemned by American pacifists and "pinks"—at that time pacifist.

stood. The Chinese boycott against Japanese goods backfired. The domination of the Chinese merchant in the Philippines, Malay, and the South Sea Islands was broken when natives demanding the cheap Japanese goods which Chinese traders ceased to stock began to be supplied by direct branches of the great Japanese mercantile houses —who also supplied the natives credit at a fraction of the old Chinese interest. And so there appeared whole new streets of Japanese shops in Manila and Cebu and Singapore, and Japanese traders in the islands and atolls, while Chinese traders were folding up and returning to the ancestral land by the thousands. Indian merchants, backed by Japanese houses, supplanted the Chinese in remote places.

Under the competitive system, to which the west clings though it becomes the rope with which we are being hung, artificial barriers against lower-priced goods cannot last. They are false to the whole competitive idea. Japan has played us into a false position toward our own basic philosophy. Says Asano, son of the cement and shipping pioneer, "Any nation depending too much on the protection of economic barriers is only delaying the day of reckoning."

Meanwhile what the west has taught the orient, what the white race has taught the yellow race is, in essence, the philosophy of the hearty Baron [5] Shibuzawa. He was called during his life Japan's Rockefeller, although he was in youth a gentler pirate than his American counterpart and in age was fortunate enough to die while still lively and handsome. This Baron Shibuzawa remarked that the most beautiful sight to the eyes of a modern Asiatic was a landscape of belching factory chimneys. The baron was, of course, looking at his belching stacks through the cherry branches surrounding his mansion.

To the workers huddled where the soot falls, the chimneys may not have appeared so beautiful. But their fathers were born serfs. Their tradition is to do as told, and to put their heart into it for the sake of the Emperor. Some went into a mine and refused to come out until better conditions were promised—a strategy which the des-

---

[5] He died Viscount Shibuzawa, but was always "the baron." Many business peers became viscounts; only statesmen of high career, Katsu for example, become counts.

perate Hungarian miners of Plecs pathetically adopted—and one did climb to the top of a stack and sit on its narrow edge for twenty days —until the company promised better wages. He came down and the police waiting at the foot took him. But he had become a hero. That satisfied him and his fellows for some time to come.

Rationalization binds up the ragged edges of Japan's trade break with the west. "The world seems to forget that we buy more than we sell," says Hoshino, economic adviser to the Bank of Chosen. "Medical authorities in Tanganyika report that cheap Japanese canvas and rubber shoes have done more against hookworm than all the medical and sanitary work of the colonial government," boasts Honolulu's *Nippon Jiji*.

And ponder this, all ye western traders who once blessed a reluctant east with your products! It is the letter of an Indian patriot to a Tokyo paper: "If Japan supplies cheap articles for the poor, she fulfils what Jesus said. Japan's heart breaks at seeing the poor pay a dollar for a thing worth fifty cents. Japan has transfigured herself into the savior of tens of millions throughout the world. . . . She does a divine and godly work. . . . Oh, Japan, true symbol of the poor and humble!"

Just this way feel millions of orientals, Indians, islanders, and Africans, who crave the commodities of the west and envy its superior standard of living. So did English moralists speak when British steam looms were condemning to death the old weavers' guilds in India and Europe. So has American industry claimed virtue to itself for every invention allowing a wider distribution of goods, and, incidentally, wider market and bigger profits. So would the average American who drives a car to-day feel about a new transportation gadget that would release him forever from tribute to his local garage man and to Detroit, regardless of the sudden stark effect upon capital and labor in the motor industry.

Sir Andrew MacFadyean of the British Labor party said Japan should be hailed as a world benefactor for her activity in cheap production: "The British policy of restricting the amount of Japanese products which the poorer inhabitants of the Empire shall be permitted to enjoy is the negation of common sense, a crime against world prosperity, and a betrayal of trust."[6] We fear Sir Andrew with his Scotch wit was using Japan as a whipping block for the capitalist fat boy. Japan's foreign office declares: "The standard of living of the Dutch East Indian natives is raised by the import of Japanese goods."

This is the divine mission in canvas shoes, cotton sheets, and bicycles.

There is truth in Japanese magnate Shibuzawa's philosophy. Humanity in the ideal state should have factory chimneys as well as cherry blossoms (until cleaner ways of providing power and heat are everywhere practicable). However, when we had converted an Asiatic nation to the belief that its national pride and safety as well as the feeding of its increasing millions required it to build nests of factories making every product in which it can undersell the western world, and to maintain economic, political and naval strength sufficient to hold open the doors of world markets for such a purse-picking trade, it was time for us to pause and consider: What price philosophy (for us!) of the survival of the fittest?

Japan had the formula for supreme success in a competitive world, the ability to undersell combined with a warlike spirit. The Jews had the former. They lacked the latter. Japan, challenger of the white man's world dominance, unexpected competer in machine industry and machine warfare upon which dominance now rests, was to be the final crown and glory—or the *reductio ad absurdum*—of history's era of unrestrained individual and national competition.

Economist Takahashi (Kamekichi) was outspoken: "As Russia and the United States of America are the theoretical objectives of our military and naval circles so should British industry be the objective of our industrial offensive."[7] Said the editor of the quoted Japanese paper in Honolulu: "Japan is badly spoken of because she has become great. It is most necessary for us not to lose our attitude as a great people."

Japan's position was confessed in a little Mitsubishi propaganda pamphlet: "That our goods spread over the world is because of our

[6] Labor publication of the national Joint Council of the Trades Union Congress and the Labor Party, first quarter, 1934.
[7] In magazine, *Gaiko Jiho*.

superior industrial ability—diligence necessitated by our dire need of maintaining our national existence. We shall never retreat." [8] This was a declaration of industrial war to the death on those unthinking white nations who pointed that backfiring blunderbus, quantity production, at Asia.

[8] *International Gleanings,* August 15, 1933.

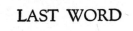

LAST WORD

Chapter XXXI

Last Word—Before War

WESTERN hope of peace and understanding with Japan is based upon her becoming western-minded and modern-minded, thinking as we do, relating herself to the world as we would. We are positive that we are right.

Japanese hope of peace and understanding with the west is based upon our acknowledgment of Japan's divine mission and acceptance of what Japanese do. Japan is certain that she is right—In fact, she never has the qualms that occasionally trouble us.

The mutual hope of peace and understanding between the two is like that between a husband and wife who have a deep sentimental wish to be considerate of one another and pull together, but whose natures, social conceptions, ideals, and aims are so fundamentally different that they drift inevitably towards a break while each, positive that he or she is right, waits for the other "to change."

If there is anything to be learned from the survey of a nation's mental growth contained in this book, it is that Japan will not change—short of disaster. Neither will the west, which feels as justified by logic in its position as a man "talking reason" with a high-strung woman.

II

At least twice in history there has risen a feminine-minded nation —intuitive, quick, adaptable, hypersensitive, brave, persistent, con-

---

[1] This was the final chapter in the edition of 1934. Some critics of that period called it "war-mongering." We include it here as historical interpretation so well thought out before the event it foreshadows that it remains the best interpretation after that event—And it goes yet further into the future—THE PUBLISHER.

scientious, egocentric, incapable of understanding or accepting the masculine logic of give and take. (I use "feminine-minded" and "masculine" only for lack of more appropriate terms in our language, realizing that there exists much of this sort of feminine-mindedness in men and that on the other hand there exist women governed by logic and reason.) To the masculine Romans, the Greeks were such a feminine-minded nation. The Romans were fascinated with Greek quickness. They admired, even though they never understood, the intuitive Greek response to beauty. They revered Greek courage, making the Greek sagas their own. But the Greek superiority complex, the Greek arrogance towards the barbarian, the Greek inability to come to definite terms and keep contracts, the Greek "heavenly impulses" and lack of political rationality, and the Greek refusal to submit when cornered or be quiet when beaten drove the Romans to cold exasperation.

There were only two ways for them to deal with Greece: to let the Greeks severely alone or to crush and scatter them. Since Rome was out to establish world rule, she crushed Greece. The operation proved messy—as the squelching of a high-spirited woman by a man, however superior in muscle, always proves.

A similar dilemma confronted France with regard to Germany after 1932. Should she allow Germany to become strong enough to challenge her concretely? Or should she strike first, and spatter all Europe with blood? But the possibility that Germany herself will change is far greater than that Japan's mind and soul will diverge from a fifteen-hundred-year-old pattern.

Japan believes we are stupid and blind. This is typical of the egocentric mind. "What puzzles the American people," writes Kawakami, "is the uncertainty of Japanese policy regarding not merely the naval but other vital questions. Does Japan really desire peace with Soviet Russia? Does she still feel the urge of territorial expansion? Does she intend to advance into China beyond the Great Wall? Is she satisfied with what she has achieved in Manchuria?" [2]

"Such questions would never be asked," comments a Japanese editor, "if there was in the west any understanding of the realities of the far eastern situation."

[2] *Japan Times,* July 24, 1934.

The clash is psychological. It is as hard for our diplomats to converse with the Japanese foreign office as for a man to argue with a woman. There can be no coöperative and peaceful solution of this clash—which goes beyond boundaries and markets into the realm of the mind—until the vast psychological as well as material distances between new east and old west are obliterated, until standards of living are leveled through catastrophe and evolution, and experience has created the same viewpoints in the parties involved.

One might justifiably make a thesis of the feminine-minded and masculine-minded aspects of nations. But the author desires to introduce these concepts here only so far as they clear our perspective of Japan. Nippon's estheticism, which is an instinctive sense of the appropriate in the grouping of concrete objects but is weak in abstractions, Japan's penchant for drastic and indignant mothering of Formosan headhunters, primitive islanders, and disorderly Asiatics —for wiping the noses of Manchurians and Mongols—these are essentially feminine traits. Japan's kindness to the conquered who absolutely submit, her harshness to those who hold out or question her right, her intuitive reaction to world forces and international currents, the serious way in which her people take pleasure and sports and their haunting fear of appearing illogical to the outsider —all these might be said to fit the theory of the feminine mind. The basic difference between Japan and the west was never more evident than in the exasperation of leonine old Briand with foxlike little Yoshizawa at Geneva. How is a mere western human going to argue with the oriental executor of a divine mission, in whose veins flows the blood of Amaterasu, Goddess of the Sun?

III

Why should Japan and America fight?—They shouldn't. What have either Japan or America to gain by war?—Nothing. It isn't that sort of a picture. It isn't two rivals in commerce or politics viewing one another masculinely.

I repeat: it is the picture of the couple who have everything to gain by seeing eye to eye and working together—everything to lose through a break. Yet the sane observer not befogged by sentiment knows that their basic senses of values, ideas of sportsmanship, spiritual and material hankerings and ambitions in life are so variant that the break must and will come.

Japan's present pride, Japan's entire history, dictate that she must have an equal navy. Common strategy dictates that the United States must fortify Alaska and the Aleutian Islands. The menace must become unbearable to Japan. When Russia "thrust a dagger at Japan's back" by entrenching herself in Manchuria and Korea, Chief Black Dragon Toyama saw to it that Japan pounced upon Russia. When America "thrusts a dagger" at Japan's front——? Logically (read all that has gone before) : Japanese Black Dragons blow Panama Canal. (Already several hundred Japanese barber shops line the locks.) Simultaneously Suetsugu's submarines raid Pearl Harbor and San Diego, à la Port Arthur in 1904, and the alien Japanese fishing community in San Pedro takes care of that base.[3]

Will Japan crash before the clash of national mentalities brings this? The west may as well cease mouthing the hopeful prediction. Let the reader of this book think whether the structure it portrays is one about to crash, or a fabric rotten. Might Japanese industry over-expand and go into depression as the west pulls out? Minister of communications Machida, "good-natured papa" as his people call him, and his council of five ministries that govern all production, quality, and sales, will guard against that. Says M. Audoyer, president of the French chamber of commerce in Japan, speaking from an experience of forty years' residence and business in Japan: "It is not for me to say what other countries should do for their own protection. But it is my duty to say to those who predict catastrophe (within Japan) that they are repeating forecasts which I have heard every year for forty years. Japan has the will to live. Its population increases almost a million yearly. Its people are enterprising, courageous, able, artistic, gay-spirited, and earnest." [4]

America could throw her weight with Russia to crush Japan. That would mean either a temporary American empire of the Pacific and far east, with perhaps its imperial capital at Honolulu—or imme-

---

[3] Of all these surprise actions in the Japanese high command's book of strategy, only the Pearl Harbor attack materialized.

[4] *Japan Times*, May 1, 1934.

diate Russian hegemony of Asia. The prospect is not enticing. Yet so may events go.

On the other hand, if the United States wishes to avoid the final showdown it must take second place on the Pacific, allowing Japan to have her own way entirely—simply run away and shut itself off. The United States may do this, getting off the seas and out of world politics and competitive international trade.

Nippon, the modern feminine-minded nation, *may* yet accomplish what Alexander, Cæsar, Genghiz, Charlemagne, Napoleon and Kaiser Wilhelm II failed to accomplish. Whatever comes, Matsuoka's warning applies:

"There may be some who dare to say that the emergency time has passed or that there is nothing disquieting to worry about. They are like people told that they are breathing air, but who deny the fact because they cannot see air." This is true for both Asiatic and white man—or it would not be true at all.

From the yellow race comes the final crisis to the white man's economic and social system. Japan, last out of feudalism, will be last out of capitalism. But not until her dog-eat-dog competition has added the last straw to the already sway-backed camel of western dog-eat-dog individualism.—Furthermore, not until it has wrecked Nippon also. Men, eastern and western, do not change through idealism. They change through trial and error. *After* disaster they try the preachments. *After* the carnage, not before, should come to fruitage the work of Kagawa in the manner expressed by an Italian author [5] of long acquaintance with Nippon:

"Japan may become a crucible in which the knowledge accumulated by the secular experience of the East and West will be fused and amalgamated, giving forth as its product a new form of civilization on a wider basis."

After disaster, after the carnage.

[5] Z. Volpicelli.

Chapter XXXII
Last Word—Before Peace

So, for sensationalists, for sober interpreters, for those who would have it and those who wouldn't have it, for those who look only at Europe and care not a rap about Asia as well as those who look more toward the Pacific because of the westward drift of this nation, and for the sentimental or commercial friends of Japan as well as for Jap-haters—for all alike—the Great War of the Pacific burst on December 7, 1941. Having come this far with the author, and with events, you see that whether begun with a treacherous blow, as this book predicted, or otherwise, the violent ushering in of the Pacific Era was as much a part of the panorama of time as the very difference between the Japanese and American mind.

Now the Pacific Era has arrived, the era which every discerning historian has seen in the westward course of empire. It has burst upon us in flame and bloodshed, the complete opposite of the import of the words which make up its name. It is here to stay regardless of who wins this war. History waited as long as it could for western man to turn his eyes Asia-ward, to complete the cycle of global oneness. Long did he remain in a state of infantile fear, refusing to sever the umbilical cord with Europe, and turning aside from the virile challenge to look ahead.

So war with Japan means much more than just to hate and lick the nation that has thus forced the birth of the Pacific Era in spite of our obstinacy and shortsightedness. We have only begun with Japan, and how we handle this violent opening of the era of the Pacific promises to be the turning point of history.

A century ago we vitalized and strengthened Japan's cocoon state and life again flowed through the hermit kingdom. She took by far the most virile and healthy place in the family of Asiatics. What did she see? Did she see white men carrying out the doctrines which they preached—did she see white men truly working for the Pacific Era as the era of equality and plenty?—Hardly. She saw race and creed discrimination being sharpened to an edge never before felt among humans. She saw imperialism under the guise of a benefactor, building trade monopolies with porcine greediness. She saw China and India held in bondage by speakers of fine words; she soon saw great America discriminating against her emigrants. Japan was quick to learn.

From the time of Commodore Matthew Perry, 1853, to the Kurusu-Hull talks, 1941, our policy was to push Japan out into the modern world while ignoring as much as we could what she did there. She was quick to use the weapons and tools offered her, quick to learn how to guise her fling at imperialism under the cloak of her "divine mission"—quick to use the slogan "save China from outside domination" as a smokescreen for her own aggression. The day for ignoring Japan was now over, though few westerners gave it a thought. The force of a people, hard-working and infuriated, was gaining momentum when America presented the ultimatum: "You have no right in China. This is the Pacific Era, whose banner is the 'Open Door' policy; there are to be no further aggressions, no more monopolies." But the words rattled like empty shells in the ears of the Japanese. Spurred on in their belief in their divine mission, they watched their opportunity to leap upon the nations which, to themselves, were champions of democracy. Our one prepared strength, our sea power, was attacked. The leap came, not upon our back, but upon our main, front rampart. Then, at last, we knew that the day of ignoring Japan, the day of ignoring our job in the Pacific, was over.

Japan unleashed the most bitter monster ever let loose in the blood-stained arena of History because it is a monster fed for generations on the rotten food of race prejudice. Japan imposed upon us the greatest war ever fought across oceans, the costliest war in men lost and captured and naval craft sunk that this nation has ever experienced; the most upsetting war to our domestic economy and habits—as witness the rubber situation. There is more to it than that, however. Japan's assault upon the United States and Britain, initially successful from mid-Pacific to mid-Indian Ocean, was the violent, final period to the temporary, tenuous, superior-race status of the white race—whose virile citadel had become North America. It leveled the prestige of the West over the East.—More on that as the very last, last word.

If we assume that once having broken Japan's power and imposed peace on our terms, we shall be through with Japan—through with the mentality and physical energy of seventy million Japanese—we will be repeating the mistake which Britain, France, and we made after the allied defeat of Germany in 1917. Repetition of this mistake in the case of Japan would have ever greater and more tragedy and more costly results than it has in that case. Victory, then, is not enough. Our American democracy came onto the stage of history destined to carry the banner of the oneness of the human family, the banner of peace not war, and never before in the evolutionary process of nations has any one nation had so magnificent an opportunity to fulfil its destiny.

Here is a challenge to prove in the case of a nation the theory that modern educators and psychologists find successful in the cases of individuals. Intolerable racial characteristics exist, just as obnoxious qualities exist in individuals, but these can only be eradicated from the human family by probing to find out what makes the offenders "tick," and by discovering the adjustments necessary to make them fall into line with a way of life which is for the good of all. To do this America will have to break through the thickening wall of hate; she will have to purge out the insidious poisons which seep into the veins of every warring nation. To hate what causes war, to hate a way of life which denies others their places in the sun, to hate industrial and trade monopolies, to hate imperialistic conquest, to hate "we-are-the-people" arrogance or "divine mission" fanaticism, to hate race and creed discrimination is the only hate that will win the lasting peace.

The mouthpieces of propaganda may have said that we cannot win the war unless we hate our enemy, unless the personal hate becomes the charioteer. That form of teaching belongs to an out-worn past—

a way of life gone forever. If the true meaning of victory becomes the language of the heart, if it means to us a Pacific Era in the truest meaning of the word—the global oneness of humanity after this strife ends—then, and only then, can its destruction and misery be justified. We are saddled with this great spiritual job, contemporaneously with the great physical job of destroying aggressive force.

The adjustments to be made for constructive peace come under two heads: social and economic. They will not be made by envisioning the Japanese as buck-toothed monkeys hanging from trees. They must be made from knowledge of Japan as one of the best-rooted and toughest national growths that has ever pushed up through the jungle of history, a growth bearing notable fruit artistically and commercially, but containing—through a combination of nature-inspired defense mechanism and warped pride—savage thorns and virulent poison which have reacted upon itself. The social adjustment after the war can only be made in a world in which a confraternity of the snubbed can no longer form, a world in which no one has the superior advantages enabling him to snub, a world in which the categorization of races and nations as either "progressive" or "backward" is forgotten. Otherwise, a defeated Japan will have little difficulty consorting with, and further embittering, two billion disappointed Asiatic souls, and inciting every other element, half-Asiatic and non-Asiatic, which wonders who got profit and power out of the war.

The economic adjustment required is plainer to most people, although not much easier to make. Its necessity from the straight, selfish angle, as well as the idealistic, if we of the high standard (hitherto) of living are to survive, is shown from the trade figures given in the footnote [1] at the end of this chapter—placed as the last thing to engage the reader's notice, because the sharpness of the economic clash will be full in our faces as soon as the military clash comes to its end.

The struggle in the Pacific is psychological, ideological, cultural, and material. Our survey of Japan's mental, social, political, and industrial growth, our understanding of Japanese senses of values at conflict with ours, reveal to us the vast intent and purpose of

Japan's revolt against the West, and the possibilities of a revolt of all the "tinted" races, and hint at the horrible chaos to overwhelm humanity East and West if we win only the war and not the peace.

The battle now reveals us in the crisis of the decision as to whether or not for the first time in man's history a truly global civilization can be established, or whether we are entering History's most disastrous period of chaos, marked by an ascendency of economically undercutting, militarily superior eastern men over a self-destroyed western world. The battle for the Pacific is vastly greater in import than any other battle because it has become the test of our race and the crucible of our civilization.

The questions before us now are (1) Why are we fighting? and (2) Whom are we fighting? We are fighting Japan because her empire builders attacked our fighting forces. They attacked our forces because our government took measures to obstruct their empire building in the Pacific. Our government obstructed Japan in China and South Asia because in the end it felt bound—in spite of shilly-shallying—to carry out the long-term policy of American statesmanship which demands an end to the old deal of "Let him take who has the power and let him keep who can" in the Pacific, and to insist upon a new deal of live and let live around the world's largest and richest ocean, in the basin which is destined to be the world center of the future. So contradictory had been our actions and words that Japan thought we were ready to compromise the basic American statesmanship regarding the Pacific. But in the final test, our President and Secretary of State backed it up. They had to, or give up all claim to stand for a new world and an ethic essentially different from that of the frank empire builders by force.

So Japan struck us. In brief, then, we fight Japan for our vision of a new world from which empires by force shall be banned. That must apply generally, no matter who may think himself entitled to rule over, or even to be good for, conquered peoples; else it cannot apply at all—else we are fighting for nothing, and will not long fight, or by temporary victory will only gain the privilege of fighting again, against greater odds. So much for why we fight.

This book, as *Challenge—Behind the Face of Japan*, was first written in the hope that if we *knew* the Japanese we would see what we must do about them—and ourselves—that we might not have to fight them. Now, as *Behind the Face of Japan,* it is reissued, with the material and thoughts of 1942, to answer the question of *whom* we *are fighting,* and with *whom* we must yet make peace and live. The author offers it as his contribution to constructive peace. It or something similar, will be needed by every American who is concerned in the establishment of peace and interested in trying to make that peace permanent. That means every American.

For that, victory is not enough. We must know how to cook and flavor the pie, as well as put our finger into it.

[1] *Footnote: Japan's Trade Challenge.*—Japan's last year of "peace-time" trade growth was 1933-1934. Japan's trade growth in 1933 over 1932 was approximately 50% by value in yen. The magazine *Contemporary Japan* states that Japanese trade growth during 1934 was even more marked than in 1933, although suffering some check during the last few months of the year. It gives the percentages of increase of Japanese export trade for the first four months of 1934 over the same period of 1933 as follows: North America, 10%; Asia, 18%; Europe, 56%; South America, 56%; Africa, 53%; and Central America, where Japanese trade is just beginning, 176%; Haiti, more than 1000%; which inspired a letter from the United States Cotton Trade Export Association to President Roosevelt's new Trade Agreement Committee, asking for some sort of bargain with the Latin American countries, saving the Latin American market for America. The following articles show more than 100% increase over 1933: rayon yarn and tissue, coal tar dyes, locomotive engines, telephone apparatus, electrical appliances, woolen fabrics, linen tissues and cotton poplin. Save for rayon yarn, Japan was seriously entering the international market in these products. The increase in rayon yarn export, which is well established, was 500%; from 1.7 million yen to 8.5 million yen. Japanese cotton goods export to East Africa increased 25%. Japanese "Bridgestone" tires constituted 85% of the total tire imports of Zanzibar.

The magazine states that the best advertisement of Japanese goods throughout the world was the complaints from western manufacturers of their scandalous cheapness.

Japan's imports of iron in all forms rose from 48,000,000 yen worth in 1931 to 136,000,000 in 1933. One company had obtained control of 99% of steel production within the empire, including Manchuria and Korea. The new Nippon Steel Tube Company, while American steel industry was operating at 20 to 30% production, made so much money that it declared a 17% dividend, gave six-to-twelve-month-pay bonuses to 2,800 factory workers and 450 official clerks and also contributions to the Japanese army and navy. This company won a contract over American bidders to build Mexico City's water system, which inspired the former Mexican President Calles to suggest a trade agreement between Mexico and the United States in preparation for a predicted economic war between the continents.

Broken-up American warships were shipped directly to Osaka for the Imperial Japanese navy yards. Japan purchased from one line alone twelve antiquated American coasters to carry metal scrap, and in late 1934 every ship which would take such cargo went out loaded.

Japan's scrap iron imports totaled a million tons in 1933, and reached between 1,500,000 and 2,000,000 tons in 1934. Scrap was costing her four to six dollars a ton in America, plus four dollars a ton carrying charges. Japanese steel concerns were using seven to eight parts scrap iron to two or three parts pig iron in the manufacture of steel.

An amusing complaint against Japanese competition came from the "Sanitary Institute of America," which is the coördinating organization of the United States waste industry. It claimed that the waste industry —rag picking—was the third largest industry in the world, and that the United States industry had lost $2,500,000 per year revenue through Japanese import of wiping rags (for machinery)—the aristocratic product of the waste industry. The institute complained that the United States navy, using 15,000,000 pounds of wiping rags per year, had let down home industry to become Japan's chief customer in this product.

Japan's investments in capitalized industry in Manchukuo leaped from 11,500,000 yen in 1932 to 443,390,000 in 1933—an increase of forty times within one year! This amount had doubled again by May, 1934.

In 1933 Japan became the world's first textile exporter, making more than two billion of the 5½ billion yards of cotton goods required to clothe the world. Showing the world's poverty since 1929 was the decrease in world consumption of cotton goods from eight to 5½ billion yards. Nearly half of the raw cotton came from the United States, and most of the remainder from India. India provided Japan's largest textile market, taking 32% of her piece goods, the Dutch East Indies, China, and England following in order named. Japan's 1932 excess of exports to India was 75,000,000 yen. For thirty years the balance was the other way, during which Japan's excess of imports piled up to 3,500,000 yen.

Japan was the largest buyer of cotton from America and the largest purchaser of wool from Australia. In 1933 Japan's sales to America were 26% of her total sales, and her purchases from America were 32% of her total purchases. Japan became the largest buyer of United States goods excepting the British Empire, taking 22% of American cotton exports. The year's trade was favorable to the United States by 300,000,000 yen. Seventy per cent of America's purchases from Japan was raw silk.

British Marxists warned that western economic rivalries would play the depressed colonial peoples of the world into the hands of the cheapest manufacturer, namely, Japan. Said Ralph Fox, in *The Colonial Policy of British Imperialism,* published by International Publishers, New York, 1933: "The path outlined by the labor party and by empire free trade and Ottawa agreements cannot raise the standard of life of the colonial workers and peasants, but only depress them still further,

preparing the way for another war for the redivision of the world between the rival robber powers. . . . Capitalism, shaken by the greatest
economic crisis in history, is trying to find a way out along the lines
of national self-sufficiency." The intensified exploitation of home market
(for American industry) and imperial market (for British), the ruthless
cutting down of imports through high tariffs, and economic war on all
countries through dumping and penal tariffs were, according to the
Marxist Fox, the last feverish spasm of western industrialism stricken
to the heart. Japan intended to take over with "eastern industrialism."

The tendency in 1934 was toward a rapid drop in American purchases
of Japanese products, due to anti-dumping embargoes on manufactured
goods and drop in American use of silk, while Japan showed indications
of plans to procure elsewhere in the future her raw cotton and other
products now taken from America. Japanese exports to the United States
for the first seven months of 1934 were worth 225,450,000 yen as
against 274,219,000 for the same period in 1933. During the same time
Japan's purchases from the United States rose from 383,000,000 yen to
447,000,000 yen—a non-permanent increase largely due to purchases
of raw materials, particularly iron and steel, for military purposes, and
of specialized machinery and airplane parts. Purchases of raw cotton
from America fell off.

American trade with China was a little more than one-third that with
Japan—however, these figures were misleading, since shipments to
Hongkong, almost entirely trans-shipped to China and comprising the
bulk of south China's purchases, were listed separately in official trade
statistics. Japanese-American trade had apparently passed its zenith.
Chinese-American trade, barring artificial interference, was still in its
infancy.

Japan's largest industries after textiles were: pulp and paper, rubber
goods, glass, chemicals, celluloid film and other products, toilet goods,
incandescent bulbs, hemp, phonographs, radios, bicycles, Diesel engines,
tires, tinplate, and sox. New industries attaining a major status in 1934:
vitamins, electric refrigerators, ice-cream plants, airplane parts, and
automobile motors. Japan's principal export products in 1933 were:
rayon piece goods, silk, canned foodstuffs, hosiery, earth and porcelain
ware, iron manufacturing, machinery, tops, and woolen goods. Woolen
goods increased from a production value of 1,500,000 yen in 1931 to
3,400,000 yen in 1932, and 16,000,000 yen during the first ten months
of 1933.

Japan had devised the clever scheme of endeavoring to compel American and Dutch companies to keep a supply of oil in Japan sufficient
to supply the Japanese navy for a long naval campaign, in return for

the privilege of exploiting the Japanese market. This was of a piece with the gradual closing of Manchuria to western business.

Perhaps the most amusing of Japan's new industries was the reproduction of old American heirlooms—New England furniture and such. Japan's toothbrush industry planned to teach Manchukuo to use toothbrushes.

To conclude these flashes of Japan's trade growth in a light vein: Said Japan's ambassador to Italy, Sugimura: "I deem that my negotiations with the papal state in Rome are important. I believe the best method to encourage trade with South America is through friendliness with the pope." This from the representative of the nation which once exterminated Roman Catholicism within its borders.

"Japan will raise China's diplomatic status to that of a nation entitled to an ambassador instead of a minister, provided China will more sincerely control the Chinese boycott against Japanese goods," said Ariyoshi, Japan's plenipotentiary in China.

"Representing Japan, Yoshioka, famous Japanese mouth-organist, went from Osaka to New York to take part in the world contest of harmonica players held there on September 16, 1934. Mr. Yoshioka used a ninety sen Japanese instrument, and it was hoped that his success would promote the sale of Japanese mouth-organs in the west."

The *Arkansas Gazette* summed up the whole matter. "Japan completely misunderstood our occidental purpose in Westernizing her. We wanted a good customer, not a cut-price competitor."

INDEX

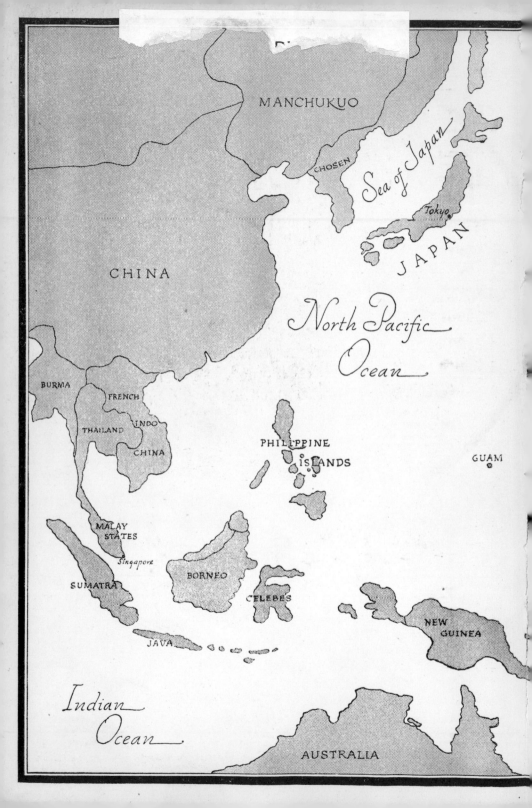